Managing a Conurbation: Birmingham and its Region

Managing a Conurbation: Birmingham and its Region

Edited by
A.J. Gerrard and T.R. Slater

Brewin Books

Studley, Warwickshire

First published by
Brewin Books, Studley, Warwickshire, B80 7LG
in 1996

ISBNs
1 85858 083 8 (Paperback)
1 85858 084 6 (HardBack)

British Library Cataloguing in Publication Data.
A Catalogue record for this book is available from the British Library

Typeset in 10pt Times by Heron Press Kings Norton Birmingham B38 9TS
Printed in Great Britain by Heron Press, Kings Norton Birmingham B38 9TS
Telephone: 0121 433 5100

Contents

I Environmental Management

II People, Economy and Society

III Managing the Built Environment

Contributors

M J Beazley *is Lecturer in the Centre for Urban and Regional Studies, University of Birmingham*

J R Bryson *is Lecturer in the School of Geography, University of Birmingham*

X Cai *is Lecturer in the School of Geography, University of Birmingham*

M Caplat *works for Soil & Water Ltd*

C M H Carr *is a graduate student in the School of Geography, University of Birmingham*

P W Daniels *is Professor and Head of the School of Geography, University of Birmingham*

A J Gerrard *is Senior Lecturer in the School of Geography, University of Birmingham*

B D Giles *is part-time Lecturer in the School of Geography, University of Birmingham*

R N Gwynne *is Reader in Latin American Development in the University of Birmingham*

R M Harrison *is Professor of Environmental Health in the University of Birmingham*

N D Henry *is Lecturer in the School of Geography, University of Birmingham*

D M Lawler *is Senior Lecturer in the School of Geography, University of Birmingham*

P Loftman *is Senior Lecturer in the Built Environment Development Centre, University of Central England in Birmingham*

D R Ingram *is Lecturer in the School of Geography, University of Birmingham*

P J Jarvis *is Reader in the School of Applied Sciences, University of Wolverhampton*

J Kings *is Meteorologist in the Weather facility of the School of Geography, University of Birmingham*

P J Larkham *is Senior Lecturer, School of Planning, University of Central England in Birmingham*

P A Lowe *is Associate Lecturer, Open University, West Midlands Region*

G R McGregor *is Lecturer in the School of Geography, University of Birmingham*

B Nevin *is Honorary Research Fellow in the Centre of Urban and Regional Studies, University of Birmingham*

M A Oliver *is a part-time Lecturer in the Department of Soil Science, University of Reading*

G E Petts *is Professor of Physical Geography in the University of Birmingham*

T R Slater *is Reader in Historical Geography in the University of Birmingham*

S Sljivic *works for RSK Environment Ltd*

M F Tanner *is Lecturer in the School of Geography, University of Birmingham*

J E Thornes *is Reader in Applied Meteorology in the University of Birmingham*

A Veal *is a graduate student in the School of Geography, University of Birmingham*

T Westlake *is Head of the International Office, University of Wales, Cardiff*

J W R Whitehand *is Professor of Urban Geography in the University of Birmingham*

Preface

The British Association for the Advancement of Science has held an annual meeting since 1831. For much of the present century those meetings have been held in Britain's universities and today these 'Annual Festivals of Science' held each September attract thousands of visitors, many of them young people, a body of international speakers, and widespread publicity in the press, and on radio and television. Section E of the British Association is devoted to Geography and geographers have always played a part in the conference. The Association last met in the University of Birmingham in 1950 and this proved a seminal year in the contributions of geographers since the Handbook, which the British Association had always produced to accompany its conference, was largely produced by the staff of the then Department of Geography in the university. It set new standards of production, content and format and proved to be a model which geography departments in other universities used subsequently when the Association visited their city and university. These collections of regional essays remain eminently collectable, a source of important information, and a reflection of the state of geographical scholarship at the time at which each successive volume was produced. Their high standard of production was enhanced by a financial subsidy from the Association. By the 1970s that subsidy was no longer available and the tradition of regional scholarship which had lingered in most geography departments was dead. The production of regional handbooks died with it, though many departments tried to maintain the tradition with in-house productions of variable quality in the 1980s and '90s.

This is the prelude to the production of the present volume of essays with its strong emphasis on the city of Birmingham and its region since, in 1996, the British Association is once more holding its Festival of Science in the University of Birmingham. However, this is not a regional Handbook. The staff of the School of Geography have been stimulated by the festival, but the primary purpose of this book is not to serve those who come to Birmingham and its university for that festival. Rather, it is to reflect some of the work and expertise which is on-going in the School and amongst colleagues involved in cooperative research ventures. We hope it will be of interest to visitors to the Festival of Science, but we also hope that it will be of interest to those who live and work in the city which we write about, and to those many students who study the region in courses of advanced, further and higher education.

The period since 1950 has been an interesting and, at times, a traumatic one for the people of Birmingham. The stories of that nearly half a century of change are the substance of this book. They are gathered into three sections. In the first, the emphasis is on the management of the physical resources of the region. There is a tendency to forget that cities occupy physical places, that the land and water and air of the city are important to its economic and social well-being. To forget, that is, until something goes wrong: until asthma cases start increasing rapidly; until there is no water from the city taps in a long hot summer, or flooding stops the city traffic. Geographers and environmental scientists are in the forefront of efforts to ensure that those responsible for managing the city do not forget.

The second section is concerned with the people of the city and the ways in which they manage the economy of Birmingham. It is within these areas of enquiry that some of the most dramatic changes of the past half century are apparent. In 1950 the first migrants from Britain's colonial empire were beginning to come in search of employment and opportunity in the 'mother country'. Many of them came to Birmingham because it was enjoying a period of unprecedented prosperity. Its car factories and all the subsidiary trades were short of workers as the period of mass production, for which geographers and others now use the shorthand term of 'Fordism', gathered pace through the 1950s and '60s. In the 1970s this period of prosperity collapsed and the West Midlands economy went from one of full employment to mass unemployment in less than a decade. Managing this period of dramatic change has inevitably been controversial and it is still far from clear that the growth of a service-based economy can replace the jobs lost. Meanwhile, the children of those first migrant workers have grown up as Black or Asian British and are seeking jobs and homes. Given the current patterns of internal migration and births, by 2020 Birmingham will have a majority of Black and Asian British residents. The sensitive management of social and economic relationships are going to be critical in this period.

The third section deals with the townscape. Buildings and streets and open spaces are also important to the economic and social well-being of a city. They also do much to produce the image of a place held by both residents and outsiders. Outsiders think of Birmingham as a dirty, industrial city which they glimpse from the railways into New Street or as they drive along the M5 or M6 motorways. Residents perceive its millions of trees, parks, playing fields, well-planned residential boulevards, and tower blocks. Both are beginning to understand that change has been dramatic in the city centre. Pedestrianization, public art, new shops, the opening out of the canal network have begun to transform the image and some of the realities. Pavement cafes and street entertainers mean that many are beginning to believe that Birmingham is indeed 'Europe's Meeting Place' - but the tower blocks are still there, and the Bull Ring, and Spaghetti Junction, the icons of sixties' Birmingham. Managing change in the physical places where people have to live and work and play and shop is just as significant for their health and well-being as the other aspects which this book examines.

An edited volume such as this incurs many debts. First, we are grateful to Mr KAF Brewin for the enthusiasm with which he received our proposed volume and his care in the publication process. We are grateful to our colleagues in the School of Geography and elsewhere for (mostly) producing their chapters to tight schedules at a time when there are many calls on academic lives. We are grateful to our colleague Adrian Passmore for providing access to the view of Birmingham city centre from his lounge window in Moseley, which forms the front cover of this book. It would have been impossible to have had the manuscript ready for the press without the dedication, enthusiasm and sheer hard work of technical and clerical colleagues in the School of Geography. The photographic expertise of Geoff Dowling, AMPA, ARPS is evident in the many illustrations which we believe to be an essential attribute of the book. Similarly, the rough sketches of maps and diagrams have been converted into professional products by Kevin Burkhill of the School's Drawing Office. The final debt is to Lynn Ford who has dealt quietly and efficiently with successive drafts of the manuscript. This is their book as much as ours. If it continues to have a life as long as its illustrious predecessor of 1950, we shall be satisfied.

John Gerrard
Terry Slater

Figures

Tables

I
ENVIRONMENTAL MANAGEMENT

CHAPTER 1

The Physical Framework of the West Midlands Conurbation

John Gerrard

The West Midlands conurbation is a densely built-up area with an immense variety of 'human landscapes'. This mass of buildings, roads, railways and canals has masked, very efficiently, the underlying landforms and topography. However, the development of the region has followed, albeit subtly and not necessarily deterministically, the configuration of the land. Thus, it may only be possible to understand some of the nuances brought out in the majority of chapters in this book if some understanding is achieved concerning the physical landscape beneath the built-up conurbation. This is what this chapter attempts. The following account of the general physical background of the Birmingham area builds on the analysis of Warwick, provided for the book published on the occasion of the British Association visit to Birmingham in 1950 (Kinvig et al. 1950). Warwick's account has been enlarged upon here using more quantitative data based on a one kilometre grid analysis of relief, drainage and landforms. The area analysed in detail is bounded by Ordnance Survey grid lines 3 8800 and 3 2800, and 3 0800 and 2 7000, making 1200 square kilometres in total. The one inch to one mile relief and drainage map was used because it lacked the obscuring built-up area. This has resulted in a certain inaccuracy because it has been necessary to change elevation data in feet into approximate metric measurements. This is a smaller area than that covered by Warwick but includes the majority of the West Midlands Conurbation. Much of the characteristic relief and drainage of the area can be explained in terms of rock type and the nature of superficial materials.

Rock type and surface materials

The geology of the region is dominated by rocks of Carboniferous, Permian and Triassic age. Small outcrops of older rock also occur, such as the Silurian limestones of the Wren's Nest and the Cambrian quartzite of the Lickey Hills, and much of the region is covered by various types of glacial deposits. The Carboniferous rocks are essentially those of the Middle and Upper Coal Measures. The Middle Coal Measure Group is dominated by what has been called the Productive Coal Measures. The coal-bearing strata consist of grey shales, sandstones and mudstones, seat-earths of ganister or fireclay, and coal. This rhythmic cycle of shale and/or sandstone, seat-earth, coal, is often repeated. Large volumes of groundwater exist within the rocks of these sequences but the water contains high amounts of chemical salts making it of little use for domestic or industrial purposes. However, natural seepage or seepage into and from old mine workings through certain rock bands may pose serious problems.

It is the Productive Coal Measures that provided the opportunity for the initial, and then sustained, industrial development of the region. In the area known as the Black Country, coal workings initially clung close to the outcrop of the principal coal seams. The presence of the Thick Coal (or the Ten Yard or Thirty Foot seam as it was often called) was the most important single feature influencing the prosperity of the industrial district. Producers of raw and refined iron were to be found on waterpower sites in and around the plateau.

The Upper Coal Measures present a completely different sequence of rocks, their 'red-bed' facies indicating weathering under semi-arid conditions. Within the Upper Coal Measures, the Etruria Marl Group comprises red or purple sandy mudstones with bands of grit. It is a highly variable facies and the various rock types may produce topographic variability. Above the Etruria Marl is a succession of sandstones and clays with coal seams and bands of limestone known collectively as the Halesowen Beds. Above the Halesowen Beds the Keele Group consists of a series of red sandstones and mudstones; many of the mudstones being calcareous. The Enville Beds are generally grouped with the Upper Coal Measures and usually succeed the Keele Group without marked unconformity. They consist generally of red 'marls' and red calcareous sandstones with locally beds of calcareous conglomerate in the lower part and breccia in the upper part of the sequence. At the boundary between Carboniferous and Permian rocks is a group of breccias which have various names depending on location. The most important, in landscape terms, are the Enville and Clent Breccias which form the well-defined ridge of the Clent Hills to the southwest of Birmingham. In the Clent Breccias the dominant pebbles are of Precambrian igneous rocks. The matrix of these rocks tends to be impermeable when compacted and footpath erosion in such areas can be significant.

The Permo-Triassic rocks (New Red Sandstone) dominate the south western, central and eastern portions of the region. They are predominantly red in colour due to the presence of iron minerals, usually hematite although small amounts of goethite also occur (Hains and Horton 1969). The rocks consist largely of sandstones, conglomerates and marls (quartzose mudstones and siltstones). The main landforming units are the Bunter Pebble Beds, Upper Mottled Sandstone, Keuper Sandstone and Keuper Marl (Mercian Mudstone). The Bunter Pebble Beds are coarse-grained, brownish red sandstones with conglomeratic lenses and layers of pebbles varying in size from 7mm to 23cm in diameter. They are a highly variable facies and the landscape response often reflects this facies-induced variation in rock properties. In some areas the pebbles are poorly cemented and readily weather into loose pebbles, in other areas they have a calcite cement and gypsum-rich bands also occur. The Upper Mottled Sandstone consists of soft bright red, medium- to fine-grained sandstones with thin red mudstone beds. Each sand grain has a coating of iron oxide which will affect the longterm weathering potential of the rock. The Keuper Sandstone, dominated in the south west of the region by the Bromsgrove Sandstone, is a red brown and buff sandstone and siltstone with red mudstone bands. Individual sand grains tend to be angular. These rock types, when weathered, produce extremely sandy soils which are susceptible to erosion. The nature and consequences of this erosion are discussed in Chapter 4.

The Keuper Marl, now known as the Mercian Mudstone Group, occurs over a large part of the region. It comprises reddish-brown mudstones and silty mudstones with subordinate bands of sandstone and siltstone. The term marl is misleading (hence the change of name) because it usually denotes a highly calcareous clay, whereas the 'marls' of the Keuper are only slightly calcareous. The 'marls' consist of clay minerals mixed with a high proportion of aeolian quartz dust plus minute crystals of dolomite and gypsum aggregates. Thin beds of grey to buff or pink sandstone, usually associated with silty shales, occur quite frequently. The Mercian Mudstone produces generally flat topography with most eminences being the result of the relatively resistant sandstones. Given the right circumstances weathered Mercian Mudstone is subject to conspicuous landsliding (see Chapter 5). In the upper part of the sequence is a group of sandstones known as the Arden sandstone. This sandstone has been used extensively for building purposes which might have been slightly unfortunate because Goudie and Evans (1970) have shown that, of the six rocks they tested, Arden Sandstone was the second most susceptible to salt weathering.

A variety of younger, surface deposits occur throughout the region. Most of the slopes are mantled with solifluction material (head) and the major river valleys possess alluvial infills. Glacial and fluvioglacial deposits are abundant but never achieve great thicknesses. Glacial till (boulder clay) dominates but there are patches of sands and gravel and occurrences of glacial lake deposits.

The rocks and surface material, collectively and individually, have exerted a major influence on the topographical development of the region. Landforms are the result of the interaction between driving and resisting forces. The driving forces or processes are the methods by which energy is exerted on earth materials and include both surface, geomorphological processes such as weathering and erosion, and subsurface geological processes. The resisting forces are the surface materials with their inherent resistances determined by a complex combination of rock properties. These properties will also exert an influence on the way in which landscape is modified by human activity. Soils developed on these surface materials will also possess distinctive characteristics which will influence factors such as surface and subsurface drainage (see Chapter 6) and habitat development (Chapter 7). Heathlands develop on sandy soils and wet habitats on heavy, poorly-drained soils.

Drainage characteristics

The major drainage component of the region is the Tame-Blythe system which eventually drains into the River Trent (Fig. 1.1). The main tributary of the River Tame is the River Rea, with the

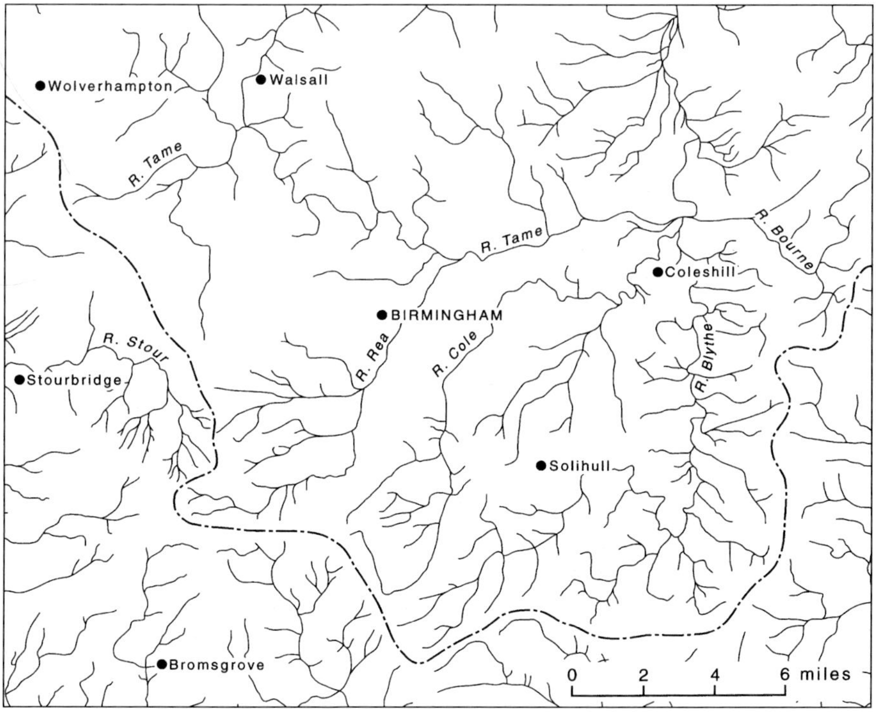

Fig 1.1 The major drainage systems of the Birmingham region

River Cole being a major tributary of the River Blythe. The River Bourne joins the Tame from the east. These drainage systems rise on the main watershed of England and have cut into the plateau-like surfaces of much of the West Midlands. This watershed, separating the Trent from the Severn drainage basins, two of the largest drainage systems in Britain, follows the Sedgley-Northfield Ridge and Clent-Lickey Hills and forms a major barrier between the comparatively gently sloping area leading to the Tame in the east from the steep slopes of the Upper Stour, Salwarpe and Avon valleys. This western area is intensely dissected and generally forms a barrier to communications.

The position of the region, astride one of the main watersheds in England, has exerted a major influence on water management schemes (see Chapter 2). It has also meant that the region is central to many water transfer schemes (Chapter 3) enhanced by the canal network linking the main drainage basins of England and Wales across the West Midlands area.

As the map of drainage shows, stream density is generally low, especially in the Upper Tame area. This can be seen on a map showing the number of stream courses in each kilometre square (Fig. 1.2). Large areas possess no or few stream courses; 26 per cent of the squares possess no stream courses and 40 per cent possess only one stream. Only 17 out of the 1200 squares possess 4 or more stream courses. This means that, as will be seen later, degree of dissection is also generally slight.

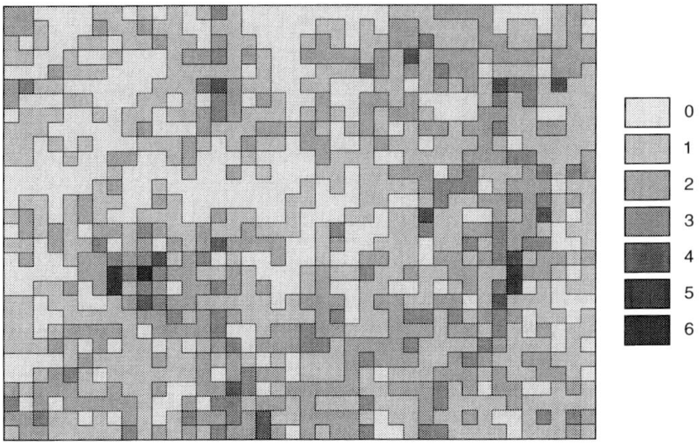

Fig 1.2 Number of stream courses per kilometre square

Relief characteristics

The city of Birmingham and most of the conurbation stands on an upland area which has been isolated by the development of the tributaries of the rivers Trent, Severn and Avon. The region has been divided, almost in two, by the valleys of the lower Tame and Blythe, and Birmingham occupies the edge of this somewhat lower area. Figure 1.3 shows the regional distribution of maximum elevation in each kilometre square. From this map it is possible to identify a number of broad relief zones. First, there is the prominent band of high ground (maximum elevation generally over 250m) trending in a N.E. - S.W. direction in the western part of the region. This is the Sedgley-Northfield Ridge and the Clent-Lickey Ridge. This is essentially the main watershed mentioned earlier. Immediately to the east of this high ground is a broad belt of land between 150m and 250m which is basically the Birmingham Plateau. There is then the combined floodplains and valleys of the rivers Tame and Blythe, forming a land area below 150m which dominates the central and eastern regions. Two minor relief regions are also visible. A western fringe of the main north-south ridge and an eastern ridge, generally above 150m, slighter higher

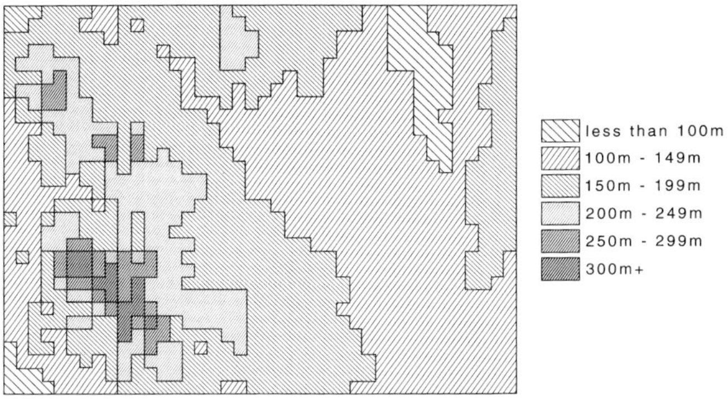

Fig 1.3 Spatial distribution of maximum elevation values

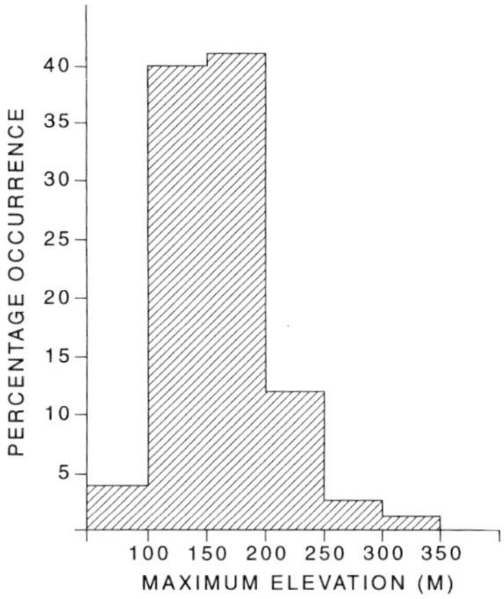

Fig 1.4 Frequency distribution of maximum elevation values

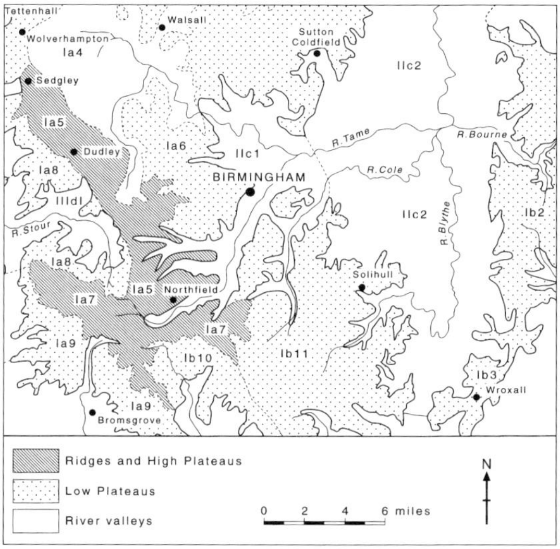

Fig 1.5 Relief units of the Birmingham region

UnitSymbol	Unit name
Ia2	South Cannock Plateau
Ia3	Sutton Plateau
Ia4	Upper-Tame Valley
Ia5	Sedgley-Northfield Ridge
Ia6	West Bromwich-Harborne Plateau
Ia7	Clent-Lickey Ridge
Ia8	Stour Valley Plateau Fringe
Ia9	South West Plateau Fringe
Ia11	Solihull Plateau
Ib1	Ansley Plateau
Ib2	Corley Plateau
IIc1	Mid-Tame, Rea, and Upper Cole Valleys
IIc2	Blyth-Lower Tame Valleys
IIId1	Upper Stour Basin
IIIe	Salwarpe Basin
IVb	Arrow Valley

Table 1.1. The relief units of the Birmingham region

than the nearby Tame-Blythe plains.

The mean maximum elevation is 142m but, as Figure 1.4 shows, the frequency distribution of values is somewhat skewed, which reflects the generally plateau-like nature of the region with areas of higher ground rising above the general topography The mean minimum elevation is 120m which, in comparison to the mean maximum elevation of 142m, demonstrates that considerable parts of the region possess gentle topography with little relative relief. Approximately 56 per cent of the area, by grid square, possesses minimum elevations of between 100 and 150m. The regional variation in relief becomes clearer when individual relief units are examined.

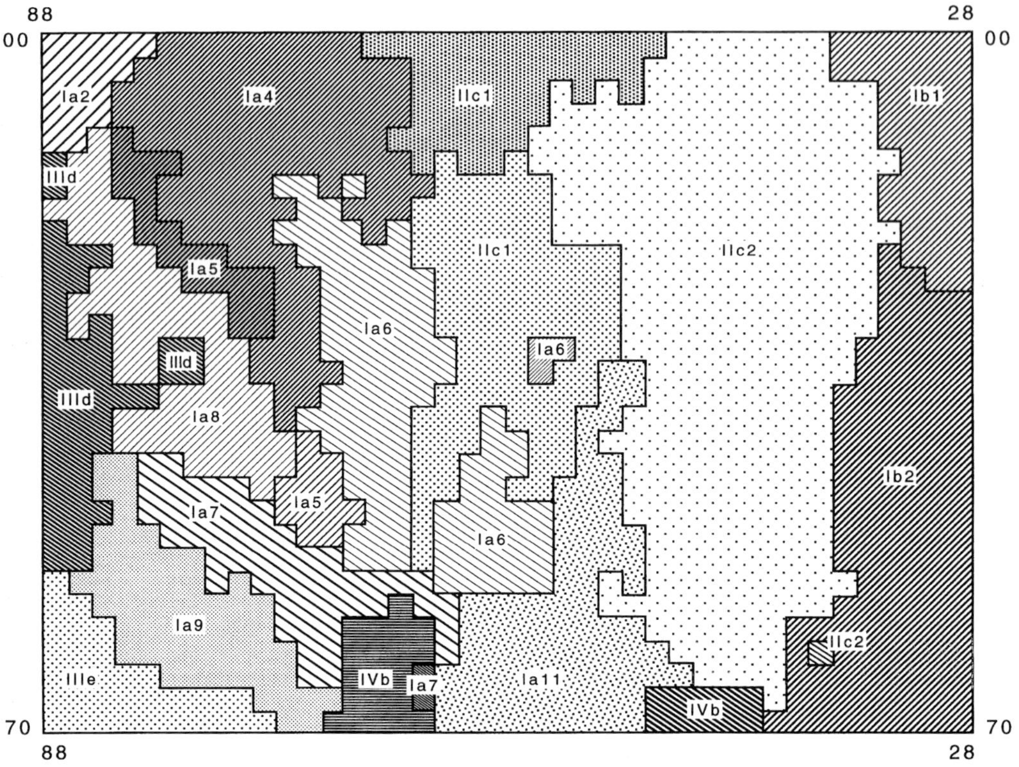

Ia2 South Cannock Plateau
Ia3 Sutton Plateau
Ia4 Upper Tame Valley
Ia5 Sedgley - Northern Ridge
Ia6 West Bromwich - Harborne Plateau
Ia7 Clent Lickey Ridge
Ia8 Stour Valley Plateau Fringe
Ia9 South Western Plateau Fringe

Ia11 Solihull Plateau
Ib1 Ansley Plateau
Ib2 Corley Plateau
IIc1 Mid Tame, Rea & Upper Cole Valley
IIc2 Blythe - Lower Tame Valleys
IIId Stour Valley
IIIe Salwarpe Basin
IIIf Arrow Valley

Fig 1.6 Relief units, based upon those of Warwick (1950), mapped on a kilometre square basis

Relief units

Warwick (1950) subdivided the region into relief units using the major changes of slope (Fig. 1.5). In places the boundaries between units are somewhat arbitrary and generalised but the subdivision does represent the main relief units of the area quite adequately. The main units are listed in Table 1.1 and their extent mapped on a grid basis is shown in Figure 1.6. The numbers are those given to the units by Warwick and are retained for consistency. The four main subdivisions are the Birmingham Plateau, which is the largest and most important physical unit in the region, the Trent Valley System, the Severn Valley System and the Avon Valley System. The characteristics of these units are now examined using the data obtained from the map analysis.

The Birmingham Plateau

The Birmingham Plateau is subdivided into the *South Staffordshire Plateau* and the *East Warwickshire Plateau.* The South Staffordshire Plateau is the largest and most significant of these two major subdivisions. It also possesses a more complex geological structure which is reflected in a greater variety of slope relief features. The southern and eastern part is drained by the Tame system whilst rivers in the north drain towards the Penk and Trent valleys. The western and southern margins are deeply dissected, draining to the rivers Severn and Avon, and provide a striking relief contrast with the land to the west and south. The major components of the South Staffordshire Plateau are the Upper Tame Valley, West Bromwich-Harborne Plateau, Solihull Plateau, Sedgley-Northfield Ridge and the Clent-Lickey Ridge. There are also small areas of the South Cannock and Sutton Plateaus to the north and plateau fringes of the South West and Stour Valley to the west and south.

The *Upper Tame Valley* (Ia4) has an average maximum elevation of 152m with a modal group of 135m (Table 1.2). This is a very uniform area as shown by the high percentage (41) of values in the modal group. The range in maximum elevation is from 120m to 210m but only 18 per cent of the grid squares possess a maximum elevation of over 165m. The boundaries of this unit are not as clear as for some of the other units and this may account for the comparatively large range of maximum elevation values. The centre of this relief unit has been dissected by the major upper tributaries of the Tame into a series of low hills and ridges. Many of these hills and ridges are capped with glacial deposits and many of the towns of the Black Country, such as Wednesbury and Darlaston, are situated on such hills. Many of the small valleys were chosen as routes for canals and parts of the rivers have been absorbed into the canal network.

Much of the city of Birmingham stands on the *West Bromwich-Harborne Plateau* (Ia6). This unit deserves its name as the maximum elevation data indicate (Table 1.2). The average maximum elevation is 177m with 45 per cent of the grid values within the modal group of 150m. The plateau has proved advantageous to the development of Birmingham and its link with the rest of the conurbation. The *Solihull Plateau* (Ia11) is demarcated by the Rea and Tame valleys on the north and north west and by the Upper Blythe and Alne valleys to the south. This latter boundary is quite prominent, the edge is steep and it has often proved to be a barrier to communications. The northern edge is dissected by the River Cole and its tributaries and is essentially covered by the southern suburbs of Birmingham. It is a variable relief region although its plateau-like appearance is demonstrated by a modal group of maximum elevation of 135m containing 35 per cent of the values (Table 1.2). The mean maximum elevation is 145m.

Relief Unit	*Mean maximum elevation*	*Modal elevation*	*% in the mode*
Ia2	*150*	*135, 150*	*24*
Ia3	*175*	*150*	*39*
Ia4	*152*	*135*	*41*
Ia5	*241*	*210*	*46*
Ia6	*177*	*150*	*45*
Ia7	*231*	*255*	*17*
Ia8	*168*	*150, 165*	*24*
Ia9	*156*	*165*	*25*
Ia11	*145*	*135*	*38*
Ib1	*120*	*120*	*35*
Ib2	*128*	*120*	*44*
IIc1	*127*	*120*	*38*
IIc2	*106*	*90*	*31*
IIId1	*113*	*120*	*37*
IIe	*98*	*105*	*27*
IVb	*148*	*135*	*30*

Table 1.2 Mean maximum and modal elevations (in metres) for the Birmingham region relief units

The striking relief units in the region are the Sedgley-Northfield Ridge and the Clent-Lickey Ridge. The *Sedgley-Northfield Ridge* (Ia5) forms the main English watershed separating the Trent system to the north and east from the Severn system to the west and south. Its highest point is 264m at Turners Hill. It varies in elevation from 180m to 264m with a mean maximum elevation of 241m and modal group of 210m. This ridge has had a considerable influence on the development of the conurbation. Road communications are possible through cols and gaps in the ridge but rail and canal routes have been forced to cut through it in tunnels. The Upper Severn tributaries have cut deeply into the ridge on the west side creating steep slopes. The ridge is composed of a variety of rock types many of which exerted an influence on industrial development in the area. The northern part of the ridge is composed essentially of Silurian limestones and shales forming the hills of Sedgley Beacon, Wren's Nest and Dudley Castle. The lower flanks of the ridge are composed of Middle Coal Measure rocks. Towards the south, rocks of Upper Coal Measure age are intruded with dolerite at Rowley Hill. The dolerite has been extensively quarried. South of Quinton, the ridge narrows at Frankley Beeches, then broadens out and becomes dissected by the River Rea. Northfield, a major southern suburb of Birmingham, stands on this part of the ridge. Here the ridge is composed of Bunter Pebble Beds, Upper Bunter Sandstone and Keuper Sandstone.

The *Clent-Lickey Ridge* (Ia7) parallels the Sedgley-Northfield Ridge to the west and south. This Ridge contains the highest land in the region, 316m at Walton Hill. Because of the nature of its dissection and its somewhat lower extension to the south, in terms of mean maximum elevation (231m), it does not appear as high as the Sedgley-Northfield Ridge. But this statistic is misleading. The modal grouping is 255m, with 17per cent in this group and a range from 165m to 316m (Table 1.2). Morphologically it can be subdivided into the Clent Hills, the Lickey Hills and an unnamed southern section. The Clent Hills have been almost isolated by the upper tributaries of the River Stour and a number of prominent gaps have been utilised by main communication routes such as the M5 and A38 roads. The Clent Hills are composed of Clent Breccias and Bunter Pebble Beds. The Lickey Hills, although part of the ridge, are composed of entirely different rock types. The core of the hills is Cambrian quartzite upfaulted into newer rocks. The gap between the Clent and Lickey Hills has been excavated from softer Keele Clays.

There is a small area of the *South Cannock Plateau* (Ia2) in the north west of the region. Much of this unit lies between 120m and 180m with a mean maximum elevation of 150m and modal groups of 123m and 150m. There are outcrops of Silurian shales and limestones near Walsall but most of the plateau is dominated by Middle Coal Measure rocks. The western edge is drained by the River Penk northwards to the River Trent while to the south is the Upper Tame Valley. In terms of elevation much of the *Sutton Plateau* (Ia3) is similar to the West Bromwich-Harborne Plateau and is probably part of the same geomorphological surface. It is virtually impossible to distinguish it from the West Bromwich-Harborne Plateau in terms of maximum elevation statistics with a mean maximum elevation of 175m and modal grouping of 150m. On its southern edge it slopes towards the Middle and Upper Tame Valley whilst on its western edge there is a conspicuous north-south ridge stretching from Shire Oak to Queslett and culminating in Barr Beacon. Most of the area is composed of Keuper Sandstones and Bunter sandstones and conglomerates. Upper Coal Measure sediments are exposed in some of the stream valleys and the eastern edge has been influenced by the Birmingham-Hints fault.

Two reasonably distinct areas of land fringe the two main ridges on their western and southern edges. The *Stour Valley Plateau Fringe* (Ia8) has a general maximum elevation of 150m and 165m (48 per cent of the values fall within these groups) and a mean maximum elevation of

168m. These generally level areas provide the location for towns such as Cradley Heath, Netherton and Brierley Hill. The *South West Plateau Fringe* (Ia9) flanks the Clent Hills and provides the divide between the rivers Stour and Salwarpe. There has been a certain amount of dissection by streams but the higher part of the plateau is essentially continuous. Average maximum elevation is 156m with a modal group of 165m; thus this unit is very similar to the Stour Valley Plateau Fringe.

The *East Warwickshire Plateau* is represented by the *Ansley Plateau* (Ib1) and the *Corley Plateau* (Ib2). The plateau, as a whole, is almost completely detached from the South Staffordshire Plateau by the valleys of the Tame and Blythe. The two relief units are similar and comparatively simple. Maximum elevation is generally between 120m and 135m with a highest elevation of just over 195m. The Ansley and Corley Plateaus are separated by the Bourne Valley. The data in Table 1.2 indicate how similar the two plateaus are, and the percentage in the modal groups (120m in both cases) demonstrate the level relief. Both plateaus are composed essentially of Middle and Upper Coal Measure sediments with occasional outcrops of Cambrian shales and quartzites. Slopes on the western edge, leading to the Blythe and Lower Tame valleys are comparatively steep, largely the result of the River Blythe cutting into this edge.

The Trent Valley System

The Trent Valley System is represented by the Mid-Tame, Rea and Upper Cole Valleys and the Blythe-Lower Tame Valleys. The *Mid-Tame Valley* (IIc1) is separated from the Upper Tame by a narrow valley between West Bromwich and Great Barr. The River Rea has incised extensively into the Birmingham Plateau and it was on the slope leading down to the river that Birmingham developed. Until the rivers Rea and Tame were controlled, the floodplains were subject to frequent inundation, as were those of the River Cole. The Mid-Tame Valley is generally at a maximum elevation of 120m (38 per cent in the modal group), occasionally rising to just over 165m and a mean maximum elevation of 127m. The *Blythe-Lower Tame* (IIc2) is a much wider and slightly lower unit (average maximum elevation 106m, with a modal group of 90m). Its greater width is probably due to the fact that it is cut into softer Mercian Mudstones. This area was also prone to flooding but this has now been controlled effectively. A single gravel terrace exists and the valley has provided easy access to the Birmingham region from the north.

The Severn Valley System

The Severn Valley System is represented by the *Upper Stour Basin* (IIId1) and the *Salwarpe Basin* (IIIe). The former possesses slightly higher relief (Table 1.2). The Upper Stour Basin is cut into Middle Coal Measure rocks and possesses steep sides and narrow valley floors. These characteristics are represented by a greater range of maximum relief, 90m to 195m, as opposed to 135m for the Salwarpe basin. The Salwarpe Basin is generally lower and possesses gentler slopes than the Upper Stour Valley.

Avon Valley System

A small portion of the *Arrow Valley* (IVb) exists in the south of the area. The river rises on the Birmingham Plateau, below Beacon Hill, and passes through the Lickey Hills at Rednal in a shallow valley cut into the plateau fringe. It has a mean maximum elevation of 148m and a modal group of 135m.

Discussion

This brief analysis has shown that the Birmingham area and the wider region of the West Midlands conurbation is characterised by a variety of landforms and relief units. However the general impression is of a plateau-like region, sloping gently to the east from a high western rim on the watershed of England. The rivers Tame and Blythe and their upper tributaries have cut into this plateau and created the topographical variety seen in the area. Much of this general physical framework is still recognisable in the built-up area and it is this combination of physical and human geography which makes the region distinctive. The significance of this framework will be seen in the subsequent chapters.

References

Kinvig R H Smith J G and Wise M J 1950 *Birmingham and its regional setting,* British Association for the Advancement of Science, Birmingham

Goudie A S and Evans I 1970 *Experimental investigation of rock weathering by salts* Area 2 42-8

Hains B A and Horton A 1969 *British Regional Geology: Central England* Her Majesty's Stationery Office, London

Warwick G T 1950 Relief and physiographic regions, in **Kinvig R H Smith J G and Wise M J** eds *Birmingham and it's Regional Setting* British Association for the Advancement of Science, Birmingham 3-15

CHAPTER 2

Providing water to an inland city: water supply in Birmingham 1826-1996

Michael Tanner

Like many other industrial cities that began to expand rapidly early in the 19th century, Birmingham was to experience serious water supply problems well before its end. These problems were compounded by the city's inland location close to the watershed between the major river basins of the Severn and Trent. The area of the present city was drained only by two minor rivers, the River Rea, which ran along the eastern fringe of the early 19th-century town, and the Cole, which ran a little further east through what was then largely open country. Both rivers flowed northwards to join the River Tame shortly before it turns north to join the Trent. The Tame and its tributaries rise in the Black Country to the north west of Birmingham, but it is still a relatively small river when it runs from west to east about 4 km to the north of the city centre. Not only was the water in the Rea and the Cole inadequate to meet the needs of a growing industrial town but they had insufficient capacity to accommodate the increasing amounts of waste which it generated. The way in which Birmingham satisfied its water needs is a classic story of municipal enterprise and Victorian foresight, which have left a lasting legacy to the city, in spite of continuing growth in demand and a succession of administrative changes.

Early water development

The early growth of Birmingham was based on its abundant groundwater resources in the underlying Triassic sandstones, which surfaced naturally at numerous springs or could be easily reached by shallow wells. These were tapped on an individual basis by their owners, but there was also some commercial distribution by water carts. The need for a more organised approach to the provision of a secure water supply was recognised in the mid-18th century when there was an attempt to establish a public supply. Other attempts were made in 1808 and 1810, but it was not until 1826 that the Birmingham Water Works Company was established by the Birmingham Water Act, which authorized it to abstract water from the River Tame and its small northern tributary, the Hawthorn Brook. The company's statutory service area was only 895 ha, but it was to be responsible for the city's water supply for the next half-century, during which time it followed a strategy which combined the provision of surface water storage with the increasing exploitation of groundwater by deep wells (City of Birmingham 1926).

The company's first major development was the construction of an 8 ha reservoir at Salford, about 4 km to the north-east of the town centre and close to the junction between the Tame and the Rea. Salford Reservoir still remains today as the centrepiece lake of Salford Park, although it is now overshadowed by Spaghetti Junction. Water was diverted from the River Tame into the reservoir, which held 136 million litres (Ml) and acted as a settling basin. Two deep wells were also sunk to supply the reservoir, at Aston and Witton. A steam pumping station was constructed at Salford to raise the water 86 m to a new storage reservoir in Edgbaston 2 km to the west of the town centre, from where it could be distributed to the company's supply area by gravity (Skipp 1983).

In spite of such developments, it was inevitable that a water supply system dependent on such locally-limited resources would find it difficult to keep pace with the rapid escalation of demand that accompanied Birmingham's urban and industrial growth, especially as both its surface and ground water sources became increasingly polluted by domestic sewage and industrial effluents. When Robert Rawlinson visited the town in 1849 to report on its sanitary condition for Edwin Chadwick's General Board of Health, he found that it was 'imperfectly supplied with water'. The waterworks company supplied only about one third of the area for three days a week with water drawn largely from the polluted Tame. Much of the population still had to purchase its water from carts or relied on public or private wells and pumps, most of which were already polluted in the lower part of the town. Rawlinson also expressed the view that a city as important as Birmingham ought to have a water supply of at least 36 million litres a day (Ml/d) (Rawlinson 1849).

During the next two decades the company promoted a series of Bills to extend its service area to include the expanding suburbs and to obtain powers to develop new sources. These authorised it to abstract water from several small rural north-bank tributaries of the Tame and from the rivers Blythe and Bourne, which flow into the Tame to the east of the Cole. A further seven small storage reservoirs were constructed and eight new deep wells sunk around the outer part of the city. These enabled the company to provide a constant supply of water throughout its area by 1853. By the mid-1860s, however, about one third of the company's water was drawn from sources that were becoming less reliable because of the effects of urban growth. It also experienced increasing problems with its use of the Tame because of pollution from the Black Country and suffered a major setback in 1872 when abstraction from the Tame was prohibited altogether, except in times of emergency (Gill 1952). It was these problems that forced it to look to the more distant Blythe and Bourne and to rely increasingly on deep wells.

The municipalisation of Birmingham's water

As a result of these growing problems, there was a great deal of debate during the 1850s and 1860s about the best way to secure a safe and reliable supply, a debate that was intensified by John Snow's establishment of a relationship between cholera and polluted water sources. This debate focused not only on the question of sources of supply but also on whether it was necessary for the Corporation to take over the waterworks, as had been done by some other major cities, most notably by Manchester. Authority to achieve this by compulsory purchase was granted by the City's Improvement Act of 1852, but this was allowed to lapse and it was not until the mayorality of Joseph Chamberlain between 1873-6 that the necessary action was taken. The acquisition of the water undertaking was to be one of Chamberlain's three major achievements during his term of office; the others were the municipalisation of gas and the city improvement scheme. Whereas the benefits which Chamberlain claimed for the other two were largely of an economic nature, his arguments in favour of the municipalisation of water emphasized its importance to the improvement of public health.

In proposing the takeover of the waterworks, Chamberlain laid down two principles which make interesting reading in the light of contemporary debate about the role of the privatised water industry. These were that "all regulated monopolies .... should be controlled by representatives of the people, and not left in the hands of private speculators", and that ".... the waterworks should never be a source of profit, as all profit should go in the reduction of the price of water" (Briggs 1952). After lengthy and sometimes heated negotiations between the City and the Waterworks Company, the necessary powers were granted by the Birmingham Corporation Act 1875 and the undertaking passed to the City on 1st January 1876 for a price of £54,491. The significance of this transfer of responsibility lay not in any immediate alleviation of the city's water supply problems but in the fact that much greater financial and other resources could now be devoted to finding long-term solutions to those problems.

Nevertheless, the first actions of the new Water Committee were to implement plans that had already been drawn up by the Waterworks Company, primarily to improve the quality of the supply as quickly as possible. Most important was the construction of a 40 ha reservoir at Shustoke near the junction between the River Bourne and the Tame, some 16 km to the north-east of the city centre. This reservoir was completed in 1883 and was designed to hold 1900 Ml of water abstracted from the Bourne. It was then taken by conduit to the nearby filter beds at Whiteacre for treatment, from where it was pumped by a 90 cm main to Edgbaston. A group of small reservoirs and associated filter beds was also built at Plant's Brook near Minworth to the north of the Tame Valley to hold water from the stream after which the works was named and which rises in Sutton Park to the north. By 1882 almost all the shallow wells within the city had been polluted by sewage and the provision of additional supplies enabled the Corporation to close 3000 such wells.

Once these works were completed, there were 14 storage reservoirs within the city, with a total capacity of 2800 Ml, although two-thirds of this was provided by Shustoke. At the time, it was hoped that this would prove sufficient for at least the rest of the century, but a combination of a growing population and increased per capita consumption meant that the provision of additional sources of supply were soon to become necessary. By 1890, the total daily supply available to the city was some 80 Ml, but the average daily consumption had risen to 77 Ml, with peaks of up to 100 Ml on some days. In spite of the investment in surface sources, these provided only 7.5 Ml (42 per cent) of the average daily supply, with the remaining 10.5 Ml coming mainly from six deep wells at Aston, King's Vale, Longbridge, Perry Barr, Selly Oak and Witton. This meant that there was already little margin for safety and, with demand increasing at 3 per cent a year, it appeared that further action was urgently required; the Corporation's Engineer estimated that demand would increase by 50 Ml over the next 25 years (Dent 1894).

The tapping of Welsh water

The Corporation therefore commissioned the eminent consulting engineer James Mansergh to advise it on the best way to meet its future water needs. He found that the additional supplies that might be obtained from local streams or new deep wells would be quite inadequate to meet anticipated demands and recommended that the Corporation should look to mid-Wales. On the basis of his advice, a plan was drawn up for the development of new sources near Rhayader, over 120 km due west of the city, a solution that Robert Rawlinson had first suggested 20 years before, when he was assisted by Mansergh. The plan required the acquisition of the catchments of the River Elan and its tributary, the Claerwen, in the upper reaches of the Wye basin, which would yield ample supplies of pure and soft water. When the scheme was announced and the necessary Bill promoted, there was strong opposition from a number of sources, including local landowners, Welsh MPs, access groups and fishery interests on the Wye. Initially it was also

Fig 2.1 Craig Goch Dam in the Elan Valley

opposed by local authorities in London which argued that the needs of the Metropolis should be considered before such a valuable source was acquired by a provincial city.

After a somewhat heated passage through Parliament, the necessary powers to proceed with the scheme were granted by the Birmingham Corporation Water Act 1892, which incorporated a number of safeguards for its opponents. It was also the first such Act to include special clauses securing public rights of access to the catchment area for exercise and recreation. These became known as the 'Birmingham Clauses' and were subsequently inserted as a matter of course into most Bills promoted by water undertakings to take over upland catchments. The Act authorized the acquisition of a catchment area of 18,450 ha and the construction of six reservoirs, three on the Elan (Fig. 2.1) and three on the Claerwen. These would store an estimated 81,800 Ml of water and would yield a total of 464 Ml/d. Although 123 Ml/d had to be released into the Wye as the compensation water demanded by fisheries and other interests, the scheme when fully implemented would provide an assured supply of 340 Ml/d to the City of Birmingham. Since the city's total consumption of water in 1895 was only 77 Ml/d, it was clear that the scheme had the potential to meet all conceivable needs far into the future.

Work on the scheme began in 1893 under the direction of James Mansergh and was to continue for 13 years, but initially only the three reservoirs on the Elan were constructed. These had a total surface area of 340 ha and were capable of storing 50,000 Ml, which could supply up to 160 Ml/d to Birmingham, far in excess of the city's then current needs. Water abstracted from these reservoirs was given preliminary treatment by 30 rough sand filters and was then conveyed to Birmingham by a 118 km aqueduct. The Elan Aqueduct was itself a major engineering achievement. The adoption of a direct route to Birmingham meant that it had to cross not only part of the central Welsh uplands and their foothills to the east but also six railway lines and 11 river valleys, including that of the Severn. It was therefore decided to adopt two modes of construction, which meant that for the next 60 years different parts of the aqueduct had different capacities. About half was constructed in the form of traditional conduits which had the capacity to carry the full 340 Ml/d potential yield of the scheme. This included nine tunnels with a total length of 19.3 km, with the remaining 38.6 km being 'cut-and-cover' channels. The other half comprised 11 siphons which were necessary to cross the river valleys, the largest of which was 28 km long across the Severn valley and included a 213 m bridge over the river itself. Initially these siphon sections were laid as a pair of parallel 105 cm pipelines which could carry only 110 Ml/d, but provision was made for an expansion to the six pipelines that would be needed to bring them up to the capacity of the conduit sections.

An important advantage of the Elan catchment was its elevation, which meant that its water could be conveyed to Birmingham by gravity. In order to achieve this, it was necessary for the aqueduct to start at a height of at least 260 m. The compensation water that was released into the Wye was discharged from the lowest and largest reservoir, Caban Coch, but at a height of only 245 m. It was therefore decided that water should be abstracted at Carreg Ddu, 2.4 km above the Caban Coch Dam where the reservoir narrowed. Here a submerged dam or weir was constructed to maintain a water level of 266 m in the upper reservoir, with the water below the weir being used primarily for compensation. The submerged dam was also used as the foundations for the viaduct which provides road access to the Claerwen valley and effectively divides the reservoir into two. The adoption of this device enabled the aqueduct to be constructed with a drop of 58 m over its 118 km length, yet still reach the new Frankley waterworks on the outskirts of Birmingham (Fig. 2.2) at a height of nearly 200 m. Frankley lies 10 km to the south west of the

Fig 2.2 Frankley Water Treatment Works and Bartley Reservoir

city centre and was selected partly because its height meant that over two thirds of the water it treated could be distributed by gravity. The works at Frankley included a 10 ha receiving reservoir to hold 900 Ml of water and 5.6 ha of slow sand filter beds. Because areas of the city above 170 m could not be served by gravity, two small high level service reservoirs were also built, at Northfield (242 m) and Warley (263 m), to which water was pumped from Frankley.

The Elan Valley works were opened with appropriate ceremony by King Edward VII and Queen Alexandra on 21 July 1904 and the first Welsh water reached the city a week later, but it was not until September that there was a sufficient quantity for it be put into the distribution system. Little more than a year later the whole of the city was supplied with Welsh water, although construction work continued into 1906. The new source of supply largely replaced the existing waterworks, which were then capable of yielding 89 Ml/d. Those that depended on sources regarded as being of doubtful quality because of pollution were quickly abandoned, while others were retained to provide a reserve supply. These included the reservoir at Shustoke, which was later developed so that some of its capacity was used to provide a supplementary supply to Coventry, and four of the deep wells, at Aston, Short Heath, Selly Oak and Longbridge. In spite of the retention of these old sources, the dominance of the Elan Valley scheme was such that the distribution system was designed so that their water could not be mixed with that from Wales and was used only to supply particular districts when deficiencies occurred (Lees 1913). The arrival of Elan water also meant that, for the first time, supplies could be spared for the city's public baths, which had previously had to rely on their own wells, one of which was 217 m deep.

20th century consolidation

The period since 1904 has mainly seen the consolidation, extension and augmentation of the Elan Valley supply rather than any major development of new resources. Only eight years had elapsed when it was felt necessary to add a third 105 cm pipeline to the aqueduct and Parliamentary approval was obtained for the necessary works in 1914. These were delayed by the outbreak of war and did not begin until 1921, by which time it had been decided that the diameter of the third main should be increased to 150 cm. At the same time, there was concern that reliance on a single aqueduct made the city vulnerable to an interruption of supply and the precaution was taken of strengthening the two original cast iron mains by the addition of 10 to 15 cm of concrete. The new concrete-lined steel pipeline was laid in sections over a period of 19 years, with each new section cross-connected to the original mains so that water could be switched between them in case of failure. By the end of 1934, 44 km of the third main had been completed, but the last section was not laid until 26 September 1939. It is perhaps indicative of the city's long-term vision in managing its water supply that a development deemed necessary two years before the start of the First World War was not completed until after the outbreak of the Second without any serious problems resulting from the delay.

The vulnerability of the aqueduct also led to another development during the inter-war period. The receiving reservoir at Frankley had a capacity of only 900 Ml, which was now only four days supply to the city and was regarded as insufficient to meet exceptional circumstances. It was therefore decided to build a new and much larger reservoir adjacent to the Frankley waterworks by damming the valley of the Senneleys Brook. Construction started in 1923 and when the new Bartley Reservoir was completed in 1930, it had a surface water area of 46 ha and a capacity of 2270 Ml, equivalent to 10-12 days consumption at the time. This additional capacity was partly needed because of another increase in the statutory area of supply in 1929, from 35,163 ha to

48,234 ha. Such extensions were always limited to Birmingham's administrative area, plus that of Solihull to the south east. Much of the Black Country, together with Sutton Coldfield, was served, as it is today, by the South Staffordshire Water Works Company, while Wolverhampton, Bilston and the Stourbridge district had their own municipal undertakings. The continued expansion of Birmingham's suburbs during the inter-war years also necessitated improvements to the distribution system and a further 65 ha of land were purchased at Frankley for future developments. At the same time, the old sources within Birmingham continued to be abandoned as the supply from the Elan Valley increased. In 1920, for example, the old deep well at Selly Oak was closed because of contamination, while it was decided that the River Blythe was no longer needed as a reserve source of supply (Jones 1940).

The growth of consumption, which almost doubled between 1904 and 1937, also meant that consideration had to be given to completing the Elan Valley scheme. Parliamentary approval was granted in 1940 for the construction of a single Claerwen Dam in place of the three reservoirs originally proposed, but a start was delayed by the needs of war. Once the war was over, the project was given high priority because consumption had continued to grow rapidly, particularly due to the increase in industrial activity, and construction began in 1946. The 62 m high Claerwen dam was completed in 1952 and created a 260 ha reservoir that could store 48,300 Ml of water, only 2500 Ml less than the combined capacity of the three existing Elan reservoirs. There was also concern that the rapid rise in demand from industry immediately after the war might mean that the Elan Aqueduct would reach its effective capacity within a few years. As a result, it was decided to add a fourth main as quickly as possible by laying another 150 cm concrete-lined pipeline, which would bring the capacity of the siphon sections up to that of the rest of the aqueduct. Work began in 1949 and again the new main was laid in sections, finishing in 1961, by which time the siphons comprised two 105 cm and two 150 cm pipelines.

River regulation and Birmingham's water supply

The construction of the Claerwen Dam was to be the last major water development to be carried out by Birmingham acting independently. Up until this time, the city, like most other large industrial cities in the midlands and north, had regarded it as its duty to develop its own sources of supply for its citizens. Such action was normally triggered by existing or anticipated supply deficiencies and the usual response was to seek additional resources from upland catchments where sources could be protected and impounding reservoirs constructed without too much opposition. The water stored in this way would then be safely conveyed to the areas of demand by a specially-constructed aqueduct, like that from the Elan Valley to Birmingham. The acquisition of catchment areas and the construction of reservoirs and aqueducts was subject only to approval by Parliament, because it was normally necessary to promote a Private Bill to carry out the necessary works. Towards the end of the 19th century, when many of the most productive catchments had already been exploited and there was sometimes fierce competition between municipal authorities for those that remained, Parliament had become increasingly concerned that it was being asked to fulfil a function for which it was not suited.

The first proposals for the adoption of a catchment-based approach to the planning of water resources were made in the 1870s and these were repeated by a succession of Royal Commissions and Committees of Enquiry. Nevertheless, the Private Bill procedure remained the main mechanism by which water development proposals were examined throughout the first half of the 20th century. The only change was that Parliament usually insisted on the establishment of a joint board or similar administrative arrangement wherever it was felt that a particular source of supply should not be appropriated by a single authority. There was some move towards catchment management in 1948 with the establishment of River Boards, but these had no control over the activities of water supply undertakings, whether private or municipal, which continued to act independently.

The arguments in favour of a more coordinated approach were reinforced during the 1950s as the rapidly escalating demand for water led to calls for action at the national level. It was also increasingly argued that the most effective way of conserving water was to use reservoir construction mainly to regulate the flow of rivers, which could then act as natural aqueducts. In this way, water could be transported over long distances at relatively low cost and abstracted as and when required, although it was recognised that additional treatment costs would be incurred. When Birmingham next found it necessary to augment its supply in order to satisfy the growing demand for water within the city, it therefore adopted a very different strategy to that which it had previously followed.

This involved the abstraction of water from the River Severn, which rises in mid-Wales to the north of the Elan catchment and runs about 25 km to the west of the city. For the first time, Birmingham agreed to develop this resource in collaboration with a number of other bodies which wished to abstract water from the river. These included not only local water undertakings but also the Central Electricity Generating Board and the Bristol Waterworks Company. The key to the scheme was the construction of a large regulating reservoir on the River Clywedog in the headwaters of the Severn upstream of Llanidloes. Work began in 1964 and when it was completed in 1967 the new Clywedog Reservoir had a surface area of 250 ha and a capacity of 50,000 Ml. The function of the reservoir is to store water for release during summer low-flow conditions to ensure that sufficient supplies are available to meet the needs of the six million people that depend on the river for their drinking water.

The first compensation water was released from the Clywedog Reservoir in 1968 and in the same year Birmingham completed the works that would enable it to abstract 136 Ml/d from the river. These were located at Trimpley on the east bank of the river to the north of Bewdley and close to the point at which the Elan Aqueduct crosses the Severn. Water abstracted from the river is stored in Trimpley Reservoir, which has a surface area of 12 ha and a capacity of 950 Ml, and is then given preliminary treatment. Because Trimpley lies at a height of less than 40 m, the water then has to be pumped up to the Elan Aqueduct for transmission to Frankley, where it is given further treatment before being mixed with the Elan supply for distribution.

River authorities and national water planning

Birmingham's freedom of action in meeting its water needs was formally brought to an end by the Water Resources Act 1963. This Act created a new system of 29 River Authorities which took over all the functions of the old River Boards, but were also given responsibility for controlling the impoundment and abstraction of water. The effect of this was that responsibility for planning the development of resources at the local level passed to the River Authorities, which were to be advised by the new national Water Resources Board. Because the boundaries of the new bodies were drawn along the watersheds between the major river basins, responsibility for the Birmingham area was divided between the Severn and Trent River Authorities. The new Trent River Authority quickly concluded that the water needs of the West Midlands part of its area would be satisfied by the regulated Severn until at least the year 2000 and turned its attention to the pollution problems caused by the discharge of effluents from Birmingham and the Black Country (Trent River Authority 1967).

It was therefore the Severn River Authority (SRA) that had the main responsibility for ensuring that Birmingham had access to sufficient resources to meet the growing demand for water in the city. The SRA also operated the Clywedog regulating reservoir as agents of the Joint Authority, including Birmingham, which had been set up to construct it. Before the Clywedog Dam was even completed, however, the SRA in conjunction with the Water Resources Board carried out a detailed study showing demand in the Severn basin was rising so fast that there would be need to further augment the flow in the Severn by the mid 1970s. It therefore decided to investigate a number of possible sites for an additional regulating reservoir in the upper reaches of the river (Severn River Authority 1968). When the Authority's consulting engineers reported, they recommended a site in the valley of the River Dulas, another tributary of the River Severn to the south of Clywedog. Accordingly, an application was made to the Secretary of State for Wales for permission to carry out detailed site investigations at what were known as the Upper and Lower Dulas Reservoir sites, an application that was supported by Birmingham Corporation, the South Staffordshire Waterworks Company, the Bristol Waterworks Company and the Central Electricity Generating Board. This application was rejected by the Secretary of State in November 1970, partly on the grounds that such a decision should await the report on the water resources of Wales and the Midlands that was currently being prepared by the Water Resources Board, although he accepted that additional supplies would be needed before 1980.

This report was published in 1971 and recommended a number of developments that should be implemented as soon as possible. Most immediate was a redeployment of the resources stored in the reservoir on the River Vyrnwy, another tributary of the upper Severn to the north of Clywedog. Lake Vyrnwy had been built in the late 1880s as a direct supply reservoir by the City of Liverpool, to which it was connected by aqueduct, but it was now proposed that some of its water should be released to help regulate the Severn. A second proposal was for the implementation of the Shropshire Groundwater Scheme. This scheme had been under investigation by the SRA for some time and involved the use of groundwater abstracted from the sandstone aquifers of north Shropshire to augment dry weather flows in the Severn. Finally, it was recommended that priority should be given to an investigation of the enlargement of Craig Goch, the uppermost of Birmingham's three Elan Valley reservoirs, with a view to using the additional supply to regulate both the Severn and the Wye (Water Resources Board 1971).

The 1973 national strategy for water

The basis of these recommendations was that further storage would be needed in the Severn basin by about 1978, although the redeployment of Lake Vyrnwy's water and the development of the Shropshire Groundwater Scheme would defer this need for a few years. In making such a forecast, the report was following the conventional wisdom of the day by assuming that the rapid increase in the demand for water would continue throughout the rest of the century. This was also the underlying assumption of the comprehensive report on the supply and demand situation in England and Wales that the Water Resources Board published shortly before the water industry was next reorganised in 1974 (Water Resources Board, 1973).

This report included a 'preferred strategy' for the development of resources up to 2001 and focused on those regions where demand could not be readily satisfied by the exploitation of local sources. Particular attention was paid to the needs of Wales and the Midlands, partly because it was felt that the Severn might be the key to a long-term solution to the water-supply problems of south-east England. As far as Birmingham was concerned, it was suggested, on the basis of forecasts made by local water supply undertakings, that its 1971 demand of 725 Ml/d would rise to 1680 Ml/d by 2001, an increase of 132 per cent. Alternative forecasts based on population growth and trends in per capita consumption gave a rather lower figure for 2001 of 1100 Ml/d. Nevertheless, when account was taken of existing and proposed resource development, the 'strategic planning deficiency' for 2001 was estimated to be 705 Ml/d, which implied a need to nearly double the supply to the city over the next 30 years.

At the national level, the Water Resources Board's preferred strategy involved the integrated development of various sources, including the building of one or more estuarial barrages, the construction of new reservoirs and the enlargement of existing ones, the development of groundwater resources and the artificial recharge of aquifers. The new and enlarged reservoirs would mainly be used to regulate the larger rivers whose function would increasingly be to transport water, while a number of aqueducts would be built to transfer water between river basins. As far as Birmingham was concerned, a solution would be found in the further development of sources in mid-Wales. A complicating factor here was the possibility that these sources would also be used to supply water to London and the South East via the rivers Severn and Thames, which raised issues reminiscent of those which surfaced when Birmingham first proposed to exploit the resources of the Elan Valley 80 years before.

It was therefore recommended that two of the proposals made in the regional report should go ahead during the next decade; the Shropshire Groundwater Scheme was to be brought into service by 1978 and the enlargement of Craig Goch implemented by 1980. In the longer term, it might also be necessary to consider the enlargement of the Clywedog or Vyrnwy reservoirs. The Board's preference for the enlargement of Craig Goch reflected the fact that its potential yield might be in excess of 1200 Ml/d, while the Shropshire sandstone could provide up to 225 Ml/d to the Severn at relatively low cost. This suggested that there was sufficient capacity to satisfy Birmingham's needs well into the next century, so long as Severn water was not needed to supply London and the south east.

The nationalisation of Birmingham's water

The passage of the Water Act 1973, which came into force on 1 April 1974, meant that Birmingham lost control of its water supply almost a century after it had become a municipal enterprise. What the Act did was to amalgamate all water management functions into 10 multi-functional Regional Water Authorities, including water supply which had previously been mainly the responsibility of local government. The South Staffordshire Water Works Company, like the other remaining private water companies, was excluded, but was to act as the agent of the water authority. Birmingham now lay at the heart of the new Severn Trent Water Authority which, because the two major river basins came under one administration, was responsible not only for the city's water supply but also for disposing of its liquid wastes. Although it was anticipated that the new water authorities would implement the 1973 national strategy, they were expected to do so without the guidance of the Water Resources Board, which was replaced by a purely advisory National Water Council without any planning functions.

Severn Trent therefore decided to go ahead with the enlargement of Craig Goch in collaboration with the Welsh Water Authority, within whose area the Elan Valley was located. Agreement was reached between the two authorities to raise the dam so that the reservoir would yield an additional 1020 Ml/d for use in regulating the Wye and the Severn. This would be more than enough to satisfy the needs of Birmingham and other areas that relied on Severn water for the foreseeable future. In spite of this agreement, the implementation of the scheme was deferred several times as forecasts of the future demand for water were steadily revised downwards. Eventually Severn-Trent decided to withdraw from the scheme in the light of its own analysis of water resource needs in its area, which was published in 1981.

This concluded that the increase in demand up to 2001 was likely to be of the order of 25 per cent, compared with a forecast of 42 per cent made only four years before. Much of this growth could be satisfied by the more efficient use of existing resources, particularly through the integration of the various water supply systems which it had inherited (Severn Trent Water 1983). The remaining deficit would be largely made up by implementing the Shropshire Groundwater Scheme, which it had continued to investigate since 1974. This was designed to be built in eight stages in response to the growth of demand and would eventually yield 225 Ml/d. The first stage was completed in 1985, when it was expected that the second stage would not be required until at least the early 1990s.

As far as Birmingham was concerned, the 15-year regime of the Severn Trent Water Authority was mainly marked by a consolidation of the existing system. This was reflected both in the greater emphasis on the integration of water supply sources and works at the regional scale and in investment in the maintenance and improvement of the infrastructure, like the £13 million spent on safeguarding the Elan Aqueduct in 1986-7. The resilience of this Victorian system of supply was demonstrated during the long hot summer and drought of 1976. Whereas the Authority's lowland reservoirs had remained seriously depleted during the previous winter, rainfall in the Elan Valley catchment was over 70 per cent of its average amount and was sufficient to virtually refill its reservoirs. As a result, Birmingham was spared the stringent restrictions on water use that had to be introduced in other parts of the country (Severn Trent Water 1977). The main changes during this period were that any increase in demand within the city was wholly met by abstraction from the Severn, a process that had begun with the completion of Clywedog in 1968, and that some of the water in the Severn was drawn from groundwater sources in Shropshire. This was the situation when there was yet another change of responsibility for the management of water resources.

The privatization of Birmingham's water

The privatization of the water industry in England and Wales by the Water Act 1989 meant that Birmingham's water supply was returned to the private sector after 124 years in public ownership. Water management functions were once again divided. The two major operational functions of water supply and sewage treatment were combined into a water service company and sold as Severn Trent Water Limited. Like other privatized utilities, the water industry has its own regulator, the Office of Water Services, which happens to be based in Birmingham. The remaining, mainly regulatory, functions were vested in a new public body, the National Rivers Authority (NRA), which operates through eight regions. Responsibility for ensuring that Birmingham's water needs are satisfied now rested with the NRA's Severn-Trent Region, although the Elan Valley reservoirs are in its Welsh Region.

This stems from the NRA's statutory duties relating to the conservation and management of water resources, which include the regulation of rivers. Its approach to carrying out these duties is based on the preparation of regional water resource strategies, which will be brought together into a National Strategy. The NRA published its strategy for the Severn-Trent Region in 1993, which emphasized the key role of the region and its two major rivers in the national development of water resources. This used a number of demand forecast scenarios to examine the regional water supply situation during the planning period to 2021. It concluded that, unless demand increased at a rate above that produced by the medium scenario, existing and planned resource developments would meet needs throughout most of this period. The NRA's preferred strategy for meeting any deficits that occurred was increased abstraction from the Severn, which could be augmented up to the levels required by the medium scenario by developing further stages of the Shropshire Groundwater Scheme, which would be managed by the NRA (NRA 1993).

The extent to which other developments would be required to support abstraction from the Severn, like the redeployment of Vyrnwy water and the enlargement of Craig Goch, would depend upon the reliance of the National Water Strategy on inter-basin transfers. Two such possible transfers from the Severn basin were under consideration, into the Trent near Stafford and into the upper Thames. Such long-term strategic issues are no longer the responsibility of Severn Trent Water, the company which supplies water to Birmingham. Severn Trent's priority in its investment programme since privatization has been in the modernization of its infrastructure. As far as its water supply functions are concerned, the emphasis has been on the improvement of quality and capital investment has included the progressive renewal or refurbishment of the distribution system and a £70 million renovation of the Frankley Water Treatment Plant completed in 1994. This latter development was partly a response to the pollution risk posed by the increasing numbers of seagulls that used Bartley Reservoir as a roost, many of which spent their days on local sewage works.

Birmingham's water supply in 1996

There have been a number of important changes in the way in which Birmingham is provided with water since the first supplies from the Elan Valley reached the city in 1904 (Fig 2.3). Until the 1960s these changes were usually a direct response to the needs generated by rising levels of demand, but since then the situation has become more complex. Whereas domestic demand has continued to increase, there has been a marked decline in the demand from manufacturing industry (NRA 1993). This has particularly affected abstraction from the groundwater resources under Birmingham itself. Large industrial users began to sink their own wells and boreholes in the 1860s and abstraction steadily increased until it reached a peak in the years after the Second World War, although the water table continued to fall in some areas until the early 1960s. Subsequently licensed abstraction within the city has declined to less than 20 per cent of its 1940s peak and groundwater levels have risen steadily so that the original water table has been restored in many areas. This has caused particular problems in the older industrial areas along the Tame and Rea valleys to the north of the city centre where basements have become flooded and some firms have had to install pumps (Knipe *et al.* 1993).

The most striking changes, however, have affected the ownership and control of the city's water supply system. Birmingham is no longer supplied by a municipally-owned undertaking that is concerned only with supplying its statutory area of supply and seeks to satisfy any increase of demand by developing its own sources. Instead, the city is now served by the Birmingham Water District, one of the 15 operational districts through which Severn Trent Water organises its activities, while the development and allocation of water resources is carried out at the same regional level by an agency of central government, the NRA. As a result, decisions about the

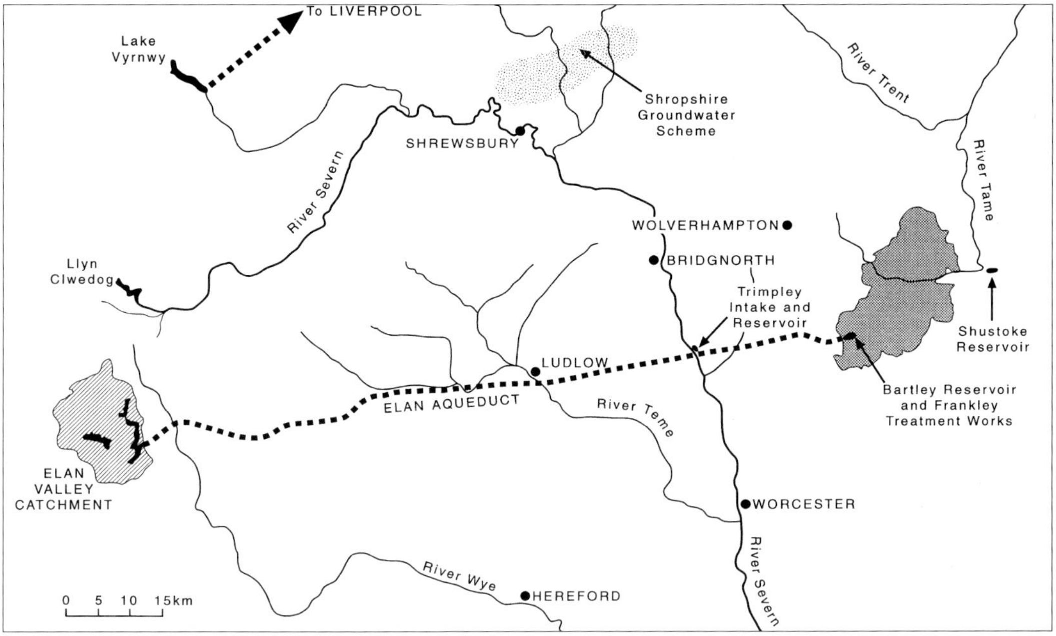

Fig 2.3 Birmingham's water supply system in 1996

city's water supply are no longer taken purely in the interests of its citizens, but reflect regional or even national needs. At one level, this may be seen as the inevitable outcome of the decline of municipal power in Britain, which was at its peak at the time when Birmingham was developing its Elan Valley supply system, but which has been steadily eroded ever since, particularly during the last quarter-century.

Such a view ignores both the importance of technical changes in the water industry and the growing recognition that water is such a scarce and valuable resource that its conservation can only be properly achieved by strategic planning and management at the regional level. In particular, the use of river regulation as the main means for transporting water has the effect of creating a common supply source which cannot be appropriated by a single user and which needs to be managed at the catchment level. There is also the fact that few cities today rely entirely on a single source for their water. Whereas Birmingham in 1905 was able to dedicate its whole water supply system to its own Elan Valley source, retaining only a few local sources to cover emergencies, it now relies to a significant extent on abstraction from the Severn, which it shares with other cities from Shrewsbury to Bristol and may, in the long term, also share with London and the cities of the east midlands. Since the Severn is itself augmented by supplies from a combination of traditional impounding reservoirs and groundwater sources, the integration and management of supply systems at a regional scale has become essential.

Not only is Birmingham's water supply in 1996 delivered by a highly complex regional system, but there has also been a massive increase in the quantities involved. In 1905, when Elan Valley water was first distributed throughout the city, the average supply was 81 Ml/d, but by 1996 this had risen two and a half times, to 320 Ml/d. Nevertheless, the basic structure of the city's supply system and the sources it uses are remarkably similar to what they were in 1905. Up to 340 Ml/d is imported from the Elan Valley and this is still treated at Frankley, one of the largest water treatment works in the country, before being distributed to the 1.2 million people within the Birmingham Supply District. It is true that this is supplemented by abstraction of up to 180 Ml/d from the Severn at Trimpley, but much of this also comes from similar sources in mid-Wales, although currently from the Severn rather than the Wye catchment. Similarly, most of the water which the city draws from mid-Wales is discharged into the Trent system, which not only has significant implications for the quality of that river but should also be regarded as a large scale inter-basin water transfer. It could also be argued that there are important parallels with Birmingham's water supply system before it was municipalised in 1875. Water is once again supplied by a private company on a commercial, if highly regulated, basis, while the city depends for its supplies on the same mixture of surface water storage, river abstraction and groundwater. What has changed is the scale of the regional system from which the city draws its supplies and the complexity of the management structure.

Acknowledgements

The photographs of Frankley Water Treatment Plant and Craig Goch dam were kindly provided by Severn Trent Water.

References

Black H J 1957 *History of the Corporation of Birmingham, Volume VI (1936-1950): Part 1* Corporation of the City of Birmingham, Birmingham

Briggs A 1952 *History of Birmingham, volume II: borough and city 1865-1938* Oxford University Press for the City of Birmingham, Oxford

City of Birmingham Water Department 1926 *Birmingham Corporation Water Works: a short history of the development of the undertaking with a description of the existing sources of supply* Birmingham Corporation, Birmingham

Dent R K 1894 *The making of Birmingham, being a history of the rise and growth of the Midland metropolis* J L Allday, Birmingham

Gill C 1952 *History of Birmingham, volume I: manor and borough to 1865* Oxford University Press for the City of Birmingham, Oxford

Jones J T 1940 *History of the Corporation of Birmingham, Volume V (1915-1935): Part 1* Corporation of the City of Birmingham, Birmingham

Knipe C V Lloyd J W Lerner D N and Greswell R 1993 *Rising groundwater levels in Birmingham and the engineering implications* Special Publication 92, Construction Industry Research and Information Association, London

Lees E A 1913 City of Birmingham water supply, in **Auden, G A** ed *A handbook for Birmingham and the neighbourhood: prepared for the 83rd meeting of the British Association for the Advancement of Science* Cornish Brothers, Birmingham 183-200

National Rivers Authority, Severn-Trent Region 1993 *Regional water resources strategy: Severn-Trent Region* NRA, Birmingham

Rawlinson R 1849 *Report to the General Board of Health on a preliminary inquiry into the sewerage, drainage, and supply of water, and the sanitary condition of the inhabitants of the Borough of Birmingham* HMSO, London

Severn River Authority 1968 *Third annual report: year ended 31 March 1968* the Authority, Great Malvern

Severn Trent Water 1977 *Report and accounts 1976-77* Severn Trent Water Authority, Birmingham
Severn Trent Water 1983 *Report and accounts 1982-83* Severn Trent Water, Birmingham
Skipp V 1983 *The making of Victorian Birmingham* Victor Skipp, Birmingham
Trent River Authority 1967 *Annual report: year ended 31 March 1967* the Authority, Nottingham
Water Resources Board 1971 *Water Resources in Wales and the Midlands* HMSO, London
Water Resources Board 1973 *Water Resources in England and Wales, Volume 1: Report and Volume 2: Appendices* HMSO, London

CHAPTER 3

Inter-basin water transfers and regional water management

Geoff Petts and Paul Wood

Water scarcity resulting from population growth, increasing water use, and climate change, is of major concern to many governments worldwide. The construction of dams and reservoirs is a solution to the problem of unreliable water supplies. Artificial transfers of water from one river basin to another are a solution to regional water shortages. Major Inter-Basin Transfers (IBTs) are those that involve the mass transfer of water from one geographically distinct river basin to another (Davies et al. 1992). They include simple schemes where surface-water abstractions supply transfers from one river to another but often require water storage reservoirs to sustain a reliable yield from the donor catchment. In some cases, the transferred water may be used before discharge as effluent water into the receiving stream.

From an international perspective, long-distance transfers over hundreds and in some cases thousands of kilometres have been used or proposed to overcome major regional water deficits (e.g Biswas et al. 1983, Golubev and Biswas 1985, O'Keeffe and De Moor 1988, Falkenmark 1989, Roy and Messier 1989, Davies et al. 1992, Dudgeon 1992, Petts 1994). Such schemes can have major environmental impacts. They can alter dramatically the seasonal pattern of river flows and water-quality (temperature, concentrations of nutrients etc.) in both the donor and receiving rivers, leading to changes of their animal and plant communities. Changes may be particularly dramatic in naturally ephemeral receiving

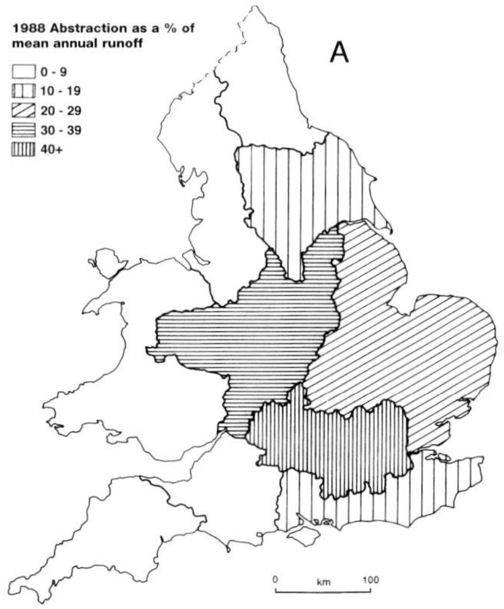

Fig 3.1 The distribution of water abstractions by region in England and Wales

streams (e.g. Hadley et al. 1987, Sherrard and Erskine 1991). IBTs break down natural biogeographical barriers, reduce the diversity of river types, assist the spread of alien fauna, flora and disease vectors, and lead to the mixing of population gene pools (Davies et al. 1992). This chapter examines the potential role of inter-basin transfers in meeting forecast water deficits in England and Wales and emphasises the environmental concerns that must be addressed.

The regional context

England and Wales comprise an area of about 152,000 km^2, characterised by small drainage basins of which only the Thames, Severn, Trent, Wye, Ouse and Great Ouse have areas larger than 3000km^2. Hydrologically and biogeographically, the river basins can be divided into two general types. The basins of the wet uplands to the north and west contrast with those of the drier lowlands in the south and east. The line between these two geographically distinct areas is between the estuaries of the Tees in the north east and the Exe in the south west, although the divide defined by different criteria is not always coincident.

Population densities either side of the Tees-Exe divide are markedly different: in 1993, a density of approximately 470 persons per km^2 to the east of the watershed, rising to 920 in the Thames area, contrasts with 260 persons per km^2 to the west with a low of 140 in the south west. Water abstractions reflect this pattern especially when expressed as a proportion of mean annual streamflow (Fig. 3.1A). One indicator of the impact of abstractions on the environment is the residual annual flow after abstractions and before effluent returns (Fig. 3.1B). Given projected increases in water demands, water resources have to be developed to be able to meet abstraction requirements during drought years whilst protecting environmental needs. After allowing for reasonable demand management and 'local' resource developments, forecasts for 2021 (Table 3.1) show deficits in some regions to the east of the Tees-Exe divide. The deficits are not related to a region-wide resource balance but indicate that one or more demand centres within a region will be in deficit (NRA 1993). Such deficits must be satisfied by strategic developments and inter-basin transfers may be an inevitable component of a national water resource strategy.

Administative area/region	Current available yield (Ml/d)	Current demand (Ml/d)	Public water supply deficit in 2021 (Ml/d)		Public water supply deficit in 2021 after local resource options developed	
			Medium scenario	High scenario	Medium scenario	High scenario
Northumbria Area	2046	1106	0	14	0	0
Yorkshire Area	1657	1506	29	261	0	0
North-West Region	2811	2579	0	164	0	0
Welsh Region	1637	1299	38	133	0	0
South-West Area	604	499	40	124	0	0
Wessex Area	1045	901	58	201	0	84
Severn-Trent Region	2724	2411	182	577	4	252
Anglian Region	2223	1764	100	195	72	128
Thames Region	4333	3975	270	867	66	629
Southern Region	1513	1220	57	152	0	0

Table 3.1 Current water resources (1991 baseline) and average public water supply deficits at demand centre level in 2021 under medium and high demand scenarios (NRA 1994)

The Severn-Trent Region, by virtue of its location, has a central role in the development of water resources nationally (NRA 1993). Birmingham is located close to the Tees-Exe divide and the watershed between the Severn and Trent catchments. Of the total population in the two catchments (about 8.4 million) over 99 per cent are connected to the public supply and more than 97 per cent are connected to the sewer system. Inter-basin water transfers between the two basins have played a major role in the development of the Midlands over the past century. They have involved not only water abstractions from the donor river (the Severn) and waste-water discharges to the receiving river (the Trent), but also the construction of canals crossing the biogeographical divide.

Historical Background

The transfer of water by pipeline, aqueduct or canal from one river basin to another for the purpose of redistributing water resources is a long-established practice. Local water redistribution schemes, involving transfers over distances of up to 30km, have been important for over 400 years. One of the earliest schemes was that made in 1590 when Sir Francis Drake obtained powers to divert the water of the River Meavy via a 29km leat or trench (2m wide) to Plymouth. The 1585 Act allocated only 2.62 megalitres per day (Ml/d), i.e. 0.03 cubic metres per second (cumecs), to sustain flows in the donor river for a yield of more than 36.4 Ml/d (Walters 1936). The issue of how much water must be allocated to meet in-river needs within the donor river remains a key area of debate today (Petts 1996).

Walters text 'The Nation's Water Supplies' describes nineteenth century proposals to transfer water more than 100km from the 'gathering grounds' of Wales to Merseyside, Birmingham and London; from Pennine catchments to Leicester; and from Thirlmere and Haweswater in the Lake District to Manchester (Fig. 3.2). The first great inter-basin scheme in the UK was the Liverpool Scheme. Prior to 1849, Liverpool was dependent upon wells in the New Red Sandstone, an important water-bearing formation which historically provided a plentiful water supply from shallow wells (Walters 1936). These sources became brackish and surface-water sources on the western slopes of the Pennines were transferred over a distance of about 30km. By the 1880s these supplies proved inadequate. To meet the growing demands, the Vyrnwy dam, in North Wales, was completed in 1892, at the time creating Europe's largest artificial reservoir which supplied Liverpool via a 100km-long pipeline (Fig. 3.2).

The West Midlands

Like Liverpool, Birmingham also developed, in part, on the New Red Sandstone. By 1891, local sources could supply over 90 Ml/d but some supplies were already polluted. In order to meet the growing demand, in 1904, runoff from a 185 km^2 gathering ground in the upper Wye valley of mid-Wales was stored in reservoirs and transported by a 118km pipeline (Fig. 3.2) to a storage reservoir at Frankley, later to be supplemented by one at Bartley; the head of 52m being sufficient to enable water to be supplied without pumping. In the donor river, the River Wye, approximately five per cent of the mean flow at Monmouth is lost because of transfers to Birmingham (Edwards and Brooker 1982).

Tanner (Chapter 2) describes the history of supplying water to Birmingham in detail. However, the Birmingham scheme was particularly significant because specific attention to environmental needs was raised for the first time in water resources developments. The Bill, by

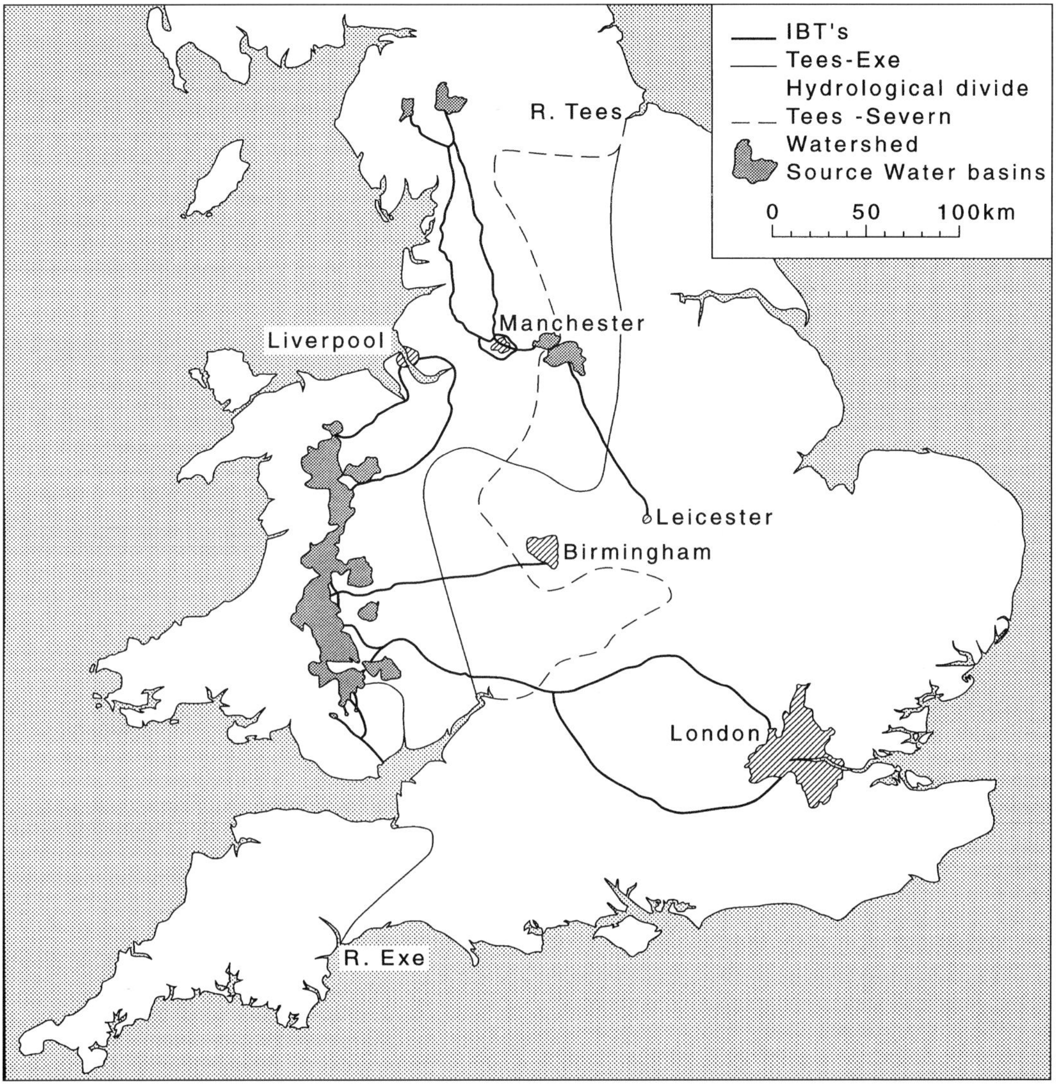

Fig 3.2 19th century plans for inter-basin transfers and their gathering grounds

the Corporation of Birmingham (1892), to build storage reservoirs in the upper Wye valley, included the setting of a 'comprehensive flow' to maintain discharges along the rivers affected by storage and abstraction. Below Caban Coch dam the compensation flow to the River Elan was fixed at 1.4 cumecs (123 Ml/d) and included a clause empowering the Wye Conservancy to demand 'freshets' (short periods of high flows) to protect the salmon fishery. The freshet volume of 477 Ml/d (2.8 cumecs for 48 hours) would be accumulated over a period of 21 days prior to the date of the release by reducing the compensation flow to 1.16 cumecs (100 Ml/d). This established a precedent for protecting the river environment using variably compensation flows regulated by control rules.

Whilst the management of donor rivers focused on sustaining minimum flows to protect river needs, the major problem for the receiving rivers was pollution caused by untreated or inadequately treated effluent discharges. By the mid-19th century over half the population of Britain lived in towns and cities and the rivers of the major industrialised areas became notorious for pollution caused by sewage and trade effluent. The innovation of using pipelines to make every urban property part of a unified water-supply and drainage system was to have dramatic consequences for rivers (Sheail 1988). The River Trent, for example, was severely affected: summer dry weather flows were increased and effluent discharges exceeded natural runoff. By 1900 salmon had disappeared from the Trent and by 1950 the upper river was virtually devoid of fish and invertebrate life (Mann 1989).

An additional problem was the break down of biogeographical divides by the building of canals. The West Midlands is at the centre of an extensive network of inland waterways (Fig. 3.3). Initiated by Acts of Parliament between 1766 and 1769, the canals were built to link the major navigable rivers: the Staffordshire and Worcestershire Canal (1. linking the Severn and Trent), the Trent and Mersey Canal (2) and the Coventry and Oxford canals (3. linking the Trent and Thames). Together with the Leeds and Liverpool Canal (4) built in 1770, these artificial waterways linked rivers draining basins on both sides of the Tees-Severn watershed. They

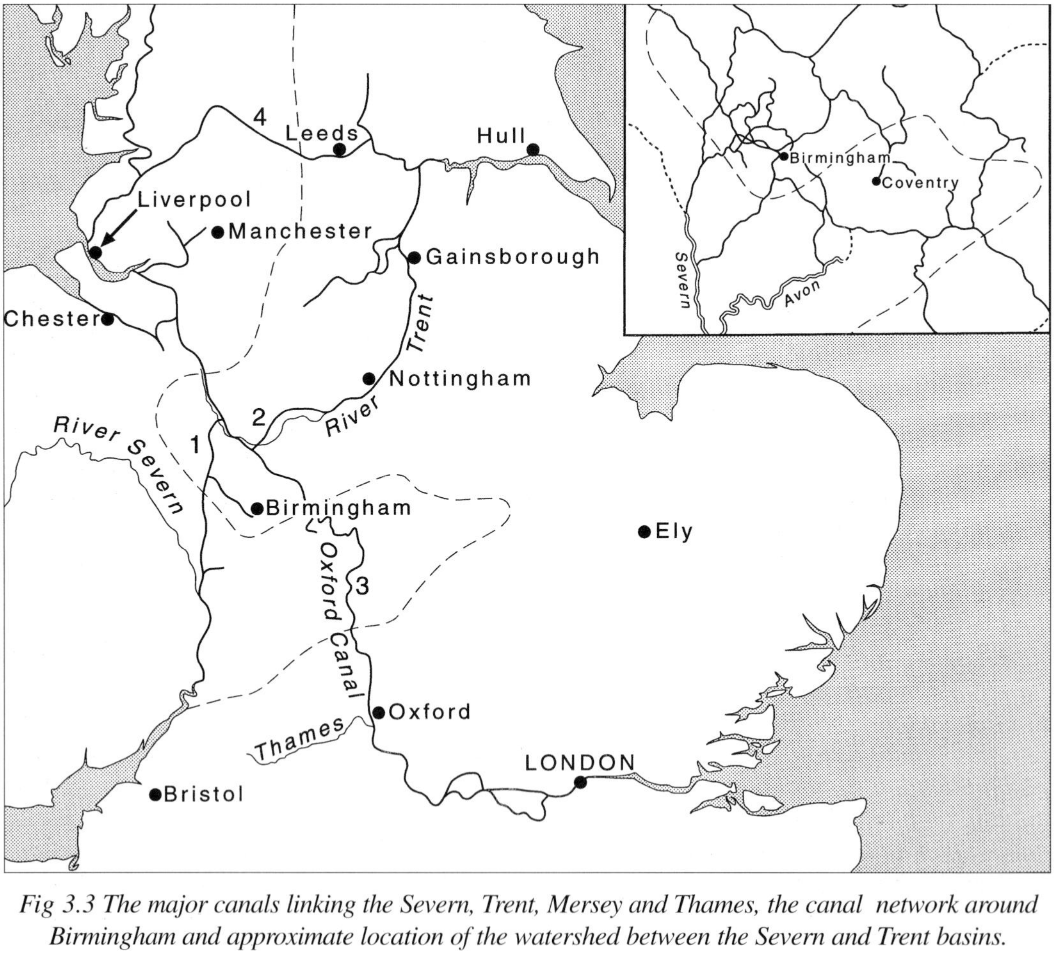

Fig 3.3 The major canals linking the Severn, Trent, Mersey and Thames, the canal network around Birmingham and approximate location of the watershed between the Severn and Trent basins.

allowed ready interchange of species. The slow-flowing canals were ideal habitats for the invasion of predominantly lowland species, such as roach *Rutilus rutilus* L., bream *Aramis brama* L., and pike *Esox lucius* L. (Mann 1989). The canals also provided unique habitats and the build-up of exotic species of fish in canals may be a significant issue. Wheeler (1974, in Mann 1988) reported the existence of the South American Guppy, *Poecilia reticulate,* in the St. Helens Canal and in the River Lee, London. In turn, these canal populations influenced the composition of the river fish communities, as seen along the middle and lower Trent (Mann 1989).

The present situation

The River Severn

The longest of Britain's regulated rivers, the River Severn, is intensively controlled (see *Operating Rules for the River Severn*, STWA 1988, Douglas 1988). The primary control point is at Bewdley (Fig. 3.4), the location of a long historic record of river levels and flows (Wood 1987), and upstream of the first major 'industrial' tributary, the Stour, which rises in the Black Country. Today, the river supports abstractions of 2300 Ml/d (NRA 1993).

Between the 1950s and the mid-1970s, intakes were constructed on the river to satisfy remote demands outside the catchment boundary, as well as local demands where water is returned as effluent back to the river close to the point of abstraction. The main intakes were built at: Hampton Loade to supply Wolverhampton and the Black Country (150+ Ml/d) and Trimpley to supply Birmingham (100+ Ml/d); and downstream of Bewdley at Upton to supply Coventry, Mythe to supply Gloucester and Cheltenham, and Purton to supply Bristol.

During the early 1960s it was realised that river flows during a prolonged period of dry weather would no longer be sufficient to support the increasing water demands. The major abstractors then joined with the newly founded Severn River Authority to form the Clywedog Reservoir Joint Authority (CRJA). The CRJA Act 1963 authorised the construction of the Clywedog Reservoir in the headwaters of the Severn to provide water storage for release to augment river flows. The reservoir, first filled in 1968, has a capacity of 50,000 megalitres of water. The CRJA Act 1963 also imposed a statutory obligation on the Authority to maintain a minimum flow in the river. A minimum flow of 727 Ml/d at Bewdley was set to protect downstream abstractions, to ensure levels for navigation, and to ensure adequate residual flows to the estuary to maintain quality. Abstractors are required to report their daily abstractions promptly during periods of active flow augmentation. Public water supply licences stipulate an annual and daily maximum quantity to be abstracted. In some cases, there is also a stipulation that average abstraction, in periods of protracted flow augmentation, may not exceed the annual licensed rate.

In order to decide on release requirements for Clywedog, flows at Bewdley had to be forecast four or five days ahead and the uncertainty inherent in these forecasts required a new approach (Douglas 1988). Thus, the Clywedog Act was varied so that a mean 5-day flow was to be maintained (not a day by day flow). Prescribed (mean 5-day) residual flows at Bewdley were raised to 850 Ml/d but a lower 24-hour minimum of 650 Ml/d was introduced, subject only that the augmentation release from Lyn Clywedog need not exceed 500 Ml/d. The first 130 Ml/d of flow augmentation releases required by the Bewdley prescribed flow are passed through turbines for hydroelectricity generation. Flow regulation has fundamentally affected the pattern of flows especially in the upper river above Shrewsbury, although the effects of low flow modification is obvious over the full length of the river (Douglas 1988). During drought conditions, regulation allows water abstractions of more than 700 Ml/d - four times that which could be supported by natural flows without regulation.

The River Trent

The River Trent (Fig. 3.4) is one of the few major underdeveloped sources of surface waters in England. To a large degree this reflects the poor quality of the river which receives large volumes of effluent water imported from the Severn basin. Major consented effluent discharges are from the Minworth (450 Ml/d) and Coleshill Water Recovery Works (65.4 Ml/d). Such discharges have markedly altered the pattern of flows from the upper catchment (Table 3.2), significantly increasing discharges especially during dry summers. Along the lower river the contribution of effluents at times of dry weather can exceed 50 per cent of the total flow.

The Trent and several major headwater tributaries rise in or near conurbations and until the mid-1960s the quality of the Trent from Stoke down to Nottingham was no better than a reasonably treated sewage effluent (Brewin and Martin 1988). This was caused by inadequate sewage treatment and a lack of capacity in the sewers and at the treatment works. Consequently, very large and polluting flows were discharged from storm overflows in the Birmingham area even under dry weather conditions.

Since the mid 1960s, following the introduction of the pollution control legislation and a new commitment of resources to improve sewage treatment, the quality of the Trent has improved dramatically. Biological Oxygen Demand exceeded 13 mg/l in the 1950s but by 1980 had been reduced to less than 5 mg/l (Mann 1989). The 1990 water-quality survey showed that the Trent is now a class 2 river, with the exception of a reach of about 20km through and downstream of Stoke. Flows at Stoke have declined since the early 1980s due to the closure of a number of small sewage works and the piping of effluent to Strongford WRW (mean flow in 1990/91 of 109 Ml/d).

Most of the inter-basin transfers of water that supply Birmingham and the West Midlands are eventually discharged as effluent to the Tame. Until the mid 1970s, the River Tame was devoid of fish (Mann 1989). The Tame remains class 4 in its upper sector but has been improved to class 3 below the Tame purification lakes constructed in the early 1980s. Populations of roach, dace, bream, chub, bleak and gudgeon had become re-established in the reaches below the lakes (Severn Trent Water Authority 1983).

Flows in the middle and lower Trent are controlled by abstraction licenses. At present, power stations are by far the largest abstractors but the heated effluent water is returned to the river a short distance downstream. Estimated peak evaporative loss is less than five per cent (NRA 1993). The power stations are licensed for their gross abstractions and the peak daily licensed quantity at the power stations, and new licenses can be permitted only when flows exceed this level. Currently, the peak daily abstraction of 3211 Ml/d at Staythorpe B near Newark is the minimum flow for new abstraction licences.

The future: strategic resource options and transfers

The national water resources strategy (NRA 1994) has examined the need for new strategic supplies to meet marginal demands for water; after taking account of the scale of existing resources, potential local options and the possible growth in water demand. These are

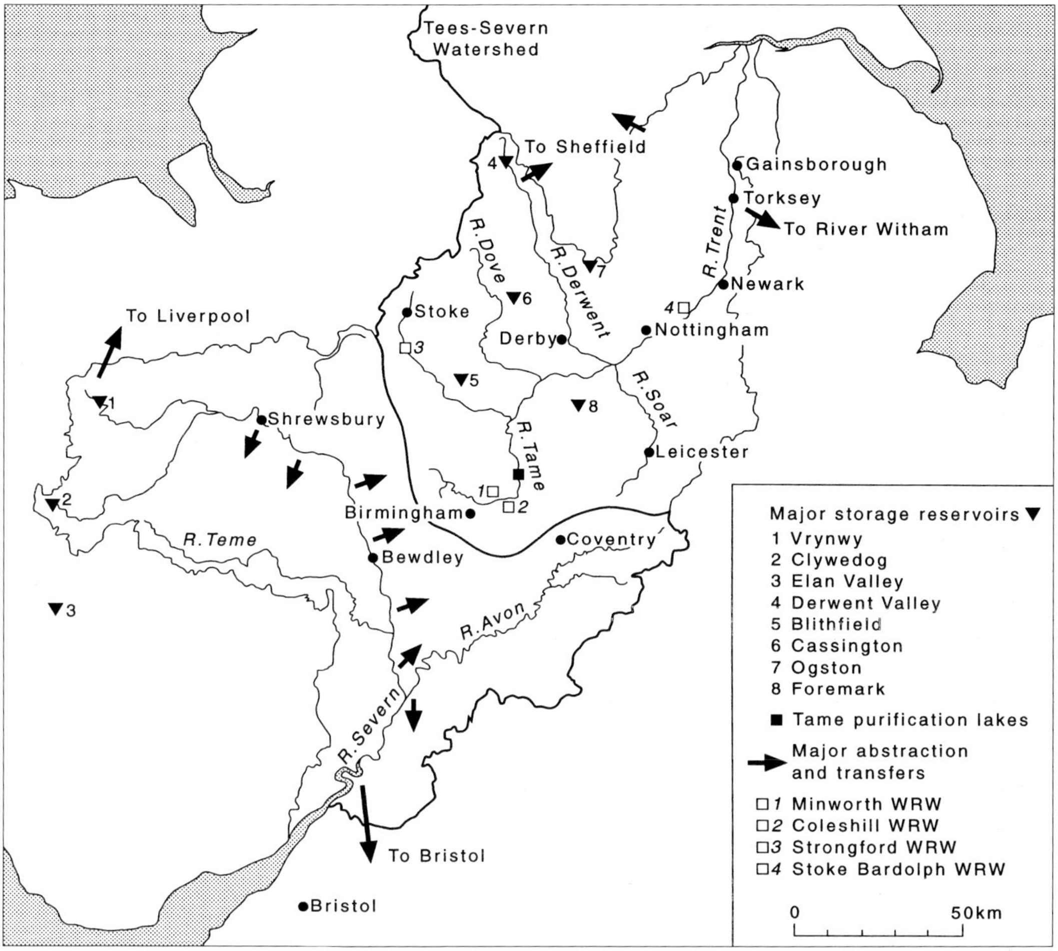

Fig 3.4 The Severn and Trent catchments showing major storage reservoirs, abstractions, transfers and effluent discharges.

Flow	Gauged (Ml/d)	Estimated Natural (Ml/d)	Net gain (Ml/d)
Average	3026	2213	813
Dry weather flow	1221	531	690

Table 3.2 Upper Trent River flows at Drakelow gauging station, having a drainage area of 3072 km² (from NRA 1993 River Trent Control Rules)

summarised below. At the present time impacts of future climate change have not been incorporated in strategic plans but the results of new research are periodically reviewed. The strategy focuses on schemes which are relatively large in scale and impact, or which would require transfer of water from one basin to another. The West Midlands is at a strategic location in these plans which seek to redistribute water to Anglian and Thames regions to supply the forecast deficits (see Table 3.1).

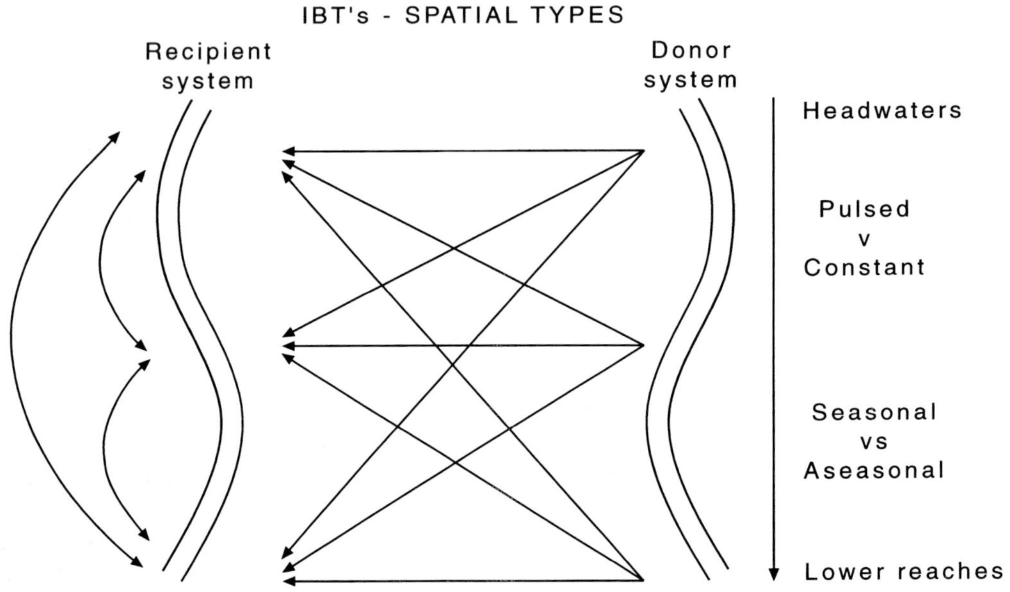

Fig 3.5 Diagrammatic representation of the major types of IBTs

Unsupported Trent

Downstream of Nottingham, artificial inputs (effluent discharges resulting from inter-basin transfers) increase dry weather flows by about 1000 Ml/d. Effluent discharges are likely to increase in the future and one estimate forecasts an increase to the upper Trent by 46 Ml/d to the year 2021. Following the improvements in water quality over the past thirty years, these artificial inputs are now being actively considered as an important water supply source for the future. Currently, the only major licensed abstraction from the Trent for water supply is the Lower Trent-Witham-Ancholme scheme. This has an intake at Torksey (see Fig. 3.4), about 25km below the Staythorpe power station, licensed for daily abstractions of up to 182 Ml/d. The largest peak daily licence below Staythorpe, for Cottam power station which is close to the Torksey intake, is only 227 Ml/d. In the future, additional transfers from the Trent at Torksey could increase supplies to Anglia Region and a new transfer could be introduced near Gainsborough in the tidal Trent to supply Yorkshire Region. An abstraction from the Trent, near Rugeley in the upper river, would supplement inflows to Blithfield Reservoir (see Fig. 3.4); an abstraction near the Derwent confluence could help to meet demands from Nottingham, Derby and Leicester; and such abstractions could be used as an opportunity to reduce groundwater abstractions from critical aquifers such as the Sherwood sandstones.

Supported Trent

In the West Midlands the Severn and Trent rivers are less than 40km apart. One proposed scheme involves abstractions of between 100 and 300 Ml/d at Coalport on the Severn and transfer to the Trent near the Sow confluence (about 15km below the Strongford WRW). This transfer could be used to regulate the Trent (i) to meet demands from the East Midlands demand centres supplied from the intake near the Derwent confluence, (ii) to support increased abstractions from the lower river to Yorkshire and/or Anglian Regions, and (iii) to supply water to the Thames via the Trent and Mersey, Coventry and Oxford canals. A lower Trent-southeast Essex transfer and the Ely Ouse-Essex transfer would require a new pipeline to link the Trent-Fossdyke-Witham transfer and the Ely Ouse-Essex transfer, and could be developed in conjunction with a new East Anglian Reservoir having a reliable yield of 268 Ml/d, adding security to the south of the region. The reservoir could be fed by water transferred from the Trent or by additional abstractions from the River Ouse at Denver.

Supported Severn

One strategic option involves the further augmentation of flows along the River Severn to supply new transfers from the river. To meet the additional demands, two options have been proposed. First, Vyrnwy Reservoir could be redeployed with resources transferred to Liverpool being partially redeployed to supply releases to the Severn. The supply to Liverpool must be sustained for operational reasons at more than 60 Ml/d but up to 147 Ml/d could be made available for regulating the Severn (NRA 1993). Secondly, the Craig Goch reservoir in the upper Wye valley could be enlarged to provide storage (190,000 Ml) with a reliable yield of up to 775 Ml/d to supply releases either to the Severn or down the Wye (see Chapter 2).

Supported Thames

Options for supplementing supplies in the Thames basin include the transfer of water from the lower Severn at Deerhurst to Buscot in the upper Thames using the river as a natural conduit to supply the London reservoirs. Abstractions made during periods of high flow could provide a reliable yield of up to 146 Ml/d: the partially redeployed Vyrnwy Reservoir could provide an additional 146 Ml/d; and an enlarged Craig Goch Reservoir, 775 Ml/d. Part of the transfer could incorporate a restored Thames and Severn Canal. Alternatively, water abstracted from the Severn could be transferred via a 90km pipeline with a capacity of 200 Ml/d directly to London. Abstractions could also be made from the Wye via an intake in the vicinity of Ross-on-Wye and a pipeline crossing the Severn near Deerhurst.

Birmingham groundwater

The decline in industrial abstraction within the Birmingham conurbation has caused a rise in water table and about 50 Ml/d could be abstracted. Although the yield is small in relation to other strategic options, this source could serve several demand centres and is seen by the NRA as a potential resource available for augmenting the River Trent or canal system. An added benefit would be to control the water table beneath Birmingham by carefully managing the abstractions.

Ecological effects of inter-basin transfers

The effects of inter-basin transfers relate to (a) the similarity between the donor and recipient stream, especially in terms of their water quality and biological communities, and (b) the magnitude of the impacts on flows, which has ramifications for in-stream and riparian habitats. In 1976, the Ministry of Agriculture, Fisheries and Food, and the National Water Council (MAFF/NWC 1976) examined the potential effects of water redistribution by artificial transfers and by using natural water courses as aqueducts on fish populations and fisheries. Their concerns focused on the influence of the changes in flow regime and water quality on the homing and upstream migration of salmonids, on spawning, and on the survival of eggs and fry; and on the transfer of biota across biogeographical divides. Little progress seems to have been made in addressing these issues which have been reiterated by the NRA (1994) - key concerns include:

- the effect on fauna and flora of changing runoff patterns and of mixing waters of different chemistry;
- the transfer of species, pathogens and diseases, and predatory species between catchments; and
- the effect of changed flow regimes and water quality on fish movement especially on water-source finger-printing for migrating salmonids.

Loss of biogeographical integrity

Rivers draining different catchments, with different climates, rock types, topographic features, and land-uses have different hydrological, geomorphological and biological characteristics. These are reflected by the classification systems that have been used widely to organise information about rivers and their catchments (e.g. Naiman *et al.* 1992). However, rivers change in character from source to mouth and simple classification systems recognise three typical divisions of a river (see Petts and Amoros 1996): headwater streams (small, steep, cool-water streams), middle river sectors where channels are often morphologically dynamic, and the large, lowland, (relatively) nutrient rich, floodplain river. These relate to distinct zones of fauna and flora, defined using one or more species of fish, invertebrates, or plants as 'indicators'. Thus, Davies *et al.* (1992), defined a wide range of different types of manipulation from inter-basin transfers (Fig. 3.5).

In England and Wales, the basins of the upland north and west have high annual rainfalls (to over 4000 mm), are underlain by old, hard rocks, and are low in dissolved substances. The lowland basins of eastern and southern areas have low rainfalls (typically below 750 mm), are characterised by young sedimentary rocks, and have relatively high concentrations of dissolved substances, often with nitrate levels of more than 10mg/l. The distribution of stream fauna and flora also reflect the west-east divide. For example, Holmes and Newbold (1984) defined four groups of rivers based upon aquatic plant communities: (i) lowland streams in southern, central and eastern England; (ii) streams where sandstone and Carboniferous limestone rocks dominate;

(iii) rivers draining basins underlain by old resistant rocks; and (iv) the mountain streams of the west and north. Similar patterns are demonstrated by macroinvertebrate communities (Castella *et al.* 1995). In terms of the fish fauna, the major difference between the regions is the more limited fish communities in the northwest (Solomon 1975).

Superimposed upon these strong regional patterns are longitudinal zonations of physico-chemical characteristics and biota. The River Invertebrate Prediction and Classification System (RIVPACS) (Wright at al. 1984, Wright *et al.* 1989) demonstrates that rivers show typical downstream patterns. Similarly, there is a well-defined fish zonation (Carpenter 1928): trout (*Salmo trutta*) and Atlantic salmon (*Salmo salar*) being indicators of headwater streams; minnow (*Phoximus phoximus*), and chub (*Leuciscus cephalus*) being typical of middle sectors; and eel (Anguila anguila), bream (*Abramis brama*), roach (*Rutilus rutilus*), and carp (*Cypriuns carpio*) characterising the lower river.

Examples already exist of unintentional, and unwelcome, introductions via IBTs. The Ely Ouse-Essex transfer led to the accidental introduction of the fish predator, zander (*Stizostedion lucioperca*), from the Great Ouse to the River Stour, Essex, despite having to pass through, or by-pass, high-pressure pipes and an 8mm mesh screen (Guiver 1976). The alga *Stephanodiscus*, rarely found in Essex rivers, also was introduced from the Ouse to the rivers Stour and Blackwater, causing in 1973 a severe algal bloom that required Essex Water Company to stop abstracting from the receiving rivers (Solomon 1975).

With regard to the Severn and Trent catchments, the watershed between the two is low, at an altitude of below 60m between the Avon (Severn) and Soar (Trent) basins. These two sub-catchments not only share many similar biogeographical features they may also share a common history, possibly being part of a much larger 'Palaeo-Soar' having its source in Worcestershire, which existed prior to the major glaciations of the Quaternary Ice Ages. The upper Severn is very different to the Trent. Although the two rivers have been interconnected by canals for some 200 years (see Fig. 3.3), concerns remain about future transfers, not least because of the possible transfer of a fish disease (*Pomphorhynchus*) known to affect chub, barbel and other species from the Severn to the Trent (NRA 1994).

Flow regulation

In the UK, impacts of flow regulation have been widely studied over the past decade (see Boon 1988). Flood reduction below dams has a highly variable effect on macroinvertebrate taxa. Regulation leads to a decline in winter floods and an increase in summer low flows leading to the stabilisation of the channel bed, and the deposition of silt at the surface and in the interstitial spaces of the substrate (Petts 1984). Armitage (1987) found that some mayfly (Ephemeroptera: *Rithrogena, Ecdynurus* and *Heptagenia*) and stonefly (Plecoptera: Perlodidae and Chloroperlidae) larvae were rare or absent below impoundments. Significant changes have also been identified where flows in donor rivers have been severely reduced (e.g. Armitage and Petts 1992, Castella *et al.* 1995).

A study of the invertebrate responses to water transfers into the River Wear, northeast England (transfer of up to 0.87 cumecs on receiving flows of as low as 0.35 cumecs) failed to demonstrate any ecological changes below the discharge point (Archer and Gibbins 1995). However, changes of faunal communities have been reported where receiving streams have benefited from flow augmentation during dry summers. One example is the Glen in Lincolnshire where summer flows of less than 0.01 cumecs are now augmented to 0.13 cumecs by local inter-basin transfer

(Petts *et al.* 1995). Similarly, flow augmentation via groundwater sources brought immediate benefit to a chalk stream subject to severe low flows (Wright and Berrie 1987). It increased river width, flushed accumulations of silt and encouraged the growth of macrophytes, and as a result recovery of macroinvertebrate fauna. However, a constant flow sustained over long periods of time, even if the flow is higher than natural low flow levels, can be detrimental to flora and fauna that depend upon flow variations during a year (Petts 1984). Moreover, river ecosystems depend upon wet and dry years to maintain them in a healthy state (Petts 1996a). In any case, flow regulation must be carefully planned, incorporating ecological needs, to avoid adverse ecological impacts on both donor and receiving rivers.

Prospect

The principal aim of the NRA's water resource function, transferred to the new Environmental Agency for England and Wales from April 1st 1996, is to 'manage water resources to achieve the right balance between the needs of the environment and those of abstractors' (NRA 1993b). Any changes in the quality and/or quantity of river flows will have ecological impacts but given the forecast of water deficits in 2021 a policy of 'no development' is unrealistic. Whilst recognising the potential problems of establishing connections across biogeographical divides, the connections between catchments through the existing canal network to some extent negates this concern. Furthermore, many rivers in the UK already show artificial flow patterns. Of 1310 gauging stations in the UK registered by the Department of the Environment only 11 per cent record natural flows; 793 gauging stations are classified as affected by flow manipulations, abstractions and discharges. The following statistics concerning gauging stations reflect the nature of flow regulation in the UK:

- 39.3 per cent are affected by inter-basin transfers for water supply. This is achieved either by abstractions from a reservoir or river intake (25.9 per cent), or by effluent return via sewage works or industrial works (26.6 per cent).
- 25.9 per cent are affected by impounding or storage reservoirs situated in, and supplied from, the catchment above the gauging station;
- 2.4 per cent are affected by hydroelectric power generation:

An integrated strategy for water resources development and environmental protection and enhancement, as a priority should seek to protect those rivers that have the highest ecological value (e.g. Hellawell 1988). These include the Welsh Wye and its tributaries the Lugg and Arrow, the Teme tributary of the Severn, the Dove and Blythe in the Trent basin, and the Windrush and Kennet in the Thames catchment. Elsewhere, the development of water resources should seek to enhance the environmental values of the affected rivers and canals.

The Greater Trent System

This short review suggests that exploiting the Elan valley-Birmingham-Trent - (i) Witham-Ouse-Essex transfers network and (ii) canals-Thames system offers considerable opportunities for water redistribution with relatively low environmental impacts. The scheme would utilise the large (and increasing) artificial component of the discharges along the Trent and abstractions from the rising groundwater beneath Birmingham conjunctively with existing sources (e.g. the

Derwent reservoirs in the Pennines). There are seven nationally recognised rivers within the Severn-Trent region which are critically affected by abstractions causing unacceptable low flows (see Fig. 3.4; NRA 1993); the scheme should also be used to enable the reduction of abstractions from these catchments.

The scheme would reduce the need for additional supplies from the upper Severn to a minimum. This is important because of the concern (NRA 1994) about the possible transfer of a fish disease into the Trent. The potential transfer of eels carrying the nematode parasite *Anguillicola crassa* from the Severn to the Thames has also raised some concern, although the parasite is already present in the eel population in the Thames estuary (R. Mann pers. comm.). If such concerns are shown to be unfounded, in the longer term additional supplies from the upper Severn could be met by redeploying the Vyrnwy reservoir. Transfers from the upper Severn to the upper Trent or via its tributaries, the Penck and Sow, would improve water quality in the receiving streams. Any further development of the River Wye should be resisted. The River Wye is nationally important, a Site of Special Scientific Interest throughout its length and a valuable salmonid fishery with class 1 water quality. Any change of the flow regime would threaten this nationally important river ecosystem.

Canal transfers from the Trent to Thames basins raise a number of issues. Most have some reaches of poor quality (high nutrient loads) and infrequent use could mean poor quality water impacting on the Thames at critical times i.e. under dry weather flow conditions, increasing the risk of algal growths. However, the transfers could improve the water supply security for the canals. Reduced barge traffic caused by controls on the frequency of lock use during drought periods can have a serious impact on navigation and amenity. The quality of the canal water could also be improved by the higher quality transfer water and by reduced retention times during droughts (NRA 1994). The national and regional benefits could be much greater than any local impacts on the artificial systems, even though some reaches of the canals are designated SSSIs.

Safeguards

To manage water resources to achieve the right balance between the needs of abstractors and instream uses - including environmental protection - is a principal aim of the NRA, and this responsibility will be transferred to the Environmental Agency. Due to potential variations in the physical, chemical and biological properties of waters from different catchments, particular care is required when planning inter-basin transfer (Davies *et al.* 1992) and river support schemes (Bryan *et al.* 1980). However, in England and Wales safeguards exist within the current legislation to ensure that environmental factors are considered fully in any proposed water resources development. Environmental Assessment procedures should ensure that all potential environmental impacts are identified and evaluated. A range of methods are available to ensure that any harmful effects on the donor and receiving rivers are mitigated. Enough knowledge is available (e.g. Petts and Calow 1996) to mitigate water quality and associated algae problems, to ensure that any dredging works, bank raising, and construction works for pumping stations etc. would have only short-term and local ecological impacts, and to direct opportunities for developing channel management programmes to enhance river ecosystems.

The transfer of organisms through IBTs can be controlled in a number of ways (Solomon 1975) including preventative measures, such as screens of various types to prevent organisms entering water intakes and destructive measures. Of the latter the most widely used is chlorination. Provision for continuous chlorination (and dechlorination to reduce dangers of toxic quantities being released into the receiving stream) is included in the Ely Ouse to Essex transfer. Environmental effects of releasing water from one river to another can be mitigated by conjunctive use of several sources, by treatment before release and/or by reservoir storage. An example of the last is the possible construction of a new reservoir in Anglian Region to receive Trent water before use within the Ely Ouse network (NRA 1994).

Safeguards also exist to ensure that the change in flow regime in the donor and receiving rivers is not damaging to in-river and riparian interests. These are elaborated within the Minimum Acceptable Flow (MAF) concept which was formally introduced in the 1963 Water Resources Act and is currently defined under section 21 of the Water Resources Act 1991. Although no formal MAFs have been set, the general approach has been widely used in an informal context to control abstractions. These controls involve prescribed flows attached to abstraction licences, which include a 'hands-off flow' below which abstractions must cease and a 'maintained flow' which is the flow that shall be maintained by reservoir release, groundwater pumping, or inter-basin transfer.

To achieve a balanced allocation of water, giving due regard to the range of abstractors, water-quality, navigation, recreation, fisheries and conservation (both in-river and riparian needs), requires the objective setting of flow targets and their consistent application. The use-related target, especially an 'ecological objective', has been recommended (Petts *et al.* 1995, Petts 1996b) as the fundamental building block for defining the Minimum Acceptable Flow. Targets may be defined for each function (at least for dilution, to meet the ecological objective, and for other in-river uses) and will vary for each river type (e.g. upland, lowland, estuary). Flow targets would be integrated to derive a River Flow Objective (RFO: defined by the NRA as the flow which is needed to sustain the ecosystem, to meet abstraction requirements and to support other legitimate water uses) for each sector of river. Petts *et al.* (1995) recommended that the RFO should be a flow regime including (i) seasonally variable flows to meet specified ecological targets, (ii) a minimum threshold flow to sustain biota during extreme drought conditions, and (iii) high flows to maintain physical habitat diversity. Whilst a single summer minimum flow may be appropriate to safeguard rivers that have limited development, a more complex set of rules may be required for rivers that are heavily developed, for example, to protect important fisheries or restore sites of special conservation interest. Abstractions are managed by licences from the NRA (subsequently the EA) who cannot issue new licences that impinge upon the protected rights of existing licence holders. In order to achieve an RFO, prescribed flows would be attached to licences which should be time-limited, whenever possible, so that future generations will not be constrained in the way they manage their water resources by decisions made by this generation.

Conclusion

The development of inter-basin transfers to provide water security to south-east England may be inevitable. Environmental impacts are also inevitable. However, through detailed Environmental Assessment within the process of catchment management planning, the use of IBTs could be expanded within England and Wales. The application of River Flow Objectives will ensure that the process of allocating water among all users will be structured, open and consistent, and that environmental needs will be given explicit recognition. Engineering works and conservation measures can be used to minimise the risk of accidental transfers of organisms and to maximise the ecological benefits of a scheme. A scheme also may provide opportunities for actions to enhance waterways damaged by the historical legacy of industrialisation and over abstraction. However, the priority of protecting those rivers of special ecological interest and high conservation value should not be compromised. The West Midlands is likely to be at the centre of strategic plans for redistributing water and the River Trent, once reduced to an open sewer, should play the key role in providing water resources for the East Midlands, East Anglia and even the Thames basin.

References

Archer D and Gibbins C 1995 Hydrological and species-specific responses to water transfers into the River Wear northeast England, in **Petts G E** ed *Mans Influence on Freshwater Ecosystems and Water Use* Proceedings Boulder Symposium IAHS Publication No 230 207-218

Armitrage P D and Petts G.E. 1992 Biotic score and prediction to assess the effects of water abstractions on river macroinvertebrates for conservation purposes *Aquatic Conservation* 2 1-17

Bass J A B and Armitrage P D 1987 Observed and predicted occurrence of blackflies (Diptera: Simuliidae) at fifty reservoir outlets in Britain *Regulated Rivers* 1 247-55

Biswas A K Dakang Z Nickum J E and Changming L eds 1983 *Long-Distance Water Transfers: a Chinese case study and international experiences* Tycooly International, London

Boon P J 1988 The impact of river regulation on invertebrate communities in the UK *Regulated Rivers* 2 389-409

Brewin D J and Martin J R 1988 Water quality management: a regional perspective *Regulated Rivers* 2 257-277

Carpenter K E 1928 *Life in Inland Waters* Sidgwick and Jackson, London

Castella E Bickerton M A Armitrage P D and Petts G E 1995 The effect of water abstraction on invertebrate communities in UK streams *Hydrobiologia* 308 167-182

Davies B R Thoms M and Meador M 1992 An assessment of the ecological impacts of inter-basin transfers and their threats to river basin integrity and conservation *Aquatic Conservation* 2 325-349

Douglas J R 1988 Regulating the River Severn *Regulated Rivers* 2 309-322

Dudgeon D 1992 Effects of water transfer on aquatic insects in a stream in Hong Kong *Regulated Rivers* 2 369-377

Edwards R W and Brooker M P 1982 *The Ecology of the River Wye* Dr W Junk, The Hague

Falkenmark M 1989 The massive water scarcity now threatening Africa - why isn't it being addressed? *Ambio* 18 112-118

Golubev G N and Biswas A K eds 1985 *Large Scale Water Transfers: emerging environmental and social experiences* Tycooly Publishing, Oxford

Guiver K 1976 The Ely Ouse to Essex transfer scheme *Chemistry Industry* February 132-135

Gustard A 1989 Compensation flows in the UK: a hydrological review *Regulated Rivers* 3 49-59

Hadley R F Karlinger M R Burns A W and Eschner T R 1987 Water development and associated changes in the Platte River Nebraska USA *Regulated Rivers* 1 331-341

Hellawell J M 1988 River regulation and nature conservation *Regulated Rivers* 2 425-443

Holmes N and Newbold C 1984 *River Plant Communities - reflectors of water chemistry and substrate chemistry* Report 9 Nature Conservancy Council, Peterborough

Large A R G and Petts G.E 1966 Rehabilitation of river margins, in **Petts G E and Calow P** eds *Principles of River Restoration* Blackwell Scientific, Oxford

MAFF/NWC 1976 *The fisheries implications of water transfers between catchments* Ministry of Agriculture Fisheries and Foods/National Water Council, London

Mann R H K 1988 Fish and fisheries of regulated rivers in the UK *Regulated Rivers* 2 411-424

Mann R H K 1989 The management problems and fisheries of three major British rivers: the Thames, Trent and Wye in **Dodge D P** ed *International Large River Symposium (LARS) Canadian Special Publication of Fisheries and Aquatic Sciences* 106 444-454

Naiman R J Lonzarich D G Beechie T J and Ralph S C 1992 General principles of classification and the assessment of conservation potential in rivers in **Boon P J Calow P and Petts G E** eds *River Conservation and Management* Wiley, Chichester

NRA 1993a *Regional Water Resources Strategy Severn-Trent Region* National Rivers Authority Severn Trent Region, Solihull

NRA 1993b *River Trent Control Rules* National Rivers Authority Severn Trent Region, Solihull

NRA 1994 *Water Nature's Precious Resource* National Rivers Authority HMSO, London

O'Keeffe J H and De Moor F C 1988 Changes in the physico-chemistry and benthic invertebrates of the Great Fish River South Africa following an interbasin transfer of water *Regulated Rivers* 2 39-55

Petts G E 1984 *Impounded Rivers: Perspectives for Ecological Management* Wiley, Chichester

Petts G E 1988 Regulated rivers in the United Kingdom *Regulated Rivers* 2 201-220

Petts G E 1994 Large-scale river regulation in **Roberts C N** ed *The Changing Global Environment* Blackwell, Oxford 262-284

Petts G E 1995 *Determination of Minimum Acceptable Flows* National Rivers Authority Anglian Region, Peterborough

Petts G E 1996 The scientific basis of managing biodiversity along river margins in **LaChavanne J-B** ed *Biodiversity and Land-water Ecotones* UNESCO Paris

Petts G E in press Sustaining the ecological integrity of large floodplain rivers in **Anderson M D Walling D E and Blake P** eds *Floodplain Processes* Wiley, Chichester

Petts G E in press The allocation of water to meet in-river needs *Regulated Rivers*

Petts G E and Amoros C eds 1996 *Fluvial Hydrosystems*, Chapman and Hall, London

Petts G E Armitage P and Castella E 1993 Physical habitat changes and macroinvertebrate response to river regulation: the River Rede UK *Regulated Rivers* 8 167-78

Petts G E and Calow P eds 1996 *Principles of River Restoration* Blackwell Scientific, Oxford

Petts G E Crawford C and Clarke R 1995 *The determination of minimum acceptable flows* National Rivers Authority Report, Peterborough

Petts G E Maddock I Bickerton M and Ferguson A J D 1995 Linking hydrology and ecology: the scientific basis for river management in **Harper D M and Ferguson A J D** eds *The Ecological Basis for River Management* Wiley, Chichester

Roy D and Messier D 1989 A review of the effects of water transfers in La Grande Hydroelectric Complex (Quebec, Canada) *Regulated Rivers* 4 299-316

Sheail J 1988 River regulation in the United Kingdom - an historical perspective *Regulated Rivers* 2 221-232

Sherrard J J and Erskine W D 1991 Complex response of a sand-bed stream to upstream river impoundment *Regulated Rivers* 6 53-70

STWA 1983 *Review of fisheries survey undertaken in the Trent area of the Severn-Trent Water Authority during the period 1975-1981* Severn-Trent Water Authority, Nottingham

Walters R C S 1936 *The Nation's Water Supply* Nicholson and Watson, London

Ward R 1981 River systems and river regimes in Lewin J ed *British Rivers* Allen and Unwin,

London 126-172

Wood T R 1981 River management in **Lewin J** ed *British Rivers* Allen and Unwin, London 173-95

Wright J F and Berrie A D 1987 Ecological effects of groundwater pumping and a natural drought on the upper reaches of a chalk stream *Regulated Rivers* 1 145-160

Wright J F Moss P D Armitrage P and Furse M T 1984 A preliminary classification of running-water sites in Great Britain based on macro-invertebrate species and the prediction of community type using environmental data *Freshwater Biology* 14 221-56

CHAPTER 4

Soil Erosion in the West Midlands

Margaret Oliver and John Gerrard

Soil erosion by wind and water are natural processes, but such erosion is often enhanced by a combination of the types of agriculture, land management practices and the nature and condition of the soil. Land under continuous arable cultivation is the most sensitive of all in Britain to erosion because the soil is inevitably exposed to the weather yearly. In some regions in England and Wales as much as 25 per cent of the land most sensitive to water erosion has eroded (Evans 1988). Recorded rates of water-induced soil erosion in lowland Britain vary from levels of less that 1t/ha/yr to extremely high rates of 20 t/ha/yr (Arden-Clarke and Evans 1993). Most rates of erosion are less than 1-2 m^3/ha/field/yr (Evans and Skinner 1987) but erosion rates will be much higher in some parts of the fields. Severe rates of more than 10m^3/ha/field/yr occur in less than 10 per cent of erosion events. The soil types that are most sensitive to erosion are those with a large sand content and to some extent those that are silty. These light-textured, freely draining soils are easily worked, they can be worked at a wide range of moisture contents and a wide range of crops can be grown on them. Their nature and the intensity of their use makes them vulnerable to erosion. Erosion occurs when the threshold at which erosional forces, triggered by the weather, overcomes locally the resistance of the soil and vegetation to soil movement. The threshold depends on the type and condition of the soil and the type and degree of development of the crop.

The five year survey (1982-86) carried out by the Soil Survey of England and Wales (SSEW) has provided information on the frequency of occurrence and rates of water erosion on lowland soils in Britain. In 1982, 297 fields at 15 selected localities were visited by soil scientists, 148 of which were found to be eroding at rates varying from 0.1 to 36.8 m^3/ha/yr or approximately 0.1 to 47.8 t/ha/y (SSEW 1983). By 1986, 1769 fields suffering erosion had been located (Evans and Cook 1986). However, this is an underestimation by an order of magnitude. By 1983, Reed (1979, 1983) had located over 1000 eroding fields in the West Midlands alone.

Relatively large depths of colluvium on the lower sections of slopes, and alluvium infills in river valleys show that erosion has been occurring for many hundreds of years. Old tenancy agreements that demand a tenant to carry soil back upslope each year support this. In a survey of past erosion, Evans (1990a) has estimated that approximately 180mm of topsoil have been removed from some slopes on the Permo-Triassic sandstones in the West Midlands. This amount is as much as that recorded for Chalk slopes in Kent which exhibit the highest rates of erosion. There is clear evidence, as we shall show, that erosion is still occurring, perhaps at even greater rates, on land in the West Midlands.

The regional context

We have studied an area bordering the western part of the West Midlands conurbation where the land, which is under continuous arable cultivation, is suffering from accelerated soil erosion (Fig.

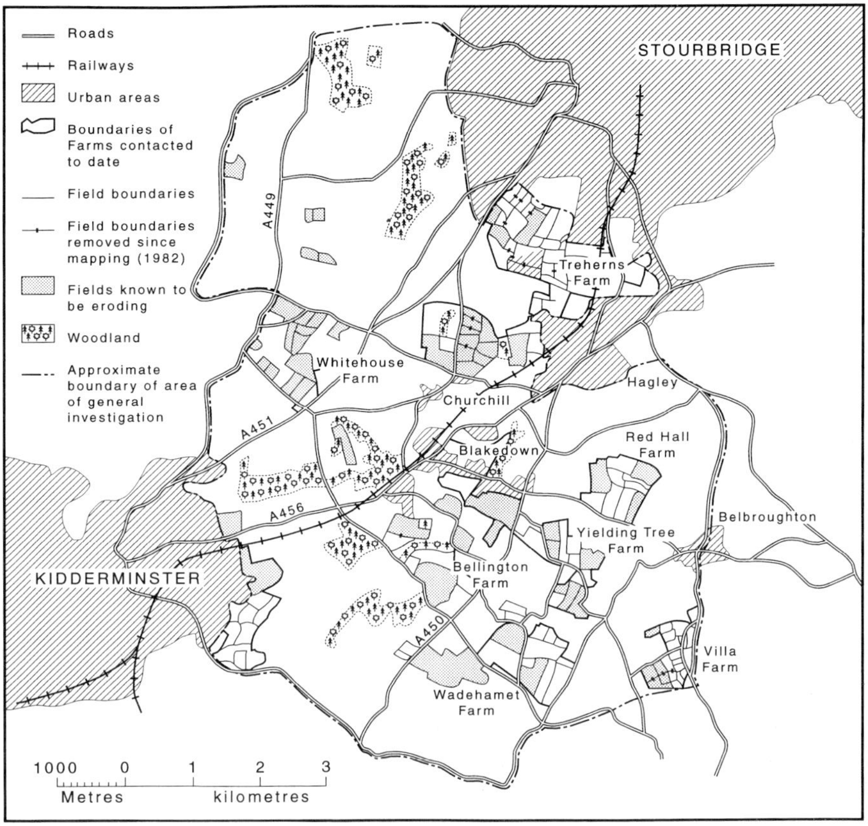

Fig 4.1 Location and extent of erodible fields in the area to the west of the West Midlands conurbation

4.1). The natural processes of soil erosion are often exaggerated by several orders of magnitude by the effects of arable farming. Almost any system of arable farming is liable to lead to soil erosion. This is confirmed by the high rates of soil erosion, noted earlier, that have been observed and recorded over a fairly extensive tract of land to the west and south of the conurbation. The former Soil Survey of England and Wales and the Ministry of Agriculture, Food and Fisheries identified it as an area of recurring soil erosion from their aerial surveys (Evans, 1980; 1984). In addition Evans (1980) and Fullen (1985) suggest that the extent and magnitude of erosion have been increasing, especially since the 1960s.

Physiographically and climatically it is an area that would be regarded as unlikely to suffer from severe erosion. The landscape is gently undulating with gentle to moderate slopes: slopes steeper than 9° are uncommon. However, Evans (1990b) has noted that water erosion can occur on slopes with angles as small as 3° and where the relief within fields is as low as 5m. Convex slope forms are common in the undulating landscape of the West Midlands. On light soil, slopes below convexities are the most at risk from water erosion (Evans and Cook 1986). The average precipitation, of 700mm per annum, is also moderate, and it falls mostly as rain. The area lies in the rain shadow of the Cambrian Mountains, the Clee Hills and the Wrekin. Convectional storms substantially contribute to the summer rainfall, yet highly erosive rainfall events of 25mm hr^{-1} are infrequent in the West Midlands.

A major factor associated with the degree of soil erosion in the area is the type of soil. The most extensive type is the Bridgnorth Association which consists of the Bridgnorth, Bromsgrove and Newport series. The soil of these series differs from one another mainly in terms of stoniness, and there are slight differences in clay and silt contents. Of these series the Bridgnorth and the Newport are the most extensive. Soil parent material is mainly solid geology in the southern part of the area, whereas in the northern part there is more glacial drift consisting of sandy clay loam till, and sandy loam to loamy sand outwash sands and gravels. The superficial deposits are mostly local having being derived from the underlying Permo-Triassic and Triassic formations (Hollis and Reed 1981). The latter include the soft red sandstones of the Lower and Upper Mottled formations which often have Bunter Pebble Beds between. The sandstones were formed under desert conditions, consequently they are only weakly cemented and generally weather rapidly. This is particularly evident where the soil is shallow because ploughing brings fragments of rock to the surface of the soil from the weathering zone. This is especially noticeable on slope convexities. In general weathered sandstone is found within approximately 80cm of the surface.

The principal soil series in the area we surveyed is the Bridgnorth series. It is a freely drained reddish brown soil, an acid brown earth with a pH of approximately 6 to 6.5. The particle size distribution is that of a sandy to coarse loamy sand, with 80 per cent to 90 per cent sand, which is important in terms of the soil's threshold of erodibility. The sand fraction ranges from coarse to fine, and the fine and medium sand fractions are a considerable proportion. The silt and clay fractions account for only 10 per cent to 20 per cent of the total, with the clay content averaging less than 5 per cent. This kind of soil texture produces a predominance of macropores which account for its generally high permeability. However, the lack of meso- and macropores inhibits the capillary movement of water, hence this soil has a limited ability to retain water and to replace water lost by evaporation at the surface. In desiccating conditions the soil at the surface is inevitably dry and friable making it susceptible to erosion, in particular by wind. Horizons are only weakly developed in the Bridgnorth series soil.

Soil with 80 per cent or more sand content generally has a weak granular or subangular blocky structure, but it is sometimes apedal. There is insufficient clay content to bind the coarser particles together to form more stable structural units. In addition to the poor aggregation the fine sand and silt fractions make it susceptible to slaking, that is structural collapse, when the soil is unprotected and exposed to rainfall. Slaking produces a surface cap or crust which leads to further impedance of infiltration of water into the soil, and also prevents the emergence of seedlings.

The soil organic matter content is small, about 1-2 per cent. The predominance of macropores encourages the rapid breakdown of organic residues added to the soil because of the oxidising environment. Furthermore, the breakdown products are subsequently removed rapidly by percolating solutions. Organic matter is a major controlling factor in stabilising soil structure. Hence for a soil with a large sand content it is the organic fraction that is vital for both creating and stabilising aggregation. Organic compounds, such a fungal hyphae and humus, bind soil particles by creating flexible bridges between them. It is difficult to increase the organic matter concentration in the short term and therefore to improve soil structure. Once the organic matter fraction approaches 1 per cent the structure of the soil becomes weak increasing its susceptibility to erosion.

The soil of the Bridgnorth series is easily worked because it is light and friable, and it can also be worked at most times of the year because it drains rapidly after rain. The gentle slopes in the region also favour cultivation, and since the 1960s much of the area has been under continuous arable cultivation. A wide range of crops is grown, including cereals (winter and spring wheat and barley), oilseed rape, sugar beet, potatoes, other vegetables and soft fruit. Permanent pasture, which used to be a major land use in the area, is generally restricted to the steeper slopes. The changing land use in this area has had two effects that increase the susceptibility of the land to soil erosion. Continuous arable cultivation has led to a widespread decline in organic matter levels in the soil even though substantial amounts of plant residue are ploughed back. Tilling also exposes the organic matter to oxidation and hence it is broken down and removed more rapidly.

Under cultivation the soil of the Bridgnorth series compacts easily because its structure is weak and breaks down easily with the weight of heavy machinery and with ploughing. This also impedes infiltration both at the surface and at depth where plough pans form. The severity of compaction has increased since the second world war because of the changes in agricultural practice. For instance mechanisation has increased, the number of operations requiring the movement of heavy machinery over the land are more numerous (e.g. spraying herbicides and pesticides, fertilising),and the machines are larger and heavier, which all lead to increased soil compaction. The increase in the use of large machinery has also necessitated larger fields resulting in the gradual removal of many kilometres of hedgerows. The larger the size of fields the greater is the risk of both water and wind erosion because they allow the momentum of water and wind movement, respectively, to increase.

Types of soil erosion occurring

In general wind erosion is not considered a significant problem in the United Kingdom, except in the eastern part of the country. Nevertheless, both water and wind are responsible for processes of erosion in the area bordering the West Midlands conurbation. Evans (1981) stated that over a long time the effects of water erosion are likely to be more serious than those of wind in an area such as this. However, occasionally there are severe wind erosion events, such as the one recorded by Fullen (1985) for east Shropshire in spring 1983.

Evidence of wind erosion is provided by material observed in suspension during strong winds, and the deposition of material against hedgerows, fences, gate posts etc. Wind deposited material is easily distinguished from that deposited by water. It tends to occur in different positions and the nature of the material and its degree of compaction are also different. It can also blanket large areas as we observed during our survey (Fig. 4.2). Wind picks up loose material, especially fine sand and silt particles, and organic matter. If there is moisture in the soil it will bind such particles together, and this limits soil loss. Since the soil of the Bridgnorth series dries out rapidly, contains fine sand and silt, and lacks aggregation it is prone to wind erosion. Weak aggregates are also broken down during the process of erosion by saltation, which is when particles are bounced along the surface by the wind. This produces more loose material for the wind to pick up and remove. Sandy soil, when ploughed does not produce large clods; the smoother the surface the less is the friction between the moving air and soil to slow down its movement and to reduce its erosivity. Large fields without hedgerows allow the velocity of the wind to increase and become more erosive: hedgerows play a vital role in creating wind breaks. Their removal over the past twenty or more years has made the area more susceptible to wind erosion. Wind removes material selectively, carrying away the fine organic matter and other nutrient rich components, leaving behind coarse infertile material.

Fullen's (1985) report of major wind erosion in the Spring of 1983 shows that the topsoil at

Fig 4.2 Field severely affected by depostion of windblown material (Photo. M Oliver)

Fig 4.3 Overland flow after 10 minute rainfall event (Photo. M Oliver)

the time was desiccated. In addition the weak structure and large sand content meant that the soil had little resistance to wind erosion. The recently cultivated fields were the most prone to severe soil loss, especially those prepared for sugar beet. Those fields with an emerging crop were affected little. Fullen considered that another major contributing factor to the degree of soil loss was the enlargement of fields and the lack of windbreaks. In general, crops that render the soil most sensitive to 'blowing' are those drilled into very fine tilths often in spring, and which take a long time to cover the ground such as sugar beet, carrots and onions.

Soil erosion by water causes more soil loss in the West Midlands area than wind. It is caused by several different but associated processes. The first is the loosening and detachment of soil particles mainly by raindrop impact, followed by the forces of running water, and by freeze-thaw action. It can cause widespread aggregate disintegration. The effect of raindrop impact is most pronounced on bare soil, especially where it has been cultivated recently, and when the rain is heavy because the raindrops are large. The full force of the raindrops is diminished where there is some vegetation cover because the leaves intercept them, although there is some evidence that suggests that leaf drip from certain crops can be significant. When plant cover is over 30 per cent raindrop impact begins to decrease and when it is more than 70 per cent there is little. Land drilled in the autumn for winter cereals is especially vulnerable because it can remain bare for a considerable length of time. The effect of raindrop impact on the soil of the Bridgnorth series is severe because the soil aggregates are weak and disintegrate easily. When raindrops hit the soil surface they splash, and this action moves fine material in all directions. This breakdown of aggregates provides loose material that can be moved in other ways and also results in slaking causing fine material to be deposited in the pore spaces. This eventually leads to the formation of a surface crust which is brittle and impervious.. It impedes infiltration and allows water to move over the surface as overland flow. The soil surface appears saturated yet the soil beneath the surface layer can be dry.

Overland flow occurs when the rate of precipitation exceeds the rate of infiltration. This can arise from heavy rainfall, impeded infiltration, or low water holding ability of the soil, or a combination of all. Overland flow occurs in the West Midlands even when rainfall is not intensive enough to be regarded as erosive: 1 to 2 mm hr^{-1} with a total of 10 mm can be erosive. The formation of a surface crust and low hydraulic conductivity arising from compaction have reduced the threshold at which rainfall becomes erosive. We have observed overland flow in a field after heavy rainfall lasting only 10 minutes (Fig. 4.3). Overland flow can pick up and carry a wide range of sizes of material depending on the velocity of the flow, which in turn is affected by the volume of water, slope angle, slope length and surface roughness.

Overland flow is more likely where heavy machinery has compacted the soil. Compaction destroys soil structure, increases the bulk density, and reduces porosity. The proportion of unconnected pores increases with compaction as does the likelihood of erosion. Infiltration is reduced at the surface where there are tractor wheelings, and at depth because of compaction and the formation of a plough pan. The absence of vegetation also reduces infiltration because the roots provide channels into the subsoil along which water can move. The interception of water by leaves also improves infiltration because it slows down the rate at which water reaches the soil surface.

Results of overland flow

The main features resulting from soil erosion by water in the West midlands are extensive rill systems (Fig. 4.4), large alluvial fans (Fig. 4.5), soil blocking roads (Fig. 4.6), light coloured patches of soil which show reworking, bright colours on the convexities of slopes where the subsoil is exposed and sometimes fragments of the underlying rock, organic matter accumulations at the base of slopes (Fig. 4.5), wilting crops where soil has been removed, and differences in height on either side of hedgerows.

Rills are ephemeral channels; some we measured were 30cm deep, but they can be ploughed out. They often start in the tractor wheelings (Fig. 4.7) where the soil has been compacted, and where slight depressions in the soil surface have been formed. The rate of infiltration is reduced in the wheelings resulting in overland flow. Once the water is concentrated it becomes erosive producing rills which gradually increase in size to become extensive and complex networks. These systems are capable of removing large quantities of soil as well as gravel and pebble sized material. The clay fraction and organic matter are picked up the most easily and are often moved beyond the field. The selective removal and transport of these fractions can be seen clearly in the material deposited in fans and also stored in the rills for subsequent entrainment. The sand and silt form alluvial fans where the velocity of the water decreases. These fans can be several centimetres thick. In any one season they can destroy up to 20 per cent of the growing crop by smothering it. They consist of fine material completely lacking in structure and they also contain relatively little air which is needed for respiration by roots. Evans (pers. comm.) used the depth

Fig. 4.4 Rill systems cutting across furrows and tractor wheelings (Photo. M Oliver)

Fig. 4.5 Build up of eroded material at the lower edge of fields smothering the sugar beet crop (Photo. M Oliver)

Fig. 4.6 Material removed from road and 'returned' to the eroding field (Photo. M Oliver)

Fig. 4.7 Rill that developed initially in a tractor wheeling (Photo. M Oliver)

of material deposited in the fans and their areal extents, together with the cross section of the rills and their extent to determine the amount of soil being moved within fields and that being removed beyond their boundaries.

General factors promoting soil erosion in the West Midlands

The soil of the Bridgnorth series is liable to erosion by both wind and water because of its large sand content, weak aggregation and its susceptibility to compaction and capping. Arable farming, with long periods when the soil surface is bare, increases the likelihood of erosion. The ploughed surface of a sandy soil is relatively smooth so that there is little hindrance to flowing water or wind, hence they can accelerate over the surface and entrain more and larger material. Ploughing perpendicular to the contours encourages water to move downhill and to form rills (Fig. 4.8). The wheelings of tractors and other farm machinery tend to concentrate water flow in the first instance. Water moves faster down steep slopes, however, we found little relation between slope angle and the degree of erosion. Rills were observed on slopes as gentle as 2°. Length of slope appears to be a more significant factor and this would explain erosion on gentle slopes. The increase in field size and removal of hedgerows has increased slope length which allows water and wind to gather momentum and to move more quickly.

Fig. 4.8 Water flow using furrows aligned parallel with the slope (Photo. M Oliver)

Reasons for the increase in soil erosion in the West Midlands

Evans (1984) and Fullen (1985b) have noted an increase in soil erosion during the past twenty years in the West Midlands. During our discussions with farmers it was clear that they were in no doubt that soil erosion had increased since the 1960s. Erosion is largely confined to soil under arable cultivation and the area cultivated continued to increase until the 1990s with the removal of grass leys and fallow from the rotation systems. The consequences of this change have been a decline in the soil organic fraction, an increase in the traffic over the land, more cultivations, and larger areas of bare soil for certain periods each year. Continuous arable cultivation is known to deplete the soil's reserves of organic matter and this is especially serious for soil such as that of the Bridgnorth series. Set-aside policy should redress some of this imbalance and allow organic matter levels to build up again, albeit slowly.

The increase in the use and weight of machinery compacts the soil. Reed (1983) showed that water erosion is closely associated with soil compaction. The latter can occur at the surface and at depth reducing the soil's hydraulic conductivity which leads to premature overland flow. Fullen (1985b) measured infiltration rates on experimental plots near Wolverhampton before and after traffic over the soil. Infiltration was reduced from 173cm per hour to 3cm per hour. Such changes mean that the thresholds at which rainfall becomes erosive are decreasing.

For herbicides to act effectively farmers have to prepare a fine seedbed which means that the smooth surface provides no resistance to the movement of water or wind over the surface. Soil clods are broken down making the small weak aggregates prone to disintegration by raindrop impact. There has also been a widespread change to growing winter cereals. This has been blamed for much of the increase in soil erosion, and it has been suggested that increased soil erosion in the West of England, Wales and Scotland has also been a consequence of the widespread change to winter cereals. However, this is questionable. If the crop does not establish well in the autumn the soil can be left bare for much of the winter rendering it liable to erosion. However, if the crop establishes itself early then the soil is protected for much of the winter. Evans (1988) observed that severe erosion occurred in the West Midlands area under spring cereals with heavy storms in April.

The widespread removal of hedgerows in the area to facilitate the efficient use of modern machinery means that there is less protection from wind, and the longer slopes means that overland flow becomes more erosive. We have often observed that hedgerows have been removed from key locations in the landscape, such as the convexities of slopes. A hedge at this point on a slope reduces the rate of flow and causes the upper part of the slope to act as a storage area for water. Once the hedgerow has been removed water can move freely and it gathers momentum as it flows over the steeper part of the slope becoming very erosive. The upper area of the slope then supplies water continuously adding to the erosivity. Also the practice of replacing hedges with wire fencing allows water and soil to pass from one field to another. It was noted earlier how convexities appear to be more prone to erosion.

Consequences of increased soil erosion

Much of the soil that is lost is topsoil, which is the most fertile part containing the already small fine fraction, the organic matter and nutrients. In general the nutrients are bound naturally to the clay fraction and organic matter so that as these fractions are depleted so too is the nutrient status. This loss of nutrients can be replaced by artificial fertilisers and manures, and the organic matter with slightly more difficulty by farmyard and green manures. The fine fraction, however, cannot be replaced. Once lost from the topsoil it has gone forever. As this fraction is naturally small in the soil of the Bridgnorth series, and there are few weatherable minerals that could replenish it, its loss through erosion is serious.

The loss of soil decreases the depth of the profile, which is a particular problem in shallow soils such as those of the Bridgnorth series. This increases the droughtiness of the soil through the removal of the water holding components and by reducing the rooting depth.

The loss of soil increases the rate of runoff because of changes in the morphology of the soil as more compacted subsoil is exposed at the surface. The decline in soil structure and increasing compactness, the fewer fines and less organic matter mean that less water is absorbed by the soil. Hence less water percolates into the subsoil and downwards to replenish the groundwater. This leads to a vicious circle with more runoff and more material being removed from the topsoil resulting in silting of roads, drains and reservoirs, and in flooding. These effects of soil erosion are all costly to remedy. Soil is not the only material washed from the soil, fertilisers, seeds and pesticides are also removed with the likelihood of pollution for which the farmer is having to take increasing responsibility. This leads to two sources of costs to the farmer - replacing the products lost from the soil and the costs of clean-up operations. One farmer that we spoke to had to replant one of his fields of sugar beet three times during the year that we were doing our survey. This also increases the traffic over the land, adding to the compaction and the cycle of increasing erodibility of the soil.

The result of erosion economically is a decline in yields and in the farmer's profit margins, which have been eroded considerably during the present decade as a result of other additional factors. The soil in this area is in urgent need of protection from erosion. There is a need for a sustainable system of farming whereby the soil is not damaged for future generations. The soil will regenerate in the long term, but in Britain the rate of its renewal is far slower than the current rate of losses.

Conservation measures

A return to a rotation system with grass leys would remove land that is marginal for arable cultivation from continuous cultivation. It would also gradually help to improve the organic matter status in the soil as the leys are rotated. There are indications that this is now happening on some farms. Alternatively a system that embraces periods of fallow helps to improve the condition of the soil. The set-aside policy has achieved this to some extent, but for different reasons. Now that farmers can rotate fields under set-aside there is a greater chance of improving the condition of the soil more widely. Grass strips in arable fields would also help greatly in reducing erosion (Fullen, 1991).

The amount of traffic over fields must be reduced to limit compaction. This is being taken seriously and farmers are doing several operations in one go to limit the movement of vehicles over the land. However, it is now well established that if fertilisers are applied in small amounts frequently to sandy soil this will limit pollution because the plants will take up what is available before the fertilisers are washed through the soil. To restrict compaction farmers use a system of tramlining so that vehicles travel over the same tracks each time and the extent of compaction is limited to these lines. There are also improvements to the tyres which reduce the forces exerted on the soil.

Direct drilling and minimising cultivation helps to reduce erosion, however, the Bridgnorth series is not particularly amenable to minimal tillage because of its poor structure. Other measures that the farmers are taking to limit erosion on their land include leaving the stubble for longer. This not only protects the soil from erosion and raindrop impact, it also increases the organic matter content of the soil. Contour ploughing is another simple measure, although many farmers appear reluctant to practice this even though slopes are relatively gentle in the West Midlands. It does not always confer a benefit however, because the wheelings can act as reservoirs of water which become erosive when they spill over.

There is now a much greater awareness of the fragility of the soil as part of our environment, Furthermore government and European Union policy should lead to some improvement in the condition of the soil. Serious damage has occurred to the soil in the area to the west of the conurbation by accelerated erosion over the past twenty or so years, and where soil depth has been reduced to little more than 15cm it will take a considerable time to repair. Measures on less seriously eroded land should show some improvement in soil condition over the next ten years.

References

Arden-Clarke C and Evans R 1993 Soil erosion and conservation in the United Kingdom in **Pimentel D** ed *World soil erosion and conservation* Cambridge University Press, Cambridge 193-215

Evans R 1980 Characteristics of water-eroded fields in lowland England in **De Boot M and Gabriels D** ed *Assessment of Erosion* John Wiley and Sons, Chichester 77-87

Evans R 1981 Potential soil and crop losses by erosion in *Proceedings of a Conference on Soil and Crop Loss: Developments in Erosion Control* Soil and Water Management Association, Stoneleigh 1-12

Evans R 1984 *Soil Survey Annual Report for 1983* Harpenden 14.15

Evans R 1988 *Water Erosion in England and Wales 1982-1984* Report for Soil Survey and Land Resource Centre, Silsoe

Evans R 1990a Water erosion in British farmers' fields - some causes, impacts, predictions *Progress in Physical Geography* 14 199-219

Evans R 1990b Soil erosion: its impacts on the English and Welsh landscape since woodland clearance in **Boardman J Foster I D L and Dearing J A** eds *Soil Erosion on Agricultural Land* John Wiley and Sons, Chichester 230-54

Evans R and Cook S 1986 Soil erosion in Britain *SEESOIL* 3 28-59

Evans R and Skinner R J 1987 A survey of water erosion *Soil and Water* 13 28-31

Fullen M A 1985a Wind erosion of arable soils in east Shropshire (England) during spring 1983 *Catena* 12 111-20

Fullen M A 1985b Compaction, hydrological processes and soil erosion on loamy sands in east Shropshire, England *Soil and Tillage Research* 6 17-29

Fullen M A 1991 A comparison of runoff and erosion rates on bare and grassed loamy sand soils *Soil Use and Management* 7 136-9

Hollis J M 1978 *Soils in Salop 1* Soil Survey Record 49 Soil Survey of England and Wales, Harpenden

Hollis J M and Reed A H 1981 The Pleistocene deposits of the southern Worfe catchment *Proceedings of the Geologists Association* 92 59-74

Reed A H 1979 Accelerated erosion of arable soils in the U.K. by rainfall and run-off, *Outlook on Agriculture*, 10, 41-48

Reed A H 1983 The erosion risk of compaction *Soil and Water* 11, 29-33

Reed A H 1986a Accelerated erosion in arable soils *Spans* 29 17-19

Reed A H 1986b Soil loss from tractor wheelings *Soil and Water* 14 12-14

SSEW (Soil Survey of England and Wales) 1983 Soil erosion in *Rothamsted Experimental Station Report for 1982*, part 1, RES, Harpenden 242-243

Whitehead T H and Pocock R W 1947 *Dudley and Bridgnorth* Memoirs of the Geological Survey UK

CHAPTER 5

Planning and Slopes

John Gerrard

It was shown in Chapter 1 how, in a very general way, the development of Birmingham and the conurbation has been influenced by the relief and drainage of the region. This statement is not meant to be unduly deterministic but the development of road, rail and canal routes has, inevitably, been influenced by factors such as slope angle, relief ruggedness and stream networks. A city must fit with the topographic limitations of the site. It will also be influenced by the geological conditions below the surface. At the present time with more advanced technology and expertise, it is possible to overcome many of these natural hindrances to development. However, there will always be a heavy cost involved in elaborate engineering projects and there is always the possibility that such projects will hit unforeseen problems.

The need for large-scale urban redevelopment together with the increase in the rate of construction and the increasing scarcity of suitable sites has meant that, in recent years, areas formerly regarded as unsuitable have been and are being considered for building purposes (Bell 1975). This statement was true in 1975 and is even more so now. This chapter makes a more detailed analysis of the natural landscape features that impinge on the planning process. The analysis is mostly conducted on the kilometre grid basis introduced in Chapter 1. The relief units, outlined earlier, will also be examined and, in addition, case studies will be used to illustrate specific points.

Planning involves the optimum use of land so that the physical development of cities and regions may best meet the needs of people. The proper use of land can be achieved only if the nature of the ground and subsurface conditions is known with certainty (Leggett 1973). Consideration of the environment is one of the most vital parts of the complex planning process. Sound information about the ground in the area being planned and for the region immediately adjoining is of major importance and basic data must be assembled to provide this information. A number of landform characteristics will have an influence on landscape sensitivity and thus on the planning process. The characteristics that appear to be most significant in this context are maximum slope angles, relative relief and landscape ruggedness. Steep angles present building difficulties and they also introduce the possibility of slope failure and general instability. The latter possibility will need to be examined in conjunction with rock type. Relative relief over a specific distance is an indication of average slope steepness but also provides an additional dimension of slope length. It is possible for an area to possess steep slopes but a small relative relief. A river cliff can be vertical but the relative relief may be low. Relative relief will provide a scale factor into the landscape analysis. Landscape ruggedness is an indication of degree of dissection. Various idealised combinations of these characteristics are possible with the characteristics being essentially independent. The most severe problems will be caused by a landscape that possesses high slope angles, high relative relief and high ruggedness.

In this analysis maximum slope angle has been assessed by the minimum distance, in millimetres, between adjacent contours on the one inch to mile relief and drainage map. Relative relief has been defined as the difference between the highest and lowest elevation in each square and ruggedness as the number of times a contour crosses the perimeter of each grid square. These are very simple measures but do provide an indication of the nature of the physical landscape.

Maximum slope angles

The variation in maximum slope angle (minimum contour spacing) across the region is shown in Figure 5.1. At this scale a contour spacing of 1mm represents an average slope of 13.5° and 2mm

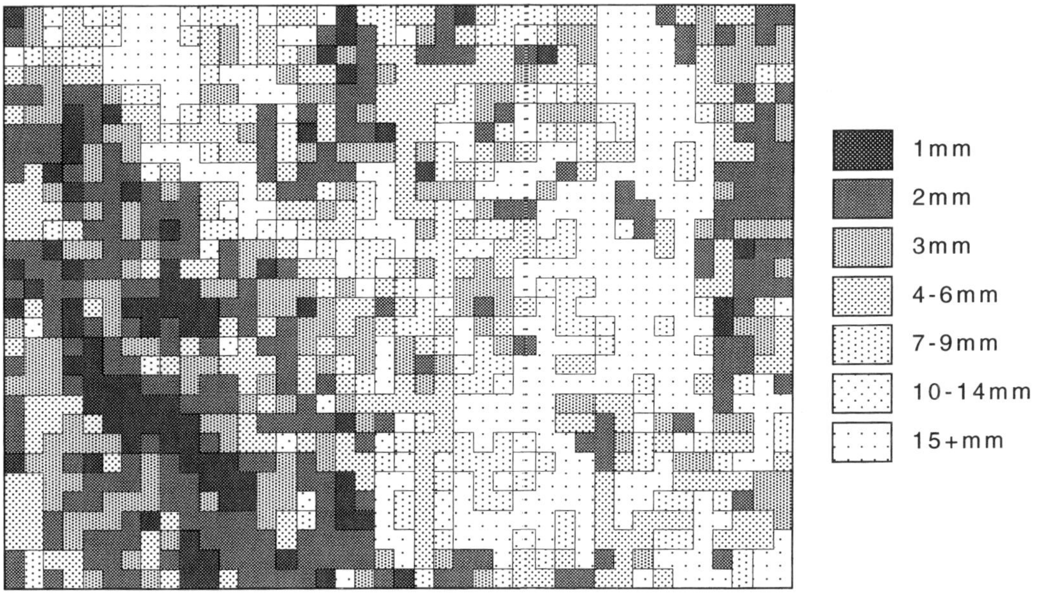

Fig. 5.1 Spatial distribution of maximum slope angle (minimum contour spacing)

represents 6.75°. These are bound to be minimum values of maximum steepness as there will probably be areas of steeper slopes not accounted for at this scale and contour interval. The dominance of steep slopes in the west and the gentler slopes in the main valley basins is clear. But there are smaller areas of steep slopes which are related to localised incision by streams. The sharply defined eastern edge of the Blythe-Lower Tame valleys was mentioned earlier. This edge forms a prominent feature in the eastern part of the region. The frequency histogram of cell values (Fig. 5.2) shows a clear bimodality between those areas with low values (steep slopes) and those with high values (gentle slopes). Thus the mean value of 7.2 is very misleading. Slightly over 29 per cent of cells possess moderately steep slopes (greater than 6.75°) while approximately 23 per cent possess extremely gentle slopes. A clear differentiation occurs when the relief units are considered (Table 5.1). The Clent-Lickey Ridge possesses the highest maximum slope angles and is the only unit in which the modal group is 1mm, followed, perhaps surprisingly, by the Stour Valley Plateau Fringe. However, it was noted in Chapter 1 how active dissection by the Upper Stour had extended into this area. Also, the boundary between the Clent Ridge and the Upper

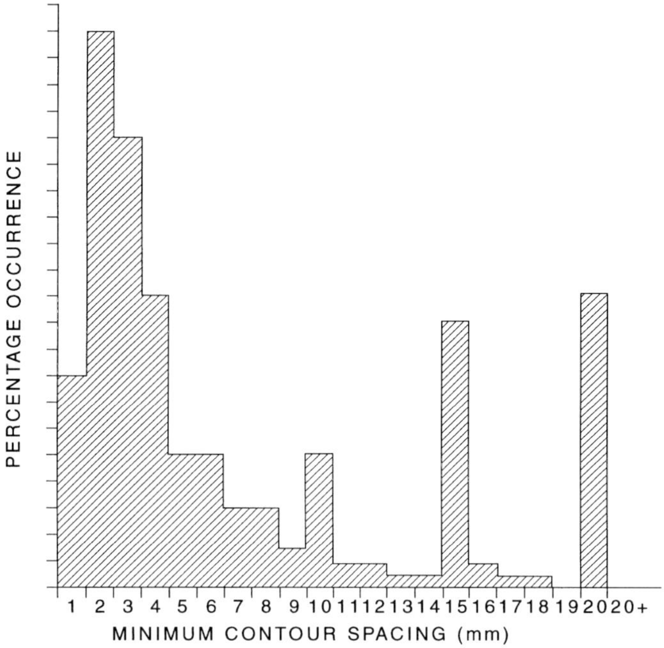

Fig. 5.2 Frequency distribution of maximum slope angle (minimum contour spacing)

Relief Unit	Mean minimum contour spacing	Modal Group	% in the mode
South Cannock Plateau	6.9	3	21
Sutton Plateau	6.0	2/4	16
Upper Tame Valley	9.9	20	13
Sedgley-Northfield Ridge	2.9	2	51
West Bromwich-Harborne Plateau	6.5	3	23
Clent-Lickey Ridge	1.6	1	52
Stour Valley Plateau Fringe	2.4	2	37
South West Plateau Fringe	10.7	10	22
Solihull Plateau	10.4	20	14
Ansley Plateau	3.2	2	47
Corley Plateau	7.8	15	18
Mid-Tame Valley	7.2	3	23
Blythe-Lower Tame Valleys	11.9	4	26
Upper Stour Basin	3.1	2	35
Salwarpe Basin	3.3	3	33
Arrow Valley	3.8	2	47

Table 5.1 Mean minimum contour spacing (mm) of the main relief units

Stour Plateau Fringe is somewhat arbitrary in places. The Sedgley-Northfield Ridge also possesses a high proportion of steep slopes. The majority of relief units possess intermediate slope angle properties with some steep but in general comparatively gentle maximum slope angles. The relief units with the smallest maximum slope angles are the Upper Tame, Mid-Tame, Rea and Cole Valleys and the Blythe-Lower Tame unit.

Relative relief

The relative relief map (Fig. 5.3) is much simpler than the maximum slope angle map, with a concentration of high values in the west and low values in the major river valleys and in the east. The frequency histogram (Fig. 5.4) shows that relative relief is dominantly less than 30m (64 per cent of all values), with 26 per cent of values less than 15m. The mean value of 21.7m is influenced by a few very high values. In terms of relief units (Table 5.2) the Clent-Lickey Ridge and Sedgley-Northfield Ridge have the highest average values followed by the two western plateau fringes. Most units possess intermediate relative relief values with the Blythe-Lower Tame possessing lowest values. The Solihull Plateau also possesses low values emphasising its conspicuous plateau form.

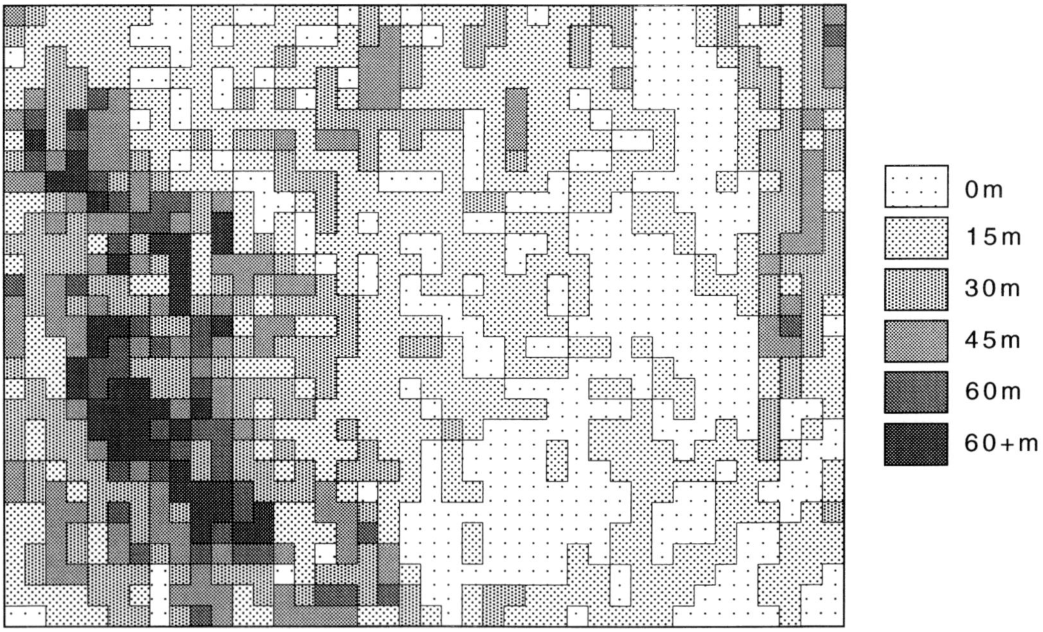

Fig. 5.3 Spatial distribution of relative relief

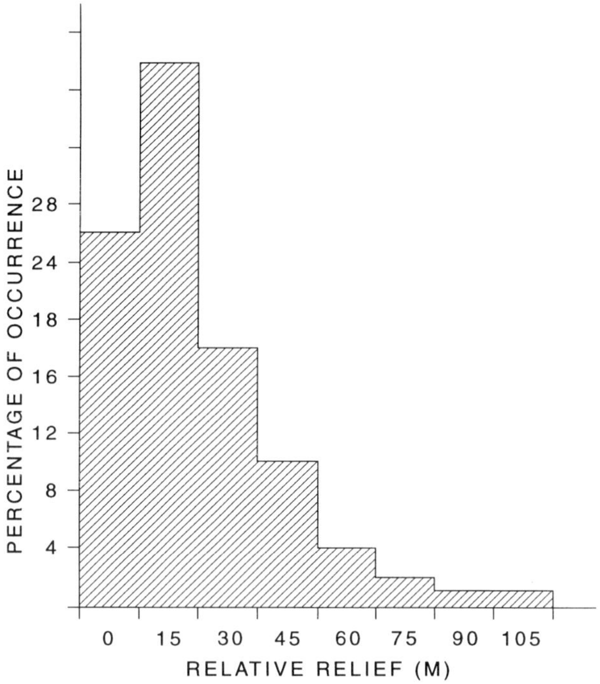

Fig. 5.4 Frequency distribution of relative relief

Relief Units	Relative Relief	Modal Group	% in modal group
South Cannock Plateau	19.5	15	64
Sutton Plateau	19.8	15	50
Upper Tame Valley	18.0	15	53
Sedgley-Northfield Ridge	52.7	45/60	26
West Bromwich-Harborne Plateau	21.0	15	47
Clent-Lickey Ridge	63.7	60	23
Stour Valley Plateau Fringe	45.1	30	31
South West Plateau Fringe	38.1	30	40
Solihull Plateau	10.1	0	53
Ansley Plateau	26.8	30	40
Corley Plateau	14.9	15	38
Mid-Tame Valley	14.0	15	64
Blythe-Lower Tame Valleys	8.1	0	53
Upper Stour Basin	32.9	15	44
Salwarpe Basin	24.4	15	48
Arrow Valley	26.8	15	47

Table 5.2. Mean relative relief (in metres) and percentage in the modal group for the relief units

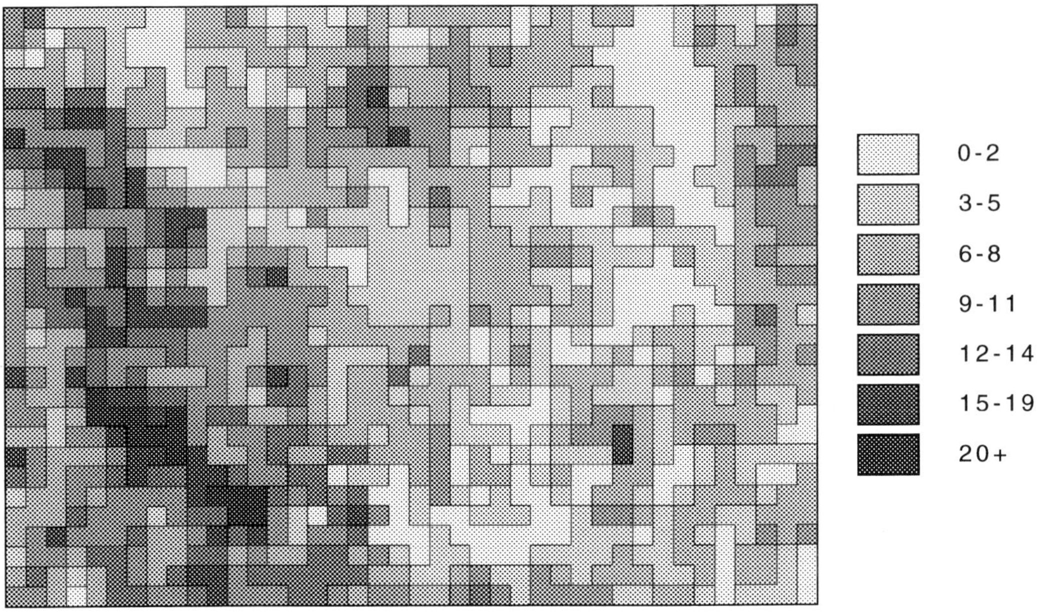

Fig. 5.5 Spatial distribution of ruggedness (number of contour crossings)

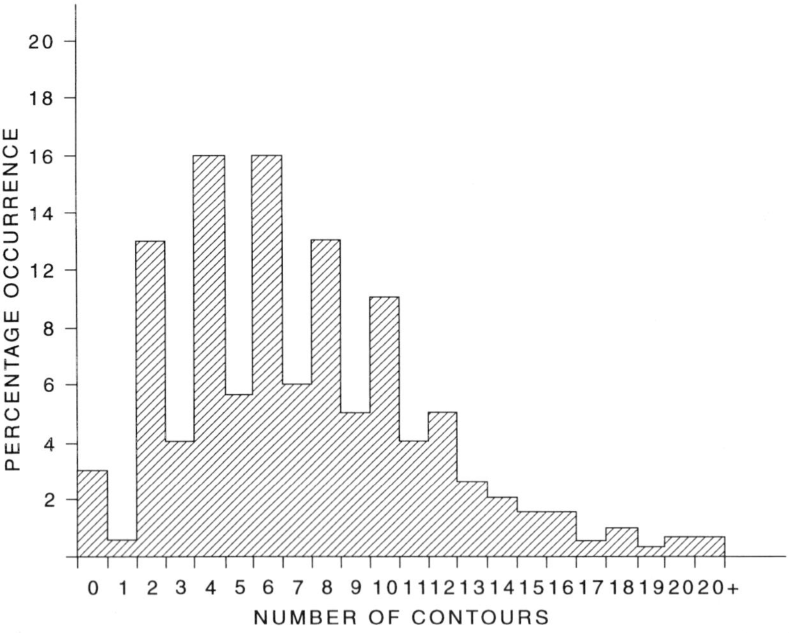

Fig. 5.6 Frequency distribution of ruggedness (number of contour crossings)

Ruggedness

Ruggedness (contour crossing) values are shown in Figure 5.5. High values in the west and south west and low values in the central and eastern portions are again evident. Apart from a tail in the high values the frequency distribution of ruggedness values is slightly more uniform with a mean of 6.4 and a double mode of 4 and 6 (Fig. 6). The slight dip for 5 contour crossings appears to be a statistical oddity. Differentiation between relief units on the basis of ruggedness is not so clear apart from the extremely high average value for the Clent-Lickey Ridge (Table 5.3). There is an intermediate group with values between 9 and 12 (Sedgley-Northfield Ridge, Stour Valley Plateau Fringe, South Western Plateau Fringe, Upper Stour Basin, Arrow Valley), a group with values between 6 and 9 (Sutton Plateau, West Bromwich-Harborne Plateau, Ansley Plateau, Mid-Tame Valley, Salwarpe Basin) and a group with low degrees of ruggedness (South Cannock Plateau, Upper Tame Valley, Corley Plateau, Blythe-Lower Tame Valleys). The Blythe-Lower Tame Valleys possess easily the lowest value.

Relief Units	Ruggedness	Modal Group	% in modal group
South Cannock Plateau	5.9	6	29
Sutton Plateau	6.5	6	27
Upper Tame Valley	5.4	4	19
Sedgley-Northfield Ridge	11.5	10	26
West Bromwich-Harborne Plateau	7.9	8	18
Clent-Lickey Ridge	15.0	12	17
Stour Valley Plateau Fringe	11.2	10	17
South West Plateau Fringe	10.7	10	22
Solihull Plateau	4.8	2	27
Ansley Plateau	8.4	6	21
Corley Plateau	5.9	6	19
Mid-Tame Valley	6.0	4	24
Blythe-Lower Tame Valleys	4.3	4	24
Upper Stour Basin	10.0	8	23
Salwarpe Basin	8.8	6	24
Arrow Valley	9.3	6/9/10/11/12	13

Table 5.3 Mean degree of ruggedness as measured by the number contour crossings

Landscape sensitivity

As mentioned earlier it is possible for a landscape to possess different combinations of the three basic relief characteristics analysed here. It is also difficult to analyse and compare areas using three separate values. Thus the values have been combined to produce what has been called a landscape sensitivity index (Gerrard 1993). The value of the index can vary between 0 and 100. A high index value would indicate high values of each of maximum angle, relative relief and ruggedness. Low values would indicate low values of each relief characteristic. Intermediate values may indicate intermediate values of each relief characteristic or some high and some low values. In either case it would indicate areas that may have some relief characteristic that may impart medium to high sensitivity. In order to produce the combined index a somewhat arbitrary decision has to be made concerning the relative importance of the three characteristics. It is assumed here that all three are important but that ruggedness imparts slightly more planning problems than maximum slope angle or relative relief. Thus the relative weighting of maximum slope angle, relief and ruggedness are 30:30:40 in the final index. There must also be a procedure to allocate the individual values of each characteristic within the 30/30/40 bands. The scheme for doing this is shown in Tables 5.4-5.6.

Contour crossings	Value in index
0 - 2	6
3 - 5	12
6 - 8	18
9 - 11	22
12 - 14	28
15 - 19	34
20+	40

Table 5.4. Scheme for incorporating ruggedness in the sensitivity index

Contour spacing	Value in the index
1	30
2	28
3	24
4 - 6	20
7 - 10	15
11 - 14	10
15+	5

Table 5.5. Scheme for incorporating maximum slope angle in the sensitivity index

Relative relief (m)	Value in the index
0	5
15	10
30	15
45	20
60	25
75+	30

Table 5.6. Scheme for incorporating relative relief in the sensitivity index

Using this scheme it is possible to assign an individual sensitivity value to each square. The spatial variation in these values is shown in Figure 5.7. This is a more complex map than has

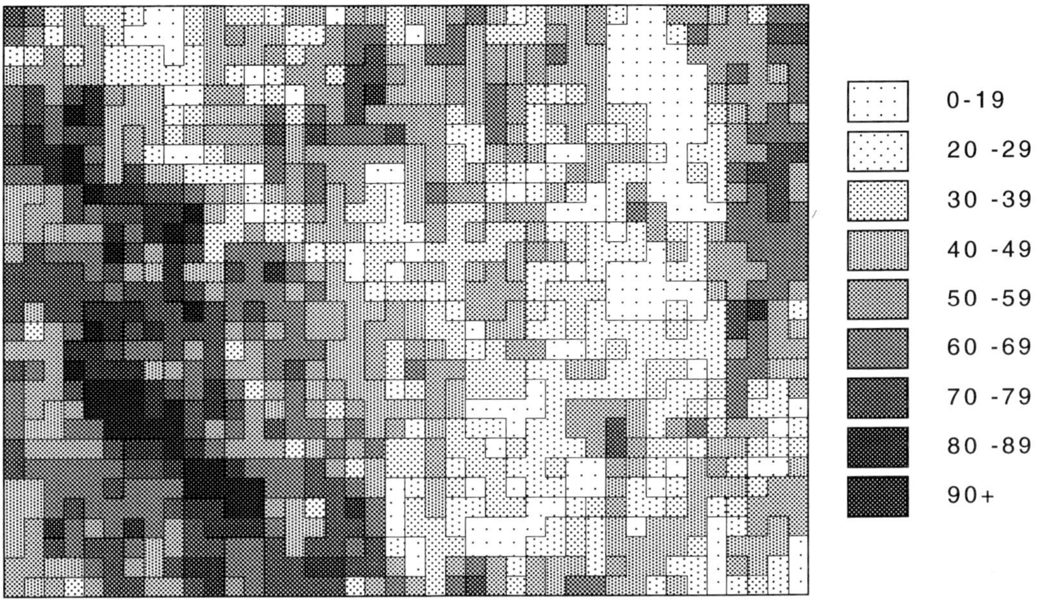

Fig. 5.7 Spatial distribution of landscape sensitivity values

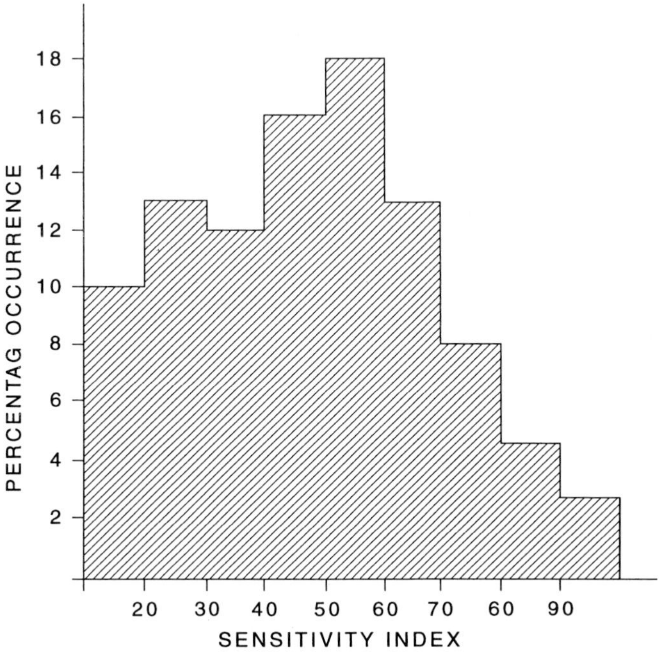

Fig. 5.8 Frequency distribution of sensitivity values

been analysed before. High values are again conspicuous in the west but high values are also scattered singly or in groups across the whole area. This implies that, although it is possible to make generalisations, it is possible to find areas with high slope angles, relative relief and ruggedness anywhere in the region, apart from the floodplains of the major rivers. A comparison of this map with that of the built-up area indicates that development has always been difficult in such areas.

Relief Units	Sensitivity Values
South Cannock Plateau	45.1
Sutton Plateau	48.0
Upper Tame Valley	42.3
Sedgley-Northfield Ridge	75.1
West Bromwich-Harborne Plateau	51.7
Clent-Lickey Ridge	80.4
Stour Valley Plateau Fringe	66.8
South West Plateau Fringe	65.7
Solihull Plateau	36.0
Ansley Plateau	57.8
Corley Plateau	42.5
Mid-Tame Valley	43.9
Blythe-Lower Tame Valleys	32.6
Upper Stour Basin	61.9
Salwarpe Basin	57.9
Arrow Valley	60.3

Table 5.7 Mean sensitivity values for relief units

The frequency histogram of sensitivity values (Fig. 5.8) shows a fairly even spread of values (average value 44.2). Nearly 15 per cent of the squares possess values over 70 which would indicate considerable planning problems. In terms of individual relief units (Table 5.7), the Sedgley-Northfield Ridge and Clent-Lickey Ridge clearly possess the highest values. Areas with values over 60 are the Stour Valley and South Western Plateau Fringes, Upper Stour Basin and Arrow Valley. All these areas will also have zones that may cause problems. The other units may have small problem areas but, in general, the topography in these units will impose few planning restrictions or problems.

Slope stability

A recent Department of the Environment survey of landsliding in Great Britain (DOE, 1994) enables the West Midlands in general and the Birmingham area in particular to be placed in a wider context. The previous section has demonstrated that areas with steep slopes and high relative relief do exist in the region but whether these slopes are prone to failure will depend on other factors, especially the nature of the bedrock and any surface materials. One of the conclusions of the British landslide survey is that maps are required combining slope steepness with hydrogeology and with rock lithologies susceptible to failure. In this way relationships and failure risk assessments can be made.

It is possible to identify three types of slope stability:

1. *Stable slopes* where the margin of stability is sufficiently high to withstand all transient forces in the short to medium term (i.e. hundreds of years), excluding excessive alteration by human activity.

2. *Marginally stable slopes* where the balance of forces is such that the slope will fail at some time in the future in response to transient forces attaining a certain level of activity.

3. *Actively unstable slopes* where transient forces produce continuous or intermittent movement.

This is not a static classification. It is possible for a particular slope to move from one category to another as a result of internal changes within the slope system, such as weathering or excess water, and as a result of changes to the transient forces. Human activity would be classed as a potentially significant modifier of these transient forces.

In the British landslide survey four broad categories of contemporary landsliding were noted.

1. Coastal landslides largely the result of wave attack;

2. Inland landslides on natural slopes for the most part unaffected by human activity which are concentrated at sites where the base of the slope is being undercut by rivers (e.g. Ironbridge Gorge).

3. Inland landslides on natural slopes largely produced by the disturbance of pre-existing ancient landslides as a consequence of human intervention; and

4. Landslides in cuttings, fills and waste dumps wholly as a consequence of human activity.

In inland areas contemporary examples of landsliding are far outnumbered by the remains of ancient landslides, many of which are difficult to identify because their outlines have been smoothed and obscured.

Marked regional differences in density of inland landsliding were noted. The West Midlands County has one of the lowest landslide densities (0.33/100km^2) with only three notable slope failures. Warwickshire also has a low density of landsliding (2.07/100km^2) with Staffordshire slightly higher (7.07/100km^2). The Staffordshire figure is mainly the result of a large number of landslides in the north Staffordshire incised river systems. In comparison Derbyshire (26.95/100km^2) has one of the highest densities of inland landsliding.

The extremely low incidence of landsliding in the West Midlands is partly a result of the comparatively gentle topography. But it is also the result of rock types which appear not to be susceptible to landsliding. No landslides have been reported in Great Britain on Cambrian quartzite, the rock exposed in the Lickey Hills. Only 44 slides (0.9/100km^2) have been reported on Permo-Triassic sandstones which includes Bunter and Keuper Sandstones, which are major

	Bunter Sandstone	Keuper Sandstone
Relative density	2.68	2.73
Porosity	25.7	10.1
Dry unconfined compressive strength (Mpa)	11.6	42.0
Saturated unconfined compressive strength (Mpa)	4.8	28.6
Point load strength (Mpa)	0.7	2.3
Schmidt hardness	10	21
Permeability (x 10^{-9} m/s)	3500	22.4

Table 5.8. Some physical properties of Permo-Triassic sandstones (from Bell, 1983)

rock constituents of the Birmingham area. Both of these rock types are relatively strong and resistant (Table 5.8) although the Bunter Sandstone does appear to be the weaker of the two types.

The frequency of landsliding on Mercian Mudstone (Keuper Marl) is greater with 212 landslides being reported at a density of 3.9 per 100km^2 of actual outcrop area. This number indicates that slopes in Keuper Marl will fail if conditions are favourable. The stability of Keuper Marl slopes is examined later. This landslide density for Keuper Marl has to be placed in context. Upper Lias rocks (essentially Upper Lias Clay) has experienced 41.6 slides per 100km^2.

Coal Measure rocks, with interbedded clays and shales, are susceptible to failure if steep slopes are created by river incision and if joints and bedding planes possess susceptible patterns and orientations. In the British landslide survey 285 slides were noted on Productive Coal Measure rocks at a density of 9.6/100km^2. During construction of the Hallamshire hospital, Sheffield, an excavation was made into a sequence of mudstones with thin sandstones and seatearths dipping at 18-19° into the excavation. During excavation a bedding plane slide occurred and it was shown that the angle of shearing resistance (ϕ_r^1) for the natural bedding surface was 16° (Bell 1975). Stimpson and Walton (1970) have shown that sheared clay mylonite bands in the Coal Measures may have ϕ_r^1 angles as low as 10°. The tremendous variation in lithology in Coal Measure rocks will make predictions of slope stability difficult. Variations in compressive strength for four Coal Measure rocks are shown in Table 5.9. These data show 3 to

Rock type	Range in uniaxial compressive strength (MN/m^2)
Sandstone	12.3-393
Siltstone	66.6-112
Mudstone/shale	4.8-73.0
Coal	9.8-81.0

Table 5.9. Unconfined strength of some Coal Measure rocks (from Price et al., 1969)

4 orders of magnitude variation in strength or deformation properties. Good examples of failures in such rocks occur in Ironbridge Gorge where incision by the River Severn has created steep slopes. Incision on such a scale and steep slopes do not occur to the same extent on the Coal Measure rocks exposed in the Black Country. Under certain circumstances glacial materials will also fail (1600 landslides in glacial materials were recorded in Great Britain) but slopes in such materials in the Birmingham region are gentle.

The most significant slope failure in the region happened in soliflucted Coal Measure rocks at Bury Hill. This landslide took place on 13 September 1960, following cut and fill operations for service roads for a proposed housing estate. Cartographic and air photo evidence suggests that a landslide approximating closely to the 1960 movement took place between about 1938 and 1955 (Hutchinson et al. 1973). The close coincidence between the southern and eastern limits of this original slide and those of the pre-existing coal tips, and the presence of a spring just below the slide toe suggest that the original slide was caused by tipping on a wet part of the slope. The 1960 landslide was a renewal of movement on a pre-existing slip surface.

Logged trial trenches showed that the stability of the slope was controlled by 6 to 10m of periglacially disturbed and soliflucted Etruria Marl. Two phases of periglacial activity have been recognised; an earlier, violent phase and a subsequent gentler phase giving rise to a layer of banded head. The early phase is characterised by irregular masses of country rock, separated from parent material but internally little disturbed, intermixed with zones of clayey silt, or silty clay head. The upper phase represents successive solifluction sheets.

The stability of slopes in Keuper Marl has been extensively studied (Chandler 1967, 1969, Davis 1966, 1968; Ward 1972). Keuper Marl is a 'soft rock' and in terms of the spectrum of rocks lies between comparatively plastic clays such as London or Lias Clays and 'hard' rocks. Weathering exerts a major influence on its strength and behaviour. Thus ' a contractor may use rock excavating techniques to move the Marl and yet when the quantity surveyor comes along in the next few days all he can see is a soft clay or even a very liquid slurry' (Ward 1972, p.4). The general weathering profile developed on Keuper Marl has been described by Chandler (1969). Zone I refers to unweathered but often fissured rock. The intial stages of weathering, represented by zone II, show the matrix starting to encroach along joints with incipient spheroidal weathering. By zone III weathered matrix comes to dominate the profile with frequent lithorelics up to 2cm long. As weathering progresses the lithorelics become less angular. Water content of the matrix is greater than that of the lithorelics. Zone IV material is almost completely weathered with little or no trace of original rock structure. Permeability is less than that of underlying layers and the weathered rock exhibits plasticity. The mode of failure of zone III and IV marls is virtually the same as in other, more plastic clays, such as London Clay. Moisture contents of unweathered Zone I marl and the lithorelics found in slightly weathered marls are of the order of 14-16 per cent whereas those in completely weathered Zone IV matrix is often over 25 per cent (Ward 1972). In his extensive study of a variety of Keuper Marl outcrops, Ward found little evidence of large-scale failure. This was mainly because steeper slopes tended to exhibit less weathering than shallow slopes. Large-scale failure tends not to occur on the steeper slopes unless the depth of weathering has been unusually increased. Tests on Zone I marl gave limiting slopes of 150m high at 70° or 530m high at 50°. Nowhere does such topography exist in the West Midlands. However, if suitably orientated joint systems occur, limiting slopes become 35m at 50°. Undercut river cliffs are a possibility at this scale. It is interesting that Ward, in his study of coastal cliffs in Devon, indicates steeper slopes in Keuper Sandstone than in Keuper Marl.

A failure, in 1970, in Zone II marl in Hartlebury Quarry, Worcestershire, just to the west of the Birmingham area, was investigated by Ward. This failure was basically rotational in type, conditioned by two sets of joints, and followed a period of exceptionally high rainfall. The only other significant failure in the Birmingham area occurred in Zone III weathered Keele Beds on cuttings near the junction of the Quinton Expressway and the M5. The Keele Group at this locality consists of red and purple sandstones with bright red marls very similar in character to Keuper Marl. The failures occurred in well weathered marl underlain at the base of the cuttings by a thin sandstone band about 0.75m thick. Slope heights were approximately 10m and slope inclination 25.5°. Residual strength tests on the shear plane produced $c^{1} = 0$ and $\phi^{1} = 18.5°$ as opposed to $c^{1} = 25kN/m^{2}$ and $\phi^{1} = 26°$ for undisturbed marl. Analysis indicated that pore water pressures were greater than would apply from a static water table at ground level. It would appear that the sandstone band had acted as a confined aquifer and had induced locally high pore water pressures. Moisture contents as high as 36% were noted even during a dry spell. The general conclusion from this survey is that failure is uncommon on Keuper Marl possibly as a result of high runoff rates which might hinder deep weathering. However, the failures in road cuttings at Quinton does demonstrate that these materials can fail if artificial slopes are constructed at wrong inclinations. The only other failure of any note occurred during the opening out of the Cofton railway tunnel (McCallum 1930). A small slide was induced in siltstone and sandstone. There may be another reason for the lack of slope failure which is related to slope changes that occurred in the past.

Threshold slopes

Analysis of shallow landsliding on thin residual soils has led to the concept of threshold slopes. For a natural slope cut in earth material, there is a single threshold angle above which rapid mass movement will occur from time to time and below which the slope material is stable with respect to rapid mass-wasting processes although subject to slower processes of creep. Two categories of threshold slope can occur. The first is termed a frictional type of threshold angle and relates to dry rock material. Most threshold slopes are termed semi-frictional and refer to situations where water flow occurs through the slope material parallel to the ground surface with the water table at the surface. It was noted, in the context of failures at Quinton, that artesian pressures, greater than normal pore pressures, can occur leading to angles lower than in the semi-frictional case. For a semi-frictional case satisfying the characteristics just noted it can be shown that $\tan\theta = 1/2\tan\phi^{1}$ where θ is the angle of slope and ϕ^{1} is the effective angle of internal friction discussed earlier.

Using this relationship it is possible to compare actual slope angles with those predicted by the stability analysis. This has been done by Goodeve (1982) for some slopes in the Birmingham area at Sutton Park and in the Clent Hills. The slopes analysed in Sutton Park are comparatively gentle compared to those in the Clent Hills and reflect the differences in slope form between the two relief units that were remarked upon earlier. Stability analysis based on the threshold slope concept has shown that the slopes in the Clent Hills are very close to their predicted angles indicating that they are very delicately balanced. Slope angles in Sutton Park are lower than those predicted by stability analysis indicating that, as regards slope failure, they are ultrastable. It is suggested that such slopes achieved their low angles as a result of high pore pressures during solifluction under a former periglacial regime. Many of the slopes in the Birmingham area are mantled with solifluction debris.

Ground subsidence

Most of the large industrial centres in the United Kingdom are underlain by Coal Measure rocks. The past extraction of coal and other materials, such as fireclay, gannister, ironstone, clays, shales and mudstones, may create problems for development. Surface waste and spoil tips are obvious problems. The Black Country conurbation is no exception and many areas have experienced or are experiencing the effects of subsidence. Subsidence is an inevitable consequence of mining. Extra problems will be caused by old mine shafts and, in the Black Country, by canal tunnels and the mining of limestone at the Wren's Nest. Subsidence can have serious effects on buildings, services and communications. It can also be responsible for flooding and can lead to extensive remedial measures and/or special constructional design in site development.

The nature and extent of subsidence will depend on the type of mining that was operated. In the pillar and stall method, stress concentrations are located at the edges of pillars and the intervening roof beds tend to sag. More serious effects can occur if pillars collapse. Even if pillars are stable the surface can be affected by void migration which may take place over a number of years. In longwall mining, subsidence at the surface follows the advance of the working face and tends to be immediate. It has been shown that the lithology of the strata between the surface and the coal seam being extracted does not necessarily exhibit a good relationship to the amount of subsidence. Superficial deposits may spread the influence of subsidence although glacial till sometimes reduces the influence.

Movements which develop at the surface can be vertical subsidence, tilt or differential subsidence, curvature or differential tilt, horizontal displacement and strain, extension and compression. The mechanical properties of the near surface rocks in the coalfields vary from brittle sandstones, through transitional siltstones to plastic mudstones and shales. With extension and compression small joints in sandstone may open and close. Bunter Sandstone sometimes fissures when affected by differential displacement. Massive Coal Measure sandstones may also suffer fissuring. Horizontal displacements are approximately proportional to the amount of vertical subsidence and inversely proportional to mining depth. Horizontal and vertical displacements create distinctive landforms including compression bulges, tension cracks, pits and depressions. Surface drainage may be disrupted. Subsidence may be enhanced by movement along faults. It has been suggested that movements are frequently greatest where the mine workings are under the hade of the fault and where a single shear plane rather than a shear zone is present.

Damage to buildings and other structures is usually caused by differential horizontal movements and the compression and extension in the structure. In buildings, cracks and jamming doors are early signs of subsidence. As stresses increase damage becomes more severe, service pipes may fracture and floors begin to slope. Most buildings require twice the amount of compression to develop damage comparable to that caused by a given amount of extension. The limit of the effect on the surface is defined by the 'angle of influence' which tends to be 35° to the normal of the seam. In a level seam the greatest amount of subsidence occurs over the centre of the working, diminishing to zero approximately at 0.7 of the mining depth outside the boundaries of the excavation. The National Coal Board (NCB 1975) has established empirically derived curves relating the amount of subsidence to the width and depth of extraction, therefore subsidence can be predicted.

Discussion

This account has demonstrated that, in comparison to many areas, the land and topography occupied by the West Midlands conurbation has imposed few major restrictions to planning and development. Landsliding and slope stability are not problems. There are no significant erosional problems. The rivers are not seriously erosive and flooding risk has been effectively controlled. However, this account has shown that there are a number of more subtle natural influences on the planning and implementation of new development. Slopes may become unstable if materials and slope angles are misrepresented. Solifluction material on slopes is capable of being reactivated. Foundations will need to take account of the nature of superficial deposits and made land will sometimes cause problems. Inheritance of relic features from past mining and industry may occasionally cause problems.

References

Bell, F G 1975 *Site Investigations in areas of Mining Subsidence*, Newnes-Butterworth, London

Bell F G 1983 *Engineering properties of soils and rocks*, Butterworth, London

Chandler R J 1967 *Shear strength properties of Keuper Marl*, unpublished PhD thesis, University of Birmingham

Chandler R J 1969 The effect of weathering on the shear strength properties of Keuper Marl *Geotechnique* 21 61-81

Davis A G 1966 *The mineralogy, structure and engineering properties of Keuper Marl* unpublished PhD thesis, University of Birmingham

Davis A G 1968 The structure of Keuper Marl *Quarterly Journal of Engineering Geology 1*

DOE 1994 *Landsliding in Great Britain* Her Majesty's Stationery Office, London

Gerrard A J 1993 Landscape sensitivity and change on Dartmoor in **Thomas D S G and Allison R J** eds *Landscape Sensitivity* John Wiley and Sons, Chichester 49-63

Goodeve G A 1982 *An examination of slope form and the concept of threshold angles in the West Midlands* unpublished Msc thesis, University of Birmingham

Hutchinson, J N Somerville S H and Petley D J 1973 A landslide in periglacially disturbed Etruria Marl at Bury Hill, Staffordshire' *Quarterly Journal of Engineering Geology* 6 377-404

Legett R F 1973 *Cities and Geology* McGraw Hill, New York

McCullum R T 1930 The opening out of the Cofton Tunnel, LMS Railway, *Minutes of the Proceedings of the Institution of Civil Engineers* 231 161-93

Price D G Malkin A B and Knill J L 1969 Foundations of multi-storey blocks with special reference to old mine workings *Quarterly Journal of Engineering Geology* 1 271-322

Stimpson B and Walton G 1970 Clay mylonites in English Coal Measures. Their significance on open-cast slope stability *Proceedings 1st International Congress, International Association of Engineering Geologists* 2

Ward A L 1972 *The stability of Keuper Marl slopes* unpublished report University of Birmingham

CHAPTER 6

Assessing the environmental impact of the Birmingham Airport Link Pipeline

D.M. Lawler, S. Sljivic and M. Caplat

Any large engineering project nowadays requires an Environmental Impact Assessment (EIA) to be produced by the developer. This includes a written report - an Environmental Statement- which details specific studies of any likely environmental effects that construction or operation could have on, for example, the ecology, archaeology and air quality of the immediate surroundings. For large companies, these Environmental Statements are normally produced by environmental consultancy companies which, in turn, commission specialists in particular environmental fields for advice on, or investigations of, specific aspects of the problem.

Despite widespread use of environmental impact assessments in the last twenty years, however, few of them are published in the 'mainstream' literature, and awareness amongst the wider scientific communities and the general public of their legal necessity, scope, depth and production mechanics is rather low. The aims of this chapter, therefore, are to:

- illustrate the nature of contemporary environmental impact assessments necessary for large development projects, using the Birmingham Airport Link (BAL) pipeline as an example;
- outline the typical planning process and timetable for such development;
- demonstrate the importance of primary and secondary physical geographic information within the planning process; and
- explore some of the concerns that may arise from various quarters and the mitigation measures available to deal with them.

The main focus here is on the archaeological, ecological and, especially, hydrological field drainage issues.

Birmingham Airport Link pipeline: the need

Pipelines designed to carry water, gas and oil now form a major part of the economic infrastructure of developed nations because, despite relatively high capital costs, they permit the rapid and efficient transport of fluid products over long distances at low running costs. In particular, pipelines increasingly meet the aviation fuel needs of airports. Modern jet aircraft consume vast quantities of kerosene, because of the huge amounts of thrust necessary for take-off and subsequently to maintain the forward momentum needed to provide the crucial lift forces.

To illustrate the scale of aviation fuel needs, Table 1 presents typical fuel capacities and consumption rates for a variety of fixed-wing aircraft of different size and thrust capabilities, many of which fly from Birmingham Airport.

Aircraft	Fuel capacity (litres)	Fuel consumption rate (litres/hour)
Boeing 747-400	216,902	12,788
Boeing 747-200	203,886	12,897
Boeing 777	168,090	8,290
DC-10-30	138,790	9,376
Concorde	119,500	25,629
Boeing 767-300	91,380	5,451
Airbus A320-200	23,876	3,025
Boeing 737-400	20,800	3,050
Boeing 737-200	19,543	2,838
Bae ATP (turboprop)	6,364	763

Table 6.1 Fuel capacities and consumption rates for modern jet aircraft, ranked in descending order of capacity (source: British Airways Engineering Communications 1995). Note that a modern car has a fuel capacity of around 50 litres.

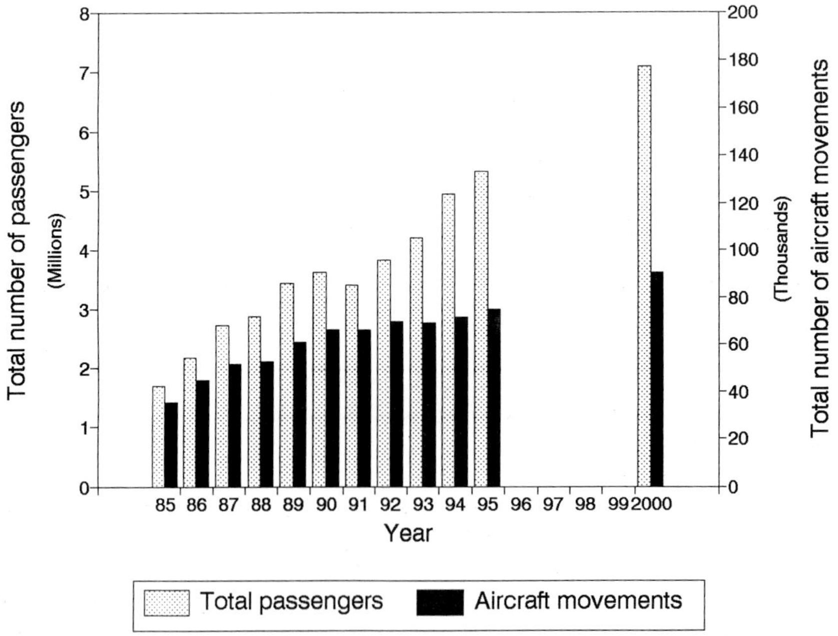

Fig. 6.1 Increase in passenger traffic and aircraft movements at Birmingham International Airport, 1985-1995

Birmingham Airport is the fifth largest in the UK, and is the fastest growing airport in the country (Summers 1994). In the 1985-1995 period traffic has risen from 1.7 million to 5.3 million passengers per annum, and projections continue this approximately linear increase to 2000 (Fig. 6.1). Aircraft movements (and fuel consumptions) have also risen significantly over this period, increases which are projected to continue into the next century (Fig. 6.1). Moreover, highly fuel-consumptive long-haul flights from Birmingham are anticipated to become especially frequent. To satisfy this increased need for aircraft fuel in a clean and efficient manner, ESSO decided in the late 1980s that a supply pipeline would be necessary. The alternative method of using a stream of tankers, was thought to be costly, less reliable, and have the undesirable environmental consequences of increased noise, pollution and energy consumption.

Environmental statements for pipelines

Planning a major development such as a pipeline is a lengthy process. In particular, under the terms of the Electricity and Pipe-line Works (Assessment of Environmental Effects) Regulations 1990 (hereafter referred to as the Regulations), any pipeline longer than 16km requires an Environmental Statement to be produced. This forms a major part of the planning application, and has to be considered by The Secretary of State for Energy before Pipeline Construction Authorisation (PCA) can be given. An Environmental Statement 'comprises a document or series of documents providing, for the purpose of assessing the likely impact upon the environment of the development proposed to be carried out, the information specific...below' (pp. 6-7). The specified information is composed of the following five elements:

a) descriptive information on the site, design and scale of the pipeline;

b) the data necessary to identify and assess its main environmental effects;

c) a description of its likely significant direct and indirect effects on the environment, in particular human beings, flora, fauna, soil, water, air, climate, the landscape (and interaction between these elements), as well as material assets and the cultural heritage;

d) a description of the measures to be used to avoid, reduce or remedy those effects;

e) a non-technical summary of the information in (a) - (d).

Throughout the Regulations, the word 'effects' is meant to include 'secondary cumulative, short, medium and long term, permanent, temporary, positive and negative effects' (p.7)

An Environmental Statement is normally a substantial document, therefore, and runs to 138 pages for the BAL pipeline. It can take many months to produce, given the range and number of stages of investigation to complete (Fig. 6.2). Planning for the Birmingham Airport Link pipeline began in 1988, when the approximate route was selected as a 2km-wide corridor running from Astwood near Droitwich, situated on an existing pipeline - the Midline - to Bromford, on the outskirts of northern Birmingham (Fig. 6.3). The 51km route passes through Birmingham Airport (Fig. 6.3B). The corridor was designed to avoid large centres of population, and so skirted the conurbation of Birmingham.

Within this broad corridor, a preferred pipeline route was identified (Fig. 6.3B) using the

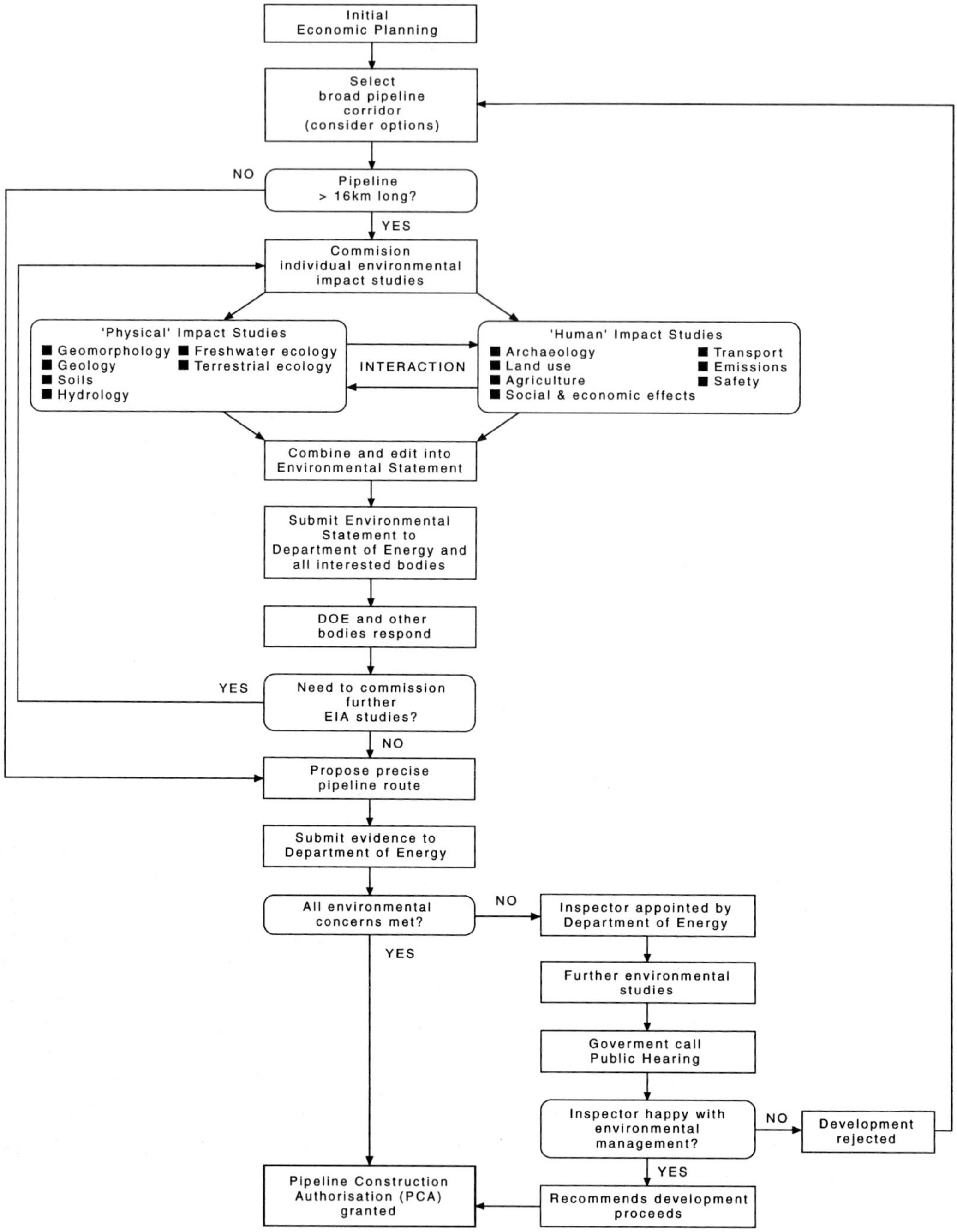

Fig. 6.2 Stages in the planning of a pipeline project

following criteria: ease of engineering; soils; geomorphology and geology; land use; special considerations such as existing services (e.g. motorways), Sites of Special Scientific Interest (SSSI) and woodlands. Specialists were then commissioned to assess the environmental impacts of this route. These individual studies formed the basis of the Environmental Statement for the pipeline (Fig. 6.2).

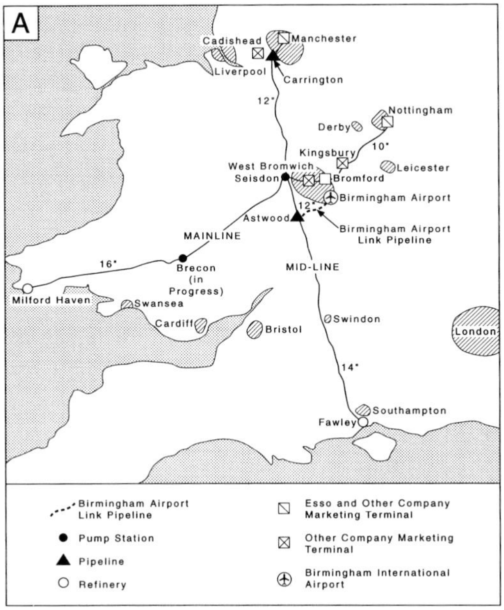

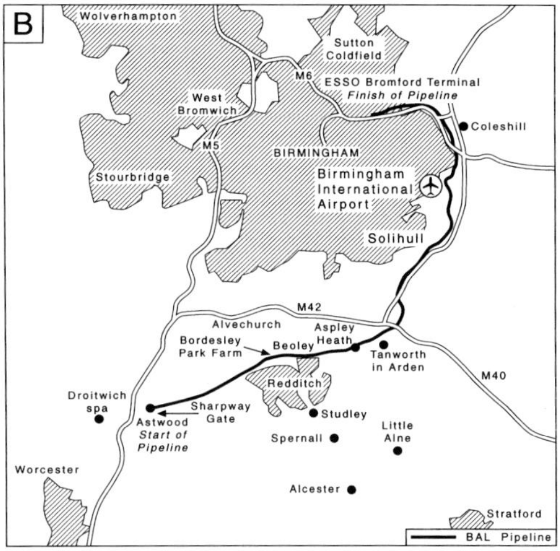

Fig. 6.3 The Birmingham airport link pipeline route: (A) national perspective; (B) regional perspective.

Birmingham Airport Link Pipeline: Environmental Statement

By some pipeline standards, the Birmingham Airport Link pipeline, with a diameter of 30cm is not large. Gas pipelines, for example, are commonly three to four times larger. Also, it was intended to bury the pipeline at shallow depth - between 0.9 and 1.5m - for most of its length. A 'working width' - this case 20m wide - would also need to be cleared either side of the pipeline trench to allow construction vehicle access (Fig. 6.4). Hence, the identification of surface and near-surface features which might affect, and be affected by, the pipeline was crucial. This is reflected in the Environmental Statement document which, following introductory sections on, for example, pipeline routing, construction and operation, includes a chapter on likely impacts on the following specific areas: land use; agriculture; geomorphology; hydrology; ecology; archaeology; social and economic issues; transport and emissions (see Fig. 6.2). Archaeology, field ecology, freshwater ecosystems and river crossings, and hillslope hydrology and drainage are examined in more detail below.

Archaeology

From the Sites and Monuments Records (SMR), a desk-top survey revealed all known archaeological sites lying within 1km of the pipeline route. Of the 185 identified, only five were prehistoric. Category 1 sites, which have statutory protection and are the most important, include Scheduled Ancient Monuments (SAM) and Listed Buildings. Although 78 category 1 sites were located within the broad 2km wide pipeline corridor - including 7 SAMs and 65 Listed Buildings - none were close enough to be directly affected by pipeline construction.

Category 2 sites numbered 93, nine of which lay close enough to the pipeline route that damage would be likely. These include two Roman roads at Sharpway gate and Beoley, ridge and furrow and a medieval fish pond at Bordesley, crop marks north of Redditch, and a variety of mounds, burnt mounds and moats (Fig. 6.3B). For some of the better preserved or important sites, plans were laid for the pipeline to be re-routed or 'thrust-bored' (passed beneath); at others, site details would be recorded by archaeologists as trenching work exposed the site for sample collection. Few category 3 sites (locations of chance finds, artefacts etc.) were found, and none lay close enough to the construction corridor to be affected.

Terrestrial Ecology

Ecological appraisal of the 2km wide pipeline corridor was first carried out by consulting records kept by county wildlife groups and the Nature Consultancy Council (NCC), now English Nature. This was followed by a more detailed survey of sites within 200m of the pipeline, including scrutiny of aerial photographs, direct ground observations and meetings with conservation groups. This was accompanied by proposals for mitigation measures. Specific sites mentioned in the Environmental Statement were targeted for special protection measures. The following five classes of habitats of ecological significance were found intermittently along the pipeline route, and are briefly discussed below: hedgerows; tree belts and woodlands; hay meadows and wet meadows; ponds surrounded by mature trees; and badger setts.

Because hedgerows provide vital evidence of ancient woodland character, contain a large variety of bird and plant species, and are important as corridors for animal migration, special precautions were taken to minimise damage and maximise reinstatement efforts where pipeline crossings were inevitable. The Tanworth-in-Arden area (Fig. 6.3B) boasts especially ancient and species-rich hedges, some dating back to Saxon times. Assuming that 15m of hedge would be interrupted at each field boundary crossing (e.g. Fig. 6.4), it was predicted that a total hedgerow length of 3.75km for the entire pipeline route would be affected. Reinstatement of each hedgerow gap following pipeline installation was planned using pre-existing and locally-grown plant species (as NCC prefers) such as hawthorn and blackthorn. The pipeline would in most cases be re-routed around sections where rare species are found. Stock- and rabbit-proof fencing would be used to protect the newly-planted hedge sections until fully established.

Woodlands act as important species refugia and plans were drawn up to avoid these wherever possible. Where tree belts had to be crossed (usually the large or linear woodlands), the pipeline would be routed along existing tracks and clearings as far as possible, and by reducing the scale of the working width. Sympathetic reinstatement (i.e. with appropriate species diversity and density) was made a priority.

Where hay meadows and wet meadows could not be avoided, turfs would be carefully removed, stored on site, watered regularly during pipeline construction, and then replaced, all within two months. Topsoil and subsoil would be stored separately in bunds either side of the trench (Fig. 6.4), and replaced to preserve the pre-existing stratigraphy. Pike Meadows, at Aspley Heath (Fig. 6.3B), consisting of two small unimproved meadow features which the Alne headwaters bisect, was one such special area and is designated as a Site of Importance for Nature Conservation (SINC).

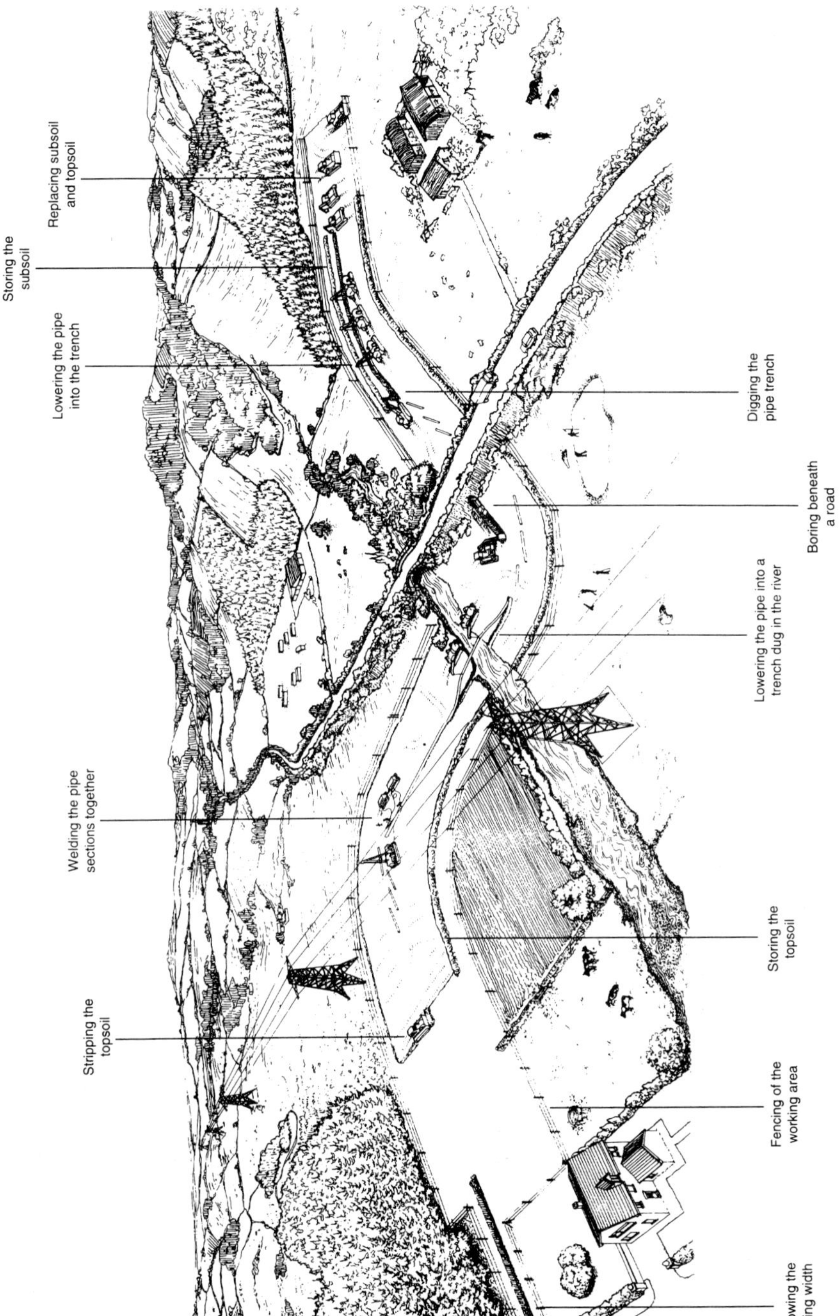

Fig. 6.4 Typical pipeling installation procedures (drawing by Andrew Wright, in Rapson, 1993)

Ponds, usually dug out from the Keuper Marl (Mercian Mudstone) and typically 20-30m in diameter, possess high ecological value, and serve as refuges for water fowl and amphibians. The pipeline route was designed to skirt all ponds and thereby minimise impact.

The Environmental Statement identifies the badger as the most important animal along the route from a conservation point of view. A number of setts had been recorded previously (e.g. by the NCC and local badger groups), and ground survey for the pipeline revealed further unrecorded examples. The line would be re-routed to avoid any setts and, during construction, pipe ends would be kept blocked to prevent ingress of animals. Well used tracks from setts were identified, and bridges provided over open trenches.

Freshwater ecology and river crossings

The 51km pipeline route crosses five drainage basins, namely (from west to east) the Arrow, Alne, Blythe, Cole and Tame. Each contains a number of headwater streams as well as ditches, and in total 20 stream crossings would be involved. Each crossing has to be handled carefully to avoid a series of potential environmental problems. Figure 6.5 summarises a range of specific effects, impacts and implications of river crossings, with special reference to aquatic flora and fauna (especially invertebrate and fish populations), channel stability, erosion, riparian zone disturbance and pollution incidents during or following construction of the crossing. We focus here on the problems of suspended sediment generation and water contamination for fisheries (Fig. 6.5).

Suspended sediment can be detrimental to (a) the survival of fish eggs in gravel river beds because of deoxygenation associated with silt deposition; (b) the survival of invertebrates if smothered in silt; (c) the health of young fish if gills are damaged by abrasive silt particles; and (d) angling conditions during periods of high turbidity (Fig. 6.5). Suspended sediment is naturally produced in most river systems by rainwash and streamflow events (Fig. 6.5). During pipeline installation, however, depending on the engineering techniques adopted and prevailing weather conditions, additional suspended solids can be generated. For example, during heavy rainfall, overland flow can develop across the surface of the working width or soil bunds lying either side of the trench and wash the finer particles into the watercourse (Figs. 6.4 and 6.5). Also, the pipe trench itself may act as a drainage channel, begin to erode, and route significant quantities of particulate matter to the river. Finally, as wet crossings are engineered, and the stream is excavated for the pipeline trench (Fig. 6.4), considerable fine sediment from the bed and banks can be liberated and dispersed downstream.

For each crossing, therefore, the following action was planned:

- Minimisation of the number of river crossings;
- Appraisal of the ecological value of the river reach at each crossing point, including existing water quality;
- Measurement of the physical characteristics (e.g. channel width, depth, velocity, bed and bank sediment grain size);
- Evaluation of river channel stability at each site;

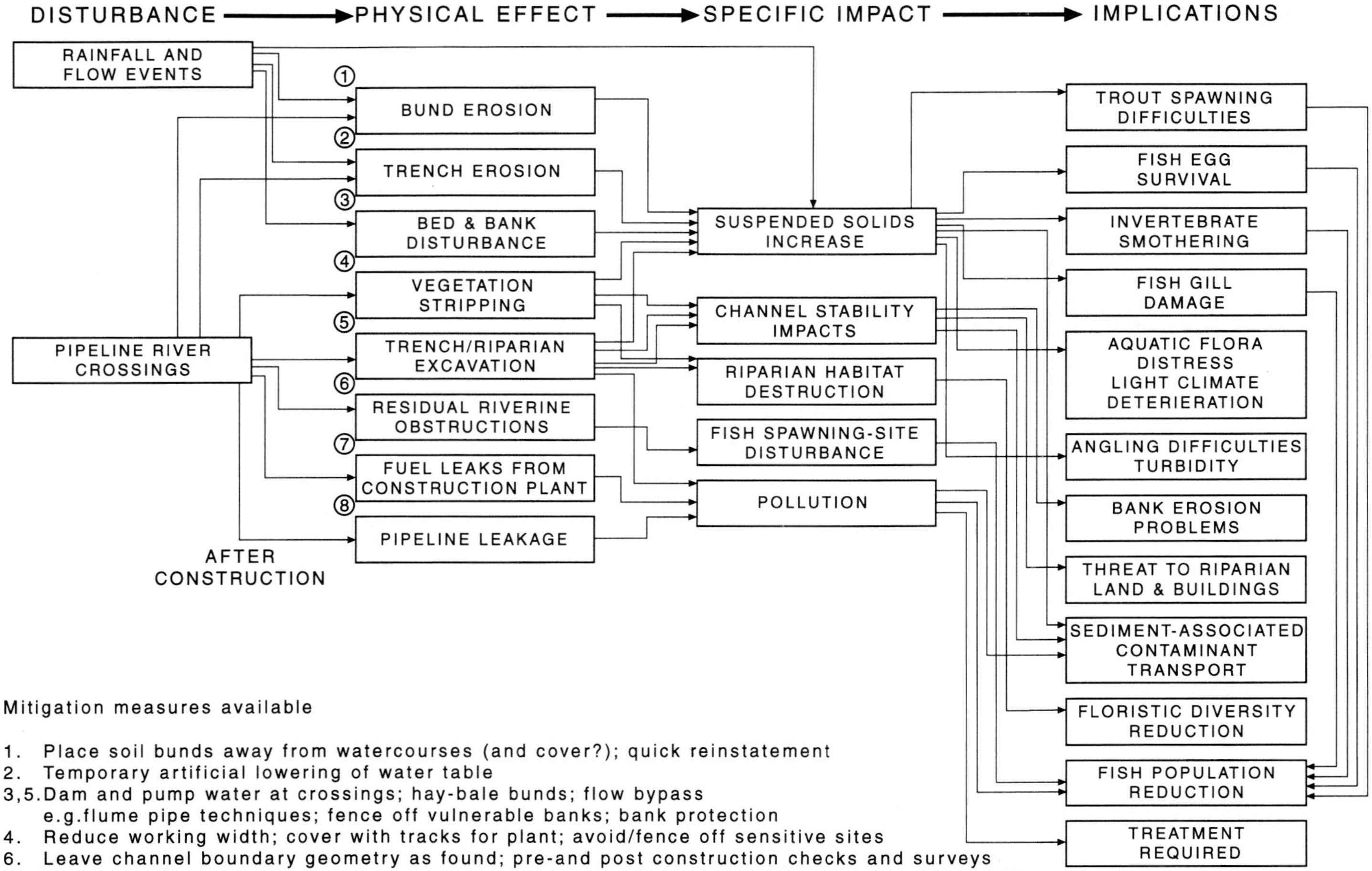

Mitigation measures available

1. Place soil bunds away from watercourses (and cover?); quick reinstatement
2. Temporary artificial lowering of water table
3,5. Dam and pump water at crossings; hay-bale bunds; flow bypass e.g.flume pipe techniques; fence off vulnerable banks; bank protection
4. Reduce working width; cover with tracks for plant; avoid/fence off sensitive sites
6. Leave channel boundary geometry as found; pre-and post construction checks and surveys
7. 'Catchment basins' around fuel tanks; locate tanks away from watercourses and working width;
8. 'Hydrotest' pipeline integrity before fuel transmission; automatic shut-off valves if breached; use thick-walled pipe

Fig. 6.5 Specific environmental effects, impacts and mitigation measures to be considered at river crossings.

- Discussion with NRA Severn-Trent region catchment managers about particularly sensitive crossings (e.g. the River Blythe SSSI), and the obtaining of necessary NRA consents for the crossing and mitigation techniques proposed;

- Rerouting of pipeline around particularly sensitive sites;

- Consideration of dry crossings/thrust-boring methods where necessary;

- Following of the NRA pipeline crossing protocol statements (e.g. NRA Severn-Trent 1989), including threshold burial depths (>600mm below 'hard bed' of the river) and bank protection and reinstatement methods;

- Drawing up of detailed 'Method Statements', including any specialised crossing techniques where necessary, to be followed by contractors;

- Training of construction personnel in river crossing protocols;

- Before and after inspection of each crossing;

- Monitoring of water quality (especially checking that suspended sediment concentrations remained within NRA specifications) at sensitive sites during construction activity.

In addition specific mitigation measures were taken to minimise the effects of construction itemised in Figure 6.5. These included placing soil bunds away from watercourse, artificial lowering of the water table (dewatering of the riparian zone) damming (e.g. with hay bales) turbid water in settling ponds before release downstream, reducing the working width, and laying tracks for heavy plant to run on.

Outstanding environmental issues

Post-submission developments

Following submission of the Environmental Statement to the Department of Energy and to all interested and relevant bodies (e.g. NCC, NRA, local authorities), a number of concerns remained (Fig. 6.2). Thus, the Government called for a Public Hearing and appointed an Inspector to preside over it, consider the environmental evidence presented by all parties, and make a recommendation to the Secretary of State for Energy on whether Pipeline Construction Authorisation (PCA) should be granted (Fig. 6.2).

Headwater streamflows, springs and wells

In particular the Council for the Protection of Rural England (CPRE)were concerned that, where the pipeline crossed the Tanworth-in-Arden area in the upper Alne basin (Fig. 6.3B), (a) it followed the main headwater of the River Alne; (b) the Aspley Heath springline (and water meadow downslope that it supported) would be adversely affected, and (c) local well supplies could be threatened.

Lawler and Lloyd (1991) interpreted the first two concerns as a reference to a possible partial interception of hillslope subsurface flows by the pipeline and its backfilled trench, because of perceived barrier effects. This could theoretically reduce spring flows and streamflows in a northerly tributary of the Alne. The headwater areas of the Alne basin are well-vegetated and gently-sloping (typical valley-side slope angle is only 4.3^{o}). The area is characterised by deep, slowly-permeable, surface water gley soils of high silt/clay content subject to seasonal waterlogging. In such environments, surface rainfall infiltration capacities tend to be relatively high so that considerable precipitation is accepted by the soil mantle, and runoff to streams and spring systems is largely by diffuse subsurface routes. With much subsurface water movement likely in the upper Alne basin, therefore (and at least potentially interceptible by underground structures), the concern of the CPRE was an understandable one which needed to be explored.

The Alne basin, with a total drainage area at Alcester of 167 km^2, is a moderately large system. However, simple sub-basin comparative drainage area analysis demonstrated that the proposed pipeline route only just clipped the upper part of the Alne catchment, with less than 2.5 per cent of the basin to the north and west (or upslope) of the pipeline. By far the largest part of the headwater zone and basin appeared to be separated some distance from the proposed route and hence unaffected by it. Furthermore, drainage network analysis suggested that the route did not necessarily 'follow the main headwater of the River Alne' but crossed and lay sub-parallel to a tributary which, although comparable in size to some headwater tributaries, was smaller than many others in the Alne basin. Even in the unlikely events, therefore, of minor, residual, hydrological effects remaining after sympathetic engineering and drainage works along the pipeline route, it was thought highly improbable that these would propagate very far downstream, given continual inputs of water from contributing hillslopes, springs and tributaries further down-valley.

Finally, Lawler and Lloyd (1991) evaluated the scale of the proposed development relative to the size of the hillslope hydrological system here. Soils and superficial materials are relatively deep here (up to 3.0m) and no water seepages were encountered in the upper 1.0m of soil cover during trial pit excavation by the drainage engineers in January 1991. The pipeline trench (maximum depth of 1.5m) is therefore small in relation to the scale of the hillslope hydrological system of the area. Any surface flows would, of course, continue to flow unimpeded over the backfilled trench. Furthermore, from previous throughflow investigations in other areas it seemed likely that considerable lateral subsurface flow would occur beneath the shallow depth of trench excavation: hence this drainage would also be largely unimpeded. Finally, we felt that near-surface throughflow would continue to drain downslope efficiently, through the trench as long as (a) it was backfilled with the original excavated material replaced to the same bulk density and overall structure, and (b) any bypass pre-construction drainage was installed where necessary. Provided these measures were adopted, and no increases or decreases in subsurface hydraulic conductivities were created, negligible interception of subsurface flows was anticipated. Pre- and post-construction monitoring of water-table levels could also be carried out to act as an 'acid test' of any pipeline trench effects, if concerns persisted.

The third concern (threat to well water levels), had already become a controversial issue in the area because of a drying up of many local (private water supply) wells about the time of the nearby construction of the M40 and M42 motorways (Fig. 6.3B). A separate hydrogeological report had earlier concluded that most of these problems had occurred because of a lack of recharge during dry winters and hot summers in the late 1980s. Four wells, however, were thought to have been adversely affected by motorway construction. However, a brief hydrogeological appraisal and scrutiny of well positions indicated that no wells were located sufficiently close to the pipeline route to be affected by derogation/drawdown processes. Moreover, Lawler and Lloyd (1991) emphasised that the shallow depth of trench excavation again suggested that well inflows would continue largely uninterrupted. A trench is very different from a motorway cutting: the latter is much larger in scale and creates a void which can lead to lowering of water tables associated with development of a cone of depression (Price 1996). The pipeline trench, on the other hand, was small (<1.5m deep and 1m across) and would be backfilled to maintain hydrological continuity across it. It was thought significant that the NRA had not voiced concerns over any of these three issues

Mitigation drainage works

Careful planning, however, was necessary, and special preparations were made by the pipeline planners to protect the spring line from damage. It is widely acknowledged, for instance, that 'a key factor in achieving (reinstatement) success is to ensure that the working area is adequately drained' (Rapson 1993, p. 24). First, the pre-construction drainage was carefully planned to intercept water run off from the upper slopes. This water would make the work of protecting the spring line even more difficult and so it was decided that in one section, a ditch should be reinstated to its former depth and width (it having fallen into disrepair), and to pipe this ditch to the river using an unperforated pipe to prevent water from the lower spring line from being intercepted (Fig. 6.6A). Secondly, the pipeline route was moved further uphill in certain sections and so to prevent the pipeline trench, at a depth of 120cm, from intercepting the strata which carried springwater. Thirdly, the protection of the soil horizons where the route was close to the spring line was considered. Here a temporary road would be constructed to prevent the need for topsoil removal and to protect the soil and the wetland flora and fauna which develop around these uncontrolled spring areas (Fig. 6.6A). Piezometers (water-table observation wells) were also planned to facilitate pre- and post-construction phreatic surface monitoring if deemed necessary (Fig. 6.6B). Although some difference of opinion existed between the drainage advisors to the pipeline and the conservationists, it was decided that drainage works would only be carried out if, in the following years, the effect of the pipeline was detrimental to the natural water progress.

The Public Hearing

These and other issues were dealt with at a four-day Public Hearing in Solihull in may 1991 (Fig. 6.2). Objectors were able to voice their (written) concerns in person, and the expert witnesses were present to discuss their opinions formed from their own, and related, investigations. Many objections had been withdrawn before the hearing itself, as a result of prior discussions between Esso, its representatives, environmental regulators, other bodies and local residents. As a result of these, Esso had undertaken to reroute, alter the engineering design or apply mitigating measures at various points in the pipeline corridor. The hydrological issues were discussed at particular length, however, and were also the subject of a site inspection visit to the upper Alne basin on the final day of the hearing, attended by one of us (DML), the inspector and a local resident.

At the close of the hearing, the inspector was satisfied that the pipeline, given its small scale and sympathetic engineering techniques agreed with the NRA, NCC and other relevant bodies,

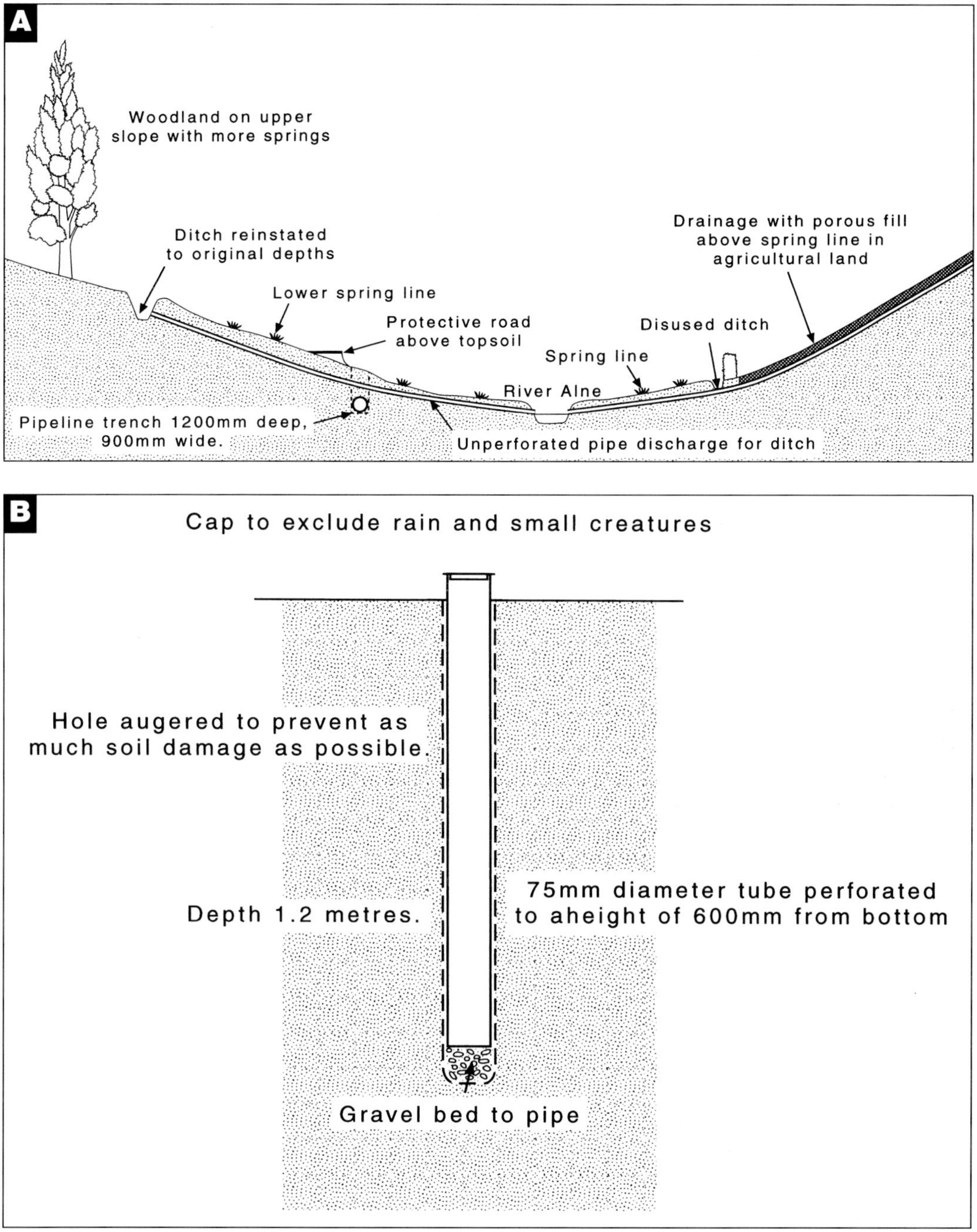

Fig. 6.6 Soil drainage issues in the upper Alne basin: (A) mitigation measures for handling spring-lines; (B) typical piezometer installation for monitoring water-table elevations.

would have no significant or lasting hydrological or environmental effect (Fig. 6.2). His recommendation, therefore, was that PCA be granted, and this was issued by the Department of Energy in July 1991. It is normal to attach a long list of conditions to such authorisation, however. In this case, the schedule asked, amongst other things, for an appointment, for the duration of the pipeline construction period, of an Ecological Liaison Officer and an Archaeological Liaison Officer. This would ensure that the best possible practices for conserving ecosystems and archaeological sites were observed, in line with the original Environmental Statement. Also, Esso were asked to undertake detailed additional ecological studies in the Blythe SSSI floodplain area, to record all archaeological information along the entire route once trenching had exposed fresh detail of the sites, and to make sure that all watercourse crossing methods were agreed with the NRA and NCC and any other relevant local authority, before construction commenced.

Post-construction developments

It is useful here to outline briefly one or two issues that arose following construction, to demonstrate the importance of long-term environmental measurement and commitment to remedial measures. Construction of the pipeline began in 1991, and finished in 1992. Testing with water (hydrotesting) to check pipeline integrity was first accomplished before aviation fuel was transmitted for the first time.

In the year following the installation of the line, however, one part of the route was badly affected by water ponding on the surface and the landowner expressed dissatisfaction. A drain was therefore laid below the pipeline at a normal agricultural depth. Observations made of the trench line during construction of the pipeline showed that the main trench had not intercepted any major soil structure change and therefore had not intercepted the spring line as had been feared. Others areas of the pipeline that ran through wetland alongside other rivers, such as the Blythe at Solihull (Fig. 6.3B), had similar consideration. Along the whole route the drainage was returned to an 'as found', or better, condition. In subsequent years, other, more minor, drainage issues have been dealt with. These have occurred mostly where heavy plant had caused undue soil compaction, or where existing drains, thought to have little or no importance, had proved to be more troublesome. Careful recording of existing drains, before and during construction of the line, have made the work of recreating the ' as found' condition a more straightforward process. The ability to identify possible causes for minor problems in years following the installation of the line has kept disruption and remedial works to a minimum.

Conclusions

The pipeline came on stream in 1992 and has run since then without significant difficulties. Fortnightly helicopter overflights and regular ground inspections are used to check for problems and third party interference. Special valves have been included which automatically shut down if a sudden loss of pressure (indicating pipeline failure) occurs. Very few concerns have been raised by landowners along the route since construction, and this is believed to reflect the comprehensiveness and thoroughness with which environmental impacts must first be assessed nowadays - a necessity which is enshrined in law. Environmental assessment legislation is perhaps less well-developed in the UK than in the USA: indeed, some have called for refinement of the guidance issued to developers and, given the multiplicity of environmental process interactions, there is probably a case for a more holistic and less compartmentalised approach to 'individual' impact appraisal (e.g. Fig. 6.2). Nonetheless, the Environmental Statement produced here, following a lengthy planning process, was a detailed and reasonably comprehensive document which appeared successfully to identify a series of sensitive issues and locations, and proposed sensible mitigation measures which, in the end, were acceptable to all. Although a wealth of useful material can be assembled from secondary sources (e.g. NCC and NRA records, maps, aerial photographs and existing reports), there is no substitute for detailed, site-specific, field investigations, especially in sensitive zones, to complete the environmental impact assessment. In addition, it is clear that post-construction responsibilities are also important, given the uncertainties surrounding the precise operation of, for example, three-dimensional subterranean hillslope hydrological systems which may only reveal their full complexity when exposed during pipeline installation.

Acknowledgements

We are very grateful to Ron Ball and Elaine Jones of Birmingham International Airport for supplying much relevant data, and to Dick Gray at Esso for assistance. Heather Lawler kindly helped with MS production. Andrew Wright of RSK Environment drew Figure 6.4.

References

British Airways Engineering Communications (1995) *British Airways Engineering Fact Book,* 2.

Lawler, D.M. and Lloyd, J.W. (1991) *Birmingham Airport Link Pipeline: hydrological assessment*, unpub. Report to RSK Environment Ltd.

NRA Severn Trent Region (1989) Summary of requirements for pipe crossings, *Land Drainage Consents - Information Sheet* 6, Fld/22/6.

Price, M. (1996) *Introducing groundwater*, Chapman and Hall, London.

Rapson, S. (1993) *The Shell North Western Ethylene Pipeline: A Workbook for A Level, AS Level and Higher Grade Geography and Environmental Science Students*, Shell UK Downstream

Summers, B. (1994) *Birmingham International Airport Vision 2005: Draft Master Plan - A Summary*, Birmingham International Airport plc, Birmingham.

CHAPTER 7

Planning for a green environment in Birmingham

Peter Jarvis

Birmingham contains a good deal of green open space within its 27,000 or so hectares. Industry, commerce, transport and housing have destroyed much of what would have been valuable habitat, but pockets of semi-natural vegetation remain, some sizeable, and many containing an interesting spectrum of plants and wildlife. Ironically, many new habitats have been created by industry and transport, such as waste sites of various kinds, quarries, canal sides and railway embankments. A number of Birmingham's formal parks have recently had a more environmentally sympathetic management, a trend echoed in many residential gardens. These patches of wildscape are often linked by habitat corridors, themselves in places sizeable enough to be considered as green wedges, linking the biodiversity of the urban matrix with the surrounding countryside. In none of these attributes is Birmingham unique, and there are certainly other urban areas where greenspace is greater in quantity, better in quality (however that may be defined), and more adventurously managed.

Essentially, all of the green environment is managed in some form. Planning therefore becomes important, especially (but certainly not only) by the City Council, and so the story of Birmingham's green environment must involve consideration of opportunities and strategies within the planning framework. Nature is also for people to enjoy, so the development of public demand for a green environment, and the extent to which such a demand has been met, is another strand to consider.

This chapter therefore reviews the nature and value of the green environment in Birmingham; considers the importance of changing attitudes to the evolution of this environment during the last quarter of a century; and discusses the significance of some of the issues, events, organisations, legislation and planning landmarks relevant to an understanding of the green landscape in Britain's second city in the mid-1990s.

The green environment of Birmingham

The most recent comprehensive habitat surveys of Birmingham were undertaken during 1986-1990 by the Urban Wildlife Group (now the Urban Wildlife Trust) following Nature Conservancy (now English Nature) guidelines for Phase 1 surveys.

An estimated 709 ha are under some form of woodland with a minimum area of 0.5 ha. Of this, the majority (around 480 ha) is broadleaved woodland, largely oak-dominated, the largest single site being the 119 ha ancient oak-holly (*Quercus-Ilex aquifolium*) woodland in Sutton Park. Sutton also contains six other blocks of ancient woodland. Locations of places mentioned in the text are given in Fig. 7.1. There are at least nineteen other sites within the city boundary that have been wooded since 1600, for example the Golf Course Woods at Moseley, Rubery Hill Woods, Woodgate Wood and Bromwich Wood. These ancient woodlands in Birmingham total 167 ha. More recent woodlands can also be extensive and species-rich. Edgbaston Pool, for instance, is noted for its beech (*Fagus sylvatica*) and wet oakwood communities. Elsewhere under damp conditions oak may give way to alder (*Alnus glutinosa*), for instance at Hill Hook, Sutton Coldfield. There are a few purely coniferous plantations, totalling around 24 ha, but there are a further 100 ha or so of mature mixed woodland, for example at Moseley Bog and again in Sutton Park. Some recent mixed plantings are located at Queslett and in the Woodgate Valley Country Park.

Land designated as scrub takes up a further 661 ha. Here, vegetation is characterised by shrubs such as broom (*Cytisus scoparius*), gorse (*Ulex europaeus*) and guelder rose (*Viburnus opolus*), and by small trees such as birch (*Betula*), hawthorn (*Crataegus monogyna*), elder (*Sambucus nigra*) and sallow (*Salix caprea*). Given time, scrub would normally develop into true woodland, but succession is often arrested by management, for example along railway cuttings and embankments.

Tall herbs characterise what are often referred to as the urban commons - waste ground or abandoned land that has been colonised by ruderal species. Ecologically, ruderals are plants that tolerate physical disturbance, but they are also often tolerant of (or even require) a low-nutrient substrate. Pioneers of these urban commons are often wind-sown plants such as Oxford ragwort (*Senecio squalidus*) and knotgrass (*Polygonum aviculare*), but other herbaceous species such as rosebay willowherb (*Epilobium angustifolium*), Canadian goldenrod (*Solidago canadensis*), mugwort (*Artemisia vulgaris*) and various thistles (largely *Cirsium* spp.) soon establish themselves, shortly followed by some woody taxa, of which buddleia (*Buddleja davidii*) is characteristic. Eventually such sites may come to resemble scrub. The 419 ha of tall herb sites noted in Phase 1 surveys greatly underestimate the contribution that this vegetation type makes to the urban landscape, because this is the kind of plant community that inserts itself into small pockets of land, or which occurs as narrow linear habitat.

The Phase 1 survey also greatly underestimated the area of improved grassland (3290 ha), since this includes the closely-mown 'green concrete' of parks and playing fields. Recently, however, the Parks Department has allowed some grassland to grow out into 'rough' areas, and indeed in places such as Cannon Hill Park, Pype Hayes and Ward End, wildflower meadows have been established (or at least attempted) within the park boundaries. Elsewhere, on embankments, in cuttings and along river courses, unimproved grassland, which may be uncut or cut once or twice a year, is quite common, with a minimum total area of 941 ha estimated in 1990. Wet natural grassland is found in the Woodgate Valley and at Plants Brook, with small patches elsewhere. The 36 ha or so of acid grassland in Sutton Park is almost certainly a remnant of a more extensive community.

Acid grassland in Sutton abuts onto heathland, which totals 448 ha. A further 45 ha of heath is found around the edges of the built-up area of Birmingham, for example in the Rubery-Rednal area and at Hodge Hill Common, as well as along parts of the railway and canal system where cuttings have been made into sandy, acidic, free-draining soils.

The 56 ha of wetland within Birmingham includes sphagnum mire in Sutton Park and also riparian swamp and marsh communities, again well-developed in Sutton Park but also found at Edgbaston Pool, Plants Brook and Queslett. Large open-water areas total 96 ha and include Edgbaston Reservoir, Edgbaston Pool, Bartley Reservoir and Plants Brook, plus 53 further lakes and reservoirs. There are also at least 167 small ponds, excluding garden examples. Furthermore there are 170 km of rivers, streams and canals in Birmingham, often of low (though generally improving) quality for aquatic life, but most of high amenity potential. Add the watercourses to their riverside plant communities, and many stretches represent attractive and ecologically valuable habitat corridors, reflected by the community-based conservation groups associated with the River Rea, River Cole and Chinn Brook.

Another important linear feature is the hedgerow, and some parts of Birmingham possess a dense network of mature, multi-species hedges. Pre-enclosure hedges are apparent in such places as Kings Heath and the Woodgate Valley. Allotments also provide wildlife habitat; and Birmingham's first bird reserve was opened in Harborne in 1993 on an abandoned allotment site. Large gardens can also serve as wildlife reservoirs. Where many of these features come together (for example the Harborne Walkway, on an abandoned railway line, has woodland bordered by allotments and extensive gardens) what might be thought of as a metahabitat patch exists, the different land-use types providing complementary habitat whose overall ecological value is greater than that of its constituent parts.

It is important to manage for and conserve what is typical and common, but Birmingham also contains a number of species that are locally or nationally rare. The small areas of heathland, for example, are important in a national context because they represent a transitional phase between lowland and upland heath, with bilberry (*Vaccinium myrtillus*) and crowberry (*Empetrum nigrum*) indicative of the latter. Nationally rare taxa include floating water-plantain (*Luronium natans*) (listed in Schedule 8 of the Wildlife and Countryside Act, 1981), recorded near to the River Cole at Stechford, though possibly introduced, and fritillary (*Fritillaria meleagris*) (in Appendix I of the Vascular Plant Red Data Book), found on wet grassland at Perry Hall, and certainly introduced; seven species of bat; water vole (*Arvicola terrestris*); and great-crested newt (*Triturus cristatus*). Lady's mantle (*Alchemilla vulgaris*), cowslip (*Primula veris*) and betony (*Stachys officinalis*) are local rarities found on unimproved neutral grassland, and wet neutral grassland supports devil's-bit scabious (*Succisa pratensis*) and southern marsh orchid (*Dactylorhiza praetermissa*), the latter also found in marshland. Acid grassland, while generally species poor, contains adder's tongue (*Ophioglossum vulgatum*). Sweet flag (*Acorus calamus*) and Cyperus sedges are found at Edgbaston Pool and Sutton Park, but at very few other sites in the region, and broadleaved helleborine (*Epipactis helleborine*) is found in damp woodland at Edgbaston Pool.

Habitat evaluation and site designation

Land is a scarce resource for which there is much competition. Land for nature conservation or amenity has to compete, in urban areas, with housing, industry, commerce, institutional use and transport routes. These latter land-uses can have some kind of a cash value placed on them. One cannot place such a value on nature or landscape (though some surrogates can be found), which makes them highly vulnerable in a profit-conscious, market-led society. It is also important to admit that not all green sites are of equal significance for wildlife or conservation. It is inevitable that some sort of evaluation be made, or some form of quantification be devised, in order to inform decisions about which sites to fight hardest for when planners sit in judgement.

For the protection of sites, some form of statutory designation is important. Two sites in Birmingham have been designated by English Nature as Sites of Special Scientific Interest (SSSIs), Edgbaston Pool and Sutton Park, the latter also having been proposed as a National Nature Reserve. English Nature has provided a set of criteria for Sites of Importance for Nature Conservation (SINCs), the next lower level in the hierarchy of conservation status (Andrews & Box 1988). Some 43 SINCS are currently designated within Birmingham, including five within the Woodgate Valley complex and two within the southeast corner of the Sandwell Valley that crosses into Birmingham. Local authorities are also able to designate Local Nature Reserves (LNRs) on council-owned land or following negotiation of management agreements with other land owners. In Birmingham, Bromwich Wood, Plants Brook, Moseley Bog and Leach Green Quarries have LNR status, with two other sites currently under consideration.

These SSSIs, SINCs and LNRs (Fig. 7.1) together cover 1335 ha, or roughly 5% of the total land area. A further 112 Sites of Local Importance for Nature Conservation (SLINCs) have been

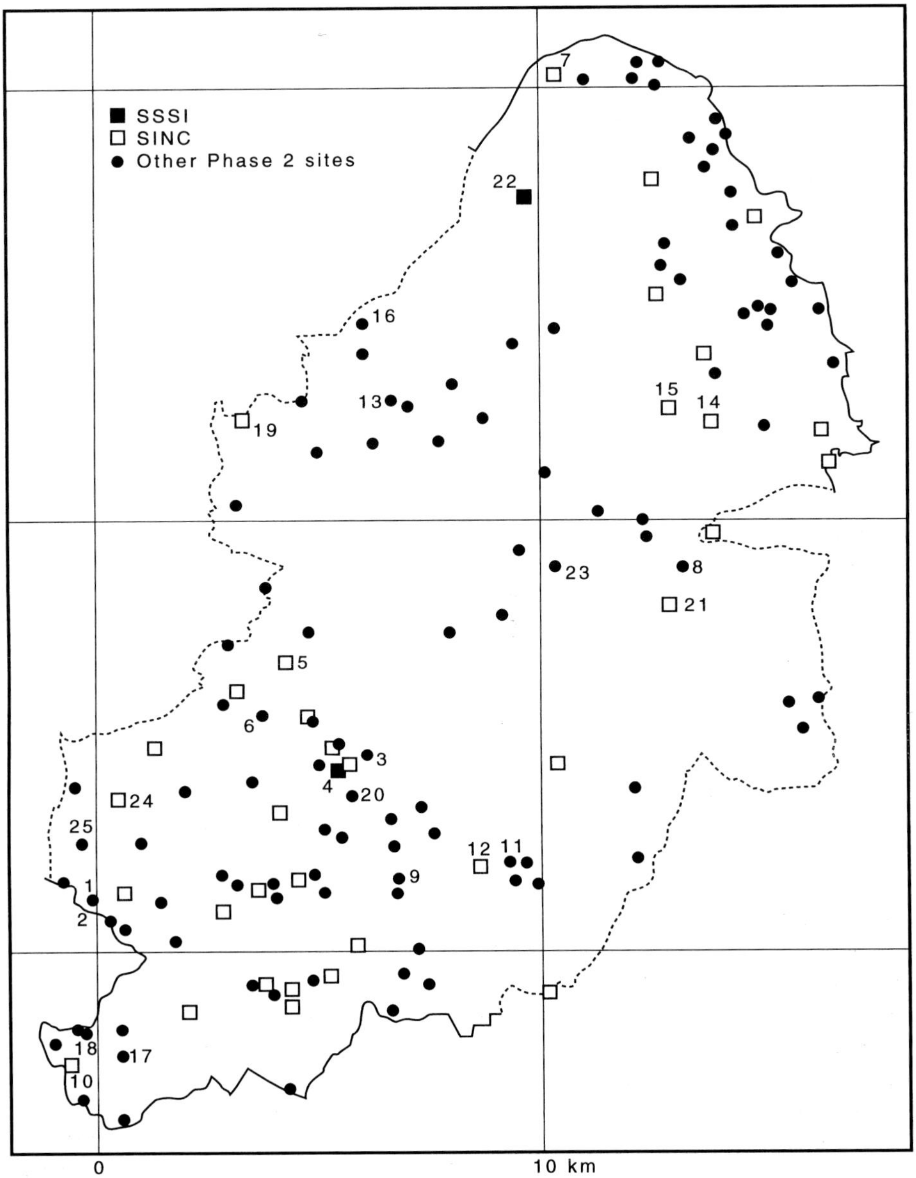

Fig. 7.1 SSSIs, SINCs, and Phase 2 sites in Birmingham, and sites mentioned in the text

proposed, totalling around 650 ha. These individually provide important links in Birmingham's open space network, and together make an important contribution to the provision of a coherent green environment.

There has been a presumption against development on all of these designated sites, though this has been weakened by a change in emphasis where the principle is agreed that such sites would 'not normally' be developed - not really the same thing. To the nearly 2000 ha of land where nature conservation value is acknowledged one can add an equivalent area of parks, golf courses, sports fields and other open spaces, some 4600 ha of agricultural and vacant land, and an estimated 7000 ha of domestic gardens. Clearly there is a substantial reserve of green space within Birmingham, albeit of varying habitat quality.

Changing attitudes to the green environment

The current acknowledgement of the value of the green environment by public and planners alike reflects radical changes in attitude that have evolved over the last twenty-five years or so. In 1970 nature conservation was an issue of little concern to most people, and green public open space was essentially viewed in terms of manicured parks with closely-mown lawns, ornamental bedding plots and (often non-native) flowering trees and shrubs. There remains a legitimate place for this approach to amenity, of course, but today this is but one of a number of options for open space management.

From around the beginning of the 1970s there was increasing public demand for different kinds of urban landscape based on different kinds of goals and attributes. One reason might have been an increased amount of urban dereliction, and certainly a number of landscaping schemes have capitalised on the availability of this kind of open space. 'The chief feature of dereliction in the 1970s was that, from being a phenomenon of mining areas and mineral workings, it arose suddenly and spectacularly in the cities' (Nicholson-Lord 1987 p.5). By 1982 Greater London and the six main conurbations in England, together accounting for 6.5% of the land, contained 32% of the country's derelict land, a figure that Nicholson-Lord stresses is a gross underestimation.

Education probably also played a role, especially with an increased awareness of the natural environment through the media, in particular television where the grainy monochrome of Zoo Quest shifted to the vivid colour of Life on Earth. People perhaps became aware of the importance and pleasures of a green environment in their neighbourhood just as they were getting disenchanted with high-rise flats and concrete urban girdles. Certainly Smyth (1987) believes in the power of television. He also convincingly stresses the role played by landscape architects, a cohort emerging in the 1970s willing to push the idea of a green landscape into design practice, sometimes for private schemes but increasingly as consultants or employees of local authorities. The role of local authorities as facilitators, providing not only schemes themselves but also a framework for grassroots action by local communities is stressed by Gordon (1983), Tyldesley (1986) and Goode (1993). The consequences of changes in attitude of people, practitioners and planners are here explored using two examples, Plants Brook and Moseley Bog.

Plants Brook Community Nature Park occupies nearly 4 ha within an 11 ha area of water, wetland, wood and meadow in north-east Birmingham. The core of the site lies in abandoned reservoirs which have left behind a series of pools or small lakes (Shirley 1988). In 1980, 7 ha of the lake area were purchased by a local developer. In the face of potential planning proposals a local residents' association was established, which discovered that the remaining 4 ha was owned by Birmingham City Council. The residents asked the City Council if they could lease the site and manage it to enhance its amenity and wildlife potential. With advice and support from the recently-established Urban Wildlife Group a proposal was made for what was essentially an innovative idea: a community nature park. A five-year lease (subsequently extended) was indeed granted for a peppercorn rent, and a management committee was established involving residents, local councillors and the Urban Wildlife Group.

Meanwhile, on the 7 ha site, the developer indeed submitted a planning proposal to drain the lake and establish a landfill site which would rise up to 10 m above the surrounding land. Permission was refused, but an appeal by the developer led to a public enquiry. This, however, found against the developer. The significance of such a result lies beyond the local issue. Previously, refusals had often been given for development proposals where wildlife value was an important contributory factor in such a decision, but this was arguably the first occasion where nature conservation was the prime consideration. Plants Brook therefore not only represented an example of local community assertiveness on a green issue but also a sea-change in attitude by a sympathetic local authority. Indeed the 7 ha site was subsequently bought off the developer by Birmingham City Council, and has been managed sympathetically, complementing the adjacent community nature park.

The nature park area was officially opened in 1985. Reed control exposed more of the pond area, but large areas of reedswamp remain, with marsh and damp alder and willow woodland also surrounding the pool. A pathway system has been established, and a boardwalk allows access across the wetland. Park rangers were appointed and an interpretation centre was constructed, though recent vandalism has destroyed this facility. Between the access point and the wetland area, a wildflower meadow has been established, and facilities for picnicking introduced. The whole site is now a Local Nature Reserve.

Moseley Bog, which lies 4 km southeast of Birmingham's city centre, comprises nearly 4 ha of damp deciduous woodland together with 2 ha of abandoned Victorian gardens. In the early 1970s the City Education Department began to infill the area as a prelude to creating playing fields, but when an interesting flora and fauna was pointed out, to its credit it desisted, and indeed the area acquired status as a nature reserve, with Nature Conservancy Council (NCC, now English Nature) input, a management committee, and hands-on work undertaken by a nearby school. The flora included garden escapes as well as some interesting native species such as skullcap *Scutellaria galericulata*, bog pimpernel *Anagallis tenella*, and the regional rarities royal fern *Osmunda regalis* and wood horsetail *Equisetum sylvaticum*. In 1980, however, a school work-party found surveyors on the former garden area adjacent to the City Council land. A planning application for housing had been submitted.

Independently of the management committee, local residents launched a 'Save our Bog' campaign. A public meeting attracted around 300 locals, and an action committee was established. There followed a 12 000 signature petition, a media blitz, and lobbying of councillors and local MPs. 'Birmingham City Planning Department, initially suspicious of "middle-class, glass-case naturalists", was eventually persuaded that Moseley Bog was also important to local kids and their vote-catching parents' (Byfield 1981 p.13). The problem was that the garden area had been designated as residential building land under a twenty-year old city plan, and if planning permission were to be refused the developers could claim compensation. The NCC had designated the woodland site an SSSI shortly after the campaign had started. SSSI status is given on scientific grounds, and the then Assistant Regional Officer for the NCC recorded that, 'Given the criteria currently applied by NCC to select sites for SSSI notification, it is impossible to justify including the bulk of the area which is the subject of this planning application (Evans 1981 p.39).

What did happen was a compromise, and eleven rather than the originally-planned 22 houses were built, leaving the wetland secure. SSSI status had almost certainly saved the day for Moseley Bog, but the criteria for designation were later more appropriate for SINC status, and the site was thus redesignated in 1991. It also has been afforded Local Nature Reserve status. The significance of this site again lay not only in the protection of one particular location but also in the broader issues of public awareness and public activism. Using this example, Nicholson-Lord refers to the parable of the bog, concerning 'riches found where they are least expected: home' (Nicholson-Lord 1987 p.82).

Pressure groups and planners

In July 1980, a few weeks after the Moseley Bog campaign began, a group of local naturalists, teachers, planners and landscape architects formed the Urban Wildlife Group, an activist body seeking a greener Birmingham and Black Country. It sought not only to influence the councils, land managers and developers but also to involve local communities. By the mid-1980s its involvement with the Manpower Services Commission meant a staff that fluctuated from eighty to well over a hundred, dealing with habitat survey, monitoring of planning applications, education and landscape design. 'In effect, it was a free-floating state-funded organ of aid, advice and environmental action combining voluntary commitment with professional skills and experimenting with newer forms of democracy, notably the making of a neighbourhood by the people who lived in it' (Nicholson-Lord 1987 p.83). Even when the Urban Wildlife Group found it was unable to work with changes in the terms of the government-sponsored training schemes, and lost all but its core professional staff, it continued with its objectives using funding from a variety of sources, including local authorities, the Black Country Development Corporation, Department of the Environment, Countryside Commission and English Nature. It has spawned the general idea of the urban wildlife group so that over sixty such groups now exist in the UK, and (having changed its name to the Urban Wildlife Trust) it has become one of the 48 trusts within The Wildlife Trusts Partnership of the Royal Society for Nature Conservation.

The Urban Wildlife Group filled an important vacant niche but it was not working in a conservation vacuum. In the 1970s the NCC had been approached by the newly-established West Midlands County Council (WMCC) for advice concerning the proposed structure plan, but it soon became apparent that little was known about the region's sites and habitats. The result was the commissioning of a survey which was subsequently published as the highly influential *The endless village* (Teagle 1978). Lyndis Cole's *Wildlife in the city* (Cole 1980) reviewed the current state of urban ecology projects: that Birmingham and London accounted for nineteen of the 27 projects mentioned reflected the limited work being undertaken elsewhere in the UK.

Teagle had indicated the richness and diversity of the region's wildlife and habitat, but his survey was neither systematic nor comprehensive. The WMCC therefore initiated a habitat survey which, by 1983, had identified over 20,000 open-space sites in the region. In 1984 it produced *The nature conservation strategy for the County of West Midlands*, which was both positive and forward-looking. The strategy identified wildlife reservoirs, green space corridors, wildlife links (habitat corridors) and extensive wildlife action areas (Fig. 7.2). WMCC also established a Wildlife Records Centre, based on the earlier habitat surveys.

In 1986, however, WMCC was abolished together with the country's other metropolitan

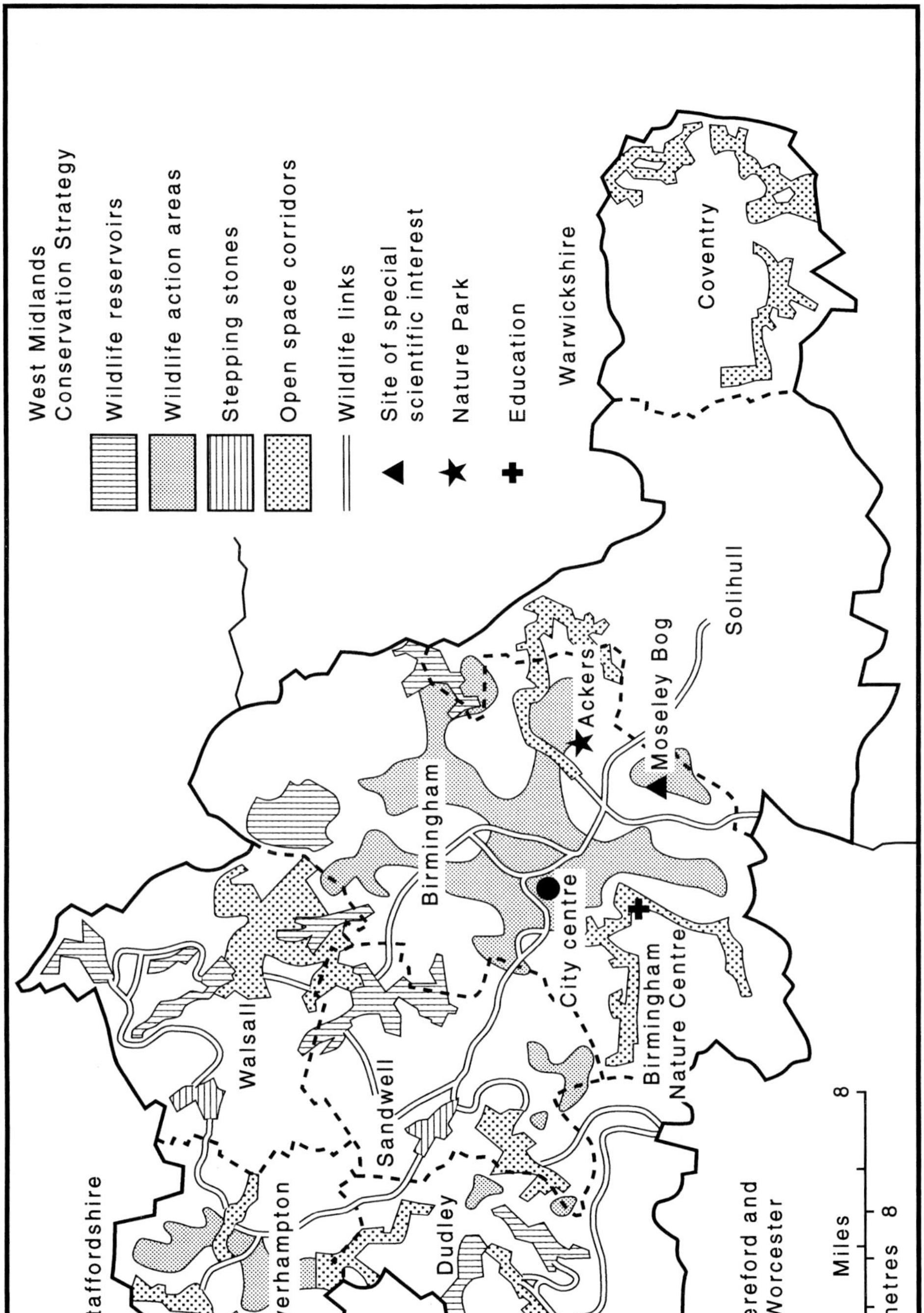

Fig. 7.2 The West Midlands Nature Conservation Strategy

county councils. The coherent, region-wide conservation strategy was abandoned, and the records centre was moth-balled. Although never implemented, the West Midlands nature conservation strategy was influential, legitimising the need to protect and enhance the wildlife network. Three new principles were enshrined: a network of 'unofficial' wildspace was recognised; traditional management of official public open spaces were identified as expensive and often wasteful of conservation and amenity opportunities; and a rich diversity of green landscape was recognised as a contributory element in economic recovery (Baines & Jones 1995). The Black Country metropolitan borough councils did initiate a Black Country Nature Conservation Strategy in 1988, the final version being launched in 1994. It was only in 1993, however, that Birmingham produced a Green Action Plan, though this was the work of the parks-orientated Recreation and Community Services Department. Shortly after, however, the City commissioned a new nature conservation strategy that went beyond in-house documentation. This strategy is scheduled for publication in 1996.

Meanwhile the Unitary Development Plan (UDP) for Birmingham was adopted in 1993. While there were a number of disappointing conclusions and omissions from the nature conservation point of view, a good deal of land was earmarked for conservation or green open space, to an extent following English Nature guidance (Nature Conservancy Council 1987). Three years later, however, even some of these sites are at risk, either from changing priorities or from UK governmental and EU regulatory policies that allow decision-makers to over-ride locally-agreed plans and which make the UDP already out of date.

Planning for a green environment in Birmingham involves participation in regional and national organisations. The West Midlands Environment Network (WMEN) began in 1984 with a membership of over fifty local bodies involving voluntary organisations, local community groups, local councils and private-sector companies. WMEN serves to coordinate, facilitate and share ideas, skills, knowledge and expertise (Jones 1988).

In 1985 the Groundwork Foundation was established as an umbrella organisation for the growing number of Groundwork Trusts, to provide a catalyst for co-operation between the public, private and voluntary sectors as a means of improving the environment.' In 1986 it moved its head office to Birmingham, and in the 1990s the Birmingham Groundwork Trust has initiated a number of local projects aimed at urban landscape enhancement (Davidson 1993). The British Trust for Conservation Volunteers is active within Birmingham, with hands-on conservation skills an important ingredient in greening the city. Birmingham also benefits from housing Friends of the Earth. While now defunct, during 1984-1991 the Centre for Urban Ecology was active as a specialist advisory centre aimed at improvements in and increased community awareness of the urban environment.

Planners and people: conflict and compromise

Cole (1983) summed up reasons for the relatively sudden rise in the popularity and promotion of nature in urban areas: 'The interest stems in part from developments in landscape architecture and land reclamation, but more importantly from the inextricable link with changing attitudes within the nature conservation movement itself..... Nature should be actively encouraged within the urban environment so that it is not the experience of the few but of the many' (p.267). Cole identified three major objectives of urban nature conservation: to conserve and press for appropriate management of urban sites deemed to have intrinsic or potential wildlife or amenity value; to increase the habitat diversity of public open space; and to create new wildlife habitats.

All of these objectives are aimed as much at people as at wildlife, with emphasis on amenity, education and participation (Johnston 1989).

In Birmingham, as elsewhere, this has led to conflict and compromise. Despite sympathy and effort from some individuals within the local authority, Birmingham has rather lagged behind other urban areas in being pro-active towards a green city environment. On balance, there does appear to have been a recent positive shift in attitude and willingness to invest time and money into greenspace. The environmental case has to be argued rather than taken for granted. Conflicts are inevitable, as is currently being seen with debate over the Draft Local Action Plan for Selly Oak, where a putative relief road, housing and new industry are proposed on land which includes a sizeable area of high quality habitat. Over the city as a whole there will be pressure on green sites as a result of the Regional Planning Guidance II document, in which the Department of the Environment has set a target for 2050 new houses in Birmingham by the year 2011, in addition to those already planned in the UDP.

At the 1992 Rio Conference the UK agreed to implement Agenda 21, an action programme for policies and actions leading to sustainable development. The proposal for each local authority to prepare a Local Agenda 21 has been adopted by Birmingham. Thus Birmingham has agreed to identify means of maintaining and enhancing species and habitat diversity, and to this end must look to all elements of the biota, not just the rarities. There has to be constant vigilance against environmentally inappropriate planning applications, however. The exhortation to those who would enjoy and guard wildlife sites has to be: watch this space.

Acknowledgements

The author is very grateful to Chris Parry, Urban Wildlife Trust, for his valuable comments on an early draft of this chapter; and to Craig Slawson , EcoRecord, for providing the initial map for Figure 7.1 Heather Hall has also helpfully confirmed a number of observations.

References

Andrews J and Box J 1988 SINCs going swimmingly *Urban Wildlife* 1(3) 32-33

Baines C and Jones N 1994 Urban forestry and landscape networks of the Black Country, England in **Cook E A and van Lier E A** eds *Landscape planning and ecological networks* Elsevier, Amsterdam 273-282

Byfield P 1981 The view from Moseley Bog *Ecos: A Review of Conservation* 2(2) 13-18

Cole L 1980 *Wildlife in the city. A study of practical conservation projects* Nature Conservancy Council, London

Cole L 1983 Urban nature conservation in **Warren A and Goldsmith F B** eds *Conservation in perspective* Wiley, Chichester 267-285

Davidson J 1993 Conservation and partnership: lessons from the Groundwork experience in: **Goldsmith F B and Warren A** eds *Conservation in progress* Wiley, Chichester 347-354

Evans M E 1981 Letter Ecos: *A Review of Conservation* 2(2) 38-39

Goode D 1993 Local authorities and urban conservation in **Goldsmith F B and Warren A** eds *op. cit.* 335-345

Gordon J 1983 Environmental management in local authorities in **Warren A and Goldsmith F B** eds *op. cit.* 411-428

Johnston J D 1989 Nature areas for city people *Ecology Handbook* 14 London Ecology

Unit, London
Jones T 1988 Green capital *Urban Wildlife* 1(3) 11-13
Nature Conservancy Council 1987 *Planning for wildlife in metropolitan areas: guidance for the preparation of Unitary Development Plans* Nature Conservancy Council, Peterborough
Nicholson-Lord D 1987 *The greening of the cities* Routledge & Kegan Paul, London
Shirley P 1988 *Wildlife walkabout: Birmingham and the Black Country* Wayside Books Clevedon
Smyth B 1987 *City wildspace* Hilary Shipman, London
Teagle W B 1978 *The endless village* Nature Conservancy Council, Shrewsbury
Tyldesley D 1986 *Gaining momentum. An analysis of the role and performance of local authorities in nature conservation* Pisces Publications, Oxford

CHAPTER 8

Birmingham Weather Through Two Centuries

Brian D Giles and John Kings

"...most men are weather-wise... some, alas are other wise"

(Benjamin Franklin, 1735)

Climate and meteorology have been synonymous with the British Association since its inauguration in 1831. At its first meeting in York, there were discussions concerning the recording of meteorological variables, as well as their temporal and spatial distribution. Instrument design and performance were also on the agenda along with a request that J.D. Forbes prepare a report on the current state of the subject (British Association 1835). It is in this latter respect that Birmingham began to take an important place in the British Association through the endeavours of one particular man - Abraham Follett Osler. During the 1830s both he and the Rev. W. Whewell invented and then described recording anemometers at various meetings of the British Association (British Association 1838, Harris 1841, Osler 1841).

There had been an interest in meteorology in Birmingham since the late eighteenth century when members of the Lunar Society, who had made their own instruments (Robinson 1957), measured and recorded the weather, producing at least two weather diaries. The Lunar Society was commuted into the Birmingham Philosophical Institute, which began in 1800 and continued an interest in meteorological measurements. It was the Philosophical Institute which organised the 1839 Birmingham meeting of the British Association. Here, Osler presented papers summarising anemograph analyses from instruments installed in Birmingham and Plymouth. The British Association returned to Birmingham in 1849 at a time when the Philosophical Institute was in a state of terminal decline. The latter was replaced by the Birmingham and Midland Institute in 1854 which was involved in the meetings of 1865 and 1886. In the present century meetings have been linked with the University of Birmingham in 1913, 1950 and 1996. Conference handbooks have all included information about the weather and climate of the area (Cresswell 1913, Seward 1950). Thus there has been a close relationship between climatology, Birmingham and the British association for over 160 years. This has meant that there are a number of accounts of the climatology of Birmingham during the nineteenth and early twentieth centuries in the Annual reports and Transactions of the British Association, the Handbooks of the British Association Local Committees, and the Annual Reports of the Birmingham and Midland Institute (Giles and Kings 1994). This chapter examines the early and more recent weather diaries, which together constitute the longest known series of monthly data for the United Kingdom.

Recording the Weather

The Lunar Society: Soho Series 1793-1830

The earliest recordings of the weather in Birmingham were made by an unknown observer or observers in a series of weather registers which form part of the Boulton and Watt Collection in the Birmingham Reference Library. These began on 4th April 1793, and continued until 29 October 1830, at a site in the Hockley area, to the north of the present city centre. Inspection of the diaries suggests that the readings were actually taken at Soho House (Fig. 8.1), the home of Matthew Boulton, one of the founder members of the Lunar Society (Bolton 1890, Wells 1951, Schofield 1963). Unfortunately, the diary covering the years 1821 to 1825 inclusive is missing and the data provided between 1826 to 1830 is fragmented. The diaries contain readings at 8am, 2pm and 8pm of pressure, temperature, rainfall, wind direction and force, humidity, cloud amount and weather experienced. Daily rainfall totals replace thrice daily readings from October 1804, though these entries are not consistent since on many occasions rainfall is mentioned in the 'remarks' column without any amount being noted in the rainfall column. Little information is given about the instrumentation other than that the thermometers were outside the house from December 1793 (in the first twenty months there was also a thermometer inside which registered up to 8°C higher in winter and about 4°C higher in summer); the outside thermometers were certainly not housed in a screen and would have been subject to radiational imbalance. It is also likely that the raingauge was located on the roof. From April 1804, a page each month is available for more detailed remarks and often these include the time of occurrence of lowest or highest temperature on a particular day. Consequently in this initial phase of analysis, the Soho Series has been examined, possible errors identified and suitably corrected, converted to present day units (°C for temperature and mm for rainfall), and averages, normals and extremes computed. These are shown in Table 8.1 which gives the 37-year period statistics.

°C/mm	Jan	Feb	Mar	Apr	May	Jun	Jul	Aug	Sep	Oct	Nov	Dec	Year
Mean maximum	3.1	5.4	7.4	10.8	14.9	17.7	18.9	18.8	16.2	11.2	6.5	4.1	11.2
Mean minimum	0.7	2.3	3.5	6.7	10.8	13.5	15.1	14.5	12.0	8.0	3.9	1.8	7.6
Mean monthly	1.9	3.9	5.5	8.7	13.0	15.6	17.2	16.7	13.9	9.6	5.2	2.9	9.6
Highmax	9.3	11.3	13.9	18.1	22.2	24.0	25.1	24.0	21.6	17	12.1	10.1	26.1
Lowmin	-6.7	-4.5	-2.5	1.4	5.6	8.9	11.3	11.1	6.7	1.4	-3.0	-6.0	-9.0
Rainfall	54.5	44.3	41.0	49.9	70.7	49.3	65.3	62.5	65.8	61.3	69.1	59.9	652.2
Raindays	10	9	8	10	11	9	12	10	9	10	11	10	112

Table. 8.1 Soho Series 1793-1830 : Temperature and Rainfall

A second set of meteorological readings at this time was carried out by William Withering over a shorter period (January 1795 to April 1796) at Edgbaston Hall, just to the southwest of the town as it was then (Withering 1822). Withering was also a member of the Lunar Society. He took readings three times a day, at 9am, 2pm and 9pm. A comparison of these two sets of data for the short period when they overlap shows that at 2pm the monthly mean temperatures were very similar in the winter but at Soho in summer they were about 1°C higher (Giles 1991). This emphasises the importance of the Soho Series since it is clearly representative of practices, and weather, at that time.

Soho House

Cannon Street

Midland Institute

Perrot's folly

Waterworks Road

Winterbourne

Fig. 8.1 Locations of weather stations within Birmingham 1793-1995

Birmingham Philosophical Institution (BPI) Series 1800-1844

This Institution was inaugurated in 1800 (as the Philosophical Society, with premises where New Street station now stands) and existed for just over 40 years. Its early years are shrouded in mystery since few records exist before 1813, prior to the Society's move to new premises in Cannon Street (Fig. 8.1) when it became part of the Institution. The extant annual reports show that although meteorological observations were made, it was not until the annual report of 1836 that weather summaries were published (Birmingham Philosophical Institution 1836). These annual summaries provide daily pressure, temperature, dew point, rainfall, and wind direction all measured at 9am and 3pm, along with the highest and lowest temperatures measured by a self-registering thermometer, and a brief description of the days weather. Annual climatological summaries continued until 1844 at which time two years of evaporation data had replaced the dew point data. The monthly data was collated into a 7-year series with averages (Table 8.2) by

°C/mm	Jan	Feb	Mar	Apr	May	Jun	Jul	Aug	Sep	Oct	Nov	Dec	Year
Mean monthly	2.7	3.6	5.9	9.5	12.7	15.5	16.5	16.6	14.5	9.7	6.1	4.9	9.9
Rainfall	48.2	56.1	41.6	32.1	47.6	51.8	64.7	66.7	59.3	58.4	82.4	35.7	644.5

Table. 8.2 Birmingham Philosophical Institute Series 1837-1844 : Temperature and Rainfall

William Ick, who had been appointed curator in 1836. Ick also produced a monthly summary which was copied verbatim in the local newspaper, The Midland Counties Herald. In December 1843, March and June 1844 he made forty successive hourly observations on each occasion from 6am on 21st to 9pm on the 22nd. This wealth of data was used in a report to the 22nd meeting of the British Association at Belfast in 1853 (Wills 1853).

Plant, Southall and Smith Series: 1860-1900

The interest in the weather in Birmingham in the middle of the nineteenth century was not limited to the Institute. Several amateurs also made their own readings and published them either privately or in the local press. One such person was Thomas Plant, who read a paper at the British Association meeting in Cambridge, in 1862. This was subsequently published, as well as a summary of climate in Birmingham for the ten years ending in 1862 (Plant 1862a, 1862b, 1863).

Other weather observers at this time were T. Southall (Edgbaston) and D. Smith (Nechells) whose observations are to be found in a local newspaper - Aris's Gazette. In the last quarter of the century, another Smith, R.T. (1912), combined the results from five stations on the northwest outskirts of Birmingham. It seems that he moved house and instruments various times between 1874 and 1901 but combined all the readings as a single series. Smith tabulated, amongst other summary data, averages of temperature and total rainfall. We have utilised part of this Smith series (1874 to 1886) to help fill the gap between the data provided by Plant and the Birmingham and Midland Institute at Perrot's Folly (Table 8.3).

Also at this time, D.H. Owen began a series of daily weather observations in Sparkhill. By 1901, with a larger array of instruments, observations became regular and continued until the mid-1950s. His manuscript notebooks are held in the School of Geography at the University of Birmingham. Owen also produced a series of annual and routine monthly summaries, both of

°C/mm	Jan	Feb	Mar	Apr	May	Jun	Jul	Aug	Sep	Oct	Nov	Dec	Year
Mean maximum	5.1	6.0	8.1	11.8	15.2	19.3	20.4	19.6	16.8	11.8	8.2	5.6	12.3
Mean minimum	0.3	0.6	1.1	3.3	5.9	9.4	10.9	10.7	9.1	5.4	3.0	0.6	5.0
Mean monthly	2.6	3.5	4.7	7.6	10.6	14.3	15.7	15.2	13.0	8.8	5.7	3.4	8.8
Highmax	10.8	11.7	14.8	18.2	21.5	25.7	26.5	25.4	22.0	17.2	13.4	11.5	27.9
Lowmin	-5.8	-4.7	-4.2	-1.3	1.2	4.9	7.1	6.6	4.1	-0.1	-2.5	-5.5	-8.2
Rainfall	59.3	47.1	37.7	45.6	57.1	61.6	61.9	73.7	63.6	74.7	65.6	61.1	709.0
Raindays	16	14	13	13	14	13	15	15	14	16	17	16	177

Table. 8.3 Plant, Southall and Smith Series 1860-1900 : Temperature and rainfall

which featured in the Birmingham Post.

Edgbaston Meteorological Observatory (EMO) series: 1881-1981

As the fortunes of the Philosophical Institute declined, moves were afoot for a new centre of learning in Birmingham and the Birmingham and Midland Institute (BMI) was founded in 1854 (Waterhouse 1954). Follett Osler was amongst those involved and arranged the transfer of the meteorological instruments to a new building in Paradise Street (Fig. 8.1) next to the Town Hall. He was also involved in providing additional instruments. Unfortunately, there was a fire in 1879 and most of the meteorological records were destroyed, although some bound volumes of monthly data for the years 1878-1881 did survive. These contain graphs of daily pressure, rainfall, extreme wind force and wind roses, mean and absolute maximum and minimum temperatures for each month. The hyetograms are drawn so that amounts can be estimated to at least one hundredth of an inch and the number of raindays can be ascertained. In 1887 it was decided to move all the meteorological instruments away from Paradise Street to a suburban site in Ladywood where the Institute had acquired Perrot's Folly (known locally as the Monument, see Fig. 8.1). Some of the instruments were located there but additional thermometers (housed in a Glaisher screen) and a raingauge were located about 60 metres away at a site known as Waterworks Road (Fig. 8.1).

Initially, for a period of 5 years between 1881 and 1885, measurements of temperature and rainfall were taken at least twice daily (at 9am and 9pm) at both sites. Later, from 1885, observations and measurements became routine at the Waterworks Road site. However, measurements of daily sunshine, using a Jordan's heliograph, wind speed and direction (at first a Robinson/Osler cup anemometer which was replaced in 1923 by a Dines Pressure Tube Anemometer) were made at the Monument. It was also at this time that a Kings barograph was installed, one of only three or four world-wide. Several instrument changes occurred between about 1900 and 1930, with the change to a Campbell-Stokes sunshine recorder and a Dines tipping bucket hyetograph. In 1923 the Observatory joined the Telegraphic Service of the Meteorological Office which required readings at 7am, 1pm and 6pm. Between 1948 and 1968 the Observatory was designated as a World Meteorological Organisation station and full synoptic observations were made every three hours from 0600 to 2100. For a short period during the 1970s additional synoptic observations were made at 00 and 03, giving complete 24hr coverage. Entries of cloud, weather and visibility became standard. Measurements from additional instruments were made from the mid 1960s onwards including evaporation readings, using

American round and English square evaporimeters and a lysimeter. It was probably at this time that black-bulb radiation measurements ceased. The use of both the Dines Pressure Tube Anemometer and the Kings barograph continued until October 1979. At this time, staff were moved to the University of Birmingham campus to the Muirhead Tower. Once a day measurements at 9am of temperature, rainfall and sunshine were continued at Waterworks Road until February 1981, when all instruments were finally removed to the University (Giles 1986). So ended the longest continuous period of meteorological records at one site in the West Midlands. Utilising this 100-year record, averages and totals have been computed and these are summarised in Table 8.4.

Cresswell (1913) published a summary of the first 25-years of this record. Data for the period

°C/mm	Jan	Feb	Mar	Apr	May	Jun	Jul	Aug	Sep	Oct	Nov	Dec	Year
Mean maximum	5.5	6.1	8.6	11.6	15.4	18.5	20.0	19.6	17.1	12.8	8.6	6.2	12.5
Mean minimum	1.5	1.3	2.2	4.1	6.9	9.9	11.8	11.5	9.8	6.8	3.9	2.2	6.0
Mean monthly	3.5	3.7	5.4	7.9	11.2	14.2	15.9	15.6	13.5	9.9	6.3	4.2	9.3
Highmax	11.1	11.6	15.1	18.4	22.6	25.2	26.3	25.5	22.8	18.1	13.8	11.7	28.0
Lowmin	-4.7	-4.0	-2.8	-0.6	2.0	6.1	7.8	7.6	4.9	1.3	-1.6	-3.9	-6.7
Rainfall	66.5	51.5	51.1	50.7	60.7	54.1	62.9	70.8	58.8	67.9	70.2	71.1	736.2
Raindays	17	14	15	14	14	13	14	15	13	16	16	17	179

Table. 8.4 Edgbaston Meteorological Observatory Series (Waterworks Road) 1881-1981 : Temperature and rainfall

from 1887 until the 1940s was collated by the superintendents of Edgbaston Observatory and published annually, until 1939, by the Birmingham Natural History and Philosophical Society (1894-1897), The BMI Scientific Society (1898-1926) and the BMI (1927-1939). Weather observers over this period of the record were Alfred Cresswell (until 1916) and Arthur Joe Kelly (from 1917 to 1938) and later his son Leslie A Kelly (from 1923 until mid 1960s).

In 1965, the Birmingham and Midland Institute transferred control of the Observatory to the University of Birmingham and, in 1968, the Department (now School) of Geography assumed responsibility. At this time additional staff were employed. Those with long service (over 10 years) at this time were Harry Brenholtz and David Osborne (mid 1950s until 1975). In 1969 Peter Howarth joined the team of weather observers, subsequently retiring in 1980. A year later Michael (Jim) Hales joined the staff and, in 1979, John Kings was the last member of staff to be attached to the EMO. Annual climatologcal summaries continued to be published by the University of Birmingham (until 1981). Both John Kings and Jim Hales maintain the weather observations today. Accounts of this period can be found in Kings (1985).

School of Geography, Winterbourne: 1979-

In 1979 a new weather station was inaugurated on the University campus. Here routine synoptic observations, at 3hr intervals between 06-21h, were continued. The Winterbourne weather station (Fig. 8.1) became part of the United Kingdom Meteorological Office climatological network in 1985. In 1989, the 21h synoptic observation ceased. In August 1989, phase one of an automatic weather station (AWS) was installed at Winterbourne. This includes air temperature and relative humidity in a Gill screen, dry- and wet-bulb thermistors, rainfall and pyrheliometer. Phase two was installed in 1991 on the roof of Muirhead Tower and included pressure, wind speed and direction as well as temperature and relative humidity. During 1964 routine synoptic observations stopped completely, being replaced with a 09h climatological observation, ending a practice extending back over 100 years. Annual summaries of Birmingham weather continue to be published by the School of Geography (1982 onwards). The Winterbourne record has been summarised into monthly averages and totals as given in Table 8.5.

	Jan	Feb	Mar	Apr	May	Jun	Jul	Aug	Sep	Oct	Nov	Dec	Year
Mean maximum	5.9	6.1	9.1	11.9	15.6	18.3	21.1	20.4	17.3	13.1	9.1	6.9	12.9
Mean minimum	1.6	1.3	3.1	4.2	6.9	9.8	11.9	11.6	9.5	6.8	4.2	2.7	6.1
Mean monthly	3.8	3.7	6.1	8.1	11.3	14.1	16.6	16.0	13.4	9.9	6.8	4.7	9.5
Highmax	10.8	11.7	14.7	18.7	22.5	25.8	27.4	26.2	23.0	18.8	14.6	13.1	28.6
Lowmin	-5.4	-5.0	-3.1	-1.1	1.3	4.4	7.4	6.7	3.9	-0.4	-2.8	-4.4	-7.2
Rainfall	79.7	50.7	67.9	57.4	61.0	57.5	58.7	65.5	70.1	72.0	71.1	85.4	796.6
Raindays	18	13	19	14	14	14	12	13	13	16	16	17	179

Table. 8.5 Winterbourne (School of Geography) Series 1979-1995

The climate of Birmingham over the past 200 years

The weather diaries, described above, can be amalgamated to form a composite, long-term time series, covering just over 200 years. Although the resulting data, the Birmingham Temperature Series (BTS) is not for a single site, and therefore not homogeneous, it is representative of an urban environment since all the locations are within 5km radius of the present city centre. Unlike the only other long-term temperature series, that of Central England (Parker et al. 1992), which consists of mean monthly temperature, the BTS incorporates five measures of temperature: mean maximum, mean minimum and mean monthly, highest maximum and lowest minimum temperature each month. It is the combination of these two properties which make the series unique and therefore worthy of further, more detailed analysis. Record length has been shown to be of prime importance when using extreme-value analysis (Kings 1992). The same is true of the Birmingham Rainfall Series (BRS) which consists of monthly rainfall totals and rainday frequency. Other long-term rainfall series consist only of total rainfall.

There are a number of ways to examine time series. Using a simple approach, one can use the actual monthly data. Anomalies (from some reference period, in this case 1961-1990) provide some measure of variability, whilst using thresholds identifies persistence. Ideally, these ought to be combined in a single climate index which provides the most useful information. Utilising all three approaches in this short initial analysis, we have examined the annual, seasonal (winter and summer) and monthly data (February and August) for the full 203 year record, computed 10yr normals (decade commencing -01) and identified thresholds. These thresholds are based on quintiles for mean temperature and terciles for rainfall. Decade normals for the full 203yr record are given in Table 8.6 and those for the present (1961-1990) climate-norm are given in Table 8.7

period	Jan	Feb	Mar	Apr	May	Jun	Jul	Aug	Sep	Oct	Nov	Dec	Year
1791 1800	1.9	3.5	4.9	9.3	12.6	15.6	17.7	16.9	13.4	9.6	5.0	3.2	9.7
1801 1810	2.5	3.8	5.3	8.1	13.2	15.6	17.2	17.5	14.3	9.7	5.1	3.3	9.6
1811 1820	1.4	4.0	6.1	9.1	12.8	15.5	16.9	15.9	14.0	9.5	5.6	2.3	9.4
1821 1830	*	*	*	*	*	*	*	*	*	*	*	*	*
1831 1840	2.4	4.0	4.8	8.4	12.4	15.4	16.8	17.0	13.6	10.4	6.3	4.3	9.7
1841 1850	2.9	3.2	7.1	10.5	12.9	15.6	16.2	16.2	15.5	8.9	5.9	5.5	10.0
1851 1860	3.1	1.7	5.0	5.3	11.0	11.4	13.2	12.9	11.3	9.4	4.4	0.9	7.5
1861 1870	1.6	4.1	5.0	7.3	11.5	12.2	14.9	15.7	12.4	10.5	3.2	4.7	8.6
1871 1880	2.3	3.9	4.8	7.9	10.6	14.8	16.1	15.5	13.0	8.9	4.5	2.7	8.7
1881 1890	2.8	3.1	4.3	6.8	10.6	13.9	15.5	14.8	12.7	8.6	5.9	2.9	8.5
1891 1900	2.7	3.6	5.0	8.1	10.6	14.5	15.6	15.3	13.4	8.9	6.4	4.3	9.0
1901 1910	3.6	3.6	5.3	7.5	10.9	13.6	15.8	15.1	13.0	9.9	5.7	3.9	9.0
1911 1920	3.7	4.3	5.0	7.6	12.1	14.0	15.4	15.7	13.2	9.5	5.9	4.5	9.3
1921 1930	4.6	4.1	5.8	7.5	11.0	13.7	16.2	15.1	13.3	10.0	5.7	4.3	9.3
1931 1940	3.7	4.0	5.9	7.8	11.2	14.7	16.1	16.4	13.7	9.5	6.8	4.2	9.5
1941 1950	3.2	3.9	6.0	9.2	11.4	14.7	16.5	16.0	14.0	10.5	6.6	4.6	9.7
1951 1960	3.5	3.3	5.7	8.3	11.7	14.4	16.1	15.8	13.7	10.4	6.8	5.3	9.6
1961 1970	3.3	3.4	5.3	8.0	11.2	14.7	15.5	15.4	13.8	11.0	6.2	3.5	9.3
1971 1980	3.9	4.2	5.5	7.7	11.0	13.9	16.3	16.1	13.5	10.3	6.5	5.3	9.5
1981 1990	4.0	3.5	6.1	7.8	11.2	13.9	16.5	15.9	13.4	10.2	6.6	4.9	9.5
1991 2000	4.4	4.3	7.0	8.6	11.6	14.4	17.1	16.3	13.1	9.4	7.1	4.1	9.8

Table. 8.6 Birmingham Temperature Series: Mean monthly temperature, decade normals

	Jan	Feb	Mar	Apr	May	Jun	Jul	Aug	Sep	Oct	Nov	Dec	Year
Mean maximum	5.6	5.9	8.6	11.4	15.1	18.3	20.2	19.8	17.2	13.4	8.7	6.4	12.6
Mean minimum	1.8	1.5	2.7	4.2	7.1	10.1	11.9	11.8	10.0	7.6	4.1	2.7	6.3
Mean monthly	3.7	3.7	5.6	7.8	11.1	14.2	16.1	15.8	13.6	10.5	6.4	4.6	9.4
Rainfall	70.4	54.1	62.2	57.6	64.4	58.7	55.7	72.1	63.9	62.3	66.7	79.0	767.0
Raindays	18	14	17	15	15	13	12	14	13	15	17	17	180

Table. 8.7 Present day climate normals 1961-1990

The Birmingham Temperature Series: 1793-1995

Mean annual temperature over the full 203yr record is 9.3°C compared with 9.4°C for the present. The series exhibits variability, some periodicity, yet little increasing trend can be perceived (Fig. 8.2). Overall, temperature has ranged from a cool 7.5°C in 1816, 'the year without a summer', to a warm 13.3°C in 1990. A cluster of cooler years occurred from the 1860s to the 1920s, and again through the 1960s to 1980s. There has been an absence of cool years in the present decade. Warm years are scattered through the series, though the 1940s, 1970s and 1990s have the highest number of such years. However, the top-ten warm years all vary within 0.3°C of each other.

Winter (DJF) mean temperature averages 3.5°C, just 0.5°C below the present. With winter temperatures there is more variability, the coldest winter (-0.3°C) was in 1963 and the mildest was in 1989 (6.4°C). Cold winters were frequent in the 1790s through to 1800s, the 1880s and 1940s and, to a lesser extent, the 1980s. The present decade has experienced just one cold winter so far, that of 1996. Conversely, mild winters are prevalent through the entire record, including the present. They reached a maximum in the 1970s. Again, there is little to support the hypotheses that either there is an increase in the frequency of mild winters or that they are becoming milder.

Summer (JJA) provides an interesting comparison. The present is just 0.1°C below the long

MEAN WINTER TEMPERATURE (degC) 1961-1990 normal is 4.0degC

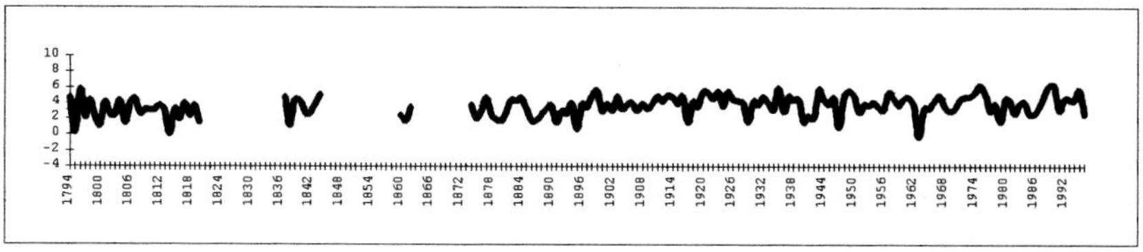

MEAN FEBRUARY TEMPERATURE (degC) 1961-1990 normal is 3.7degC

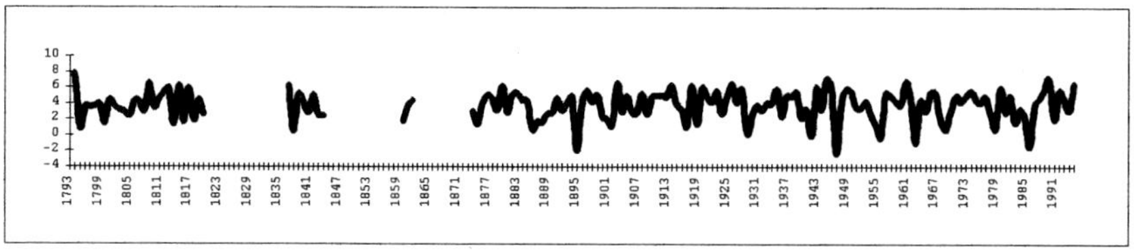

MEAN ANNUAL TEMPERATURE (degC) 1961-1990 normal is 9.4 degC

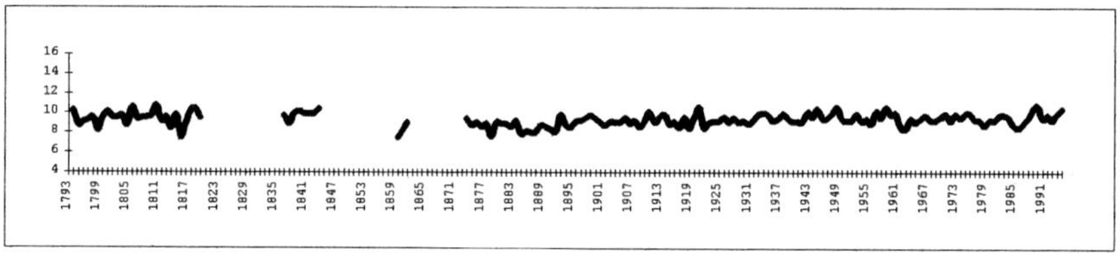

MEAN SUMMER TEMPERATURE (degC) 1961-1990 normal is 15.4degC

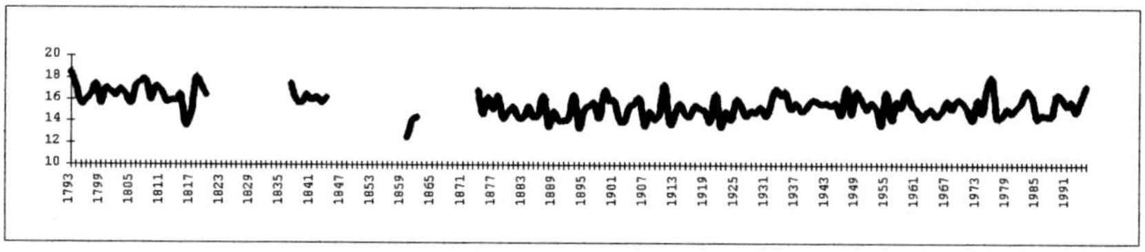

MEAN AUGUST TEMPERATURE (degC) 1961-1990 normal is 15.8degC

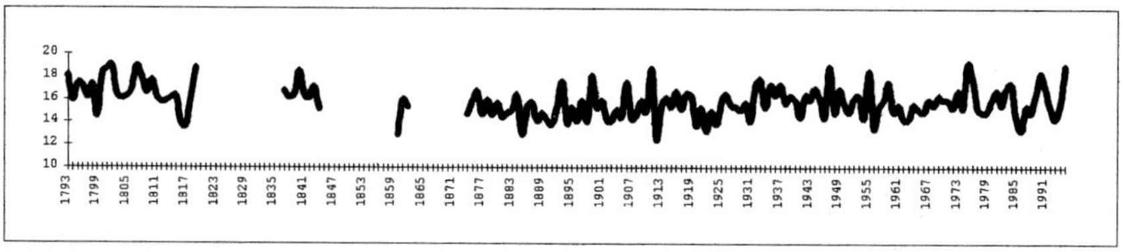

Fig. 8.2 Birmingham Temperature Series 1793-1995

term average, though the variability is much less than that of winter. During the 203 years, summers have ranged from a cool 12.5°C in 1866 to a tropical 17.3°C in 1995. Cool summers were most frequent from the 1860s to the 1920s and again from the 1950s through to the 1980s, whilst warm ones were prevalent between the 1790s and the 1810s, and have remained constant at 2 per decade since the 1930s. Recent summers (except 1995) cannot be classified as warm.

With respect to individual months, February with a long-term mean the same as the present, shows a great deal of variability. It was colder between in the 1850s, 1880s to 1900s and the 1950s to 1960s, with the coldest in 1947 at -2.3°C. Mild months have been scattered with time, the mildest with a mean temperature of 7.8°C occurred in 1794, some 0.6°C above that of 1990. There is some association between this month and the character of the winter.

It can also be related to the nature of the year itself. August, on the other hand, is often the warmest month both of the year and of the summer. The present is exactly the same as the long-term average. Temperatures have ranged from a cool 12.5°C in 1912 (the poorest summer in Birmingham) to a balmy 19.2°C in 1975, closely followed by 19.0°C in both 1802 and 1995. Warm Augusts have occurred scattered through the record, though the 1800s, 1930s and the 1990s have the highest numbers. Interestingly, the present decade is similar to those during the 1840s and the 1930s. A succession of decades between the 1880s and the 1920s (with the exception of the 1910s) experienced cool months. Taking the two months and both seasons together there is some evidence of an increasing variability, or even a climatic fluctuation from the 1790s through to the 1830s. This manifested itself as combinations of, or alternating sequences of, a cold or mild February or winter and a warm August and summer. This period is, of course, well known as the latter part of the Little Ice Age.

The Birmingham Rainfall Series: 1793-1995

Rainfall is slightly more difficult to deal with, since it is not (strictly) normally distributed. The data can however be transformed and statistics derived (Table 8.8). Undertaking a similar analysis as with temperature, inspection of total annual, winter and summer rainfall (Fig 8.3) as well as the months February and August provides the basis of the following summary. Total

Period	Jan	Feb	Mar	Apr	May	Jun	Jul	Aug	Sep	Oct	Nov	Dec	Year
1791 1800	65.3	37.1	37.8	69.7	68.6	51.6	62.0	105.3	118.6	69.1	83.2	62.7	831.0
1801 1810	54.7	36.1	35.6	40.6	67.8	50.2	71.7	57.0	54.3	58.0	74.1	72.2	657.2
1811 1820	49.5	55.8	48.4	50.4	74.4	47.4	58.9	47.8	55.1	61.5	56.5	45.1	575.7
1821 1830	*	*	*	*	*	*	*	*	*	*	*	*	*
1831 1840	51.1	58.9	29.2	36.8	40.1	66.6	72.9	67.7	52.2	49.7	86.4	38.4	650.1
1841 1850	45.4	53.3	53.9	27.4	55.0	37.0	56.4	65.6	66.4	67.1	78.4	33.0	639.0
1851 1860	97.5	23.6	52.3	30.0	61.5	163.6	38.4	164.6	57.9	50.0	74.4	91.9	905.7
1861 1870	48.7	43.0	92.2	38.2	53.9	79.1	109.8	32.2	94.5	56.5	45.6	41.0	735.0
1871 1880	48.3	50.3	31.9	50.7	60.6	66.5	77.5	93.5	86.3	78.3	67.8	57.6	769.3
1881 1890	68.3	48.8	44.9	46.2	62.1	62.2	63.5	66.3	62.1	74.0	75.0	57.7	730.9
1891 1900	58.1	43.2	34.4	41.6	49.8	57.6	49.4	67.2	49.4	72.7	54.7	66.9	645.0
1901 1910	43.2	42.9	55.1	49.2	56.5	58.1	55.5	77.7	39.2	78.3	53.8	70.8	680.2
1911 1920	60.4	48.8	64.7	46.6	54.2	57.6	70.5	67.0	50.5	61.0	57.0	84.9	723.3
1921 1930	74.1	53.2	37.6	53.1	57.2	42.2	74.9	77.4	63.3	75.3	81.4	72.6	762.2
1931 1940	75.4	52.9	41.5	65.0	63.0	49.2	72.8	51.5	52.3	74.0	86.8	60.8	745.2
1941 1950	73.6	57.3	48.0	48.2	67.7	45.0	64.4	73.4	58.6	64.7	78.0	65.2	744.2
1951 1960	77.8	52.9	60.5	46.0	59.7	56.8	69.9	82.9	72.0	68.0	86.0	75.1	807.7
1961 1970	56.8	52.6	55.6	67.9	79.2	58.9	64.4	77.2	65.8	53.9	72.3	73.0	777.7
1971 1980	79.1	61.4	62.8	44.0	54.7	56.6	47.3	69.2	65.5	55.9	59.3	79.1	734.8
1981 1990	75.2	48.2	68.2	60.9	59.2	60.6	55.4	70.0	60.4	77.1	68.4	84.9	788.5
1991 2000	94.2	46.5	52.2	56.6	56.8	50.1	73.2	50.2	88.3	61.2	82.0	81.4	792.7

Table. 8.8 Birmingham Rainfall Series: decade normals

TOTAL WINTER RAINFALL (mm) 1961-1990 normal is 203.9mm

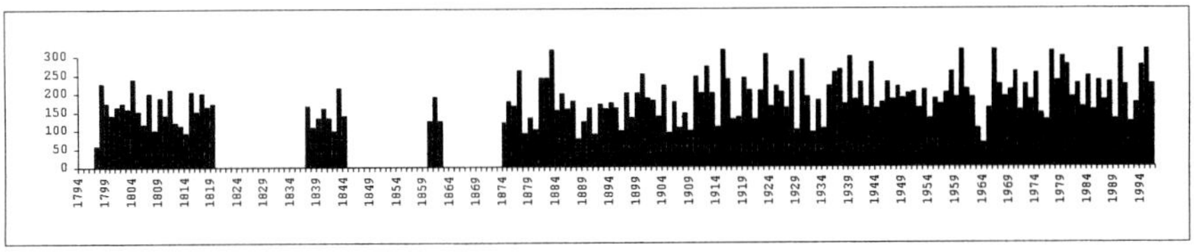

TOTAL FEBRUARY RAINFALL (mm) 1961-1990 normal is 54.1mm

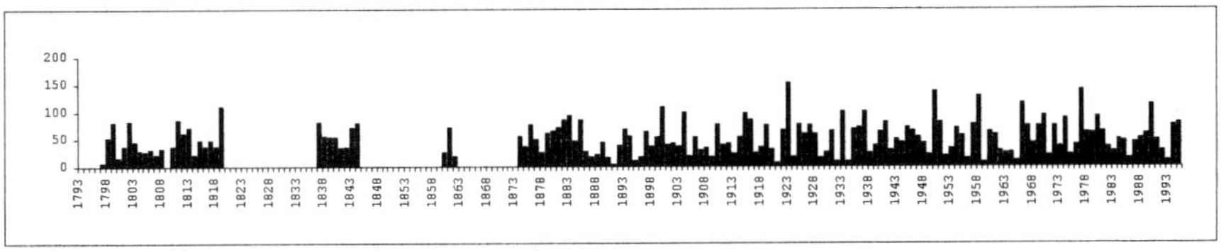

TOTAL ANNUAL RAINFALL (mm) 1961-1990 normal is 773.3mm

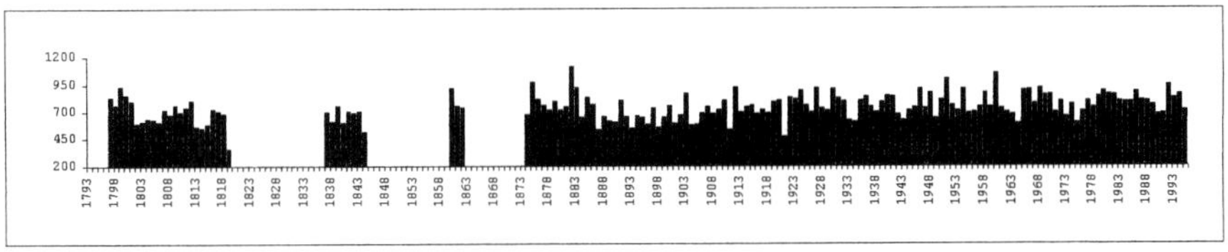

TOTAL SUMMER RAINFALL (mm) 1961-1990 normal is 186.5mm

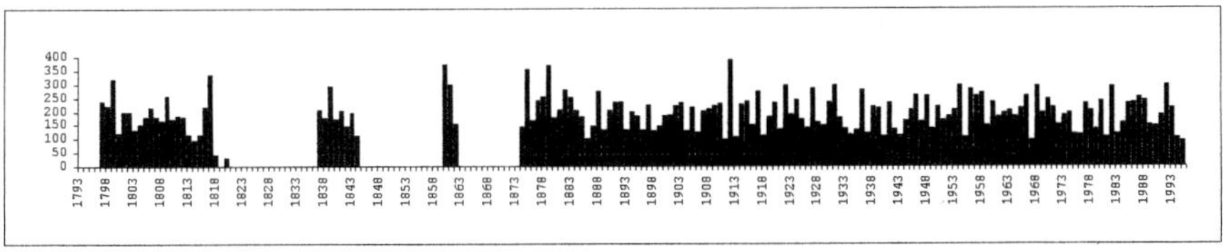

TOTAL AUGUST RAINFALL (mm) 1961-1990 normal is 72.1mm

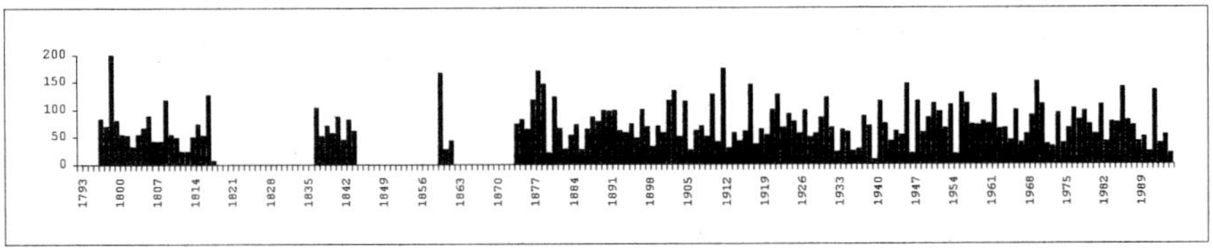

Fig. 8.3 Birmingham Rainfall Series 1793-1995

annual rainfall at present is 767mm.

Summer dryness and winter rain seem to be more frequent recently, and this combination is claimed to be a feature of enhanced global warming suggested by numerical models and is currently attributed as the first signs of such warming. However, the BRS does not lend itself to that conclusion. A more detailed inspection of annual totals identifies ±100mm from the mean as the difference between a dry and wet year. Given such a small margin, both dry and wet years are scattered through the period. The years 1819, 1820, 1844 and 1921 all had below 500mm. However, there is some clustering of the driest years between the 1890s and the 1910s. The year noted for the best summer in Birmingham (1911) had just 517mm. This is almost 30 per cent below that of 1995, when water shortages and drought hit the headlines. Conversely, the wetter years have tended to be most frequent since the 1920s, with the 1980s the wettest (also globally) so far. In Birmingham, the 1930s came a close second. Both the wettest years had in excess of 1000mm (1882 and 1960), whilst those of 1951, 1968 and 1992 had just over 900mm.

Winter rainfall at present is just over 200mm, about 12 per cent above the long term average. Winters were generally wetter from 1910 to the 1930s and again more recently since the 1970s. The wet winters, with up to 200 per cent of normal rainfall, include 1990 (the wettest), 1923 ,1960 and 1979. Dry winters tend to be more scattered, being most prevalent during the nineteenth century. There was a virtual absence of these events between 1930 and the 1950s. Winter rainfall at its lowest can be under 50 per cent of normal; for example 1820, 1863, 1932 and 1964. Over the whole period the average summer rainfall was 186mm compared to 187 mm at present.

The frequency of both dry and wet summers is fairly evenly balanced through the record. The most variable decade included those of the 1930s, 1940s and the 1970s whereas there was a near absence of dry summers during the 1860s, 1870s and the 1950s to the 1960s. Dry summers have occurred with an above average frequency during the present decade, with the driest 1995 (88mm) similar to the previous driest (1964). Rainfall reached just over 200 per cent in the wettest summer, 1912, closely followed by several in the 1870s, 1954 and 1992.

Whilst dry winters are not necessarily cold, there is an association between summer wetness and depressed temperatures. In dry summers (1911, 1955 and 1994), rainfall is often associated with thunderstorms, as evidenced in the 1995 season. A deficit of rainfall in both February and August will indicate a predominance of blocking anticyclones or prolonged easterly winds. February presently receives 108 per cent of the long-term average, whilst August receives 104 per cent. Both months have shown marked decrease over recent decades, with February becoming similar to those between 1900 and 1930. In August the decrease has been near 30 per cent since the 1950s. This has made the month the driest of the summer, a feature not evident for over 50 years. This is clearly reflected in a cluster of dry Februaries until the 1960s and a decline since, coincident with an increase in the number of dry Augusts since the 1970s. The current decade total is similar to those experienced in the early years of the nineteenth century. On the other hand wet Augusts hit their maximum frequency in the 1950s and again during the 1970s. This may well indicate a climatic fluctuation connected with these months or a return to a previous climatic norm.

Conclusion

This account of the climate of Birmingham has utilised a number of data sets that previously have not been studied in any detail and linked them with the development of observational meteorology. Diaries kept by the Lunar Society, and its various successors through to the present day within the School of Geography, have enabled the *Birmingham Climate Series* to be constructed and analysed. Long-term climatological series are an invaluable link between past and present climate and a key to the likely future climate. In addition they provide an important vehicle for validating climate model output. Once models can be shown to replicate more recent climate, then confidence can be attributed to predicted states of the atmosphere. This is important since many socio-economic and environmental decisions are being made, based upon model scenarios. Present day concerns about global warming and environmental change are not new, and as yet require to be proven. The Victorians were equally concerned about urbanisation, air quality, acid rain and global warming. However, they were at a disadvantage, since long-term weather records did not exist at the time. What this preliminary analysis has demonstrated is the scientific value of weather diaries and the useful information which can be extracted.

In summary the analysis has shown that climate oscillates on a variety of time scales and is often likely to exhibit patterns which represent either earlier phases or conditions which have not been experienced before. Whatever the past or present state of climate there is always a physical limit to its variability. Weather observations taken at present will be as valuable in the near future. Clearly the School of Geography now has a responsibility to ensure that the climatological record for Birmingham continues well into the next millennium. Only then will we be able to confirm present concerns or worry about new ones.

References

Auden G A 1913 *A handbook for Birmingham and the neighbourhood* Cornish Brothers Ltd, Birmingham

Birmingham Philosophical Institution 1836 *The report presented by the committee of managers to the annual general meeting ... together with the Meteorological Journal kept at the Institution* Belcher and Son, Birmingham

Bolton H C 1890 The Lunar Society *Birmingham and Midland Institute Archaeological Section Transactions* 15 79-94

British Association for the Advancement of Science 1835 *Report of the First and Second Meetings at York in 1831 and at Oxford in 1832* John Murray, London 48-51

British Association for the Advancement of Science 1838 *Report of the Seventh Meeting at Liverpool in 1837* John Murray, London 32-34

Cresswell A 1891-1916 *Records of meteorological observations taken at the Observatory of the Birmingham and Midland Institute* Birmingham Natural History and Philosophical Society until 1897; Birmingham and Midland Institute Scientific Society 1898-1916; continued as Kelly 1917

Cresswell A 1913 Meteorology in **Auden G A** ed *A handbook for Birmingham and the neighbourhood British Association for the Advancement of Science*, Cornish Brothers, Birmingham 539-545

Giles B D 1986 Screen temperatures at two urban sites in Birmingham *Occasional Paper* 16 Department of Geography, The University of Birmingham

Giles B D 1987 Edgbaston Observatory: its early years 1885-1900 *Meteorological Services Unit Annual Climatological Summary* Department of Geography, University of Birmingham

Giles B D 1991 Late eighteenth century temperatures in Birmingham, England *Journal of Meteorology* 16 40-45

Giles B D and Kings J 1994 Meteorology in Birmingham in **Giles B D and Kenworthy J M** eds *Observations and climatological research* Occasional Publication 29 Department of Geography University of Durham and Royal Meteorological Society 58-70

Harris S 1841 *Report on Professor Whewell's anemometer now in operation at Plymouth* British Association for the Advancement of Science 10th Meeting in Glasgow John Murray, London 157-162

Kelly A J 1917 *Records of meteorological observations taken at the Observatory of the Birmingham and Midland Institute* Birmingham and Midland Institute Scientific Society, Birmingham

Kings J 1985 The meteorological record at Birmingham (Edgbaston) England *Weather* 40 (12) 388-395

Kings J 1992 *An examination of outliers in meteorology using the Birmingham temperature record* unpublished MSc Thesis School of Geography, The University of Birmingham

Kinvig R H Smith J G and Wise M J 1950 *Birmingham and its regional setting* British Association for the Advancement of Science, Birmingham

Osler A F 1841 *Report on the observations recorded during the years 1837, 1838, 1839 and 1840 by the self-registering anemometer erected at the Philosophical Institute Birmingham* British Association for the Advancement of Science 10th Meeting at Glasgow John Murray, London 321-347

Parker D E Legg T P and Folland C K 1992 A new daily central England temperature series 1772-1991 *International Journal of Climatology*, 12 (4) 317-342

Plant T L 1862a *Meteorology: its study important for our good and for the prevention of loss of life and property from storms and floods* T L Plant, Birmingham

Plant T L 1862b *Meteorological Report for 1861* W H Smith and Sons, Birmingham

Plant T L 1863 *Report of the weather of 1862* W H Smith and Sons, Birmingham

Robinson E 1957 The Lunar Society and the improvement of scientific instruments *Annals of Science* 12 296-318 and 13 1-8

Schofield R E 1963 *The Lunar Society of Birmingham A social history of provincial science and industry in eighteenth century England* Oxford University Press, Oxford

Saward B 1950 Climate in **Kinvig R H Smith J G and Wise M J** eds *Birmingham and its regional setting* British Association for the Advancement of Science, Birmingham 47-54

Smith R T *Weather Bound* Cornish Brothers, Birmingham

Waterhouse R 1954 *The Birmingham and Midland Institute 1854-1954* Birmingham and Midland Institute, Birmingham

Wells R V 1951 The Lunar Society *School Science Review* 33 31-48

Wills W 1853 *Observations on the meteorology of Birmingham* in British Association for the Advancement of Science 22nd Meeting at Belfast John Murray, London 297-316

Withering W 1822 *The Miscellaneous tracts of the late William Withering Md FRS* Longman, London

CHAPTER 9

Air Quality in the West Midlands

G.R.McGregor, X. Cai, R.M. Harrison, J.E. Thornes & A. Veal

Air quality is an important environmental issue as it affects the utility of an area as a place to live, work and relax. Although the threat of sulphur dioxide and smoke inducing smogs to health has almost disappeared, due to the enactment of the 1956 and 1968 Clean Air Acts, public concern about urban air quality is again rising. This is due to a change in the air pollution mix and an associated concern, for pollutants associated with motor traffic. Accordingly, air quality issues have received considerable levels of media attention throughout the 1990s, mainly due to a number of severe and prolonged pollution episodes which have resulted in the exceedance of international health guidelines in a number of the United Kingdom's urban areas. In response to increasing concern about urban air quality the UK government has commissioned a number of reports so that the current state of and the possible factors that control air quality in UK urban areas may be established (QUARG 1993a, 1993b, PORG 1993). As these reports pay little attention to the West Midlands the purpose of this paper is to review, for the West Midlands, the impact that air quality control legislation has had on air quality, the current state of air quality, the dependence of air quality on meteorology and the potential application of numerical modelling as an air quality management tool.

Air Quality Legislation

The West Midlands was the cradle of the Industrial Revolution and not surprisingly the area to the north of the region is still affectionately known as the 'Black Country', named after the huge quantities of black smoke from thousands of industrial chimneys that blackened the landscape in the last century. Birmingham became known as the 'city of a thousand trades', some of which polluted the air freely.

It was not until 1863, when an Act of Parliament set up the Alkali Inspectorate, that air pollution control began to curb industrial emissions. This Act was amended several times to cover more industrial processes until it became the Alkali & Works Regulation Act in 1906. This Act was not superceeded until the Environmental Protection Act of 1990. Her Majesty's Inspectorate of Pollution (HMIP) has now taken over the role of the Alkali Inspectorate and Part A of the Act requires that operators of any of 5000 industrial processors have to obtain authorization from HMIP for which they pay a fixed fee. Part B of the Act lists smaller operations that are regulated by the local authorities. The Environment Act of 1995 set up the Environmental Agency which from 1st April 1996 will take overall regulatory control of HMIP, the National Rivers Authority and the waste control functions of local authorities to give an integrated approach to air, water and solid pollution. Large scale processes such as an iron and steel works will come under HMIP standards for emissions whereas small furnaces, of which there are dozens in the West Midlands, will now come under local authority control.

Thus industrial processes which have been monitored since 1863 are now very closely regulated. Domestic air pollution was not tackled however until much later when the first legislation - The Clean Air Act - was passed in 1956. This Act was extended in 1968 and both Acts were then consolidated into the Clean Air Act of 1993. This Act also covers the emissions from heating boilers in factories, sets maximum heights for new industrial chimneys and stipulates that smokeless fuels must be used in urban areas. The dramatic effects that these pieces of legislation have had on SO_2 levels in the West Midlands is clearly shown in Figure 9.1.

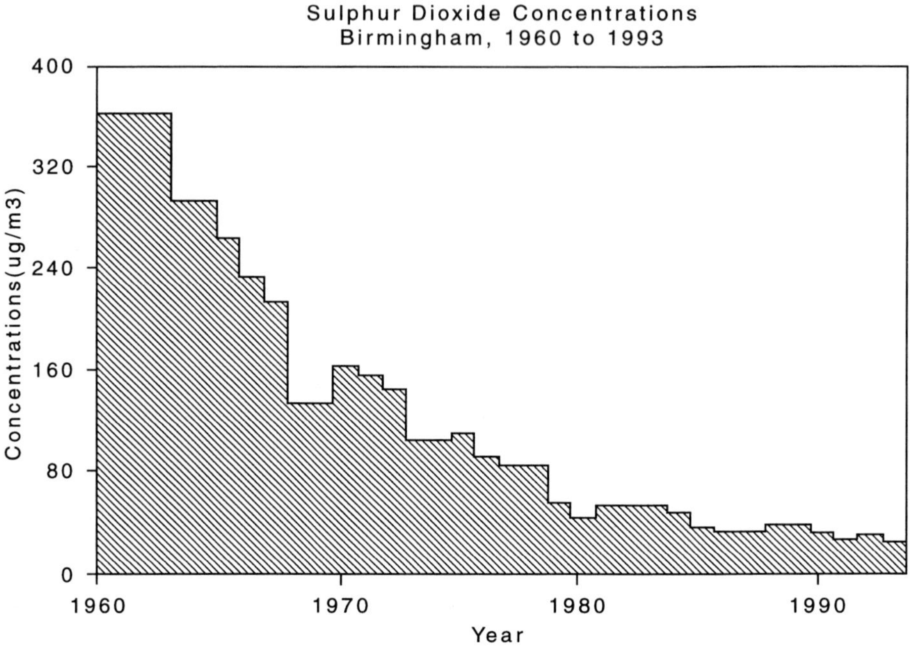

Fig. 9.1 Decrease of SO_2 concentrations for Birmingham (supplied by Birmingham City Council)

The other major source of air pollution is that from road traffic. Legislation in this area has mostly come from the European Union in a series of Directives culminating in the compulsory fitting of three-way catalytic convertors to all new petrol cars. In addition the MOT test, that has to be taken when a car is 3 years old and then annually, has been expanded to consider exhaust emissions for both petrol and diesel cars. Emission controls for heavy duty vehicles (lorries and buses) which virtually all use diesel, have also been introduced. In order to enable the development of catalytic convertors and particle traps for diesel, legislation to reduce the sulphur content of diesel will come into force on 1 October 1996.

Thus there has been a flurry of legislation, particularly in the last 10 years, that has tried to control the air pollution from the rapidly increasing number of cars on UK roads. Historically industrial air pollution was seen to pose the greatest threat to health, but today vehicular air pollution has taken over that role.

Air quality monitoring activity

Air quality monitoring within the West Midlands has improved dramatically during the 1990s. Whilst there has been a decline in the manual stations monitoring 24 hour average concentrations of smoke and sulphur dioxide, continuous automated stations measuring a range of pollutants have been introduced and integrated within national monitoring networks. The first of these was the station monitoring oxides of nitrogen at Walsall, which was installed originally as part of the NO^2 Directive Network. Subsequently, Enhanced Urban Network Stations were opened in Birmingham Central and Birmingham East. These stations are now part of the Automatic Urban Network, and monitor oxides of nitrogen (NO and NO_2 by chemiluminescence), sulphur dioxide (by UV floresscence), ozone (by UV absorption), carbon monoxide (by infra-red absorption) and particulate matter (PM_{10} by Tapered Element Oscillating Microbalance). Data are recorded as hourly means and transmitted by telemetry to a central control. Recently, (December 1995) a further Automatic Urban Network Station has opened in Wolverhampton, and one is planned for Stoke-on-Trent. A national Hydrocarbon Network site also operates at Birmingham (East) measuring some 26 individual hydrocarbon compounds, most notably benzene and 1,3-butadiene which are the subject of ambient air quality standards. Lead is also monitored in Walsall at a number of EC Lead Directive sites. In addition to the national monitoring network, a number of West Midlands Local Authorities are highly active and operate their own monitoring surveys for a range of pollutants.

Current air quality

The most recent data published by the Department of Environment in the Digest of Environmental Statistics is for 1993, which shows concentrations of smoke and sulphur dioxide well within EC Directive limit values. More recently, the Expert Panel on Air Quality Standards (EPAQS) has recommended an air quality for sulphur dioxide of 100 ppb as a 15 minute average. Currently, data are available only as hourly averages and it is not possible to evaluate compliance with this standard. EPAQS has also recently recommended a standard for PM_{10} of 50 mg m^{-3}/24 hour rolling average. Currently, this is exceeded many times each year at all monitoring sites in major urban areas within the UK, including urban sites in the West Midlands.

The EC Nitrogen Dioxide Directive specifies for hourly mean concentration a 98th percentile limit value of 104.6 ppb and a 98th percentile guide value of 70.6 ppb. In 1993 the 98th percentile concentrations at Birmingham Centre and Birmingham East sites were respectively 52 and 36 ppb and at Walsall, 47 ppb. The figure for Birmingham East is based on a short run of data at the end of the year and longer term means indicate rather similar concentrations at the two Birmingham stations.

EPAQS has recommended a standard for carbon monoxide of 10 ppm/8 hour rolling average, which was not exceeded at either Birmingham site during 1993. Concentrations of lead in air at the EC Lead Directive sites at Walsall have declined significantly since the mid 1980s, and in 1993 ranged from 0.16 to 1.22 mg m^{-3} annual average, well within the EC limit value of 2 mg m^{-3}. The annual average concentrations of benzene and 1,3-butadiene in 1994 at the Birmingham East monitoring site were 1.03 ppb and 0.2 ppb respectively. These may be compared with the EPAQS recommendations of 5 ppb for benzene and 1 ppb for 1,3-butadiene.

The EPAQS recommended standard for ozone is 50 ppb/8 hour mean. At Birmingham Centre, this was exceeded over 13 periods on two days in 1993. Since UK urban concentrations of ozone are generally below those in rural areas, it is likely that a greater number of exceedences occurred at rural sites in the West Midlands.

Table 9.1 shows the 1994 annual means and maximum hourly concentration of a range of air pollutants, at a number of urban monitoring stations across the UK, together with the latest Department of the Environment Guidelines. These guidelines are constantly being reviewed but give a snapshot view of the current situation in Birmingham relative to other UK urban centres. For the two sites in Birmingham (Centre and East) air quality is similar. The recorded mean ozone levels in Birmingham are similar to the rest of the country, but the maximum

	Ozone		NO2		CO		SO2		PM10	
	(ppb)	(max)	(ppb)	(max)	(ppm)	(max)	(ppb)	(max)	(µg/m3)	(max)
Birmingham Centre	17	82	24	136	0.6	14.1	8	105	23	311
Birmingham East	18	97	20	189	0.5	13.8	6	79	21	319
London Bloomsbury	11	95	34	207	0.6	8.3	10	168	27	307
Liverpool	18	61	26	101	0.6	5.8	11	237	25	257
Bristol	19	74	24	91	0.7	8.7	7	116	24	612
Belfast	18	57	21	100	0.7	16.3	17	351	26	490
Leeds	15	71	28	131	0.7	12.8	10	433	26	310
Edinburgh	15	55	27	91	0.6	5.5	8	122	20	307
Leicester	17	91	23	97	0.6	8.8	7	137	21	203
DOE Guidelines	V Good < 50 Good 50-89 Poor 90-179 V Poor >= 180		V Good < 50 Good 50-99 Poor 100-299 V Poor >= 300		AQS 10 ppm 8-hour av		V Good <60 Good 60-124 Poor 125-399 V Poor >= 400 AQS 100 ppb 15-min av		AQS 50µg/m3 24-hour av	

Table. 9.1 1994 Annual Mean in a range of UK Cities and Maximum Hourly Concentration recorded

concentrations are amongst the highest, getting into the 'Poor' air quality class. Nitrogen Dioxide mean levels in Birmingham are typical of other urban areas, but the maximum hourly concentrations are high and well into the 'Poor' air quality class. The mean Carbon Monoxide levels are again typical of the rest of the country but the maximum levels are high, almost 75% higher than the London Bloomsbury site. The Sulphur Dioxide levels are quite low and even the maximum concentrations fall into the 'Good' class. This confirms that the more traditional air pollutants like SO_2 no longer present the threat to human health that they once did. Smoke pollution, like SO_2, is no longer considered to be a significant problem, however, the mean and maximum levels of PM_{10} in Birmingham are typical of UK urban areas as a whole, but as can be seen from Table 9.1 the maximum concentrations across the UK are very high and way above the AQS of 50 mg/m^3.

The quantitative figures of air quality presented in Table 9.1 are for the mean situation. However, on a daily basis air quality levels vary due to emission rates and the ambient meteorological conditions. It is the latter of these two factors which we will turn our attention to in the next section.

Synoptic climatology and the study of weather air pollution relationships

Variations in the physical and dynamic properties of the atmosphere on timescales from hours to days can play a major role in influencing the level of air pollutants. This is because the state of the atmosphere at both the synoptic and meso-scales determines the transportation and diffusion of pollutants. At the synoptic scale day to day variations in the atmospheric circulation as manifest by the passage of fronts, cyclonic and anticyclonic systems modulate the mesoscale meteorological processes that influence air quality. At the mesoscale the wind field is important for pollution dispersion. Vertical thermal gradients can determine the extent to which pollutants are diffused through the atmospheric column or the rates of dry/wet deposition. Meteorological conditions through controlling reaction rates also influence the chemical and physical processes involved in the formation of a variety of secondary pollutants. Because of the links between the state of the atmosphere and air quality, synoptic climatologists have been naturally drawn to the study of weather-air pollution relationships.

The traditional approach taken by most British synoptic climatologists when analysing weather air quality relationships has been the use of Lambs Weather Types (LWT). The literature on the LWT themselves is extensive (Barry and Perry 1973) and will not be discussed here. Briefly the Lamb classification is made up of seven major circulation types and 27subtypes (anticyclonic, cyclonic and directional) with an additional unclassifiable type.

Application of the LWT scheme to the analysis of air quality in the Birmingham area has revealed the predominance of LWTs associated with poor ventilation conditions and the possible development of inversions at times of poor air quality. Bailey (1976) for example in an analysis of the relationship between LWT and SO_2 concentrations in Birmingham for the years 1961 to 1971 found 4 of the 27 subtypes were related to high SO_2 concentrations. These were anticyclonic, northerly, easterly and anticyclonic easterly. Of these the highest concentrations were associated with anticyclonic conditions. Bailey (1976) attempted to evaluate the role of anticyclonic persistence in forcing SO_2 levels but was unable to draw firm conclusions regarding a steady rise in SO_2 levels with the longevity of the anticyclonic event. This lack of relationship may be more to do with the nature of the LWT classification than a lack of actual relationship as the LWT scheme is essentially a circulation pattern scheme with no information provided on circulation system intensity, a factor of undoubted importance in periods of persistently building air pollution levels. Scott (1994) similarly, in a study of daily pollution levels in the vicinity of a single stack, found that Lamb's anticyclonic and northerly circulation types produced the highest concentrations for a range of pollutants, although because pollution was measured at a single receptor, wind direction was also of importance. This confirms the earlier work of Pass (1981) who highlighted the importance of wind direction for determining the air pollution climatology of sites downwind from single emission sources in the Birmingham area. More recently McGregor (1996) in a study of air pollution affinity areas in Birmingham has suggested that the behaviour of SO_2 concentrations in the air quality affinity areas identified is responsive to the synoptic scale windfield which is determined by the circulation pattern. He identified anticyclonic easterly types equivalent to the Lamb's ACE type as important for possible downstream loading from the east and north for locations in the northern Districts of greater Birmingham, while subdued westerly flows, as produced in weak cyclonic situations often with occluded fronts (a weak version of Lamb's cyclonic type) caused elevated SO_2 levels in central Birmingham due to possible transport of pollutants from the Black Country districts to the west of the city centre.

Harvie (1994) applied the LWT to an analysis of the daily variability of methane (CH_4) emissions as measured from individual boreholes for landfill sites in Birmingham. The underlying rationale to this application was that atmospheric pressure has been used to model volumetric changes in landfill emissions of CH_4 (Young, 1990). Despite an exhaustive analysis of spatially averaged data Harvie (1994) was unable to establish clear relationships between LWT and daily landfill CH_4 emissions rates. This is undoubtedly due to the fact that the intra-landfill site emission rate variation, on any day, is far greater than day to day spatially average variations for any one landfill site. Although spatially averaged data showed no relationships, some of the high CH_4 producing boreholes did display some sensitivity to LWT. For example, low emission rates were found on days characterised by anticyclonic conditions. This makes physical sense given the fact that low emissions are generally related to high atmospheric pressure (Young 1990). Conversely high emission rates at 75 percent of the boreholes studied were found to be associated with Lamb's southerly (directional) type. Such synoptic situations are associated with an area of low pressure to the west of the UK and an area of high pressure to the east lying over central and northern Europe and falling pressure over central to western districts of the UK. Flows are southerly as the UK lies between these two circulation systems with a meridional orientation of isobars over the UK. Harvie (1994) suggests that the transition from a predominantly continental anticyclonic to maritime cyclonic situation with the related pressure fall may well explain the elevated CH_4 emissions for this synoptic situation compared to the low emission rate anticyclonic situation.

Although the LWT demonstrate a reasonable degree of utility in assessing circulation air quality relationships there has been a move away from the application of manually derived circulation classification schemes to semi-automated statistically derived classification schemes for the analysis of weather air pollution relationships. The impetus for this approach came with the early work of Christenson and Bryson (1966) in the US who developed objective weather typing methods based on the use of principal components analysis. This methodology was later tested and improved on by Ladd and Driscoll (1980). Based on the methodological philosophy of these papers Kalkstein and Corrigan (1986), using a combination of principal components and cluster analyses, demonstrated clearly the application of objective synoptic climatological classification schemes in air pollution climatology studies. This approach has subsequently been developed further and applied mainly in the United States (Davis and Gay 1993). These studies are in the classic mould of the circulation to environment approach in synoptic climatology (Yarnal 1992) in that, based on a multivariate analysis of a range of meterological variables representative of airmass characteristics, a number of airmass types and associated circulation patterns are identified. These are used to interpret the daily variation in air quality levels. Although the US based studies have shown clearly that such an automated synoptic typing approach works well, has the ability to consistently replicate results and can be applied quickly and easily, there has been little application of this approach in the UK.

Perhaps the first published application of synoptic typing to the understanding of weather air pollution relationships in the UK has been that of McGregor and Bamzelis (1995) for the Birmingham area. This study followed the methodology of Kalkstein and Corrigan (1986) in attempting to identify the main air masses that affected the Birmingham area for the period 1992-1993. Six airmass types were identified and described in terms of their climatological, meteorological and pollution characteristics. In terms of extreme pollution events a sub-polar North Sea mixed maritime continental anticyclonic type (Type 5) with warm, sub-humid and calm conditions stood out as the most important for NO_2, O_3, NO, CO and PM_{10}. This was the warmest of the airmass circulation types identified for the study period. A related summer binary northern continental anticyclonic southern cyclonic type (Type 4) characterised by moderate warmth and moisture levels and low cloud cover, as well as high radiation inputs and calm to weak northerly and easterly flow was also found to be of importance for O_3 and SO_2. McGregor and Bamzelis (1995) explain the high incidence of extreme pollution events for these two anticyclonic types with reference to their inherent airmass characteristics. Anticyclonic airmasses generally possess weak winds, which limit ventilation and thus transport and diffusion of pollutants. Anticyclonic types with little cloud cover and high receipts of solar radiation are conducive to the development of nocturnal inversions which reduce the possibility of pollutants being diffused vertically due to the suppression of the atmospheric layer mixing height. Such a configuration of calm conditions and atmospheric stability is suggested by McGregor and Bamzelis (1995) to account for the high NO and NO_2 levels on these anticyclonic type days. Furthermore, warm anticyclonic conditions with high solar radiation inputs, especially in the summer months, provide the requisite conditions for the production of secondary pollutants such as O_3. The very fact that the majority of severe O_3 pollution days were associated with McGregor and Bamzelis' (1995) Type 5 airmass attests to the importance of this circulation type for photochemical pollution episodes. Type 5 days will also enhance the oxidation of NO to NO^2 as long as O_3 does not become limited. For SO_2, airmass circulation type 2 is associated with the greatest occurrence of extreme SO_2 events. Like types 4 and 5 this is basically an anticyclonic type but with a non-seasonal distribution. This contrasts with types 4 and 5 which are essentially summer types. Type 2 is a blocking mixed maritime continental anticyclonic type characterised by temperate, moist cloudy to foggy conditions with light northeasterly veering to southwesterly flows. McGregor and Bamzelis (1995) consider this type to be important for extreme SO_2 events as northeasterly flows may transport SO_2 into the Birmingham area from the north and east where distant pollution sources such as coal burning power generation plants exist.

The fact that air quality responds to daily weather variations and sets of ideal meteorological conditions has been clearly shown by Veal (1994) in an analysis of the often discussed Christmas 1992 pollution episode. Although most discussions of this event have referred to London it appears that this was a nationwide event as far as major urban centres are concerned. Certainly Birmingham experienced elevated pollution levels during this time. A time series of the hourly pollutant concentrations for the December 1992 pollution episode is presented in Figure 9.2.

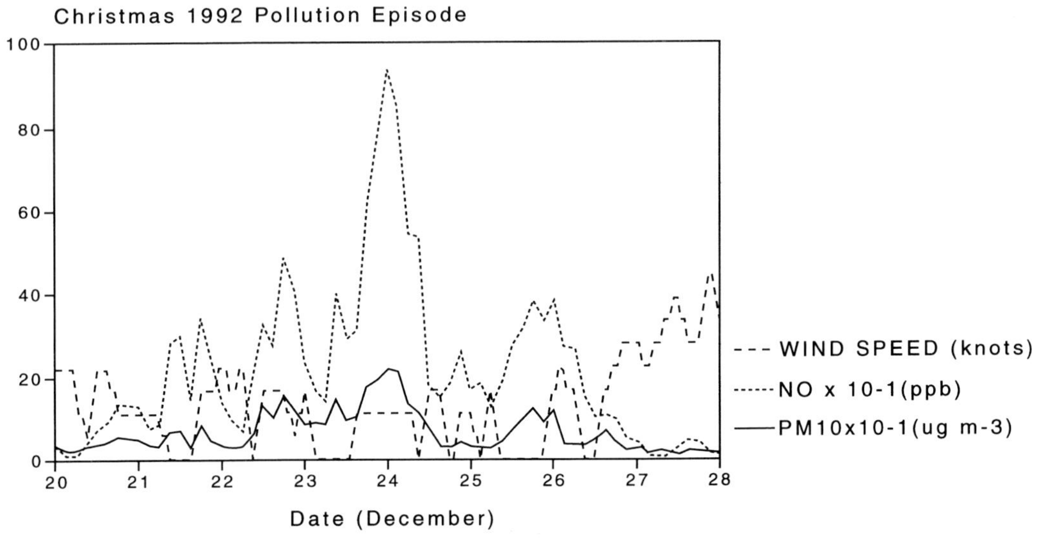

Fig. 9.2 The Birmingham Christmas 1992 pollution episode

During the period December 20-28, the WHO 24 hourly guideline limit of 80 ppb for NO_2 was exceeded on December 23 and 24. Application of the UK Department of Environment guidelines to this period results in 16 hours being classified as possessing poor air quality. The highest hourly mean NO_2 concentrations were recorded on the night of December 23-24 with peak values of 207 ppb recorded at 0200 hours in the morning of the 24th, 3 ppb below the WHO limit of 210 ppb. This level was the highest recorded since air quality monitoring started in central Birmingham in April 1992. Record hourly mean concentrations for CO, NO, and PM_{10} were also reached. They were 14 ppm (23/12/92 at 2300hrs); 1000 ppb 23/12/92 at 2400hrs); 231 ug/m^3 (23/12/92 at 2200hrs) respectively; all recorded within an hour of each other.

In terms of the airmass and circulation characteristics all days from December 20 to 28, were generally anticyclonic with an average pressure of 1029 hPa. A westward extension of the Siberian high lay over the southern half of the UK (Fig. 9.3). The persistence of synoptic scale subsidence associated with the anticyclonic conditions suppressed vertical mixing heights as reflected in a general reduction of visibility to distances of 1000 m (Fig. 9.2). Low windspeeds during the majority of the episode, particularly for the period December 22-25, helped preserve high pollution concentrations. The sensitivity of pollution levels to meteorological conditions is well demonstrated for the earlier and latter parts of the episode. Bursts of wind activity on December 22, 25 and 26 and consistently building wind speeds from early on December 27 onwards are closely related to distinct drops in pollution levels. Visibility levels also demonstrate inverse behaviour with wind speed. The reverse can be said for periods for which almost stagnant atmospheric conditions occurred. In addition to the impressive magnitude of the pollution peaks, the timing of the peaks are of interest as these demonstrate the possible role of anthropogenic factors as opposed to meteorological factors. The highest daily peaks all tended to occur during the late evening hours. This diurnal behaviour may well be related to the diurnal activity cycle within Birmingham city centre. Although no traffic volume data is available to substantiate this idea, it is suggested that elevated evening Christmas traffic activity, may account for the timing of pollution peaks. The magnitude of the peaks are therefore both a response to increased emission rates and the requisite meteorological conditions. The Christmas 1992 pollution episode was brought to an abrupt halt with the recession of the Siberian anticyclonic ridge and the increase in southwesterly airflows as a well developed cyclonic system approached the UK from the west.

Veal (1994) has also presented a clear example of the role meteorology plays in summer time photochemical pollution episodes in Birmingham. Although the requisite meteorological conditions for elevated O_3 levels existed throughout the period (Fig. 9.4) the long range trajectory of air during this episode also appears to be important as the airmass that moved over Birmingham had its origins over northwest Europe, where emissions of photochemical precursors would have been incorporated within the northeasterly flows moving over the central UK region. Such a trajectory in association with warm and dry continental airmass characteristics allowed O_3 levels to build from the 12th to a maximum on June 14. From June 15 O_3 levels began to drop as wind speeds increased and temperatures dropped (Fig. 9.4).

Although SO_2 is currently less of a problem than in the 1950s-1970s because of the enactment of the 1956 Clean Air Act and the adoption of the 1980 EC directive for SO_2, increasing levels of fine particulate matter are of some concern as they have been suggested as having important health effects. Little is known of the behaviour of PM_{10} (particulate matter less than 10 microns in size) in Birmingham's atmosphere as PM_{10} has only been measured in Birmingham since 1992. However the temporal behaviour of SO_2 appears to be a good proxy of the likely behaviour of

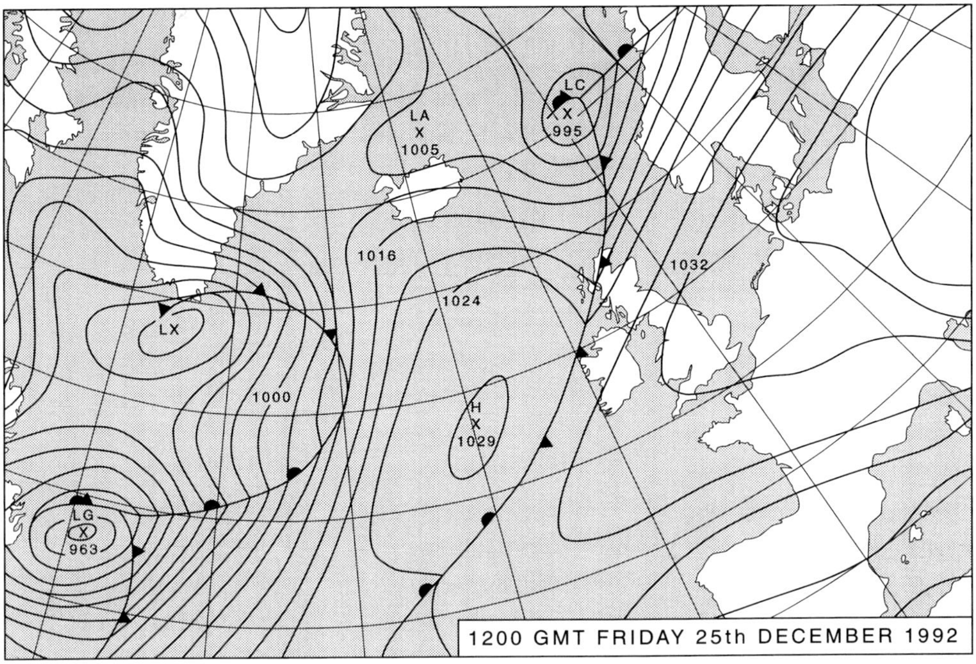

Fig. 9.3 Synoptic scale situation leading to christmas 1992 pollution episode. Note extension of siberian anticyclonic ridge over the UK

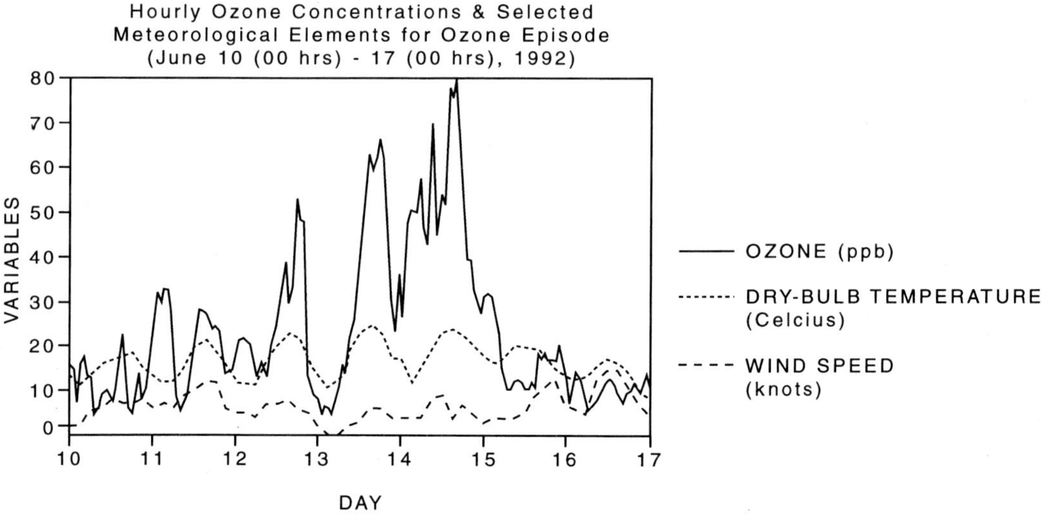

Fig. 9.4 Ozone episode, Birmingham, 10-17 June, 1992

Met Variable & Pollutant	TYPE 7				TYPE 13			
	Mean	Lower Quartile 25%	Upper Quartile 75%	Standard Error of the mean	Mean	Lower Quartile 25%	Upper Quartile 75%	Standard Error of the mean
Cloud 0900	7	6	8	0	3	0	5	0
Cloud 1500	7	6	8	0	2	1	4	0
μ 0900	-3.9	-8.0	0	0.5	-2.5	-6.0	0.3	0.7
μ 1500	-4.6	-9.0	0	0.5	-3.6	-10.0	1.7	0.7
V 0900	-0.1	-2.6	2.7	0.4	-2.3	-5.8	0	0.5
V 1500	0.7	-2.6	4.1	0.5	-1.4	-5.6	0.5	0.6
Press 0900	1017.1	1010.8	1023.0	0.8	1022.8	1016.6	1029.9	0.9
Press 1500	1015.5	1008.8	1022.7	0.8	1021.6	1015.7	1027.3	0.8
Ta 0900	-0.3	-2.2	1.8	0.2	-2.6	-4.3	-0.3	0.3
Ta 1500	2.1	0.5	4.1	0.2	2.2	0.4	-0.7	0.3
Tw 0900	-0.8	-2.6	1.2	0.2	-3.1	-4.9	-0.7	0.3
Tw 1500	1.2	-2.0	3.0	0.2	0.3	-1.5	2.0	0.3
Td 0900	-1.8	-3.6	0.2	0.2	-4.2	-6.3	-1.8	0.4
Td 1500	-0.5	-2.8	1.8	0.2	-3.3	-5.1	-1.4	0.3
SO_2*	72.10	43.20	86.60	3.46	82.98	53.10	98.75	5.40

Table. 9.2 Meteorological characteristics of the two winter airmasses associated with the highest daily mean SO_2 concentrations (adapted from Jowett, 1995)

PM_{10} as SO_2 and PM_{10} have been shown to demonstrate highly covariant behaviour especially in the winter months (McGregor and Bamzelis, 1995). Based on this idea Jowett (1995) applied principal components and cluster analyses to meteorological data for the winters 1980 to 1990 in order to identify the main winter airmasses associated with high mean daily SO_2 concentrations. Of the fourteen airmass types identified two were found to produce on occasions excessively high (greater than 140 ug m^{-3}) SO_2 concentrations. Meteorological and pollution characteristics for the two airmass types are presented in Table 9.2. These airmass physical characteristics favour stagnant non- dispersive and non-diffusive atmospheric conditions and are likely to provide the requisite meteorological conditions for high PM_{10} concentrations. Preliminary analyses of winter weather types and Birmingham PM_{10} data for the period 1992-1994 support such a contention. These analyses indicate that such conditions may also be related to slightly elevated hospital admissions for respiratory complaints (McGregor et al., 1996).

Potential application of air quality models

An air quality model (AQM) can be considered as a numerical laboratory which simulates the real world. It can provide air quality managers with guidance for regulatory decision-making by simulating future emission scenarios which may be potentially realised in the real atmosphere. Furthermore, AQMs are essential in developing a scientific understanding of transportation and dispersion processes of air pollutants in the atmosphere. Therefore, AQMs become indispensable tools for air quality management purposes.

AQMs vary in their treatment of atmospheric physics and chemistry, as well as in their temporal and spatial resolution. Once pollutants are emitted into the atmosphere, their fate is determined by transportation due to the mean wind, dispersion due to turbulence in the air, chemical reactions among the pollutants, and dry/wet deposition onto the ground. Thus the level of sophistication of an AQM depends on how these processes are represented or parameterized. Atmospheric pollution involves different scales: near-source scale (smaller than a few tens of kilometres), urban scale (from a few tens to a few hundreds of kilometres), meso-scale (from a few hundreds to a few thousands of kilometres), and regional or continental scale (larger than a few thousands of kilometres). At the near-source scale, the nature of the thermal plume and local turbulence dominate the dispersion processes, while at the urban scale, turbulent mixing and chemical reactions are important processes. At the meso-scale, chemical reactions and wind transportation are the controlling factors, whereas at the continental scale, wind transportation and deposition are major processes.

Among all kinds of AQMs, the Gaussian dispersion models are the simplest ones, involving only a small amount of computation. They produce fairly reasonable results under some restricted conditions. Therefore, these models have been favoured by most air-quality managers and have become popular management tools in many countries. However, the basic assumptions behind the models are very restrictive. For example, most of them assume a continuous emission source, steady-state meteorological conditions, and a Gaussian (normal) distribution for pollutant concentration, in both the crosswind and vertical directions. Many modifications through different kinds of parameterizations have been made to the Gaussian models so that they can handle, for example, multiple sources, line sources, area sources, instantaneous sources, or topography effects. Nevertheless, a fundamental level of model uncertainty always exists due to errors in measurements, stochastic fluctuations of the plume, and an inability to treat complicated processes by highly empirical (therefore less physical and universal) parameterization schemes in the models (Hanna 1993). Consequently, applications of the Gaussian plume models are still confined to relatively ideal conditions. Furthermore, the Gaussian plume models cannot produce good results for ground-level sources or under very convective meteorological conditions in which winds are weak and thermal plumes are strong.

There are currently available dozens of alternate forms of the Gaussian dispersion model, most of which apply to those locations downwind of continuous point sources. Some examples include the UK model ADMS (Atmospheric Diffusion Model System) and the US Environment Protection Agency (EPA) models: CRSTER (for single point source), MPTER (for multiple point sources), HPDM (Hybrid Plume Dispersion Model), CTDM (Complex Terrain Dispersion Model), and ISC (Industrial Source Complex model). All these models assume a uniform meteorology (or "non-uniform meteorology" modified entirely by topography, not by atmospheric dynamics), a symmetric Gaussian distribution of pollutant concentration, and a instantaneous dispersion process. The required inputs include the location of the source, the stack height, the emission rate and temperature of the pollution source, wind and temperature data from standard weather station(s), an atmospheric stability class (i.e., Pasquill class), and the atmospheric boundary layer mixing height. Extension of the application of a point source (a single stack) Gaussian model to a line source (a road for example) has been implemented in some models, for example, the CALINE series, developed by the California Department of Transportation. In addition to the weaknesses inherited from the Gaussian model, these line models have difficulties dealing with the situations in which wind directions are nearly parallel to the road. For low-level area sources, an example is PAL (Point, Area and Line source model), which adopts the integrated line source-segment approach to represent area sources and exhibits a reasonable predictive behaviour.

At a higher level of modelling sophistication, three-dimensional Eulerian grid-based models may parameterize the most important physical and chemical atmospheric processes and use a fine resolution to represent temporal and spatial variations of the chemical species. The basis of the models is the atmospheric diffusion equation, which expresses the conservation of each chemical component in turbulent air when chemical reactions occur. This type of model is essential for examining the complex interactions among emissions, meteorology, and atmospheric chemistry. In general, these models are more universal and their results are more reliable when compared with the Gaussian plume models. The computations are of course much more intensive, but the costs have been dramatically and persistently reduced due to the rapid evolution of computer technology over the recent decades. Many countries have already adopted the models to guide emission control strategies. The continued development of computational power will allow photochemical studies using more chemically and dynamically comprehensive models for air quality management purposes.

The three-dimensional Eulerian grid-based models generally perform much better than the Gaussian models in terms of the temporal evolution of pollutants over space and complex terrain, in weak winds, for area sources and for general physical and chemical atmospheric processes at the urban scale. The Urban Airshed Model (UAM), (Systems Applications Inc, USA), the CIT model, (California Institute of Technology and Carnegie Mellon University), and the CALGRID model, (Sigma Research, USA), are some examples. These models are designed to calculate the concentrations of both inert and chemically reactive pollutants by simulating the physical and chemical processes in the atmosphere that affect pollutant concentrations. They represent a significant departure from the steady-state, spatially homogeneous Gaussian formulations used to evaluate air quality, because the latter can only treat first-order chemical transformations, and are therefore not capable of fully characterising ozone dynamics in urban and regional areas over multiple days, nor the response of ozone to pre-cursor emission changes. Among the three models, the UAM is the most widely used. In 1984, the United States' EPA's Office of Air Quality Planning and Standard proposed that the UAM be a "recommended model for photochemical pollutant modelling applications involving entire urban areas". Regional scale equivalents of the urban scale models are the Regional Acid Deposition Model (RADM) developed by the State University of New York, the Regional Oxidants Model (ROM) developed by US EPA, and Acid Deposition and Oxidant Model (ADOM) developed by the Ontario Ministry of Environment and Energy, Canada. A EURopean Acid Deposition model (EURAD) has been developed, based on the RADM. To date it appears that urban scale Eulerian models have not been applied in or developed for the UK situation.

In the West Midlands the emissions of primary species for photochemical processes from line and area low-level sources have been increasing due to increasing vehicle numbers. The primary vehicular species of NOx, CO and VOC also coexist with other sources of VOC from both biogenic and anthropogenic origins. Topography in the West Midlands is fairly flat and weather conditions are dominated by typical midlatitude cyclonic, anticyclonic and frontal systems. Given the situation of increasing levels of photochemical pollution precursors and the fact that local authorities will soon have to assess air quality standards and identity air quality management areas, there is mounting interest in the application of available modelling technology to the development of strategies to meet air quality assessment and management endeavours. Considering these facts, possible applications of AQMs in the West Midlands may consist of both Gaussian models for single sources and nonreactive components such as SO_2 and CO under relatively stable meteorological conditions, and Eulerian grid-based photochemical models for NOx, O_3 and VOC etc. under more complicated meteorological conditions.

Currently the School of Geography and the Institute of Public and Environmental Health at the University of Birmingham, are involved with local authorities in the West Midlands in assessing an AQM system which is based on a Gaussian dispersion approach. While the system should provide valuable information for the development of air quality control strategies at the suburban scale for non-reactive components, the development of an overall management strategy for the West Midlands especially for photochemical species will most likely be based on the application of a three dimensional modelling approach using a full meteorological model to drive a photochemical model such as the UAM.

Air quality in the West Midlands: future prospects

The introduction of catalytic converters on all new petrol cars since the beginning of 1993 has led to a reduction in emissions of carbon monoxide, hydrocarbons and oxides of nitrogen from road traffic. Coupled with a tighter control of pollutant emissions from industry, it is anticipated that concentrations of the major gaseous pollutants will decline over the next 10 years or so. The main sources of airborne particulate matter are road traffic (mainly diesel vehicles) and secondary sulphate and nitrate particles. Tightening European limits on emissions of particulate matter from diesels and of the precursor gases from which secondary particles are formed will lead to a significant improvement with respect to PM_{10} concentrations. These legislation forced improvements in urban air quality are likely to continue as long as reductions in emissions per vehicle are not outweighed by greater emissions due to increased traffic growth.

Although air quality is likely to improve in the West Midlands the ability to develop effective air quality management strategies for the future will depend on us first understanding how general pollution levels are affected by legislation and how day to day variations in air quality are controlled by daily variations in emissions and meteorological conditions. Developing the right air quality management strategies for the future therefore involves making decisions in complex systems. Perhaps the only way to achieve this is by the use of traditional field data from the disciplines of climatology and atmospheric chemistry to validate numerical meteorological and atmospheric chemistry models, the results of which will allow scientifically based decisions about what type of strategies should be adopted to manage the complex environmental issue of air quality.

References

Bailey M L 1976 *A study of the effect of circulation types and other climatic factors on Sulphur Dioxide concentrations in the area of Birmingham* Unpublished MSc Dissertation School of Geography, The University of Birmingham

Barry R G and Perry A H 1973 *Synoptic Climatology* Methuen, London

Christiansen W L and Bryson R A 1966 An investigation of the potential of component analysis for weather classification *Monthly Weather Review* 94 697-707

Davis R E and Gay D A 1993 An assessment of air quality variations in the south-western United States using an upper air synoptic climatology *International Journal of Climatology* 13 755-781

Department of Environment 1995 *Digest of Environmental Statistics* No 17 HMSO, London

Hanna S R 1993 Uncertainties in air quality model predictions *Boundary-Layer Meteorology*, Vol. 62, 1-4 3-20

Harvie L 1995 *A synoptic climatological approach in the assessment of volumetric changes in landfill Methane flux* Unpublished BSc Dissertation School of Geography, The University of Birmingham

Jowett S 1995 *A study of the relationships between Sulphur Dioxide and smoke concentrations and winter synoptic types in Birmingham* Unpublished MSc Thesis School of Geography, The University of Birmingham

Ladd J W and Driscoll D M 1980 A comparison of objective and subjective means of weather typing, an example from west Texas *J. Applied Meteorology* 19 691-704

McGregor G R 1996 The identification of air quality affinity areas in Birmingham *Applied Geography* 16 (2)

McGregor G R and Bamzelis 1995 Synoptic typing and its application to the investigation of weather air pollution relationships, Birmingham, UK *Theoretical and Applied Climatology* 51 223-236

McGregor G R Walters S and Wordley J 1996 Winter airmass types and hospital respiratory admissions in Birmingham, UK Paper to be presented at the 14th International Congress of Biometeorology, September 1-8 1996 Ljubljana Slovenia

Pass A 1981 *Smoke and Sulphur Dioxide pollution in Birmingham* Unpublished MSc Dissertation School of Geography, The University of Birmingham

Scott S 1995 *Air pollution in Kitts Green, Birmingham, and its relationship to meteorological applications* Unpublished BSc Dissertation School of Geography, The University of Birmingham

Veal A 1994 *A Synoptic climatological classification to assess variations in vehicular pollutant concentrations in Birmingham, UK* Unpublished MSc Dissertation School of Geography, The University of Birmingham

Yarnal B 1992 *Synoptic Climatology in Environmental Analysis* Belhaven Press, London

II
PEOPLE, ECONOMY AND SOCIETY

CHAPTER 10

The Structure of Birmingham's Population in 1991

D. R. Ingram

This chapter is concerned with the spatial variation in the age and gender structure of Birmingham's population at the time of the 1991 census. Previous work on the population of Birmingham has been concerned with its changing size as a function of boundary extension (Wise and Thorpe, 1950) and the role of the vital and migrational processes (Rugman and Green,1977). In terms of the attributes of the population, Jones (1970,1976) has examined the development and diffusion of the 'New Commonwealth' population within Birmingham. However, relatively little attention has been paid to the demographic structure of the population. Within any city the distribution of the population in specific age-groups is related to the presence of areas of attraction to particular stages of the life-cycle. The demographic composition of a population reveals not only the past operation of fertility, mortality and migrational behaviour, reflecting broad economic and social factors, but it also has relevance to the formation of policy within local government.

Age is one status-defining variable that exhibits extreme variation in its effect on the social structure and character of communities. Age and gender determine many of the needs, activities and attitudes of individuals and the communities in which they reside. The extent to which age structure affects social stratification is unclear but it has been noted as important in employment practices and thus it can bear on occupation and income. However, little work has been concerned with the spatial variation of intra-urban age structures. What generalizations do exist on the geographic patterns of the various age groups in urban areas (Knox,1995; White,1984) suggest that new residential areas on the outskirts are child dominated, in contrast to the older suburbs and central areas that are populated by young adults and elderly people. It has been suggested that explanations for elderly concentrations in and near to the centre of cities relate to the out-migration of the more youthful components of the population, particularly young families, to the periphery; and to the lower incomes of the elderly which inhibits their propensity to relocate.

Age structure is an important component in the development of policy for the delivery of public goods and services (Coulson,1968). This is readily apparent in the provision of educational facilities for the younger elements of the population. But the provision of domiciliary services for the elderly (such as meals-on-wheels, domestic help and home-based nursing care) is perhaps a more costly and difficult task given the different locational constraints. Educational facilities are provided at locations to which their pupils travel. Domiciliary services, which are designed to allow the elderly to remain within their own homes for as long as possible, require the movement of the providers of the service to their clients.

The lack of comprehensive studies of intra-urban demographic structures in Birmingham, and other urban places, is associated with the lack of appropriate analytical tools. The most common graphical technique for displaying data about age and gender composition of a population is the population pyramid. Such diagrams (Fig. 10.1) provide a useful summary of a single population

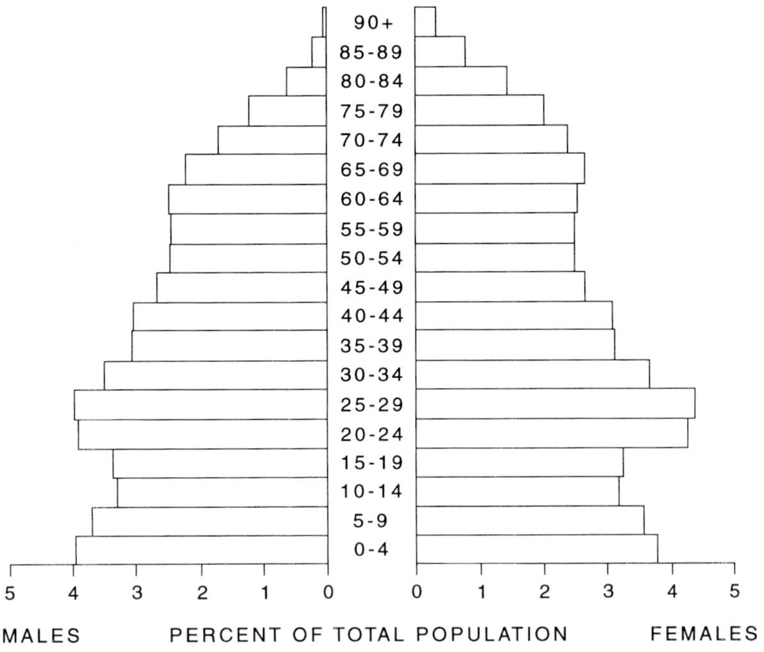

Fig. 10.1 Age and gender structure of Birmingham: 1991

suggesting particular social, economic and historical events that have been experienced by particular cohorts. However, when used for comparing the populations of many areas they tend to be overwhelming in the information that they provide. For example, in a study of Belfast, Emrys Jones (1966) used only a few of the total number of possible areas within that city to depict the types of demographic structures found within an urban area. In this chapter a simpler graphical device, a ternary or triaxial diagram (Ingram, 1984), is used to classify graphically the demographic structure of the thirty-nine wards within the city of Birmingham. Population pyramids are then used to illustrate particular types.

The Age-Gender Structure of Birmingham

Despite several changes in the administrative boundary of Birmingham, which have resulted in small population gains from the population resident in the newly-incorporated areas, the pattern of overall population change in the 1981-1991 census decade has continued the decline from the peak in 1951. The population present on census night (April 21/22, 1991) was 923,800 representing a decrease of 7.3 per cent from 1981 (996,252). There was net out-migration of 11.3 per cent from Birmingham in the 1981-91 census decade. This loss was partially counteracted by the greater number of births than deaths; net natural change was 4 per cent, the highest rate experienced by the districts in the former West Midlands County (OPCS,1992).

The age and gender structure of the population of Birmingham in 1991 (Fig. 10.1) has the rectangular appearance of a mature structure that illustrates the effect of both low rates of fertility in the past and the concentration of mortality within the older age cohorts. The pyramid demonstrates, through the 'bulge' for the 20-34 age cohorts the effect of the slightly higher rates of fertility in the 1956-71 period. This generation is also responsible for the rejuvenation at the base of the pyramid in the 1980s. During the 1980s there was an increase in the number of births, echoing the 'baby-boom' twenty to thirty years earlier.

The gender structure is representative of a population that has similar age specific rates of mortality, for both males and females, below the age of 60. At birth the ratio of males to females is approximately 105 males to 100 females. The male/female ratio remains similar (Fig. 10.2) from one cohort to the next up to age 20. However, the three five-year cohorts between ages 20-34 are female dominated possibly reflecting the in-migration to Birmingham of females for educational and employment purposes rather than the out-migration of males.

There is a slight preponderance of females in the 60-64 age cohort (Table 10.1). This is a consequence of the onset of the period of rapidly increasing age-specific rates of male mortality, which occurs at an earlier age than that for females. After age 65 the male/female ratio for the five-year cohorts declines rapidly. The greater number of females than males in both the young adult cohorts and in the elderly population results in Birmingham's population being 51.60 per cent female with a total male/female ratio of 93.78.

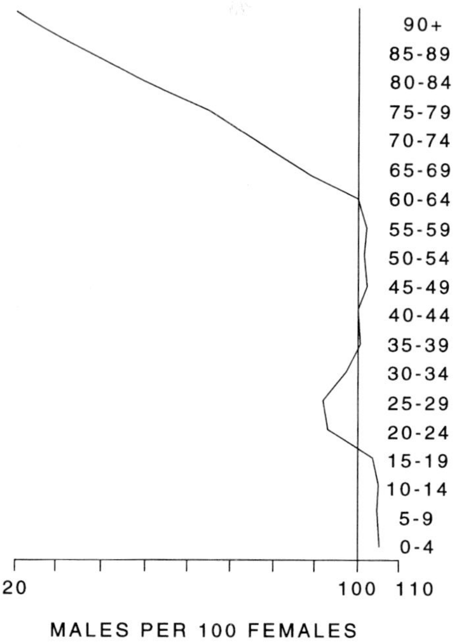

Fig. 10.2 Male - Female Ratios by five-year age cohort

Age Cohort	Males	Females
60-64	24107	24295
65-69	21583	25361
70-74	16776	22505
75-79	12181	19125
80-84	6468	13576
85-90	2471	7138
over 90	650	2904

Table. 10.1 Number of Elderly population: Birmingham 1991

Spatial Variation in Age structure

For ease of spatial analysis, a population may be regarded as consisting of three broad age components: first, children, defined as those under the minimum school-leaving age of sixteen; secondly, adults, those between 16 and pensionable age; and, thirdly, pensioners, those over pensionable age (that is age 60 for women and 65 for men). The first component, children, has traditionally been the most important for public policy because of the demands it creates for health-care facilities and for the provision of pre-school, school and recreational facilities. At the other end of the age spectrum the population above pensionable age is increasing in number, particularly those over 75, creating a concomitant increasing demand for community-based services.

Ternary diagrams

A ternary diagram or trigraph (Ingram, 1984) is a useful graphical method for displaying information which consists of three components. Each component is expressed as a percentage of the sum of the absolute values for an observation and is associated with a particular axis within an equilateral triangle. In a full ternary diagram each axis has a range of values from O per cent to 100 percent. However, in the context of population structure each observation, a ward in this study of Birmingham, the population consist of a mixture of all three components and therefore only a part of the full triangle is used (Fig. 10.3). There are significant differences between wards in terms of the relative size of each component. One method of classifying the observations is to use certain indicator or 'key' values; the indicator lines shown on the ternary graph are the percentage of the total Birmingham population in each component age group.

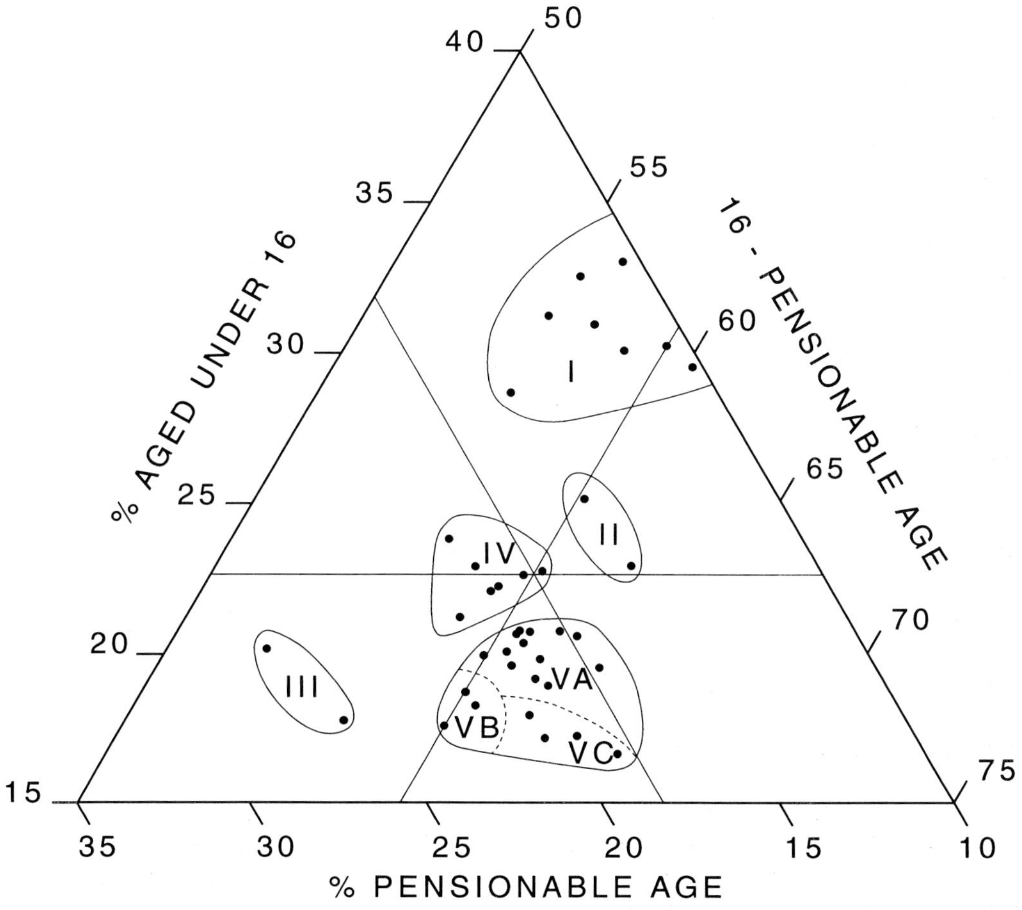

Fig. 10.3 Birmingham wards in three component demographic space

Children under 16 years of age comprised 22.6 per cent of the population resident in Birmingham in 1991. This value was the highest for the Districts comprising the former West Midlands Metropolitan County and is associated with the high rate of net natural change (4 per cent) experienced by the population in the 1981-91 period. The adult age group formed 59.1 per cent of the total population and 18.2 per cent were above pensionable age. The percentage of pensioners increased from 17.4 per cent in 1981, because of declines in the size of the other two components (OPCS,1992).

Observations near the vertices of the triangle are dominated by one of the three components; observations near the middle of the sides are characterised by a mixture of two components. Those with broad age structures similar to Birmingham as a whole are located near to the intersection of the three indicator lines on the ternary diagram. In addition to a visual examination of the graph, a numerical grouping algorithm was used to create a typology of wards with similar demographic profiles in terms of the three components. The two methods produce five well-defined clusters of observations; the largest group can be further subdivided into three subsets. At one end of the spectrum there is a cluster of eight child-dominated or 'young' wards and at the other a pair of ' elderly' wards dominated by pensioners.

Considerable variation exists between wards in the relative size of the three age components. The under-16 component is the most variable of the three components; Edgbaston (16.7 per cent) had the lowest value and Sparkbrook (33.0 per cent) the highest. Shard End had the largest percentage of pensioners (27 per cent) and Sparkhill (10.3 per cent) the lowest. The adult population is not only the largest component in each ward but also the least variable; the ward with the highest percentage of adults was Edgbaston (64.5 per cent) and the lowest was Shard End (52.8 per cent).

Child-dominated Wards

Eight wards are clearly child-dominated having more than 28 per cent of their population below the minimum school leaving age. These wards all have less than 16 per cent of their population above pensionable age. The wards in this group are located in an arc to the north and east of the centre of Birmingham (Fig. 10.4). The area was developed primarily in the second half of the nineteenth century and now consists of high-density terraced housing with some patches of post-war redevelopment (see chapter 17). This inner city area has been the focus for the initial location and expansion of immigrant communities from the Caribbean and the Indian sub-continent (see chapter 12).

The most extreme ward is Sparkbrook with 33.0 per cent of the population less than 16 and only 10.5 per cent above pensionable age. The disaggregated data for Sparkbrook (Fig. 10.5A) has a well-developed base to a very triangular pyramid, which is reminiscent of many developing nations. There is, as expected from the birth ratio, a greater number of males than females in each of the four youngest age cohorts. The six cohorts between the ages of 20-49 are excessively dominated by females in comparison to Birmingham as a whole; the reverse is the case for the five cohorts between ages 50 -74 which are male-dominated. This curious pattern may relate to male-dominated flows of Asian immigrants to this area in the 1970s and 1980s (Upton,1993:209) and the subsequent migration of younger wives.

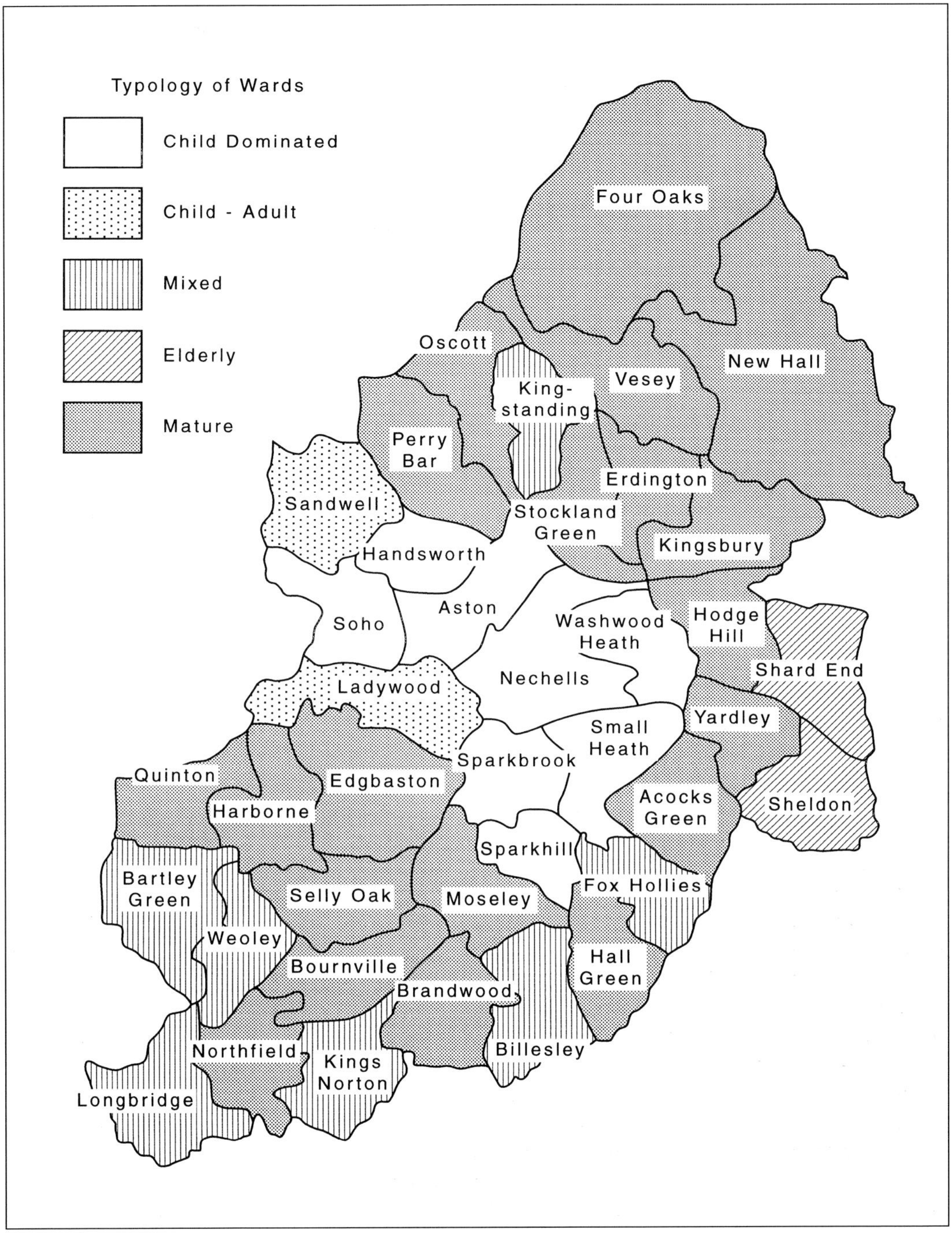

Fig. 10.4 Location of Demographic Groups

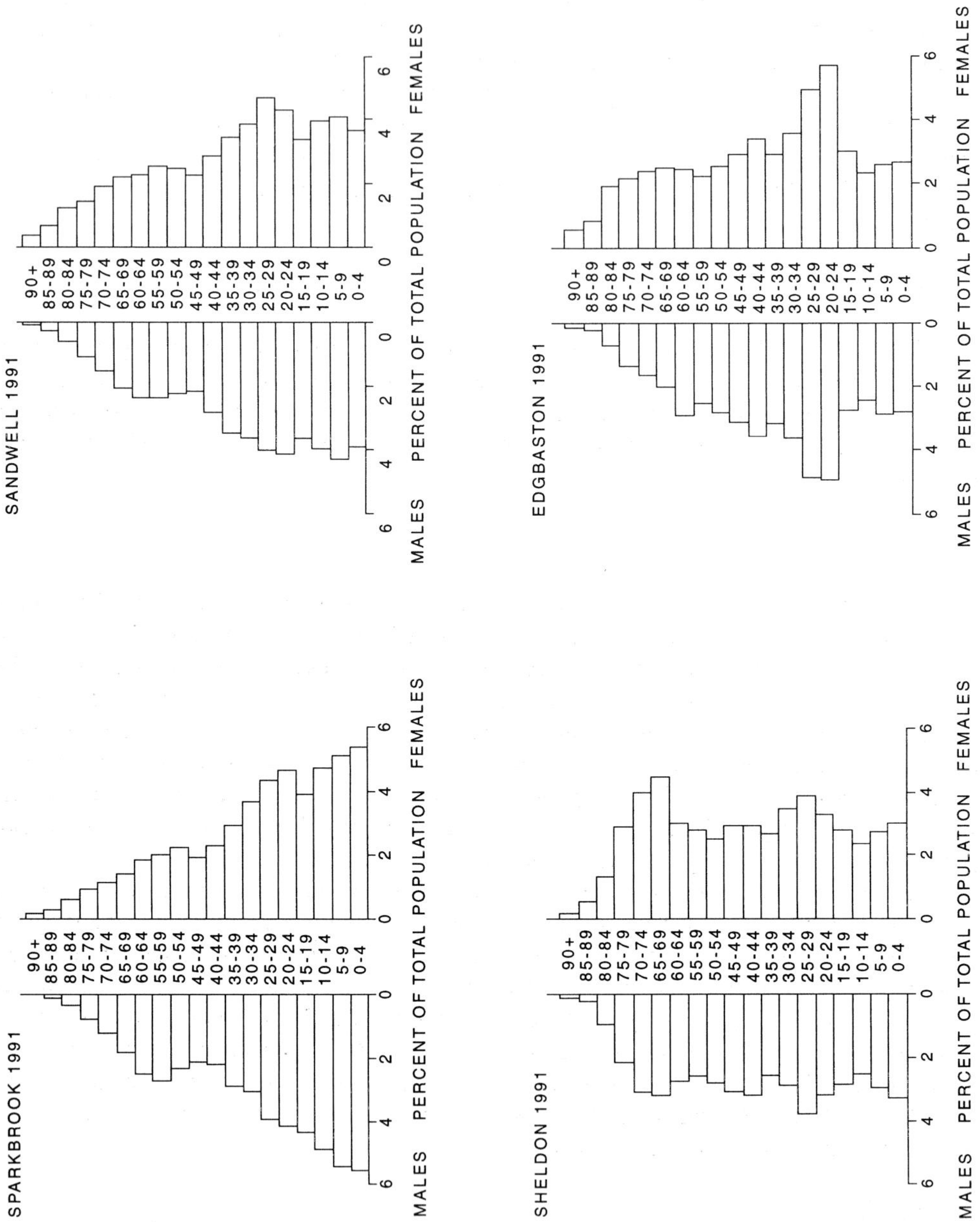

Fig. 10.5 Age and gender structures of selected wards: A) Sparkbrook B) Sandwell C) Sheldon D) Edgbaston

Child - Adult Wards

Two wards, Sandwell and Ladywood, are spatially adjacent to the eastern end of the child-dominated cluster. This pair of wards occupy a position on the ternary diagram between the child-dominated and mixed clusters in terms of their broad demographic characteristics. They have small percentages of pensioners but are above the Birmingham norm for both children and adults. In process terms these wards possibly represent an ageing of the younger elements of previously child-dominated wards. The adult population of Sandwell ward (Fig. 10.5B) is dominated by the under 45 cohorts and, similarly to Sparkbrook, these are also female dominated. The 20-39 age cohorts are likely to be the parental generation to the children in the three youngest age groups.

Mixed Wards

A group of seven wards have a mixture of the three age components similar to their proportion in the total Birmingham population. The disaggregated age structures of these wards are also similar to that of the total Birmingham population. The members of this group, with the exception of Kingstanding, are located to the south of the city in areas of pre- and post-second world war housing.

Elderly Wards

Two wards, Shard End and Sheldon, on the eastern edge of the city are characterized by having extremely large percentages of their population above pensionable age. In Sheldon 26.0 per cent of the population was above pensionable age and 17.73 was less than 16 years of age. The percentage of pensioners in Shard End was higher (27.0 per cent) but the proportion of children was also higher (20.2 per cent). Both of these wards are located on the eastern side of the city. and were developed for housing in the inter-war period; the major contrast being that Shard End has a high proportion of council housing whereas the housing in Sheldon is mainly owner-occupied. It can be suggested that the current demographic situation has resulted from in situ ageing of a long-term resident population in both areas.

The disaggregated population structure of Sheldon (Fig. 10.5C) has a very mature structure with a narrow base and an almost rectangular appearance to the middle section of the diagram with only small differences between the relative sizes of adjacent cohorts. Although there are large percentages of women in the 60-74 age cohorts in comparison to the male cohorts, the contraction due to the onset of elderly mortality is not apparent until the very elderly age groups. The population pyramid also suggests that the elderly nature of Sheldon's population is gradually being rejuvenated. The 20-34 age cohorts, for both males and females, are larger than those above and below. As a consequence of the inevitable mortality amongst the elderly, housing is slowly being released for younger households.

Mature Wards

The percentages of adults in the remaining 20 wards are all above the Birmingham norm and, with the exception of three wards, above the norm for pensioners. All have less than 20.7 per cent children. The grouping algorithm produced three subsets within this cluster a large set of 13 wards, and two small sub-groups containing three and four wards respectively. The three member subset (Harborne, Oscott and Quinton wards) have higher percentages of pensioners than other members of the cluster. These wards may well be progressing demographically towards a similar age structure to that of the elderly wards. The four member sub-group, consisting of Edgbaston, Selly Oak, Perry Barr, and Four Oaks, have low percentages of children. With the exception of Four Oaks, these wards contain or are adjacent to the University of Birmingham or the University of Central England.

The most extreme ward in this sub-group, and the mature cluster as a whole, is Edgbaston, which is characterized by the lowest percentage of children and the highest percentage of adults of all the wards in Birmingham. The four youngest cohorts (Fig. 10.5D) are very small in comparison to the very large number of people in their twenties. The presence of large numbers of young adults may be partially associated with the University of Birmingham and partially to the large proportion of single-person households in this ward. For the cohorts over age 30, the female side of the population pyramid is rectangular in comparison to the declining size of the corresponding male cohorts. However, the number of males is greater than that of females for each age cohort between 30-65.

Conclusion

Birmingham, in common with many cities of Western Europe (White, 1984), has a population that has become increasingly aged in recent decades. This situation is unlikely to alter in the near future and will result in an increased dependency of the elderly in the population with concomitant demands for increased domiciliary services. The ageing process has already resulted in a predominance of females in the older age groups and also in the total population. However, in contrast to generalizations concerning the location of children in other West European cities, the central and inner-city areas of Birmingham have young age structures reflecting a pattern similar to the inner-city residential location of 'New Commonwealth' families. From the perspective of local government these areas require investment in educational and recreational facilities appropriate to the needs of the population.

The lack of child-dominated wards in the outer city may be associated with the high level of net out-migration from Birmingham in the last two decades and the lack of areas of extensive new housing within the city for such families. Young couples and families have tended to move to the New and Expanding Towns (for example: Redditch, Tamworth, Droitwich and Worcester) outside the West Midlands Green Belt. Areas dominated by the elderly tend to be the peripheral wards which were extensively developed in the inter-war period.

References

Coulson M R C 1968 The distribution of population age structures in Kansas City *Annals, Association of American Geographers* 58 155-176

Ingram D R 1984 Simplifying Ternary Diagrams *Area* 16.2 175-80

Jones E 1966 *Towns and Cities* Oxford University Press, Oxford

Jones P N 1970 Coloured Immigrants in Birmingham 1961-1966 *Transactions Institute of British Geographers* 50 199-219

Jones P N 1976 Colored Minorities in Birmingham England *Annals Association of American Geographers* 66 80-103

Knox P L 1995 *Urban social geography, an introduction* Longman, London 3rd edition

Upton C 1993 *A history of Birmingham* Phillimore, Chichester

OPCS 1992 *1991 Census County Monitor: West Midlands* London, HMSO

Rugman A J and Green M D 1977 Demographic and Social Change in F Joyce ed *Metropolitan Development and Change* Teackfield Ltd, Farnborough, 50-74

White P 1984 *The West European City* Longman, London

Wise M J and Thorpe P O'N 1950 The growth of Birmingham 1800-1950 in Kinvig R H Smith J G and Wise M J eds *Birmingham and its regional setting* British Association for the Advancement of Science, Birmingham

CHAPTER 11

Birmingham's Black and South-Asian Population

T.R. Slater

Birmingham has one of the most ethnically diverse populations in Britain and there is a long history of academic investigation into the characteristics and distribution of this population (Jones, 1961; Jones, 1978; Rosing and Wood, 1971). The 1991 census included a question on ethnicity for the first time and, though controversial, since it came at a time when questions of nationality were high on the political agenda, it does allow for a more detailed analysis of the ethnic make-up of the population of British cities than was previously possible using the census information on birthplaces. However, that analysis is still necessarily limited to the categories of ethnicity determined by the census. This chapter provides a temporal review of studies on Birmingham's minority non-European ethnic population groups, discusses some aspects of their present geography within the city and some of the ways that they impact on the culture and politics of Birmingham.

National patterns

A recent study by Peach (1996) provides a useful starting point since he provides a national context for the 1991 ethnicity data. He does this in the course of asking the question 'do British cities have ghettos'? It is a question which has dominated the geographical discourse since the 1960s. Peach defines a ghetto in terms of the concentration of a single ethnic group into an exclusive residential area. His answer for all British cities, including Birmingham, was that they do not have ghettos, though a very few urban wards have high concentrations of non-white populations generally. He is, of course wrong. All British cities have ghettos of 'white' or 'European' people. In Birmingham, wards such as Kingstanding or Sutton Coldfield are more than 95 per cent 'white'. What is revealed here is the racialized nature of the geographical discourse and the equation of a word, 'ghetto', which carries an enormous amount of denigratory cultural baggage, with black and Asian residential areas.

What Peach (1996) reveals is that, in 1991, Britain's non-European ethnic populations were highly concentrated in the English metropolitan counties. In total, black and south-Asian groups constitute 5.5 per cent of Britain's population, a little over 3 million people. However, of these, 79 per cent of Black Caribbeans, 83 per cent of Black Africans, 74 per cent of Bangladeshis, 65 per cent of Indians, and 64 per cent of Pakistanis live in the four metropolitan regions of Greater London, the West Midlands, Greater Manchester and West Yorkshire (Peach, 1996). The total figures for the eight main ethnic groups recorded in the census for the West Midlands metropolitan county and for Birmingham are shown in Table 11.1. This shows that 21.5 per cent of Birmingham's population categorized themselves as other than 'white' in the 1991 census, the largest single group being the Pakistanis who now constitute nearly seven per cent of Birmingham's population.

Ethnic Groups	West Midlands Population	West Midlands % of Total	Birmingham Population	Birmingham % of Total
Total Population	2,551,671	100	961,041	100
White	2,178,149	85.4	754,274	78.5
Black Caribbean	72,183	2.8	44,770	4.7
Black African	4,116	0.2	2,803	0.3
Black Other	15,716	0.6	8,803	0.9
Total Black	92,015	3.6	56,376	5.9
Indian	141,359	5.5	51,075	5.3
Pakistani	88,268	3.5	66,085	6.9
Bangladeshi	18,074	0.7	12,739	1.3
Total South Asian	247,701	9.7	129,899	13.5
Chinese	6,107	0.2	3,315	0.3

Source OPCS (1993, Table 6)

Table 11.1: Ethnic groups in the West Midlands and Birmingham, 1991

This spatial concentration of the ethnic population into the major urban areas of Britain is further compounded within cities where they are concentrated into a comparatively small number of wards in each of these four city regions. However, there are only a very few wards where a single non-white ethnic group forms a majority of the population in that ward, the most concentrated being the Indian population in Northcote ward in Ealing, London at 67.2 per cent. What is true, is that when all non-white ethnic groups are taken together, very high concentrations of residence are found; Northcote again being the highest with 90 per cent non-white. No Birmingham ward has a non-white population of more than 75 per cent (Peach, 1992: Table IV). I shall return to this discussion later but the majority of this chapter is concerned to examine the chronological build up of these populations within the city.

Black and Asian people, 1945 to 1965

The first non-white residents of Birmingham pre-date the Second World War. Chinn's (1994) historical researches and oral histories have shown that both Caribbean and Indian people were living in the city in small numbers before 1945. The 1950s, however, saw substantial in-migration to Britain, first from the West Indies and a little later from the Indian sub-continent. Jones's research (1967), using the birthplace data from the 1961 census, showed that, of Birmingham's total population of 1,107,187, some 16,290 (1.4 per cent) were immigrants from the West Indies and 10,232 (0.9 per cent) were from the Indian sub-continent. He estimated that it was unlikely that more than 3 per cent (35,000) of the city's population were black or Asian in 1961, allowing for children born in this country and therefore not recorded in the birthplace statistics of the census. However, it is also important to note that Peach (1966) has estimated that the 1961 census may have under-enumerated West Indians by as much as 20 per cent because of these and other factors.

What was already clear in 1961 was that these population groups were highly concentrated into particular areas of the city, notably the middle ring of Victorian and Edwardian bye-law housing. Thus Soho and Handsworth Wards, to the north west of the city centre, together already contained more than 27 per cent of the West Indian population, whilst Aston, Market Hall, Sparkbrook and Balsall Heath Wards, to the east and south east of the city centre, contained nearly 35 per cent of the Asian population (Jones, 1967: Table 1). In other words, these two ethnic groups were also already geographically separated from one another. The middle-ring wards to the north of the city centre was the residential area favoured by a majority of Caribbean immigrants, but by less than 20 per cent of south Asians; the middle ring wards to the south of the city centre were more favoured by south Asian immigrants. In Handsworth and Soho some 23 enumeration districts (EDs) had more than 10 per cent of their population as of 'new Commonwealth' origin. A few EDs had 40 per cent in this category. Nowhere in Birmingham were black or south-Asian people in the majority in 1961.

A majority of the first generation of immigrants were males in the 20-35 year age groups seeking economic advancement and with the intention of returning home. In the West Indian population, with their greater assimilation of British educational, cultural and social patterns, this initial phase was already being substantively modified by the early 1960s. Female migrants had followed within a few years and more normal population structures and family patterns were already being established. This was less so with the south-Asian population which was still dominated by young males. However, by 1964, the city Education Department recorded more than 7,500 'new Commonwealth' children being taught in the city's schools, a clear reflection of the development of more normal patterns of family structure. 24 primary schools had 20 per cent of their pupils in this group and three had more than 50 per cent black and Asian pupils (The Times, Jan. 1965). Unrestricted immigration continued until the passing of the 1962 Commonwealth Immigration Act. Thereafter, south-Asian households repeated the pattern of West Indian, with wives and parents joining the initial young male migrants leading to the birth of British Asian children.

Geographers investigating black and Asian residential patterns in British cities were quick to point out the links between spatial concentration and particular types and tenure of housing (Glass, 1960; Jones, 1967; Peach, 1968). Formerly prosperous, middle-ring, bye-law housing (see chapter 17) was ideal for absorbing large numbers of new tenants quickly. The courtyard housing which made up the great majority of Birmingham's inner-ring slum housing was both too small to allow for sub-letting and had already been compulsorily purchased by the city council in 1946 in preparation for comprehensive redevelopment. By contrast, middle-ring housing had bathrooms, numerous reasonably-sized rooms, and was often leasehold and let on short leases. They were consequently less popular with the increasingly prosperous, upwardly-mobile white population since mortgage finance was not usually available, they were too large for modern living (many had attic bedrooms intended for servants), and they lacked garages (Jones, 1967). Consequently, they proved ideal for multi-occupation. The large rooms enabled several individuals or family groups to be housed in tolerable comfort, though often with shared bathrooms and kitchens, giving large profits to often unscrupulous landlords. Purpose-built conversions were rare and the rapid deterioration of the property followed quickly as maintenance was also neglected. High residential densities, overcrowded houses and a general environment of neglect and decay with overgrown gardens and streets choked with parked cars was characteristic of these areas in the 1960s.

For the city council the problems posed by these deteriorating middle-ring suburbs took second place to the rehousing of those displaced by the inner-ring comprehensive redevelopment areas. Consequently, though overcrowding was severe and living conditions often appalling, black and Asian households were effectively excluded from council-house provision in this period by the greater perceived needs of white, working-class, inner-city residents. Rex and Moore (1967) demonstrated clearly how this perception of need and fairness on the part of the city council, with its points system for council-house allocation, led to the rapid deterioration of housing in the middle ring. However, subsequently, the city was a pioneer in attempting to exert some control over multi-occupied housing through a private Act of Parliament (Birmingham Corporation, 1965) which allowed it to register such housing and enforce minimum standards.

A 10 per cent sample census was, uniquely, conducted by the Office of Population Censuses and Surveys (OPCS) in 1966 and the changes between 1961 and 1966 in Birmingham have also been analysed by Jones (1970). Within this five-year period, with the total city population declining by more than 50,000 people due to out-migration, the black and south-Asian population almost doubled to nearly 50,000, or some 4.7 per cent of the total. By 1966 the West Midlands was clearly established as the largest centre of black and south- Asian people outside of Greater London. Geographically, this new influx of immigrants was concentrated into the southern middle-ring districts of Balsall Heath, Small Heath, Sparkbrook and Sparkhill so that, by the mid-1960s, the concentrations of black and south-Asian residents approached those already apparent in Handsworth and Soho in the 1961 enumeration. One reason for this is that in the 1960s south-Asian immigration had begun to supercede West Indian and the initial migrants from the Indian sub-continent had located in these areas. In all middle-ring areas there were greater concentrations of black and south-Asian households but they had also begun to disperse outwards from initial core areas of residence, especially along the main radial roads of the city towards the suburban village and town centres of Gravelly Hill, Kings Heath, Selly Oak and Stechford. Within the middle-ring housing zone concentrations of black and south-Asian population reached 25-30 per cent of the total population in Balsall Heath, 20-25 per cent in Handsworth, Soho and Lozells, and 20 per cent in Small Heath, Saltley, Sparkbrook and Summerfield Park. The computer-mapped atlas of the 1966 census published by Rosing and Wood (1971) demonstrates clearly that these communities were not only assailed by the poor housing conditions already apparent in 1961, but that these areas were already showing high levels of unemployment of between 5 and 10 per cent at a time when the West Midlands economy was still booming. However, their analysis also points to the increasing differentiation in the housing conditions of the 'new Commonwealth' population. Whereas half of West-Indian households still occupied privately-rented, and often multi-occupied housing, the south-Asian population were predominantly (75 per cent) owner-occupiers of their housing (Rosing and Wood, 1971: 122-4).

Rex and Moore's classic study of Sparkbrook (1967) showed why this was so and also went some way towards demonstrating the complexity of the minority ethnic communities in Birmingham at a time when race relations were high on the local and national political agendas. The loss of Patrick Gordon Walker's Smethwick seat by the Labour Party in the 1964 General Election to a Conservative candidate campaigning openly on the race issue, when there was a national swing to Labour, was one manifestation of this. Wolverhampton M.P. Enoch Powell's now notorious 'rivers of blood' speech, delivered in the city's Midland Hotel in 1968, again meant that the national spotlight was on the city. The recent study of Birmingham politics by Solomos and Back (1995) has dissected the racialized nature of those politics in some detail. They show how this period was one in which the white, working-class core of the Labour Party in the city maintained their power through a carefully-managed system of clientage within the black and Asian communities. The complex intersection of class, race, housing, religion and politics was dissected by Rex and Moore in seeking to explain where official policies had gone wrong and where different housing and planning policies might ameliorate developing tensions.

This, and other studies sponsored by The Institute of Race Relations, was instrumental, nationally, in the passing of The Race Relations Act of 1968.

Ethnic Geography, 1971-1981

Between 1961 and 1971, Birmingham's population fell by 8.6 per cent to a little over one million people, largely as a result of out-migration (Jones, 1976). The enumerated 'new Commonwealth' population of the city was 92,632 in 1971, a 160 per cent increase in a decade. For the first time, the census included a question related to the children born of 'new Commonwealth' parents enabling more accurate statistics to be compiled of the total black and south-Asian population. In 1971, these British-born children in Birmingham already represented 35.6 per cent of the total (Jones, 1976: note 8). By the 1970s, academic writers were also becoming more aware of the ethnic diversity within the black and south-Asian populations, though not yet of the important cultural, religious, political and gender issues. Rex and Moore (1967) had drawn attention to the very specific localities from which the first south-Asian immigrants in Birmingham had derived and the chain migration that had followed. These first migrants had arrived in the 1940s: Bengalis from Sylhet in East Pakistan (now Bangladesh); Punjabis from the Campbellpure district of the North West Frontier Province of West Pakistan; and Kashmiris from the Mirpur district of Azad Kashmir (officially in India). These were areas where colonial shipping companies recruited seamen (Sylhet and Mirpur) and the British army recruited cooks and bearers (Campbellpore).

What was not appreciated until some time later was the recreation of Asian village social and political systems. The support of extended kinship networks were crucial in the early days for the immigrant seeking to establish himself and, subsequently, when he arranged for the immigration of his family and the purchase of a house. Caste was an important feature of these support networks, too, even amongst the Muslim Pakistani and Kashmiri population, and was to become an important feature of the politics of the city in the 1970s and 1980s (Solomos and Back, 1995). There were similar distinctions of culture and community within the West-Indian migrant population where different island origins betokened differences of education, class, and Christian denomination. A further important distinction in the south-Asian population was between those migrating from the Indian sub-continent and those who came to Britain from east Africa largely as a result of the political upheavals in Uganda in 1972. This latter group were more highly educated and engaged in businesses of one kind or another in east Africa, experience which was put to good use after the initial trauma of their forced migration.

The analysis of the 1971 census data by Jones (1976) showed that the patterns of residence already in evidence in 1961 had been consolidated. To the north of the city centre, the EDs in the cores of Handsworth, Lozells and Aston had proportions of 'new Commonwealth' residents that varied from 45-55 per cent. To the south and east of the city centre Balsall Heath, Sparkbrook, Sparkhill had proportions of 40-45 per cent, Small Heath and Saltley slightly less (Jones, 1976: 95). His analysis is also sensitive (in so far as the census data allows) to the different communities in different areas: West Indians and Indians in Handsworth, Aston and Summerfield; Pakistanis and some West Indians in Small Heath and Saltley; Pakistanis, Indians, West Indians and east Africans in Balsall Heath, Sparkbrook amd Sparkhill. It was notable, Jones reported, that these southern districts, in particular, were more heterogenous than they had been in 1961. The one exception was Saltley which was emerging as distinctively Pakistani (Kashmiri).

Given the wide academic interest in the censuses of 1961-1971, It is surprising that there are few studies in print of the ethnic dimension of the 1981 census in Birmingham. The ward profiles developed by the city statisticians (Birmingham City Council, 1991a) show that by 1981 a number of wards had 'new Commonwealth' populations of more than 50 per cent. They included Handsworth, Soho, Sparkbrook and Sparkhill. Wards with 'new Commonwealth' population between 25-50 per cent included Aston, Ladywood, Nechells, Sandwell and Small Heath, whilst Washwood Heath, Moseley and Edgbaston were fast approaching the 25 per cent level, suggesting that the dispersal outwards to more prosperous housing areas was well under way by 1981. Hodgins (1985) estimated a population of some 49,000 Pakistanis and nearly 8,000 Bangladeshis in Birmingham by 1985, and Joly (1995) suggests that the total Muslim population was 80,000 (8 per cent of the city population). A mid-censal estimate of the black and south-Asian communities suggested a total population of 180,000 in Birmingham, some 18 per cent of the total population and a 17 per cent increase on 1981 (Birmingham City Council, 1991b). This rapid growth was in part a consequence of the completion of family migration to Britain, but much more a consequence of a high birth rate in the south-Asian communities in particular because of their younger age profile. In 1981, 40 per cent were under 16 years of age, while only 2 per cent were over 65.

The 1980s in Birmingham are dominated socially and politically, however, by the so-called 'Handsworth riots'. Civil unrest was first manifested in Britain's larger cities in 1981, including disturbances in Sandwell, Smethwick and Birmingham. However, these paled into insignificance compared with the events of 9-10th September, 1985 when, amidst widespread unrest centred on the Lozells Road, two Asian shopkeepers died in the flames of their burning property. Solomons and Back (1995: 81-5) have shown how these disturbances were 'relocated' to better-known (and black) Handsworth by the national press and racialized through the dramatic picture of a young Afro-Caribbean man throwing a fire bomb. They show that the reporting presumed that the cause of the disturbance was West Indian antagonism towards south-Asian shopkeepers, despite the arrest of Asian and white rioters on the streets and the charging of a white man with the murder of the two shopkeepers. Whatever the causes of this unrest, it sent a clear message to local politicians that they were failing young people in the inner ring of the city and failing to allow a proper black and Asian voice in the political process. What had become clearly apparent towards the end of the 1980s was that growing numbers of black and Asian British young people were being severely disadvantaged by the multiple deprivations of poor housing, inadequate education and lack of employment opportunities consequent on the disintigration of Birmingham's industrial base (see chapter 12).

The 1990s

Mapping the 1991 ethnicity data is an exercise fraught with interpretational problems. None the less, the census provides more detailed information than any previous one thanks to the new questions that were asked. The 'black' population map of the central Birmingham wards (Fig. 11.1) combine the three census categories Black African, Black Other and Afro-Caribbean. Even in 1981 there had been no wards in the city in which there was no 'new Commonwealth' population. By 1991, the 'black' population is shown to be widely dispersed in the city. What is most noticeable, compared with Jones' mapping of the 1971 census data, is the way in which the inner-city zone of post-1945 redevelopment, largely characterized by estates of high-rise blocks of local-authority housing, no longer stands out as an area of 'white' ethnicity. Many of the EDs in these areas have 'black' populations of between 15-30 per cent. These areas include the high-rise estates of Highgate, Nechells and Ladywood. This can be related both to the positive housing

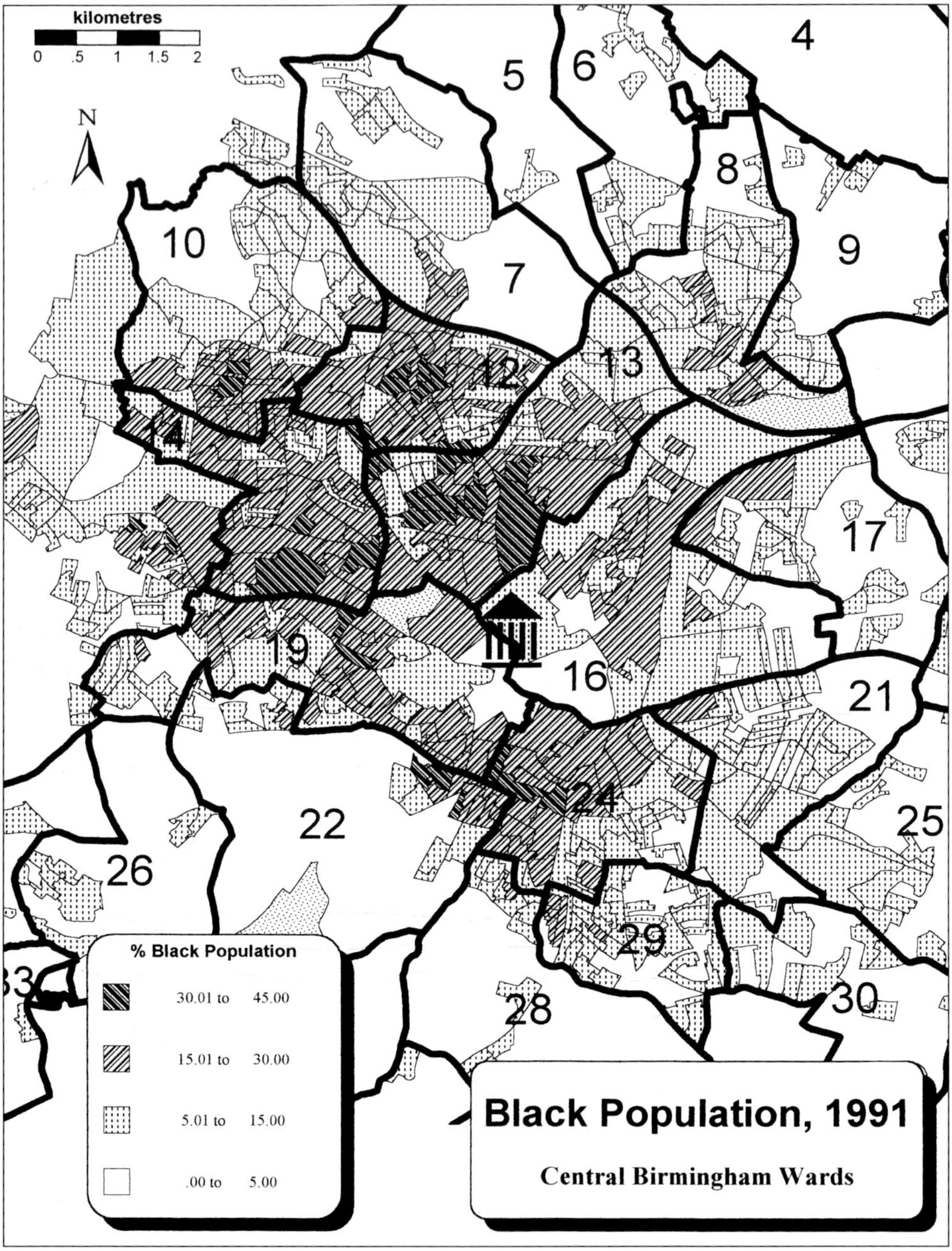

Fig. 11.1 Birmingham's Black population, 1991: central wards. (Source: OPCS)
Wards: 5. Oscott, 6. Kingstanding, 7. Perry Barr, 8. Erdington, 10. Sandwell, 12. Handsworth, 13. Aston, 14. Soho, 16. Nechells, 17. Washwood Heath, 19. Ladywood, 21. Small Heath, 22. Edgbaston, 24. Sparkbrook, 28. Moseley, 29. Sparkhill.

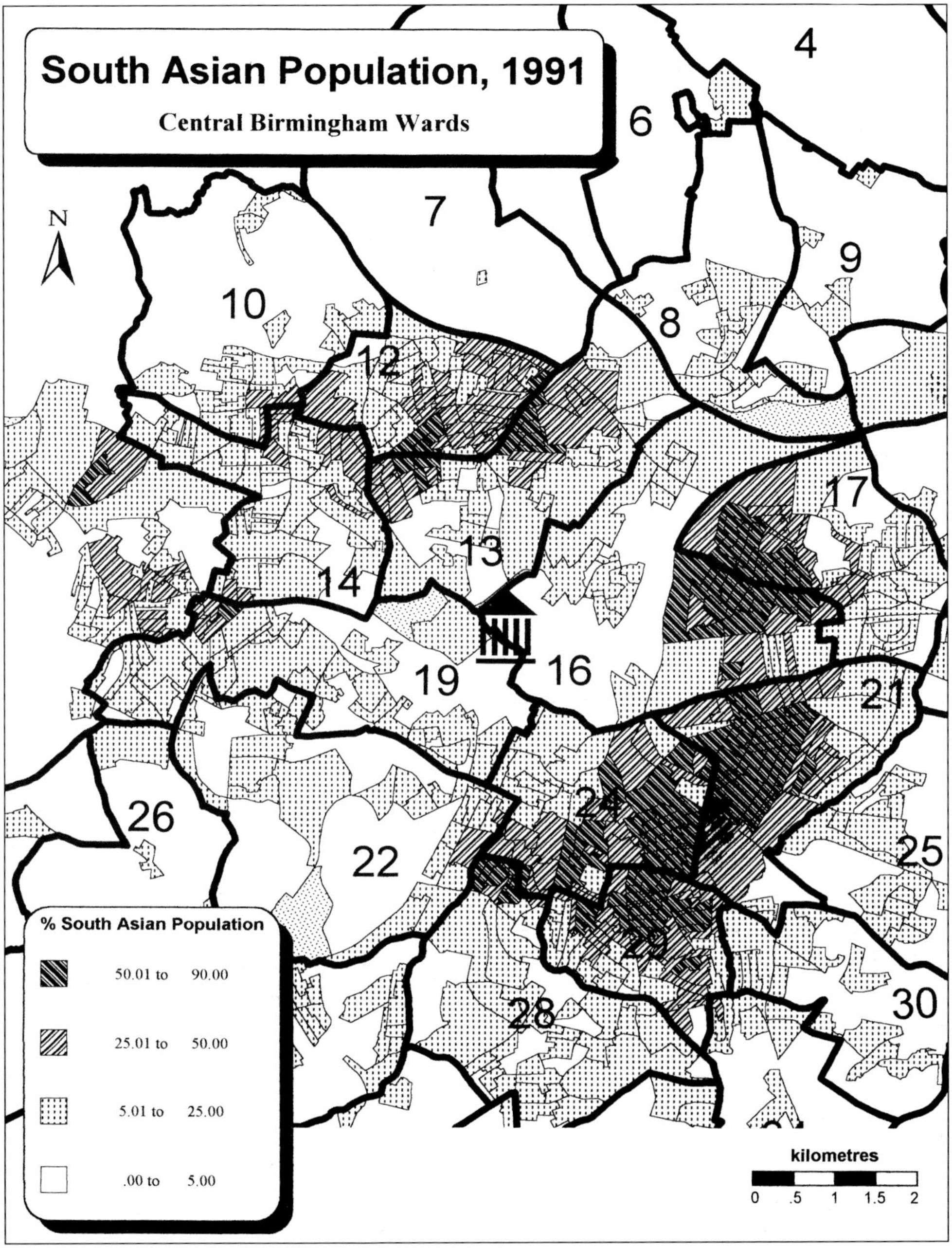

Fig. 11.2 Birmingham's south Asian population, 1991: central wards. (Source: OPCS) wards as Fig 11.1

policies of the city in removing the discriminatory points system of council-house allocation, and to the increasingly negative perceptions of high-rise estates on the part of their first (white) occupants. Their removal to suburban council-house estates, or to private occupancy, left these high-rise estates free for families in housing need from the multi-occupied houses of the middle ring. It is notable that no ED has a 'black' majority population, the highest proportion of 'black' population being a fraction under 45 per cent. Though the concentration of 'black' people to the north west of the city centre in Soho, Aston and Handsworth Wards and, to a lesser extent in Highgate, in Sparkbrook Ward, which has been apparent since the 1961 census data became available, is still present, this concentration is declining and the 'black' population is beginning to follow the Irish in dispersing throughout the city.

The south-Asian population map (Fig. 11.2) combines the Indian, Pakistani and Bangladeshi census categories of the 1991 census. With this group the pattern is very different. The concentrations to the north, east and south east of the city centre mapped by Jones (1976) for 1971 are still very clear and for a significant number of EDs in these areas south Asians are in the majority. For a few areas, that majority rises to the level of nearly 90 per cent. However, it must be noted that the different class intervals on Figure 10.2 emphasise this concentration. When the map is examined more closely it is clear that the south Asian population, too, is beginning to disperse outwards. That dispersion has been especially into the more desireable private housing of adjacent neighbourhoods such as Moseley, Handsworth Wood and Erdington. Here mosques and community shops, cinemas and the like are still accessible, but higher quality, and larger, houses are available for extended families. The most notable difference between the two ethnic groups is the relative absence of south Asians in the inner-ring, local-authority high-rise estates

Fig. 11.3 House Extension, Lordswood Road, Harborne, 1996. Many of the large 1950s' family homes on Lordswood Road have been substantially extended in the 1980-1996 period by south Asian owners moving out from the Summerfield area of north Edgbaston or from Smethwick (photo: Geoff Dowling)

and, even more so, from the suburban local-authority estates such as comprise most of Perry Barr, Oscott and Kingstanding Wards.

The association between south Asians and owner-occupied housing remains very strong in all parts of the city. The trend, noted by Jones as already apparent from the 1960s, for south Asians to become significant landlords of privately-rented housing has also continued to the present. In Selly Oak, Bournbrook and north Edgbaston, for example, where there is a substantial market for private rented accommodation from students, a high proportion of the landlords of these properties are south Asians. South-Asian homes were also strongly represented in the General Improvement Area policies of the city council to improve poor inner-city housing through the 1980s. Birmingham's pioneering 'enveloping' scheme, where the city financed improvements to the roofs, windows, chimneys and boundary walls of entire streets of houses, led to the formation of many resident's associations to improve liason with the officers of the city council, and to the appointment of local caretakers to carry out minor repairs (Joly, 1995: 104-6). The presence of south Asians in the more prosperous middle-ring suburbs is signified in the townscape through new iron paling boundary fences, the conversion of garages into additional rooms, of front gardens into block-paved parking spaces, and sometimes of substantial extensions (upwards as well as outwards) to already large houses (Fig. 11.3).

The most distinctive townscape features of south-Asian areas are, however, the mosques. To non-Muslims only three or four such mosques are readily apparent because of their size and prominent locations. The Central Mosque (Fig. 11.4), with its white dome and minaret, has long

Fig 11.4 The Central Mosque, Highgate (photo Geoff Dowling)

been a feature of the Birmingham street scene, beside the middle ring road in Highgate. It was built in 1975 after a long fund-raising campaign by a number of associations. The Saddam Hussein Mosque in Perry Barr is similarly prominent, but its completion was long delayed when funding from Iraq ceased. Most recently, the mosque built to serve the Muslim community in Small Heath is soon to be completed on a third prominent site beside the Small Heath by-pass. These large mosques are not typical, however. The majority of Birmingham's many scores of mosques occupy converted houses in residential areas. In the 1970s, this was a source of considerable tension since many were converted without planning permission. Once three or four houses had been adapted into a single communal building with attached school (madrasa) several hundred worshippers could have been using it on Eid feast days. Such mosques are numerous because the numerous sects within the home areas of south-Asian Muslims have been reproduced in Birmingham. The theological differences between these sects can sometimes be expressed with considerable antagonism (Joly, 1995: 28-29).

The radial roads which bisect the main south-Asian ethnic community areas act as the principal commercial zones and many of the businesses have been Asian-owned for several decades. Stratford Road through Sparkbrook and Sparkhill (Fig. 11.5), Coventry Road through Small Heath, Alum Rock Road through Tyseley, and Soho Road through Handsworth are examples of this. There are four Pakistani banks operative in these areas so that Muslims can have financial facilities without falling foul of the usury laws of Islam. Sparkhill has become the south-Asian jewellery quarter, mainly dominated by the Gujrati Hindus who also are prominent in the retailing of sarees and clothing on the Stratford Road and the Soho Road. Carpet shops and textiles are also the chosen retail trades of many of the Campblepuris in Sparkhill (Chinn, 1994: 102). The Saltley Kashmiris dominate Birmingham's taxi trade, whilst Sikhs, as well as being prominent in the professions, own a number of firms which utilize their skills as carpenters and

Fig. 11.5 Statford Road, Sparkhill. This major arterial road is an important social and commercial centre for the south Asian community with banks, cinema, jewellers, halal butchers and restaurants (photo: author)

builders. There are more than fifty halal butchers in the city and many sub-post offices, newsagents and small grocery stores in all areas of the city are owned by south-Asian people. However, their most notable contribution to the cultural milieu of Birmingham has been the Kashmiri balti restaurants which now have a national reputation for their cuisine (Chinn,1994: 100-1).

Balsall Heath

The details of the minority ethnic communities of Birmingham can be obscured by general maps of census data. A brief analysis of Balsall Heath is therefore provided to illustrate the complexity of ethnic communities. Balsall Heath is both one of the earliest areas of the city to be affected by the in-migration of 'new Commonwealth' people, and the area with the greatest diversity of ethnicities. Its commercial core is the Moseley Road and it stretches from the Pershore Road in the west to the Ladypool road in the east (Fig. 11.6). The majority of the district is in Sparkbrook Ward, but other parts extend into Edgbaston, Moseley and Sparkhill Wards. The way in which the community is politically divided in this way is itself a topic of some significance since it prevents the black and south-Asian community being the majority in any of the wards. That is of some consequence for the racialized academic debates on ethnic ghettos with which this chapter began but it is of far more consequence for the proper political representation of the concerns of black and south-Asian communities. This has not prevented the election of 21 councillors from the ethnic minority communities to the Labour-dominated administration of the city, however (see Solomos and Back, 1995; Joly, 1995: ch. 5 for further details).

Balsall Heath also has a long-standing function as one of the city's red-light districts. Solomos and Back (1995) show how, as early as the mid-1950s, constructs of 'black men', 'kept women',

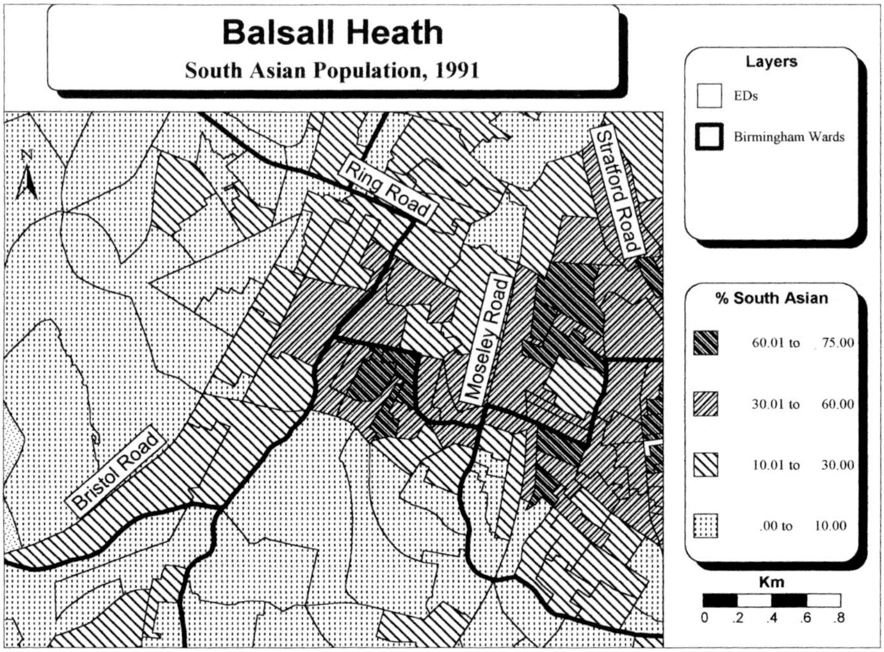

Fig. 11.6 Balsall Heath, south Asian population, 1991 (source: OPCS).

overcrowded lodging houses, 'little India', drug-taking, criminality and the like were racializing the imagery of Balsall Heath in the local newspapers and the minds of the people of the city. That remains true through to the present. Recent high-profile campaigns, led by the imams and elders of local mosques, to rid the streets of prostitutes and drug-takers have simply confirmed the reputation of the district in the eyes of the rest of the city.

The variety of Balsall Heath's ethnic make-up is impossible to convey from the census ethnicity statistics. For example, one of the earliest mosques in the city was that established in Edward Road by the small Yemini community in 1951 (Chinn,1994: 99). The first migrants from this group had come to the city from the British colony in Aden setting off a classic process of chain migration so that the community is now some 2000 strong, but they are invisible in the census. Also invisible are the second and third generations of those of Irish, Italian, Cypriot, Polish, Hungarian, Serbian and Jewish descent whose parents or grandparents migrated to the city in the 1930s and 1950s, settled in Balsall Heath, but then moved on leaving only some of their religious institutions or commercial premises to signify their former presence.

Today, however, it is south Asians who are the dominant ethnic group. Over much of the district they constitute from 30-60 per cent of the population and in two areas up to 75 per cent of the population are south Asian (Fig. 11.6). Since one of those areas is the block of streets which backs on to the Edgbaston County Cricket Ground and which coincides with the perceived red-light district, the involvement of the community in trying to remove this nuisance is readily understood. The area between the Bristol Road and the Edgbaston Ward boundary (the River Rea), is a good example of the upward mobility of more prosperous Asian families. Much of this area is made up of larger inter-war houses or estates of modern four-bedroom houses built speculatively for owner-occupation. Since they are close to the commercial and religious facilities of Balsall Heath, some 20-30 per cent of the population in this area is now south Asian.

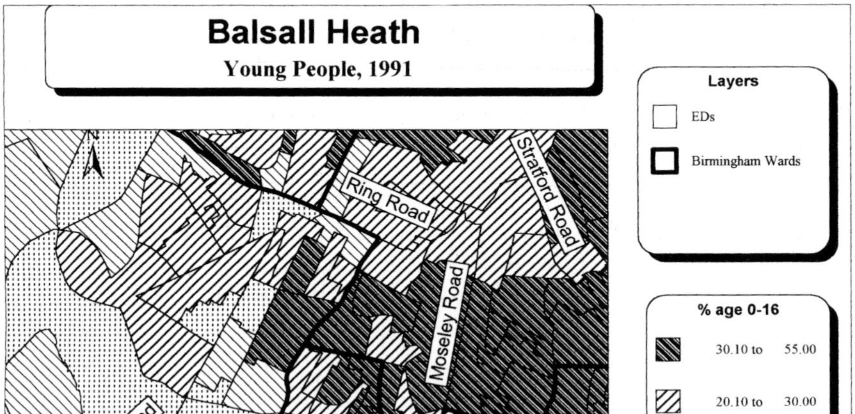

Fig. 11.7 Balsall Heath, percentage of people under 16, 1991 (Source: OPCS).

The 'black' population is concentrated in the northern part of Balsall Heath where they constituted between 15-30 per cent of the population in 1991. Beyond the middle ring road, in Highgate, the proportion increases to up to 45 per cent.

The extreme youth of this population is well shown by the 1991 census (Fig. 11.7). For most of the EDs in the core of Balsall Heath between the Pershore Road and the Stratford Road between 30 and 55 per cent of the population was under 16 (see chapter 10). Such proportions mean that one of the key concerns of the ethnic population of these areas is the quality of schooling provided for these young people. It has consequently seen the provision of new-built junior schools and the refurbishment of older schools to cope with the large number of children in this and similar areas (Slater, 1996). It also provides a source of political conflict between the Muslim community and the city council concerning topics such as the provision of halal food for Muslim children, the separate education of girls from boys, and the provision of religious education (Joly, 1995: 101-4).

The other key dimension of this area is that it suffers from multiple deprivation. In the northern parts of the district between 75-95 per cent of households have no car, 10-20 per cent of households are single parents, whilst no part of the area suffers from less than 20 per cent unemployment (Fig. 11.8). In more than a third of EDs unemployment varies between 30-60 per cent of the work force. The southern part of Balsall Heath has the additional problem of a high proportion of homes in multiple occupation and therefore lacking basic household amenities. The Low Income Predictor score devised by the Applied Social Studies Department at Oxford as a measure of multiple deprivation shows Balsall Heath with a score of 35.4 placing it amongst the 15 per cent most deprived areas in the country (Diocese of Birmingham, 1996). This is a characteristic of all the major concentrations of black and south Asian populations in Birmingham. In the 1960s, physical deprivation was not matched by economic deprivation as it

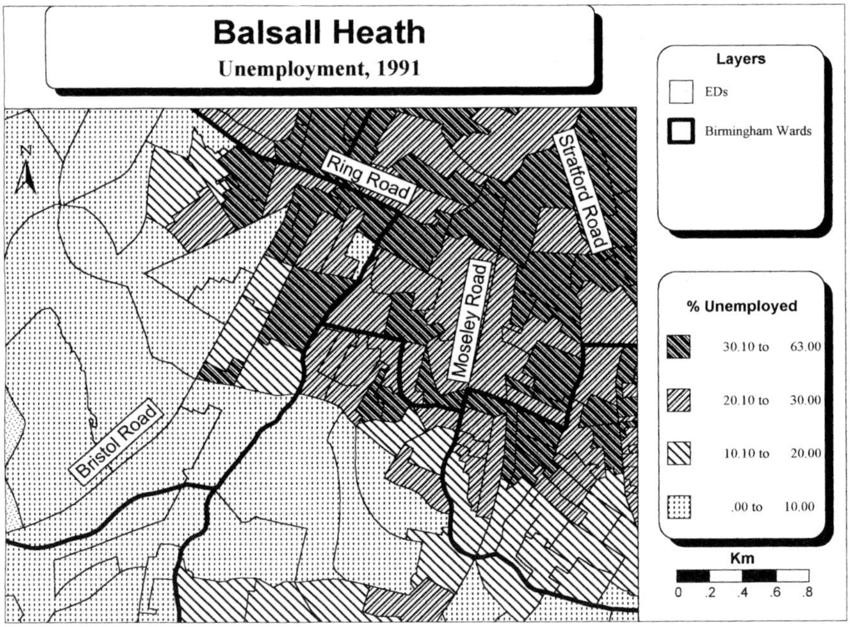

Fig. 11.8 Balsall Heath, percentage of working population unemployed, 1991 (Source: OPCS).

has been since the dramatic changes in Birmingham's economy and prosperity from the 1970s onwards.

Conclusion

The geography of black and south-Asian residence has been remarkably stable over the past forty years. The initial zones of residence, first discerned from the 1961 census data and largely determined by the patterns of housing age and tenure in the city, are still readily apparent in the townscape of today. Whereas the Irish community, which was almost equally concentrated in the 1960s, have now dispersed throughout the city, that process of dispersion is only now gathering force in the black and south-Asian communities. In part there are structural reasons for this as we have seen: the access to council housing only from the mid-1970s; in part there are cultural reasons: the desire for house ownership on the part of south-Asian households; and in part there are economic reasons: the concentration of multiple deprivation in the inner-city ethnic areas preventing movement. All of this is set within the context of global structures of economic change and Britain's slow adaptation to a post-colonial world since 1945. That colonial past was a clear determinant of 'new Commonwealth' immigration in the 1950s and 1960s and it was the economic prosperity of Birmingham's car assembly industries and their associated suppliers (see chapter 12) which brought those immigrants to the West Midlands. Today, as Birmingham attempts to transform itself into a post-Fordist and service-based economy, high unemployment, multiple deprivation, low skills and poor education records are concentrated in those areas where the black and south-Asian communities are trapped by the circumstances of their lives. Those communities are no longer largely communities of 'immigrants' but are communities of Black British and Asian British people, a high proportion of whom are under 25. Many play valued parts in the life of the city through their political, administrative, professional, cultural, practical, or sporting skills (Chinn, 1994). But others are dissolusioned or despairing of the lack of opportunities they perceive, the racism they meet in their lives and the poverty that is their lot.

Acknowledgements

Thanks are due to Nick Henry for comments on a draft of this chapter and its initial inspiration; David Ingram for assistance in providing the figures on which table 11.1 is based; Adrian Passmore for relevant reading material. The maps are based on OPCS data provided with the support of ESRC and JISC and use boundary material which is copyright of the Crown and the Post Office. They should not be reproduced without the permission of the copyright holders.

References

Birmingham City Council 1965 *Birmingham Corporation Housing Act*

Birmingham City Council 1991 *Birmingham city trends* Birmingham City Council, Birmingham

Birmingham City Council 1991 *Ward profiles* Birmingham City Council, Birmingham

Chinn C 1994 *Birmingham the Great Working City* Birmingham City Council, Birmingham

Diocese of Birmingham 1996 *Together in ministry and mission* Diocese of Birmingham, Birmingham

Glass R 1960 *Newcomers, the West Indians in London*

Hodgins H 1985 *Ethnic minorities in Birmingham: population statistics* Birmingham Community Relations Council, Birmingham

Joby D 1995 *Britannia's Crecent: making a place for Muslims in British Society* Avebury, Aldershot

Jones P N 1967 The segregation of immigrant communities in the city of Birmingham, 1961 *University of Hull Occasional Papers in Geography 7*

Jones P N 1970 Some aspects of the changing distribution of coloured immigrants in Birmingham, 1961-66 *Transactions of the Institute of British Geographers* 50 199-220

Jones P N 1976 Coloured minorities in Birmingham, England *Annals of the Association of American Geographers* 66.1 89-103

O P C S (Office of Population Censuses and Surveys) *1993 Ethnic groups and country of birth, Great Britain* HMSO, London

Peach G C K 1968 *West Indian migration in Britain, a social geography* Oxford University Press, London

Peach G C K 1996 Does Britain have ghettos? *Transactions of the Institute of British Geographers* NS21.1 216-35

Rex J and Moore R 1967 *Race, community and conflict, a study of Sparkbrook* Oxford University Press, London

Rosing K E and Wood P A 1971 *Character of a Conurbation: a computer atlas of Birmingham and the Black Country* University of London Press, London

Slater, T R 1996 A cluster profile: St Anne's, St Paul's, SS Mary & Ambrose, Balsall Heath *Diocese of Birmingham GIS Working Paper 2*

Solomos J and Back L 1995 *Race, politics and social change* Routledge, London

The Times 1965 *The dark million: a series of ten articles*

CHAPTER 12

From Widgets to Where?: The Birmingham Economy in the 1990s

J R Bryson, P W Daniels and N D Henry

In 1950, the British Association volume was optimistic in its examination of the future of the Birmingham economy suggesting that:

> 'the industries of the district rest secure...upon that facility for work in metal which the local folk have inherited from their forefathers...(and) which the rest of the world demands.' (Walker and Glaisyer, 1950, p.259)

Moreover:

> 'The latest stage in the growth of Birmingham has been a time of industrial progress and prosperity in, particularly, the motor car and allied trades...A particularly important example (of the modern industrial pattern being) the motor tyre and rubber factory at Fort Dunlop.' (Wise and O'N. Thorpe, p.226-27)

In contrast, today, the disused and dilapidated Fort Dunlop, clearly visible from the M6, stands as a testament to the hard times which Birmingham fell upon in the intervening years and the legacy from which the city is still struggling to recover. Fort Dunlop also stands for the process of economic restructuring experienced by the economy as the building is converted into a new research and development centre for Jaguar cars.

This chapter describes how, in 1950, Birmingham and the West Midlands was about to enter an era of sustained growth and prosperity - the 'post-war boom'- which was centred on the core industries of motor vehicles, metal goods and electrical engineering. It was this economic growth which the writers of 1950 foresaw. However, what was not seen was the intense period of deindustrialization which the region, the nation and, more widely, the advanced economies of the West, were to experience. Following a discussion of the years of both boom and subsequent decline, the chapter asks the question 'where is the West Midland region now?'.

In these times of competing characterisations of the future economy as, for example, 'post-Fordist', 'service-dominated' and 'part of the global economy', to answer this question is by no means easy. In essence, Birmingham and its wider region is seeking to distinguish its function in today's economy. Yet for our predecessors of 1950 the issue of the region's function was similarly critical in understanding its future possibilities. In 1950, Wise and O'N. Thorpe wrote:

> 'Birmingham today exercises three functions. The city is, firstly, a major industrial centre; secondly, the commercial capital of the Birmingham-Black Country Conurbation. Birmingham provides, thirdly, a growing range of services for a large and widening region.' (op.cit., p.228)

In 1996, the notion of an industrial centre is under scrutiny whilst Birmingham similarly appraises its role as a service provider and commercial capital for a 'large and widening region' which may extend across, and lead to competition with other cities around, the world.

From Fordism to de-industrialization: The heyday of Fordism

While 1966 is etched in to the country's historical consciousness due to exploits with a football in the World Cup, it is significant also as the high-point of manufacturing employment in the United Kingdom and the high point of the post-war economic boom. This was the period when the term 'consumer durables' came to the fore: an era of 'white goods', growing car ownership and Macmillan's famous dictum 'you've never had it so good'. In the language of economic geographers, it was the heyday of Fordism in the UK.

When using this term, what is implied is the characterisation of a distinct period of capitalist production. Its distinguishing features included the widespread 'mass production' of price-competitive, standardised goods through the use of assembly lines and the ability for the first time for the population to buy such goods. In other words, the widespread ability to take part in 'mass consumption' with the balance of this system managed, at least in principle, through government-led Keynesian demand management.

The relationship of Fordism to the West Midlands region was critical yet, basically, simple. For the heyday of Fordism in the UK was, also, this region's industrial heyday. Essentially, a high proportion of the 'core' industries of Fordist growth, for example, electrical and light engineering and the motor industry, were concentrated in the region. Just as previous periods of capitalism had been characterised by a geography of primate economic regions - most famously, Lancashire and the Industrial Revolution - so the West Midlands along with Greater London were core regions in the geography of Fordism. The region's subsequent decline, in line with the decline of Fordism and its associated processes of restructuring and de-industrialisation, was similarly part and parcel of a renewed period of capitalist transition accompanied by a geographical shift of capitalist manufacturing towards new economic regions, both within the country and across the world.

The foundations for the post-war boom had been built up over several decades and have been traced back by Allen (1929) to the post 1870s. It was during this period, especially within the traditional gun and military arms industries, that the process of replacement of a 'large number of small masters employing a few workmen' (Wise and O'N. Thorpe, 1950, p.222) by the factory system accelerated. Moreover, as the West Midlands' economy restructured and adapted at the turn of the century it found itself with a new set of industries: cycle production, electrical apparatus and motor cars inclusive of the emergent practises of manufacture including automation and standardized factory production (Spencer et al. 1986, p.6). The advent of World War I and its particular industrial demands reinforced the move towards standardized factory production and this trend continued throughout the following years of economic fluctuation, alongside the growth of light and medium engineering industries. Indeed, some commentators suggested how such a trend, so critical to the forthcoming Fordist boom, was disguised by the inter-war recession and World War II, leading Wood (1976) to write that 'this is the special problem with analysing the manufacturing base of the West Midlands, for its tradition of continuous and subtle adjustment hides the true nature of its economic life'(p.37). Its 'true nature', however, became clearer as Britain entered the post-World War II phase, with the West Midlands poised to become a powerhouse region of the Fordist boom, a boom already apparent in the US but thus far stifled in its progress across the advanced Western economies.

After the Second World War, the West Midlands enjoyed a period of growth and prosperity as a consequence of exports to European markets whose domestic capacity had been destroyed during the war. As European producers recovered during the 1950s the loss of this market was compensated for by the expansion of the home market. During this period the region was the industrial heartland of the United Kingdom, and 'the industrial region par excellence' (Wood, 1976). The West Midlands was the centre of the United Kingdom's car industry (see Chapter 13) at a time when Britain made more cars than any other country in the world except the United States (Waymark, 1983). Indeed, the West Midlands conurbation alone accounted for over 8 per cent of UK manufacturing net output (Fig 12.1) (Keeble, 1976, Table 2.1). Such was the vitality of the West Midlands that in 1955 it accounted for 13.1 per cent of total research and development professionals in private industrial establishments (DSIR, 1958).

Between 1951 and 1961, the region's employment increased by 14 per cent compared to a national average of 8.5 per cent (Wood, 1976, p.43). This decade of employment growth in the West Midlands led Wood (1976) to describe it as the region's own 'economic miracle'. The backbone of this growth was provided by five manufacturing sectors: vehicles, metal goods, metal manufacture, mechanical engineering and electrical engineering. In 1961, just under 65 per cent of the labour force was employed in manufacturing compared to 39 per cent for the United Kingdom. Throughout the period between 1961 and 1981, these five sectors accounted for 80 per cent of manufacturing employment (Spencer et al. 1986). Indeed, between 1961-1993, the West Midlands consistently had a higher proportion of its total employment in manufacturing than the national economy. This was not difficult to achieve when between 1961 and 1971, for example, mechanical and electrical engineering both increased employment by over 22 per cent, closely followed by motor vehicles and metal goods with employment growth rates at just under 20 per cent and, finally, metal manufacture which posted employment growth of 12 per cent. This represented 120,000 additional jobs in these five sectors alone over the decade of the 'economic miracle'. Thus, driven by these five key sectors and combined with associated growth in service industries, the region was to gain 361,000 jobs between 1951-1966. The region was certainly at the heart of the Fordist boom.

In addition to significant employment gain, the Fordist boom created a distinctive industrial structure within the region. As Spencer et al. (1986) and Wood (1976) have highlighted, the metal industry complex of the West Midlands was slowly and methodically transformed from its historical character of a localised economy encompassing many independent, but interdependent, firms horizontally integrated across a range of industries. As Fordist production took hold, so its wider organisational characteristics emerged to leave their imprint on the region. In particular:

> *"(a) ownership was diffused as family firms were replaced by limited companies with a large number of shareholders - managers took over control of firm policy from individualist entrepreneurs;*
>
> *(b) ownership and control were delocalised by mergers which drew local firms into national and international combines- 'one effect of these mergers was to diminish the economic independence of Birmingham industry. Many decisions affecting the city's factories came to be taken elsewhere...' (Sutcliffe and Smith 1974, p.166);*

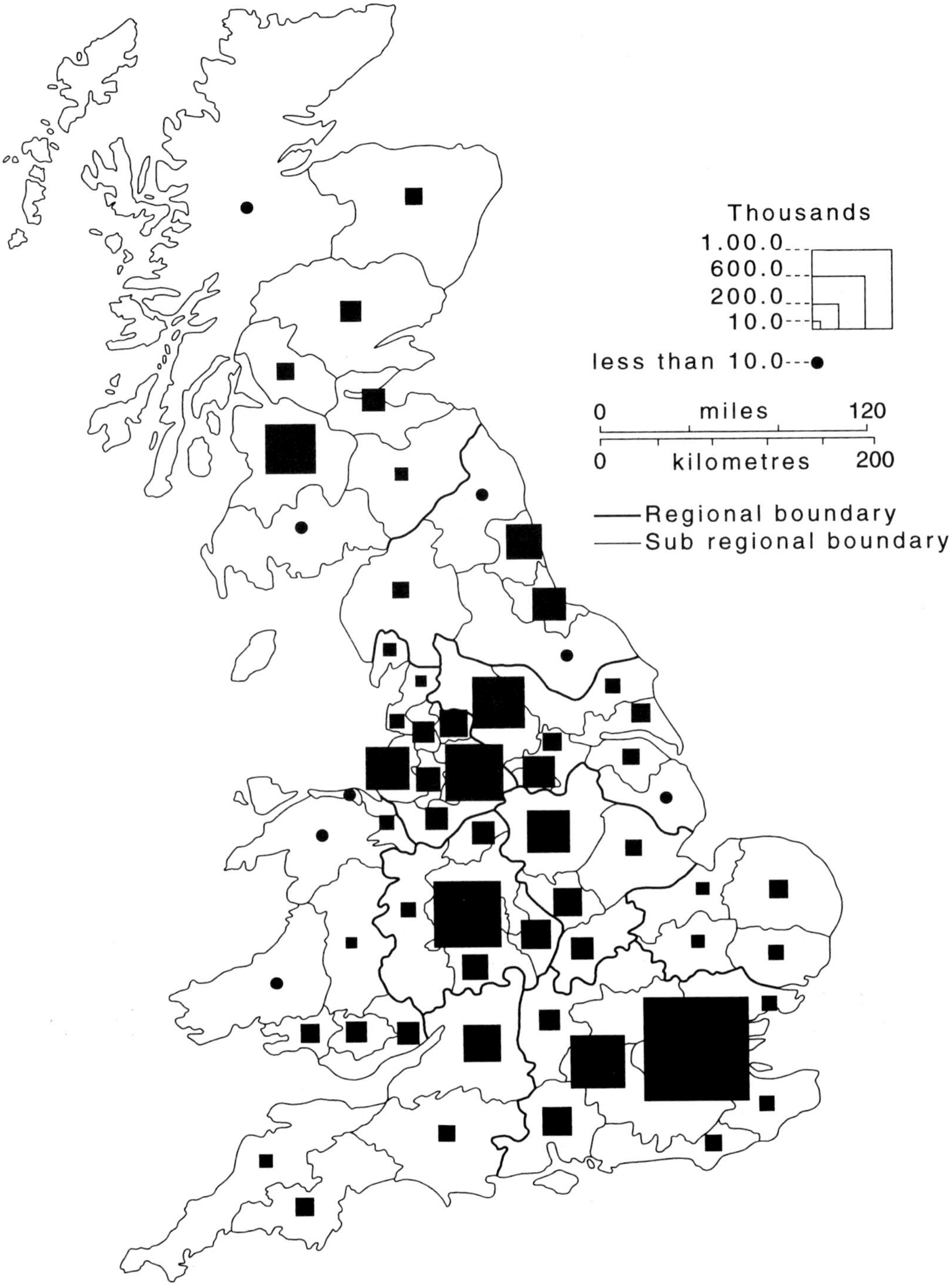

Fig. 12.1 Sub-regional manufacturing employment in the United Kingdom, 1959. Source: adapted from Keeble, 1976.

(c) the scale of production increased and became a nationally (and internationally) and not just locally integrated process;

(d) the larger firms were increasingly vertically integrated, or self-contained, with more of their production and marketing being carried out within the same company (Allen, 1929, p.331; Briggs 1952, p.287)."

(Spencer et al. 1986, p.16-17).

Yet the Fordist boom was to end. In hindsight, the growth rate of 1961-1966 was seen to have failed to match that which could have been expected considering the region's industrial structure (Wood, 1976, p.58). As Fordism faltered across the advanced Western economies so, too, did the regional bases of this production era, including the West Midlands.

De-industrialization and the crisis of Fordism

The crisis of Fordism emerged in the early 1970s, throwing into reverse the post-war industrial boom. This crisis was caused by the combination of a series of economic pressures including the inflexibility of Fordist industrial production, the high cost of production in the heavily-unionised advanced economies and increasing overseas competition. At an international scale, industrial production was reorganised away from high-cost to low-cost locations and a new spatial division of labour evolved. One of the most pronounced consequences of this crisis was the decline in the industrial manufacturing base of the advanced economies. This decline was most evident in former core industrial zones like the West Midlands. De-industrialization affected all areas of the region's economy as spiralling multiplier effects undermined the client base of small subcontracting firms, and rising long-term unemployment and industrial dereliction discouraged new inward investment.

	West Midlands						UK	
Year	Metal Goods, engin-ering & vehicles	Metal manufac-turing & chemicals	Distri-bution, hotels & catering; repairs	Banking, finance, insurance & business services	Manu-facturing West Midlands	Services West Midlands	Manu-facturing	Services
1971	696	189	315	87	1,107	908	7,890	11,388
1975	634	180	339	98	1,025	1,001	7,351	12,545
1980	580	155	368	120	933	1,087	6,801	13,384
1985	407	116	368	152	693	1,118	5,254	13,769
1990	381	103	425	196	680	1,286	4,994	15,609
1993	314	83	405	204	558	1,291	4,269	15,327
Change 1971-1993	-382	-106	+90	+117	-549	+383	-3621	+3939

Source: Department of Employment (1994) *Employment Gazette : Historical Supplement*, London

Table 12.1 Employment in manufacturing and service activities in the West Midlands and the United Kingdom, 1971-1993 (000)

Between 1971 and 1993, just over half a million manufacturing jobs were lost in the region (Table 12.1), a decline of 50 per cent in total manufacturing employment (WMCC, 1978). During the same period, manufacturing employment in the United Kingdom declined by 45 per cent. The post-1979 recession (1979-1982) had a particularly severe impact on the West Midlands' economy with a loss of 26 per cent of its manufacturing jobs (Fig 12.2). This recession accentuated the long-standing North-South disparity in the United Kingdom, and Damesick (1987) suggests that 'the 'North' now moved south to embrace the West Midlands'. The loss of manufacturing employment in the West Midlands had consequences also for employment in those service sectors which depended on manufacturing firms for their business. During the mid 1980s the economy of the West Midlands shifted from being one of the most prosperous regions in the United Kingdom to being one of the most depressed "peripheral" regions.

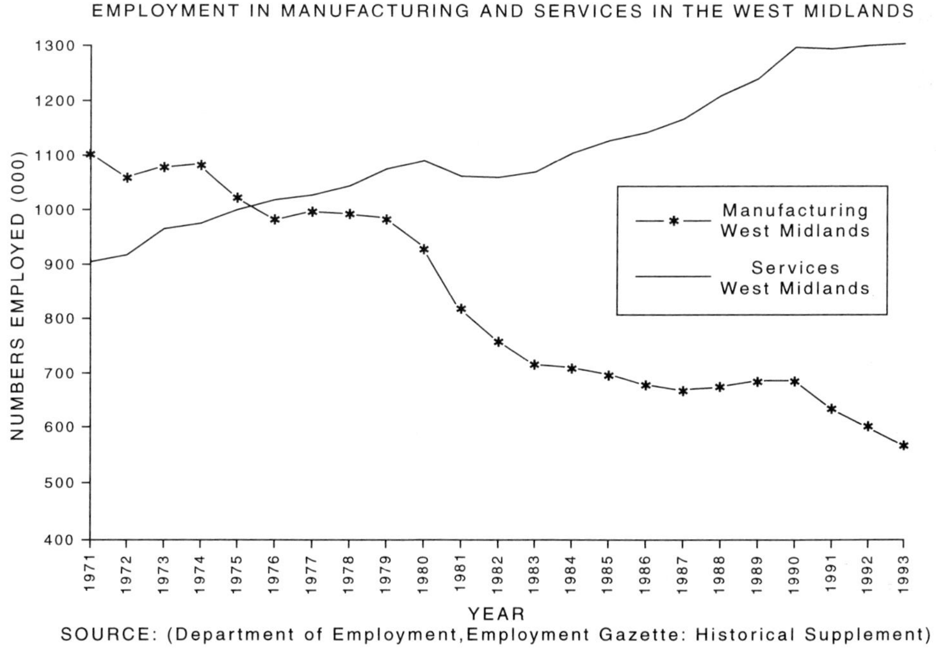

Fig. 12.2 Employment in manufacturing and service activities in the West Midlands, 1971-1993. Source: Department of Employment (1994), Employment Gazette, Historical Supplement, vol 102, 10.

The post-war prosperity of the West Midlands depended on a few key successful metal manufacturing and engineering industries, but this strength became a fundamental structural weakness in the local economy. During the post-war boom companies expanded through the acquisition of competitors and many West Midlands' companies became part of national and international industrial conglomerates. In 1952, the two largest car firms, Morris and Austin, combined to form the British Motor Corporation (BMC), and in 1969, BMC merged with Leyland to form British Leyland. At the same time these larger companies absorbed smaller ones. Cadbury's acquired a number of small companies before being taken over by Schweppes in 1969. By 1973, the region had a much higher proportion of medium to large firms than the national average (Wood, 1976). By 1977, twenty-five companies accounted for approximately 48 per cent of manufacturing employment in the region (Spencer et al. 1986). Employment was also concentrated in a small number of large plants.

One effect of these mergers was to diminish the economic independence of a high proportion of West Midlands' companies. Decisions affecting the region's economy were increasingly being taken outside the region (Sutcliffe and Smith, 1974). It is important to remember, as illustrated in the emerging organisational characteristics of firms in the region referred to earlier in this chapter, that many of these large conglomerates were operating in declining, mature industrial sectors. When overseas competition and cheap imports undermined the profitability of any one of these companies, closure or employment rationalization had a dramatic impact on the local economy.

The concentration of capital and control that occurred had important implications also for specialist component suppliers who became increasingly dependent on orders from a small group of companies. The West Midlands' car companies were predominantly assemblers of components produced by sub-contractors (see chapter 13). Generally between 60 and 70 per cent of the value of components in the car industry came from outside suppliers (Wood, 1976). The suppliers of most of the components for the Austin plant at Longbridge were clustered in a ten-mile radius around the plant (Sutcliffe and Smith, 1974). In 1976, Wood estimated that the proportion of West Midlands' output and employment that depended on the car industry was approaching 30 per cent. The increasing dependence of suppliers on the performance of a limited number of large companies was a structural weakness in the West Midlands economy. Increasing competition from overseas producers led to the collapse of many of these inter-firm linkages as major firms were forced to renegotiate conditions of trade and product quality with local suppliers. Competition, combined with the increasing external control of West Midlands' companies, led to the replacement of local subcontractors by non-local and even overseas suppliers.

As early as 1965 the West Midlands Economic Planning Council warned that:

> 'national and world demand . . . may well continue to rise but whether this is reflected in the order books of the West Midlands will depend increasingly on the extent to which the region's firms keep up in research mindedness, invention, innovation and production and marketing efficiency' (Department of Economic Affairs, 1965, cited in Spencer et al. 1986).

From 1965 to 1981, however, investment in manufacturing in the region was consistently below the national average (Spencer et al. 1986). Consequently, during the 1970s, the West Midlands' industrial plant became gradually obsolete, and the region's manufacturing companies found it increasingly difficult to compete with technologically-advanced manufacturing companies located in low-cost production regions.

The downturn in organisational performance forced a number of West Midlands' firms to introduce major changes in their management personnel, culture and policies. Cadbury's share of the total chocolate market fell from 31.1 per cent to 26.2 per cent between 1975 and 1977, with significant decline in products targeted at the same market segment as Mars and Rowntree-Mackintosh (Child and Smith, 1990). Intensification of competition in this sector increased the secrecy between competing chocolate manufacturers in the United Kingdom and Cadburys now had to rely on the recruitment of staff from competitors and technology transfer and knowledge from equipment suppliers. These transformations in the confectionery sector forced Cadburys to alter its operational practices. Manufacturing personnel was reduced from 8,565 in 1978 to 4,508 in 1985 and, at the same time, the product range was reduced from 60 items down to 32 (Smith et al. 1991). These alterations led to an overall productivity gain of 75 per cent between 1978 and 1985. The key labour elements in this transformation were a shift to short-term profitability, labour elimination as a proclaimed objective, continuous shiftwork, and an attack on traditional rigidities in labour deployment (Smith et al. 1990). Thus one response to the crisis facing Fordist manufacturers was to improve productivity by the rationalization of working practices.

The industrial decline of the West Midlands left a legacy of industrial dereliction, empty obsolete factory units, and high long-term unemployment. By the early 1980s many of the large West Midlands companies had closed down, or severely rationalized their production. For example, Guest, Keen and Nettlefolds (GKN) in the early 1970s had a workforce of around 17,000, but by 1980 this had fallen to 5000 (Spencer et al. 1986). To Spencer et al. (1986) the industrial heartland of the UK economy had become an industrial wasteland. The future economic prosperity of the West Midlands was not to be in large-scale manufacturing employment, alternative sources of employment would have to be identified.

The story of deindustrialization as part of the crisis of Fordism has been identified with the shift to 'flexible production methods', and the development of flexible labour markets. These changes are identified with the emergence of post-Fordism as a distinct period of capitalist production. Job demarcation in the factory is replaced with functional flexibility or multi-skilling; full-time permanent employees are replaced with temporary, part-time or casual employees, subcontraction replaces vertically-integrated companies, and flexible technology or customized production transforms the rigidity of the assembly lines of the Fordist factory (Amin, 1994; Harvey, 1988). These transformations in the production process lead to the development of lean corporations which concentrate on core activities and are surrounded by a web of formal and informal supplier relationships. Economies of scale are replaced with 'economies of scope', that is the use by large companies of flexible manufacturing technologies to produce for several relatively small or segmented markets (Kumar, 1995). Related to these changes is a revival in the growth of new small and medium-sized enterprises (University of Cambridge, 1992; Bryson et al. 1996).

The shift of employment from the internal labour market of the corporation to the external labour market initially resulted in a transfer of service activities to independent service suppliers. Thus, the economy of post-Fordism is one of a decline in manufacturing employment and a growth in service employment (Fig. 12.2). Transformed service industries are primarily the key to future employment opportunities. This does not mean that fewer manufactured commodities are produced, but that the way in which they are produced has altered and led to an improvement in productivity levels. The replacement of manufacturing employment with service employment does not produce a stable employment structure as many service jobs are low-paid and part-time. Greater social polarization in society develops between low-paid, insecure employees and those in well-paid, relatively permanent, employment.

The geography of post-Fordism is one of restructuring, rationalization and the development of new industrial spaces and innovative regions (Kumar, 1995). The future economic prosperity of the West Midlands as it emerged from the crisis of Fordism, thus, depended on rapid industrial restructuring as the region and its companies responded to the new post-Fordist regime. The key question which has to be addressed is how successful has the West Midlands been in this process of restructuring ?

Where is the Birmingham region now?

The demise of Fordism and the advent of post-Fordism is part of a restructuring process that has seen the decline of manufacturing and the rise of service industries. This has exposed the region, and Birmingham in particular, to even more diverse and intensive national and international competition. In all, the region lost an aggregate of 300,000 jobs between 1979 and 1992; a fact that disguises the disappearance of 430,000 jobs in manufacturing alone because of the creation of employment in the service sector (European Commission, 1994). Moreover, even though its economy expanded, output across the city lagged behind the national average in the manufacturing sector - the local economy's key wealth creator - at some 15 per cent lower than the UK. Investment in the city was also about 10 per cent below the national average (Birmingham Economic Information Centre, 1994).

Nevertheless, the Birmingham Economic Information Centre (1994) takes the view that Birmingham's overall economic prospects very much depend on the lead taken by motor-vehicle production, mechanical engineering, metal goods production and electronic engineering. These are the activities most likely to underpin the growth of the service sector, especially transport services, communications and business/financial services. This, in part, results from the strong links between the city's manufacturing and business/financial services. This might also be expected to underpin continuing development of Birmingham as a regional service centre with some prospect, although probably constrained by proximity, of receiving activities decentralized from London. Recent examples include the headquarters of the Trustee Savings Bank or the imminent relocation of the regional headquarters of British Telecom (Fig 12.3). Service industries in their own right, such as Mercury and Birmingham Cable, could also be vital engines of locally-based growth as new national and international multi-media markets develop. In any event, most new service jobs are likely to be in the public sector, in public-sector supported services such as education and training (the city has three universities as well as a number of further education colleges) and in services-related activities such as government agencies (such as OFWAT). There are therefore a number of separate poles of wealth creation and employment growth from which the city and region can benefit.

Ultimate success will, in part, also depend on how well Birmingham positions itself relative to external influences on its economic restructuring. This is well recognised in a recent report on the West Midlands labour market (Government Office West Midlands, 1995) which refers to the growth of international trade, the elimination of trade barriers (the European Single Market, GATT), the growth of multinational enterprises and the continuing advances in technology as both an opportunity and a threat. Even if Birmingham is right to promote manufacturing firms as the key to its future prosperity they will need to develop new, innovative products and markets as well as to update and improve existing products and processes that can compete in international markets. However, the numerous small and medium-sized enterprises in Birmingham, some of which are long-established, family-owned business while others such as textile and clothing firms have been developed by the south- Asian community during the 1970s and 1980s, tend to lag behind their competitors in, for example, new product development (Birmingham Economic Information Centre, 1994). Indeed, one recent and authoritative report (Price Waterhouse, 1995) indicates a deterioration in innovation activity among West Midlands firms with 43 per cent of the respondents (1,066) reporting no new product innovations. It is also noted that over a five-year period since 1990 there is little evidence of improvement in innovation activity. This fact is worrying because an ability to process and interpret knowledge and

Fig. 12.3 The new regional Headquarters of BT is under construction in Brindleyplace. Source: Argent Group PLC.

information is vital to the innovation activity of Birmingham firms, together with the availability of workers with the appropriate skills. These will be the key to success.

There are also indications that the skill gap (the discrepancy between the skills that employers need and those that the labour force are able to offer) is wider in Birmingham (and the West Midlands Region in general) that in many other parts of the UK (Government Office West Midlands, 1995). Employers in Birmingham have found it difficult to recruit employees with good personal and management skills who are comfortable with information technology. This can lead to the "drawing down" of workers with higher-level skills, such as graduates, to undertake tasks at a lower level. This results in an under-utilised labour force which is probably associated with less competitive, less flexible businesses. The occupational vacancies that are hardest to fill in the West Midlands (and by implication, Birmingham) are those that have an important contribution to make to its innovative capacity, namely managers and administrators, professional and technical occupations and those occupations based on craft skills.

One way to compensate for these serious structural problems that are confronting manufacturing is to diversify the city's economic base. This is a key part of the regeneration strategy for the city in the 1990s with projects such as the expansion of the National Exhibition Centre, the development of business tourism and the construction of the International Convention Centre leading the way (see chapter 14). The European Union (EU) has stimulated this approach: Birmingham has Objective 2 status which has enabled a wide range of schemes to be undertaken involving both physical and human resources. The aim of such EU initiatives, which have been in place since 1988, is to bring together public, private and voluntary sectors to achieve an increased level of investment in economic activities, a diversification and strengthening of the economy and the creation of conditions for regeneration of the region (training, education, research and development, business support, environmental and infrastructure improvements). The EU made a contribution of £50 million towards the cost of the International Convention Centre, making it the largest EU-supported project in England. Further European Regional Development Fund (ERDF) assistance has gone into the development of Paradise Forum and the Arcadian shopping, office and leisure scheme. EU funding has been used in the building of further halls at the National Exhibition Centre, where an estimated 1,600 jobs have been created (but see chapter 14), and where visitors and exhibitors enhance the local economy. Birmingham is now one of the top five fair and exhibition cities in Europe where it must compete with more than 350 fair-hosting cities that generate more than 60 million visitor trips annually (Cuadrado-Roura and Rubalcaba-Bermejo, 1995). As it strives to diversify its economic base it has also been important for Birmingham to consolidate its function as a regional banking and financial centre; most of the leading banks have regional offices in the city-centre financial district along with branch offices of some of the country's leading management consultants, legal firms and engineering consultants.

The economic recession in the early 1990s has not helped Birmingham's future prospects. It has lowered the demand for manufacturing output and redundancies have largely reflected efforts by companies to stay in business with leaner workforces. Since 1992, the Birmingham economy has bounced along the lower reaches of the recessionary cycle with some signs of improved use of the output capacity (improved take-up of vacant office and manufacturing floorspace, for example) only since late 1993. This largely reflects the performance of service firms which generally lag behind the economic cycle, but are certainly the most likely to be optimistic about the future (Price Waterhouse, 1995). This being the case, longer term prospects depend upon diversification of the economic base of the city, thus stimulating the requirement for tourism and leisure-related services such as hotels and transport or personal services, as well as manufacturing continuing to increase its output and thereby raising the demand for business and other producer services (Birmingham Economic Information Centre, 1995). But there may be a price to pay in so far as the jobs created will be more precarious, part-time, contract-based and in relatively low-paid work. In recent years there has been a trend towards temporary rather than permanent posts and according to BEIC's vacancy database, for example, some 16 per cent of the job vacancies in the city in 1993 were for temporary posts (Birmingham Economic Information Centre, 1994). Many of these (almost 50 per cent) are for fixed-term contracts with professional staff and clerical workers particularly affected. Such restructuring of the labour market is of course very much in line with the more flexible models of production being adopted by firms in Birmingham (and elsewhere).

As the twenty-first century beckons, Birmingham is far from being a post-industrial city founded on a strong and diverse service economy with a relatively small, but high value-added, manufacturing sector. The "widgets" that were the basis of its economic prosperity and competitiveness in the early years of this century still exert a major influence on its future, perhaps more so than might have been expected. The recent decision by Jaguar (via its American owner, Ford) to make a major investment in new plant (including research and development) in the city has perhaps reinforced the belief that its long manufacturing tradition should be nurtured rather than allowed to wither away in the manner typical of many other cities of similar size (Birmingham City Council, 1995). It remains crucial, however, for manufacturing industry to invest in the technology that will keep its products competitive and to remain innovative. This may be achieved through partnership with, for example, the three universities in the city or involvement in the Technology Foresight Programme developed by the government's Office of Science and Technology. This approach has become integral to the city's unsuccessful attempts to devise a suitable proposal for funding from the Millenium Programme and is also an important element in the City Pride initiative that has brought together private, public and voluntary sectors committed to charting the development of a sustainable city.

By attempting to diversify the economy to include a larger share of professional and financial services, and developing activities such as business tourism, Birmingham is trying to shake off the legacy of its past. This is a forward-looking approach but many other major cities in Britain, and Europe more generally, are pursuing a similar approach. One key problem is the difficulty that Birmingham has in developing a large service base simply because London is too close and easy to get to. However, the creation of a sound, diversified service economy supporting the needs of local manufacturing as well as exporting its output to other parts of the UK and overseas cannot be neglected. The difficulty for Birmingham may be that it is trying to 'hedge its bets' by committing itself to several possible sources of economic regeneration rather than focusing on a small number of clearly defined sectors that can be clearly identified by investors and national or European agencies providing funds for infrastructure, training or business development (see for example, Birmingham City Council, 1995). Indeed, we may wonder whether, despite some of the changes that have been outlined, Birmingham and the West Midlands now performs a range of functions that are really very different from those highlighted by our predecessors in 1950. In that event, from "widgets to where?" would be better expressed as from "widgets to a partially-restructured economy?".

Acknowledgements

Thanks are due to Sally Churchward for the collection of data on the West Midlands region and the Birmingham economy.

References

Allen G 1929 *The industrial development of Birmingham and the Black Country, 1860-1927* Allen and Unwin, London

Amin A (ed) 1994 *The geography of post-Fordism* Blackwell, Oxford

Birmingham City Council 1995 *Economic development strategy for Birmingham 1995-98* Economic Development Department, Birmingham

Birmingham Economic Information Centre 1994 *The Birmingham economy: Review and prospects (Recent Trends, Medium Term Prospects 1994-97, Longer Term Prospects 1997-2005)* Birmingham City Council and Birmingham Training and Enterprise Council, Birmingham

Birmingham Economic Information Centre 1995 *Birmingham economic review 1995-96* Birmingham Economic Information Centre, Birmingham

Briggs 1952 *History of Birmingham*, Vol 2 Oxford University Press, Oxford

Bryson J Keeble D and Wood P 1996 The creation and growth of small business service firms in post-industrial Britain *Small Business Economics* forthcoming.

Child J and Smith C 1990 The context and process of organizational transformation: Cadbury limited in its sector in **Loveridge R and Pitt M** eds *The strategic management of technological innovation* Wiley, Chichester

Cuadrado-Roura J and Rubalcaba-Bermejo L 1995 Specialisation and competition between

European cities: a new approach through fairs and exhibition activities. Paper presented at V Annual RESER Conferenc, Aix-en-Provence, September.

Damesick P 1987 Regional economic change since the 1960s in **Damesick P and Wood P** eds *Regional problems, problem regions, and public policy in the United Kingdom* Clarendon Press, Oxford

Department of Economic Affairs 1965 *The West Midlands: A regional study* London

Department of Scientific and Industrial Research 1958 *Estimates of resources devoted to scientific and engineering research and development in British manufacturing industry* DSIR, London.

European Commission 1994 *West Midlands: A region of the European union* HMSO, London

Government Office for the West Midlands *1995 West Midlands labour market and skill trends*, 1995-96 Government Office for the West Midlands, Birmingham

Harvey, D 1989 *The condition of postmodernity* Blackwell, Oxford

Keeble, D 1976 *Industrial location and planning in the United Kingdom* Methuen, London

Kinvig R Smith J and Wise M eds 1950 *Birmingham and its regional setting* British Association, Birmingham

Kumar K 1995 *From post-industrial to post-modern society* Blackwell, Oxford

Mawson J and Taylor A 1983 The West Midlands in crisis: an economic profile *Working Paper No. 1, Inner City Project, West Midlands Study* University of Birmingham.

Price Waterhouse 1995 *The West Midlands business survey* Price Waterhouse, Birmingham

Smith C Child J and Rowlinson M 1990 *Reshaping work: the Cadbury experience* Cambridge University Press, Cambridge

Spencer K Taylor A Smith B Mawson J Flynn N and Batley R 1986 *Crisis in the industrial heartlands: A study of the West Midlands* Clarenden Press, Oxford

Sutcliffe A and Smith R 1974 *Birmingham, 1939-1970* Oxford University Press, Oxford

WMCC 1978 *County structure plan: report of survey: Employment* WMCC, Birmingham

University of Cambridge 1992 *The state of British Enterprise: growth, innovation and competitive advantage in small and medium-sized enterprise* Small Business Research Centre, University of Cambridge

Wise M and O'N. Thorpe P 1950 The growth of Birmingham 1800-1950 in **Kinvig R Smith J and Wise M** eds *Birmingham and its Regional Setting, British Association* 213-228.

Walker G and Glaisyer E 1950 A survey of the industrial population of Birmingham and the Black Country in **Kinvig R Smith J and Wise M** eds *Birmingham and its Regional Setting, British Association* 249-260.

Waymark P 1983 *The car industry: A study in economics and geography* Sewells, Bath

Wood P 1976 *The West Midlands* David and Charles, London

CHAPTER 13

From Craft to Lean: Technological change and the motor-vehicle industry in the West Midlands

Robert N Gwynne

The motor-vehicle industry has been a key manufacturing industry throughout the twentieth century. For a country to reach industrial maturity, it normally must develop a rapidly expanding and technologically dynamic vehicle industry - as with the United States, Germany, France, Italy, Japan, South Korea and Brazil. Furthermore, in each of these countries, the industrial firms, consisting of both finished vehicle assembly and component production, have tended to concentrate spatially in one or two metropolitan areas, and not normally that of the capital city - Detroit, Wolfsburg, Turin, Nagoya, Ulsan and Sao Paulo. In Britain, the concentration of motor-vehicle assembly and component plants has been in the metropolitan area of the West Midlands.

This chapter will elaborate the broad patterns of technological change in the motor-vehicle industry during the twentieth century and how the West Midlands vehicle industry has adapted to these changes. The evolution of technological change during the twentieth century can be examined in the form of three distinctive stages (Womack et al. 1990):

- Craft production
- Mass or 'Fordist' systems of production
- Lean or flexible systems of production - these can be referred to as 'post-Fordist', but given that they originated in Japan, post-Fordist can seem an inappropriate, even ethnocentric, label. Within each stage, the aim is to examine the nature of technological change, the evolution of the key vehicle firms and the impacts of technological change on labour markets, supplier relationships, product variety and the spatial evolution of the industry within the West Midlands region. The changing nature of government policy on the motor-vehicle industry will also be considered.

Craft Production

The Nature of Technological Change

The early years of the motor-vehicle industry were characterized by craft production of the custom-built car. Production was characterised by short runs of individual models and by a great number of manufacturers. These manufacturers assembled vehicles with 'craft' components; the production of many components was sub-contracted out to workshops that initially built vehicle components as a sideline. As a result, assemblers benefited greatly from being located in a large industrial city which could offer agglomeration economies, or large numbers of production linkages within a relatively restricted geographical area. Such production linkages (a physical movement of goods from one firm to another as part of the production process) were offered by Birmingham and the West Midlands, where assemblers had the benefit of sub-contracting the manufacture of small numbers of components to a wide variety of workshops with which relatively informal arrangements could be made.

Early Growth in the West Midlands Region

Allen (1929) argues that it was Birmingham's industrial model of the nineteenth century in which a factory would be linked to a large number of workshops that proved so important for the craft production of the motor vehicle. Allen saw the motor vehicle assembler forging production linkages with workshops as varied as:

- Non-ferrous workshops specialising in brass, copper and wire and providing tubes and wire for the assembler.
- Screw makers producing wood screws for car bodies and metal screws for the chassis.
- Lock-making workshops (concentrated in Willenhall) supplying door fastenings to the assembler.
- Mirror-making manufacturers who diversified into the production of windscreens.
- Lamp manufacturers that diversified into supplying lighting equipment for the assembler.
- Metal-working workshops that specialized in weldless steel tubes, mainly located in Wolverhampton, which produced the frame of the car.
- Spring-making workshops (concentrated in West Bromwich) that supplied laminated and coil-springs.
- Leather-making workshops (concentrated in Walsall) that produced the upholstery.
- Workshops that specialised in stampings in the Black Country and diversified into the production of gear-wheels.
- Metal-working manufacturers that produced wheels, mainly located in Dudley and Bilston.

It was this wide variety of suppliers that provided such assemblers as Wolseley (started production in 1896), Standard (started 1903), Rover (started 1904), Austin (started 1905), Singer, Hillman, Vanden Plas, Triumph, Jaguar, with the components for their short runs of custom-built cars (see Fig 13.1 for the subsequent evolution of these firms). Furthermore, the relationship between assembler and supplier was very close, with a free flow of technological knowledge between them. Rapid innovation and improvements in vehicle and component design resulted.

By 1911, there were already 16,300 people employed in the motor-vehicle assembly industry (Allen, 1929). Most of these were highly skilled workers in most aspects of production. In

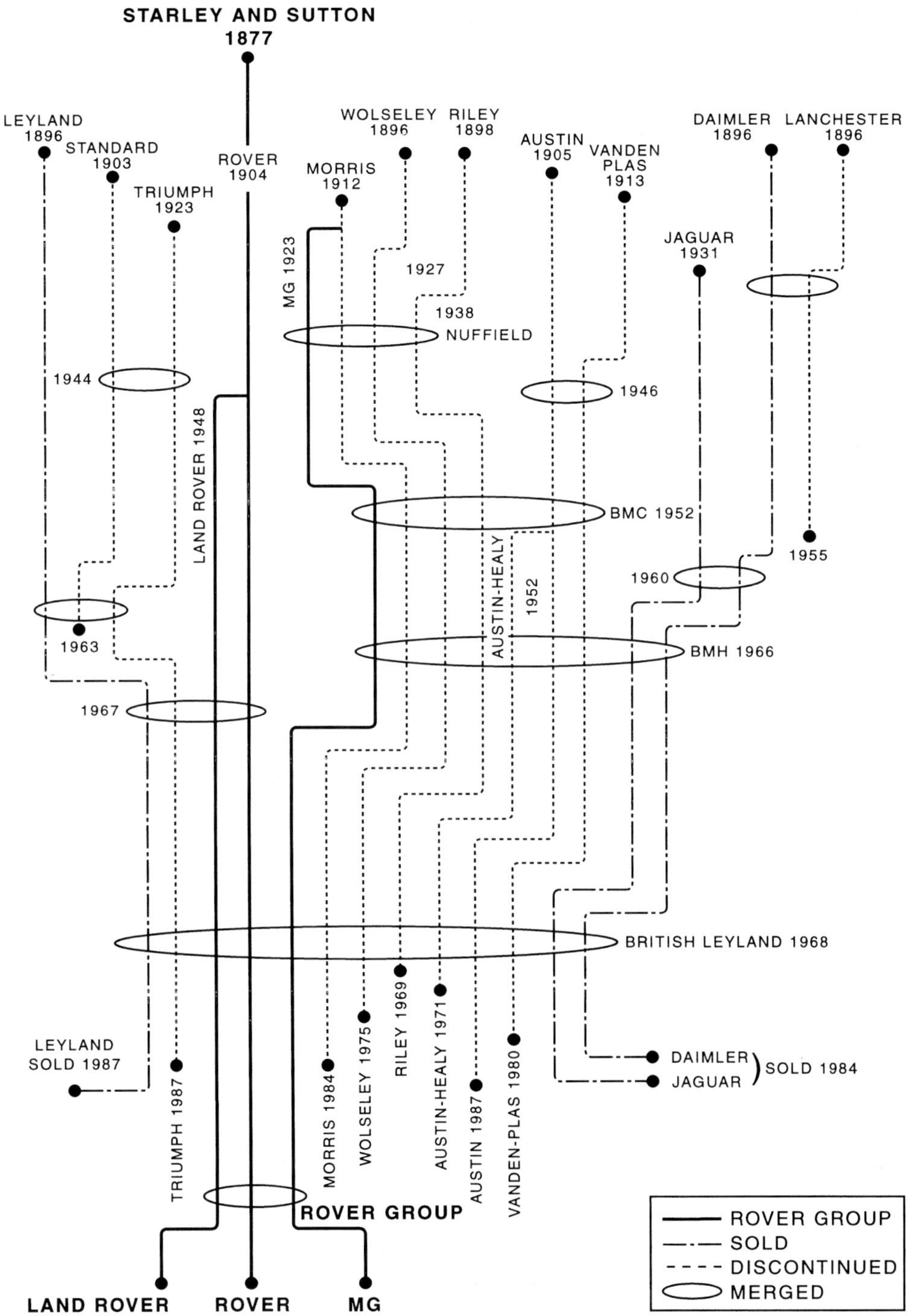

Fig. 13.1 An organigram of some UK car assembly firms

Fig. 13.2 Building Morris Cowley Bodies, early 1920s. Probably a subcontract to Kellick and Pratt in Coventry. Workers are organised in teams of two or three, and each workbench shows the body at a different stage of completion. Cutting machinery is to the right of the picture. The welding is being carried out manually (Source: BMIHT/Rover Group)

Fig. 13.3 Coach builders working on ash-framed early Austins, pre- First World War, Longbridge. One of the few examples of carpenters being employed on a large scale in motor car production. However, this only happened during the craft production stage (Source: BMIHT/Rover Group).

addition, large manufacturers had appeared in tyre production; Fort Dunlop and other tyre manufacturers in Birmingham employed 3,350 in 1911. Combined with workshops producing for the motor vehicle industry as a sideline, the motor vehicle industry was probably employing around 30,000 people by the outbreak of the First World War.

Production volume in this phase of craft production was extremely low. The building of bodies was a particularly labour-intensive process, and often done in fairly rudimentary workshops, where teams of two or three workers would manually cut and weld the body together on fixed work benches (see Fig 13.2). The labour-intensive nature did temporarily permit the employment of carpenters in the construction of wood-framed bodies (see Fig 13.3). However, product variety was very wide with each product customized to specific requirements. The phase saw considerable change in the technology of the product itself but relatively little in how the product was made (process technology). Changes in process technology were to be distinctive of the subsequent stage of mass production.

It is difficult, however, to define when the era of craft production came to an end. Unlike the United States, the Fordist era of mass production and mass marketing did not arrive in Britain in the 1920s. There were some elements of mass production introduced in the 1930s, particularly by Austin, but it was not until after the Second World War and the decade of the 1950s that mass marketing of the motor car began.

Mass production

The Nature of Technological Change

The growth of mass production during the 1950s in the West Midlands motor-vehicle industry brought rapid increases in the volume of production. At the same time, the range of vehicles narrowed as standardized models were designed; for example, the Austin plant at Longbridge became characterized by the production of the A30, A40 and Austin Cambridge/A50 models during the 1950s (see Fig 13.4). Only minor product differentiation was permitted within these standardized designs. In contrast to the craft-production phase, process technology became much more complex with the assembly line dominating production. The assembly line, however, brought its own rigidities as single-purpose machinery was installed along it. It took a long time and heavy investment to set up a new assembly line. Hence, once an assembly line was established for a model, such as the Austin A50, that assembly line would normally stay in place (with only minor subsequent modifications) until the end of the life of that model.

Furthermore, components became increasingly standardized and many assemblers followed the Detroit model of investing in large inventories of these standardized components (see Fig 13.5). These would be stored at the assembly plant or neighbouring warehouses, a system that was supposed to safeguard the assembler against supply problems - either those of production at the component firm or transport between the component plant and the assembly line. The relationship between the assembler and component firms became more formalised and based on long-term contracts with lowest unit price the crucial determinant. Technological cooperation between the assembler and component firms became much reduced, particularly compared with the era of craft production.

With the shift from craft to mass production, the nature of the labour force also radically changed. Under craft production, assemblers had relied on relatively small amounts of highly-skilled labour. With mass production, not only was there a much greater demand for labour, but

Fig. 13.4 The Austin Cambridge Assembly Line, Longbridge, 1954. An example of the rigidities of the assembly line. It took considerable investment to set up an assembly line. Once in place, the assembly line would normally stay in place until the end of the model's life. The Austin Cambridge was a sturdy, heavy model that was popular in rural areas (Source: BMIHT/Rover Group).

Fig. 13.5 Massive Inventory of Engines, Coventry, 1950s. Dramatic example of the assembler wishing to ensure supply at all costs and being prepared to invest large amounts in stock (Source: BMIHT/Rover Group).

Fig. 13.6 The Tedium of Assembly Line Work (Morris Minor Production at Cowley, early 1960s). Labour on the assembly line was classified as semi-skilled. Each worker would perform a simple task repetitively and in a predefined time and sequence. Here, on a slowly moving assembly line, one worker is screwing in the winding mechanism. These simple tasks would be repeated without change throughout the year (Source: BMIHT/Rover Group).

Fig. 13.7 Female labour did not constitute part of the assembly line, although women had worked in these areas during the Second World War. Women only worked in offices, catering or the trim shop (Cowley, 1955) (Source: BMIHT/Rover Group).

also this labour was essentially unskilled, or semi-skilled after a small amount of training at a specific task. On the assembly line, each worker would perform a very simple task repetitively and in a predefined time and sequence (see Fig 13.6). Male labour dominated the assembly line, with female labour being restricted to office work and the trim shop (see Fig 13.7). There also developed a distinct division between assembly-line workers, on the one hand, and the managerial and skilled professional workers on the other. Relationships between them became increasingly mediated between trade unions representing above all the assembly-line workers.

According to Altshuler et al. (1984), the process technology of mass production and the development of a standardized product on a moving assembly line was developed in the USA from the 1910s to the 1940s. However, during the 1950s and 1960s, west European producers were able to differentiate "standardized" products and introduce new vehicle designs. Those west European producers that came to dominate production in their own country contributed their own distinctive designs and also advanced product technology, as with the development of the transverse engine and front-wheel drive.

Corporate Growth and the West Midlands

The most fundamental point about the mass production of motor cars was that it required size, both in terms of plant and firm. Larger assembly plants enjoyed greater economies of scale than smaller plants and thus were able to manufacture cars at lower per unit cost. Meanwhile, the huge investments required for the construction and expansion of large assembly plants meant that vehicle firms had to expand as well. In addition, vehicle firms identified the benefits of vertical integration - purchasing component firms further back in the production process - and horizontal integration - purchasing or merging with competing assembly firms.

Indeed, it was through horizontal integration that the West Midlands motor-vehicle firms expanded. A series of mergers between 1952 and 1968 (Fig. 13.1) transformed a large number of small vehicle producers into one merged giant, the British Leyland Motor Corporation (BLMC). BLMC was created in 1968 as a result of the merger of the Leyland Motor Corporation and British Motor Holdings. British Motor Holdings was the final result of mergers between Austin, Morris, Pressed Steel (that produced car bodies adjacent to the assembly plants) and Jaguar. The Leyland Motor Corporation had been the more aggressive corporation in terms of growth during the 1960s as it bought up Standard Triumph of Coventry in 1961 and Rover of Solihull in 1967. As a result, four of the assembly firms of the West Midlands (Austin, Jaguar, Standard Triumph and Rover) had been merged into one massive and unwieldly corporation by 1968 (Fig. 13.1). The other two assembly firms (Singer and Hillman of Coventry) had been purchased by the United States corporation, Chrysler, during the mid-1960s.

This whole series of mergers and corporate purchases was supposed to facilitate growth in the number of vehicles produced through new investments in assembly lines, new plant, new models and foreign sales. However, growth occurred in a rather amorphous way, without any significant rationalization, for example, in the number of models being produced.

Government policy and the West Midlands

One significant problem for the vehicle assembly firms of the West Midlands in the late 1950s and early 1960s was that government did not allow them to expand significantly in the West Midlands - or if they were allowed to, they had to build large new plants in other regions of Britain.

The British governments of the 1950s firmly believed in governments intervening strongly in industry. One key priority of industrial policy was to distribute industrial growth around the various regions of Britain. As the motor-vehicle industry was geographically concentrated in the West Midlands and the South-East in the 1950s, this became one major candidate for government intervening in locational decision-making. Vehicle firms had to expand during the late 1950s as the capacity of older plant became too small for supplying the rapidly expanding demand of the domestic market; the decade of the 1950s had seen the anual consumption of motor vehicles in the UK jump from 100,000 to 800,000.

The main instrument of government intervention in the West Midlands was the Industrial Development Certificate (IDC), an instrument that dated back to the 1945 Distribution of Industry Act. Any vehicle firm wishing to erect or expand a plant in excess of 5,000 square feet in the West Midlands had to apply to government for an IDC. At the end of the 1950s, a desire for new plant was expressed by most of the motor-vehicle companies located in the West Midlands. The granting of IDCs was the responsibility of the Board of Trade. Decisions from this government department normally indicated that vehicle firms could expand their plants in the West Midlands as long as they created new plants in other regions - Wales, Northern England and Scotland. As most vehicle firms had to expand capacity in some form, they had no alternative but to increase the capacity of their existing plant alongside creating new plants in what were then described as 'depressed' regions.

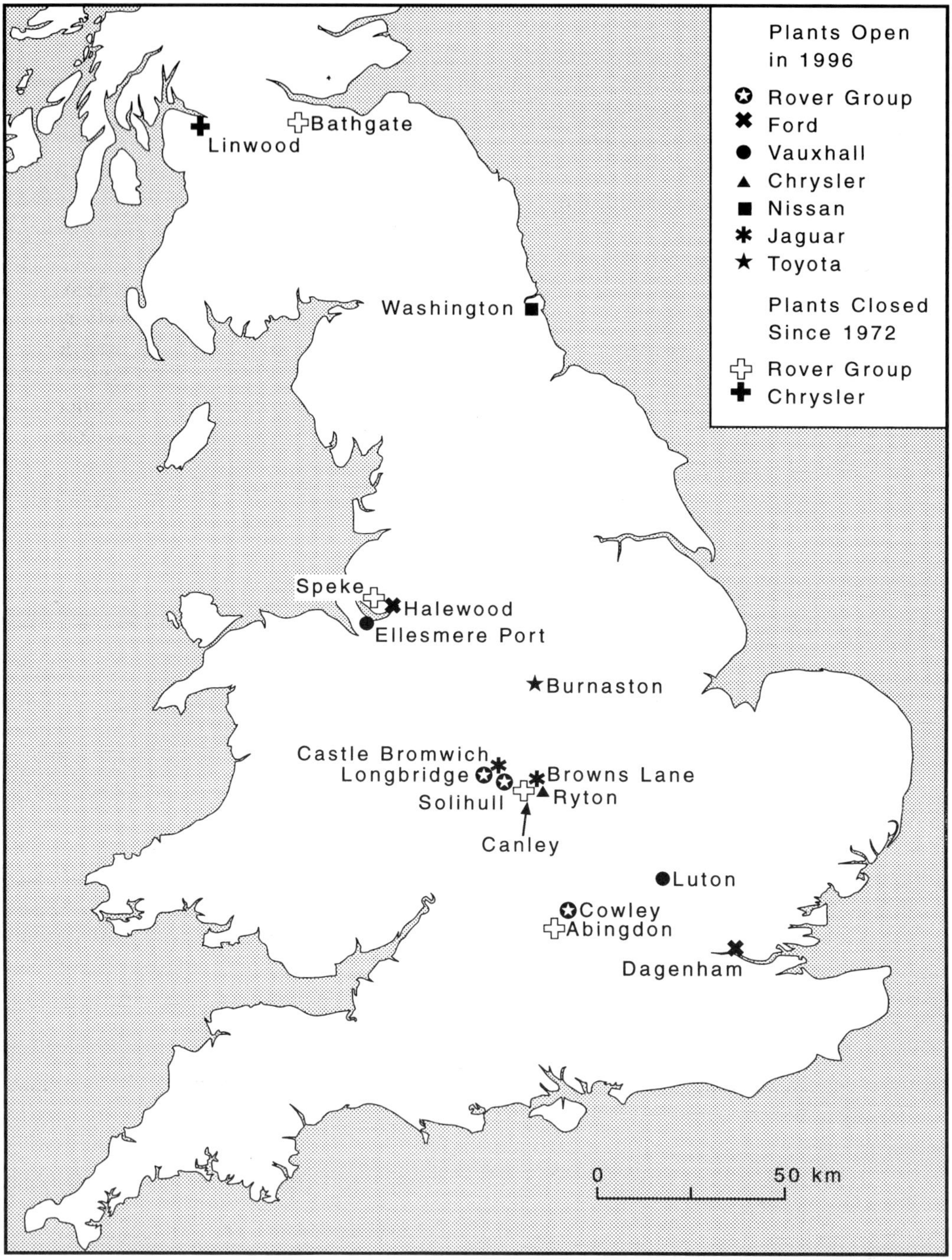

Fig. 13.8 Major UK assembly plants 1972 and 1996

Thus, Standard Triumph International, in order to expand production at its Coventry plant, was forced to establish a large assembly, bodywork and components plant at Speke, near Liverpool (Fig. 13.8). "The STI move to Speke must have added significantly to their costs. STI's total output even from a single plant was clearly too small to exploit potential economies of scale" (Dunnett 1980: 79). Austin and Morris had merged in 1952 to form the British Motor Corporation (BMC). In order to expand at Longbridge and Oxford, BMC had to agree to transfer all tractor and truck production to Bathgate, near Edinburgh (Fig. 13.8). In a similar way, Rover had to agree to build a new components plant in South Wales before it was allowed to expand capacity at Solihull.

Perhaps the most disastrous locational decision was forced upon the Rootes Group that controlled the Hillman and Singer assembly plants in Coventry before selling out to Chrysler in the mid-1960s. The Rootes group were not allowed to expand in Coventry and chose a location in central Scotland (at Linwood) for their new assembly plant (mainly to assemble the Hillman Imp). The high costs of this location were later emphasised by Chrysler in 1972 in evidence to the Trade and Industry subcommittee of the House of Commons Expenditure Committee (Keeble, 1976: 186). Chrysler asserted that "our Linwood plant was opened as a new plant in March 1963 as a result of Government policy of not granting planning permission, other than of a minimum nature, except in a development area".

As a result, Chrysler complained of two sources of additional costs at the Linwood location. First, there were the transport costs of bringing engines, gearboxes and most components from the West Midlands; nearly 80 per cent of Chrysler's total purchases of externally-supplied parts were obtained from the West Midlands and the south of England. Secondly, the cost of distribution of cars was increased by the Linwood location, particularly as compared with the Coventry plant - thus, 85 per cent of all Chrysler's cars produced at Linwood for the national market were sold to dealers situated within 150 miles of Coventry, whereas only 15 per cent were sold to dealers within 150 miles of Linwood. Chrysler thus argued that expansion should have taken place at the original Coventry location and that the government was responsible for forcing the company to locate in an uncompetitive location.

Government regional policy also meant that there were few cases of short-distance decentralization of motor vehicle plants away from the two core cities of Birmingham/Solihull and Coventry (Wood 1976: 160). In 1966, 85 per cent of vehicle employment in the West Midlands region was concentrated in these two centres with only 15 per cent of regional vehicle employment being generated in the whole of the Black Country. New assembly plants were not allowed to locate there and component firms tended to locate near the established production centres.

Government regional policy effectively penalised the further development of a successful regional specialism. Indeed, it can be argued that government regional policy lost the motor vehicle region of the West Midlands three assembly plants (Linwood, Speke, Bathgate) and one component plant. Assembly plants using mass production techniques were particularly land-intensive and hence were caught up by the regulations of the IDC policy. However, expansion of component firms were not normally so large-scale and hence generally avoided the IDC restrictions. Thus, the West Midlands continued to remain the centre of the components industry - though no longer of the assembly industry. This is reflected in Table 13.1 in which vehicle output and employment data is compared for different European regions in the early 1970s (Bloomfield 1978: 187). The effects of government regional policy had successfully restricted the growth of vehicle output in the West Midlands compared to other European regions - thus the

West Midlands ranked only sixth amongst vehicle-producing regions in Europe in 1973. However, the West Midlands still remained very significant in the components industry; as a result, in terms of overall employment in the vehicle sector, the West Midlands still ranked as the second most important region in the whole of Europe.

Region	Vehicle Output 1973 (000)	Rank	Employment 1971 (000)	Rank
Paris (F)	2,015	1	178	1
Niedersachsen (WG)	1,473	2	125	6
Piemonte (I)	1,197	3	144	4
Belgium	1,059	4	40	14
South East (UK)	871	5	151	3
West Midlands (UK)	783	6	163	2

Source: Bloomfield, 1978: 187.

Table 13.1: European Regions Ranked According to Vehicle Output and Employment, early 1970s

However, it was in the early 1970s that the British Leyland conglomerate also lost its way in terms of new investment, new technology and keeping up with rival European and US producers. In terms of fixed assets per person (a simple indicator of investment), British Leyland only achieved £920 in 1974 - compared with £2,657 by Ford (UK), £3,632 by Volkswagen and £5,602 by Ford (US) (Dunnet, 1980). Value-added per person in British Leyland was only about one-half of that of Ford (UK) and one-quarter that of Ford (US). It was becoming difficult to keep up with the rival companies of Europe and the USA, using similar technologies of mass production, let alone the corporations of Japan that had successfully come to implement lean production technologies.

Lean Production

The Nature of Technological Change

The system of mass production had been developed in the United States, most particularly during the 1920s. Lean production, however, originated in Japan. The origins of lean production go back to the early attempts of Japanese corporations, and particularly Toyota, to develop a motor-vehicle industry in the 1950s. However, it was not until the 1970s that this form of production made Japanese vehicle corporations the most competitive in the world. Mass production had managed to produce cheap cars for a mass market. Lean production, however, added quality to cheapness and was able to produce an increasingly wide range of differentiated products.

In the aftermath of the Second World War, Japanese manufacturing corporations were notoriously short of capital. They could not afford to keep the large inventories that characterized mass production. They therefore developed a just-in-time system of component delivery and forged considerable virtues from this necessity. First of all, they developed very close relationships with a relatively small number of key suppliers. Long-term contracts between assembler and component suppliers normally included mutual investment, technological cooperation and frequent and structured communications. In contrast to mass production, the emphasis was on lowest overall cost (rather than lowest unit price) - a crucial distinction which linked component manufacture to the overall assembly of a quality vehicle. To this end, component production was increasingly modularized, with the final assembly line installing sub-assemblies rather than a whole series of individual parts.

The suppliers would be committed to deliver components to the assembler on the day that they would be required. Apart from freeing up capital, this system had another clear advantage - the quality-control division of the assembler could immediately and closely monitor all aspects of the component; if problems with components were discovered they could be rectified rapidly - a distinct improvement on the mass production system where faulty components could wait in inventory stores for long periods of time. Such a just-in-time delivery system encouraged geographical proximity betweem assembler and supplier.

The assembly plants of Japanese corporations were also organised on much more flexible lines so that production could be rapidly shifted from one product to another. These methods took longer to perfect but, by the 1970s, highly flexible methods of production were in place. It became increasingly easy to switch production from one model to another on the assembly line - a marked improvement on the rigidities of the mass production system (one line - one model). The introduction of robots (particularly in the car body plant - see Fig 13.9) and computer-controlled automation significantly enhance productivity and improved quality of production.

The type and organisation of labour also changed significantly under lean production. With more flexible systems of production, workers operated in teams (see Fig 13.10). The

Fig. 13.9 Rover 400 bodies on the robotic finish weld line. With lean production techniques, the manufacture of car bodies can now be done without any direct labour input (Source: Rover Group)

Fig. 13.10 The MGF wheel and tyre fit station. Under lean production, workers are organised in teams and normally have to employ state-of-the-art machines in order to ensure quick, efficient assembly and high quality (Source: Rover Group)

responsibilities of each worker included participating in several manufacturing operations as well as responsibility for simple maintenance and quality control. The workforce under lean production was thus more highly skilled and motivated than under mass production. The Japanese model also tried to reduce distinctions between the shopfloor workforce and those working in management. The idea was for workers to identify strongly with the corporation and to this end corporate unions became the rule. Workers benefited from job security but work practices were both more flexible and demanding than under mass production.

Industrial Restructuring in the West Midlands

Initially, the impact of lean production in the UK in general and the West Midlands in particular was seen in terms of competition from Japanese motor vehicle corporations. Indeed, in 1978 the UK government placed what was euphemistically called a 'voluntary' quota on Japanese vehicle imports, so that that they could not constitute more than 11 per cent of sales in any one year.

Otherwise, Japanese imports would have cut deeply into the market share of the vehicles being produced by the British Leyland Motor Corporation, which had been taken over by the state in 1974. Through the mid-1970s the losses of the company mounted and, in 1978, the Labour government of the day brought in Michael Edwardes to rationalize the company. He renamed it BL and divided it into four divisions: Austin Rover (mass market cars); Jaguar (specialist cars); a commercial vehicle division which included trucks, vans and Land Rover; and a parts division, called Unipart.

Realising the huge technological gap that had now developed between British car assembly plants and those of Japan, Michael Edwardes negotiated a far-sighted link-up with Honda in

1979. This provided substantial assistance in both product and process technology; there were also the occasional marketing arrangement (such as the marketing of the Land Rover Discovery in Japan). Ultimately, in 1989, Honda took a 20 per cent stake in the Rover Group and Rover took a 20 per cent stake in Honda UK Manufacturing. It could be argued that the Honda link saved the West Midlands motor vehicle industry by gaining immediate access to the product and process technology of a company at the then frontier of lean production techniques.

Furthermore, the restructured BL started a process of spatial retrenchment in the West Midlands heartland. Most of the vehicle plants located in peripheral regions were closed down in the late 1970s and 1980s - for example, the Speke plant in 1978 and the Bathgate plant in the early 1980s (Fig. 13.8). The Rover components plant in South Wales went to management buyout in 1986. Furthermore, in 1978, Peugeot-Citroen purchased Chrysler UK and soon decided to close down the Linwood plant, concentrating both assembly and parts production in its Ryton plant in Coventry. Plant closures did take place in the West Midlands and South - for example, the former Triumph plant at Canley and former MG plant at Abingdon terminated production in the 1980s (Fig. 13.8). However, production of vehicles at Austin Rover was concentrated at its

Fig. 13.11 The Longbridge Assembly plant, Birmingham. This is now the largest and most technologically-advanced car assembly plant in the West Midlands, having been in the vanguard of the application of lean production techniques during the 1980s. Car manufacturing has existed here on the southern outskirts of Birmingham ever since 1905 when Herbert Austin bought a disused printing works to start making cars (he had previously been the chief designer for Wolseley) (Source: Rover Group).

plants in Longbridge (Fig 13.11), Solihull and Oxford, whilst Jaguar production continued at the Browns Lane plant in Coventry. Components production also became more concentrated in the West Midlands region.

The shift from mass production to lean production techniques in the West Midlands motor-vehicle industry dramatically reduced employment in the industry even though production and productivity were rapidly increasing - as at Longbridge where Japanese process technology was concentrated in the first instance. Between 1979 and 1986, employment in the motor-vehicle assembly industry in the West Midland region declined by half. In components industries, the reduction in employment was nearly as severe as components companies also incorporated lean production techniques into their manufacturing systems. Employment in the Lucas components division fell from 24,000 in 1981 to 12,000 in 1986.

The 1980s and 1990s have seen the privatization and subsequent selling off of much of the West Midlands motor vehicle industry to foreign companies (Fig. 13.1). Austin Rover, later renamed Rover, had the Land Rover division subsequently added to it and was purchased from government by British Aerospace in 1988. However, in early 1994, British Aerospace sold all of its 80 per cent stake to the German company, BMW. Meanwhile, Jaguar was privatized in 1984 through a £297 million flotation; but its exports markets dried up in the late 1980s and it was purchased by the US company, Ford, in 1990. In the commercial vehicles area, Leyland Trucks and Freight Rover (with its plant in Castle Bromwich) were sold to DAF of Holland in 1987; subsequently, Freight Rover went to management buyout, and was renamed as LDV. The parts division, Unipart, which was privatized in 1987, has not been purchased by a foreign company.

The Arrival of Japanese Vehicle Corporations

Meanwhile, after the restrictions placed on Japanese vehicle imports in the late 1970s, three Japanese corporations have invested in assembly plants in Britain - Nissan at Washington, Honda at Swindon, and Toyota at Burnaston, near Derby. All these three companies wanted to establish plants in the European Union (EU) before the end of 1992 so that they could enjoy unrestricted access to all markets of the EU. In Japan, the UK was seen as a large market dominated by foreign corporations. Therefore, the UK government was identified as not discriminating against the technologically-advanced Japanese corporations in favour of domestic corporations - as was perceived as occuring in such countries as France and Italy, where Japanese imports from Japan are allowed either no market share (Italy) or only 3 per cent of the market (France). Around each of these new Japanese plants in the UK, a number of Japanese component suppliers have also decided to locate.

Toyota's decision to locate at Burnaston in the East Midlands can be seen to have regional explanations. For Toyota thought that its just-in-time delivery system would function better when there was geographical proximity between its plant and suppliers (the component manufacturers of the West Midlands). It has also been argued that Toyota wished to locate its plant in an area where there was no local record of motor-vehicle assembly. The perceived advantage for the Japanese corporation was that there was no legacy of restrictive trade union practices linked to the traditional motor-vehicle industry and that the local culture would be more open to a corporate union structure.

The implementation of lean production technology has operated to re-concentrate the UK motor-vehicle industry in the West Midlands, particularly in terms of the components industry. This industry does contain some large UK companies such as GKN and Lucas. However, the sector is still characterised by large numbers of small- and medium-sized firms that have been accused of being parochial (Tomkins, 1989) given that only 10 per cent of their output goes for export.

At the same time, the vehicle assembly industry has come to be completely controlled by foreign companies - BMW, Honda, Ford, Peugeot-Citroen in the West Midlands and Toyota in the East Midlands. The decisions that will now affect the future of the West Midlands assembly industry will now be made in Germany, the United States, Japan and France. Lean production has transformed the product and process technology of the West Midlands vehicle industry but it has also made that industry more dependent on outside influences that at any time in its history.

Concluding Remarks

The motor-vehicle industry has been a technologically dynamic industry throughout the twentieth century. It has been at the cutting edge of new manufacturing technology in all three phases of technological change during the twentieth century. In the stage of craft production, the emphasis was on product technology. With the era of mass production, the emphasis shifted to process technology. With the most recent era of lean production, there have been considerable strides made in both product and process technology and a greater integration between them.

In addition, the vehicle industry has become one of the most global of all manufacturing industries. It has become an industry of giant corporations that are increasingly organizing their activities on internationally integrated lines. The geographical hubs of these corporations are at their head office locations where investment in research and development is concentrated and where the crucial decisions about the future priorities and strategies of the vehicle corporation are made. Detroit, Paris, Turin, Wolfsburg, Stuttgart and Toyota City still constitute such hubs. Unfortunately, the West Midlands no longer constitutes such a major hub of the global vehicle industry. It can be seen as an important secondary hub due to a range of assembly plants owned by foreign companies and due to a wide range of components industry. But the actions of government, domestic and foreign corporations and the pace of technological change have reduced it global significance since achieving some prominence on the world stage in the 1950s and 1960s.

However, for Birmingham and the West Midlands, there may be a 'silver lining' to this loss of international stature in the global vehicle industry. In the early 1970s, Miller (1983: 53) could complain that "the West Midlands has become an over-specialized, dependent economy based on a small number of very large firms, many of which are involved directly or indirectly with the vehicle industry". This regional specialization has been reduced during the 1980s and 1990s as both other manufacturing and new service sectors have been developed. The emphasis of employment growth in the West Midlands has returned to the region's traditional source of strength - the small adaptable firm (Chapman and Walker, 1987: 223).

Acknowledgements

I would like to thank: Karam Ram and Anders Clausager of the British Motor Industry Heritage Trust for assistance in providing material from their excellent photographic archive; Pam Wearing, Corporate Communications Manager, and Ian Strachan, both at Rover Group, Longbridge for assistance with contemporary photographs and data accuracy. I would like to dedicate the chapter to Geoffrey N Gwynne, who experienced at first hand the rapid changes in the British motor vehicle industry over a period of two decades.

References

Allen G C 1929 *The Industrial Development of Birmingham and the Black Country* Cass, London

Altshuler A et al. 1984 *The Future of the Automobile* Allen & Unwin, London

Bloomfield G 1978 *The World Automotive Industry* David and Charles, Newton Abbot

Chapman K & Walker D 1987 *Industrial Location* Blackwell, London

Damesick P & Wood P A 1987 *Regional Problems, Problem Regions* Oxford University Press, London

Dicken P 1992 *Global Shift* Paul Chapman, London

Dunnett P J S 1980 *The Decline of the British Motor Industry* Croom Helm, London

House of Commons 1987 *The UK Motor Components Industry* Third Report from the Trade and Industry Committee HMSO, London

Keeble D 1976 *Industrial Location and Planning in the United Kingdom* Methuen, London

Miller D 1983 The role of the motor car industry in the West Midlands economy *Regional Studies* 17.1 53-6

Tomkins R 1989 West Midlands *Financial Times Survey* October 18

Wood P A 1976 *Industrial Britain: the West Midlands* David and Charles, Newton Abbot

Womack J Jones D & Roos D 1990 *The Machine that Changed the World* Rawson Associates, London

CHAPTER 14

Prestige Urban Regeneration Projects: Socio-Economic Impacts

P. Loftman and B. Nevin

Inter-urban competition for footloose private investment and central government resources has been a long-standing feature of British urban policy. During the 1980s and 1990s, in the context of intense global competition between cities for service-sector investment, urban local authorities (and also central government urban development corporations) have increasingly adopted 'civic boosterism' or city-marketing strategies as a means of placing their respective areas on the international map. Key elements of such strategies have been the promotion of new and dynamic images for cities, and the development of prestige (flagship) property development projects such as convention centres, commercial office space, sports arenas and shopping malls (Loftman and Nevin, 1996).

This chapter examines Birmingham City Council's aspirations to create a new economic future for its area through the development of the International Convention Centre (ICC) and the National Indoor Arena (NIA) during the 1980s. These prestigious developments have been subject to wide media, professional and academic acclaim, however, they have also, in recent years, met with much criticism. The chapter sets out the local economic and political context surrounding the development of the ICC and NIA; the perceived economic impact of these projects; and the perceived benefits and distributional consequences of significant public-sector investments in the ICC, NIA and central-area revitalization in Birmingham. The chapter concludes by examining the change in the city's approach to flagship developments which occurred following the election of Theresa Stewart as Leader of Birmingham City Council in 1994.

Going for growth - the rationale for the development of the ICC and NIA

The economic prosperity enjoyed by Birmingham in the post-war years was critically undermined by a change in the pattern of world trade in the 1960s and 1970s and the recessions of 1973-74 and 1980-82. Within a decade, the West Midlands was transformed from being one of the nation's most prosperous regions to a low-wage, low-productivity economy (see chapter 12). Birmingham, traditionally dependent on manufacturing industry, was not immune from the impact of the region's decline. Between 1971 and 1987 the city lost 191,000 jobs (amounting to 29 per cent of total employment in the city). In particular, 149,000 manufacturing jobs were lost during this period, accounting for 46 per cent of this sector's total employment. The collapse of Birmingham's manufacturing base, however, was not mitigated by expansion in service-sector employment in the city, which only provided an increase of 9,000 jobs over the same period. By 1982, the unemployment rate in Birmingham had risen to more than 20 per cent, (twice the national average) with its inner areas worst affected.

Following the collapse of the city's manufacturing industry, Birmingham City Council sought to broaden the economic base through encouraging service-sector investment and promoting a new dynamic image for the 'Second City' (Loftman, 1990). A political consensus (incorporating the city's Labour and Conservative parties, the local media and local business interest groups) emerged around the need to pursue local economic development policies focused on the expansion of Birmingham's central business district and reshaping the jaded image of the city held by outsiders. This political consensus reflected Birmingham's long-standing tradition of local cross-political party support for major urban initiatives and public-private partnerships such as the development of the National Exhibition Centre in the 1970s and the establishment of the Birmingham Heartlands initiative in the 1980s.

At the heart of the city's local economic development growth strategy were four prestige projects located in the Broad Street Development Area, located on the western fringes of Birmingham city centre. These projects are;

- The £180 million ICC complex opened in April 1991, with a maximum conference capacity of 3,700 delegates and a concert hall providing a venue for the City of Birmingham Symphony Orchestra (Fig 14.1).

- The £31 million four-star Hyatt Hotel, built as an integral part of the ICC development (Fig 14.2).

- The £57 million National Indoor Arena (NIA), built to enhance the city's position as an international centre for sports and entertainment.

- The £250 million Brindleyplace development - located on a cleared 15-acre (6.1 ha) site adjacent to the ICC, which includes plans for the development of 850,000 sq. ft of offices, 123,00 sq. ft of retail space, 140 luxury flats and a national aquarium development (Fig 14.3). The scheme is currently under construction after many years of delay, following the collapse of the commercial property market in the late 1980s.

It is estimated that the city council has directly invested over £276 million in these projects and other city-centre redevelopment between 1986 and 1992 (Loftman and Nevin, 1996).

Local authority investment in city-centre prestige developments, was justified by officers and elected members of Birmingham City Council in terms of the anticipated city-wide and regional economic benefits which would accrue from their construction and operation. The city council initially claimed that the ICC alone would directly and indirectly support 1,900 jobs in the city (Birmingham City Council, 1983). By 1990 it was projected that the ICC would generate 12,000 new jobs. However, unlike the previous estimates (made in 1983) no explanation was given or methodology as to how this figure was calculated (Birmingham City Council, 1990a).

The public-sector investment made in Birmingham's city centre in general, and the Broad Street area in particular, during the 1980s has achieved the widely acclaimed physical transformation of the central business district (Fig 14.1) (see for example, The Planner, 1991; Planning, 1991). However, whilst it is acknowledged that the physical appearance of Birmingham's city centre has been dramatically improved by the city council's investment, it is also argued that the city council's job creation estimates for its prestige projects have been grossly exaggerated; that a significant proportion of the new jobs created by the ICC, and NIA are in

Fig. 14.1 The International Convention Centre from Centenary Square (photo: Terry Slater)

occupations where poor employment conditions and low pay are common, and that disadvantaged residents have failed to secure access to quality employment. More fundamentally, it is argued that the local authority expenditure on flagship projects has entailed massive opportunity costs for local people (Loftman and Nevin, 1992, 1996).

Prestige developments and employment creation: myth or reality

In 1990 Birmingham City Council reported that an increase in commercial activity in the city centre has "...been fuelled by the city's commitment to construct the ICC which is frequently stated as having influenced the decisions of firms to relocate and expand" (Birmingham City Council, 1990b). By 1992, the city council was also claiming that the ICC had helped to attract £2 billion of public and private-sector investment into Birmingham (Birmingham City Council, 1992a). However, these investment claims are from notional figures derived from planning applications, made in the city centre, which patently does not prove a causal link between the ICC and the claimed investment and job creation totals. Similarly, it is argued, the city council's claimed levels of job creation did not give any indications as to the quality of employment generated by the prestige projects and which groups in the population benefited from these new employment opportunities (Loftman and Nevin, 1992).

Publically available evidence to support claims made by the city council that the development of the ICC and NIA has acted as a prime factor in attracting inward investment into Birmingham is limited. During 1991-92, the consultants KPMG Peat Marwick conducted a survey of 282 foreign-owned companies which had invested in premises located within the West Midlands.

None of the firms interviewed mentioned the ICC or the proximity of high profile cultural and arts facilities as a factor which influenced their investment decision (KPMG Peat Marwick, 1992). Additionally, it is argued that historical trends in office development within the city centre do not support the city council's claim that the ICC has facilitated a 'boom' in commercial investment in Birmingham's CBD in the late 1980s (Loftman and Nevin, 1992).

Following vigorous local debate relating to the economic impact of the ICC and NIA, the city council in 1992 commissioned consultants (KPMG) to estimate the global economic impact of business tourism (generated by the ICC, NIA and NEC) on the region and the city, the study's findings (relating to the ICC and NIA), are set out in Table 14.1.

Venue	Employment generated in West Midlands	Employment generated in Birmingham	% of Jobs in B'ham
ICC/Symphony Hall	2,700	1,094	40.5
NIA	1,900	753	39.6
Total	4,600	1,847	40.1

Source: KPMG

Table 14.1: Total economic impact of ICC and NIA

The consultants estimated the number of jobs directly and indirectly supported by the expenditure generated by the prestige projects, and concluded that the operation of the ICC and NIA was supporting around 4,600 jobs in the West Midlands during 1993. However, only 40 per cent of these jobs were estimated to be filled by residents of Birmingham. Thus, according to these figures, £237 million of investment in the two prestige projects had secured 1,847 jobs for Birmingham residents, at a capital cost of around £130,000 per job.

Employment creation: who benefits?

The development of the ICC and NIA, and the associated efforts to promote Birmingham as an international city, were predicated on the belief that the economic benefits of such initiatives would 'trickle-down' to most disadvantaged areas and residents of the city. However, it is argued that the most disadvantaged areas in the city gained few benefits from the growth of employment in Birmingham's city centre. Between 1971 and 1989, the city centre saw employment growth of 9 per cent. However, in 1992 a survey of the Newtown area, which is located adjacent to the city centre, revealed that only six per cent of Newtown residents (aged between 16 and 65) worked in the central business district. Similarly, the relative unemployment rate in the Ladywood Ward (a deprived inner-city ward) increased throughout the mid- to late-1980s, despite the ICC and NIA (and most of Birmingham's city centre) being included within its boundaries (Loftman and Nevin, 1992).

In addition to the criticism that Birmingham's prestige developments did not result in substantial opportunities 'trickling-down' to disadvantaged communities, it has been noted that, where employment directly generated by the projects can be identified, much of it is of poor quality - being insecure and poorly paid. For example, in 1991, 42 per cent of the 275 permanent jobs at the ICC, and 73 per cent of the 71 permanent jobs at the NIA, were defined as cleaning,

Fig. 14.2 The four-star Hyatt Hotel, Broad Street (photo: Terry Slater)

catering and security occupations (Loftman and Nevin, 1992). Nonetheless, the development of the ICC and NIA has stimulated employment generation indirectly, through the expansion of the hotel and catering industry in the city centre area. The construction of six new hotels in the 1980s in close proximity to the ICC, was estimated to have created over 700 new jobs (Fig 14.2). However, the city council estimated that 80 per cent of new hotel and catering vacancies advertised in Birmingham Job Centres between 1988 - 1990 were poorly paid with the median salaries for most occupations falling below the Council of Europe's "decency threshold". The preponderance of poorly-paid lower-status occupations within the sectors (promoted by developments such as the ICC and NIA) appears to run counter the city council's stated commitment to an economic development strategy which builds ".... a strong local economy, capable of offering employment of a reasonable quality to all Birmingham's residents who wish to have a job" (Birmingham City Council, 1986, para 4.1)

The distributional costs of investment in flagship projects

Birmingham City Council's enthusiasm and support for prestige property developments in the 1980s and early 1990s, is reflected in the scale of resources pumped into such projects. Between 1986 and 1992, the city council invested £276 million in the ICC, NIA and the refurbishment of the city centre, and a further £103 million in developing the National Exhibition Centre, located on the city's periphery. Of this investment, £163 million was raised by the NEC Ltd (a public-private partnership controlled by the city council) with the debt being underwritten by the city council. The remainder of the necessary funds for these projects was raised from capital receipts, borrowing approvals and the European Regional Development Fund.

Whilst considerable local-authority resources have been expended in financing Birmingham's prestige schemes, public debate of their wider cost implications for residents was limited by the enforcement of the strict financial confidentiality rules, and the concentration of decision-making power and information in the hands of a select band of senior city-council politicians and officials. Few reports relating to important council sub-committees dealing with the complex financing arrangements of the ICC, NIA and NEC have been made available for public inspection. One such sub-committee met 17 times between September 1988 and February 1993, producing 41 substantive reports. Only two of these reports, however, were made available to the public — their content relating to £3 million of expenditure on general city-centre refurbishment work.

By the early 1990s, it became clear that the scale of investment in the flagship projects considerably distorted the city council's capital expenditure programme over a six-year period from 1986. For example, over the period 1986-92 public-sector investment in Birmingham's housing stock was 28 per cent below the average performance of English local authorities and, in the late 1980s, capital expenditure on education in the city fell by 60 per cent, compared with big expenditure increases in other cities such as Liverpool, Manchester and Leeds. The diversion of capital resources from housing, towards the construction of prestige property developments in Birmingham, has had a disproportionate impact upon disadvantaged groups and areas within the city. The severity of the city's housing problems cannot be underestimated. In 1992, it was estimated that 83,413 homes were unfit for human habitation and the outstanding repair bill for the public-sector housing stock was estimated to be £980 million (Birmingham City Council, 1992b). In response to the deepening crisis in the city's housing stock Birmingham City Council's Housing Department has stated that:

Fig. 14.3 Development proposals for Brindleyplace (Source: Argent Group PLC)

> "unless the city is allowed to raise far greater sums than it has been able to in the past, housing conditions will deteriorate. The city may then be forced to re-introduce policies of large scale clearance which will be very costly in the long run and will produce many adverse social effects." (Birmingham City Council, 1990c, p.1)

Similarly, the effect of Birmingham's capital under-spending on education has had a major impact on the quality of Birmingham's schools. It has been estimated that more than two out of every three school pupils in Birmingham are being taught in sub-standard buildings and that an investment of £100 million is needed to rectify the disrepair in school buildings in the city (Tully, 1990). The city's Chief Education Officer, commenting in the local press, noted the impact of such conditions on staff and school pupils stating that "poor buildings affect the morale and self-esteem of those who work in them. I believe it sends bad signals to children about the values we place on education and that it can affect their learning chances adversely" (Palmer, 1992).

The operational costs of the ICC and NIA, have also had a major impact upon the local authority's revenue budgets. Birmingham City Council estimated that in the first year of operation the ICC and NIA incurred deficits of £31 million, of which the majority related to the cost of servicing the outstanding debt on the two prestige developments. By 1 April 1996, the cumulative deficit relating to these two facilities will have reached £146 million.

Local authority financing of the costs of supporting both the flagship projects and the city's wider civic boosterism strategy has proved to be increasingly difficult in the 1990s. Central government rigidly controls local-authority spending by declaring a Standard Spending Assessment (SSA). The SSA for Birmingham, however, does not take into account debt charges and operational deficits associated with running large commercial prestige projects such as the ICC and NIA. This situation led, in the late 1980s and early 1990s, to the local authority spending significantly less on city education services than the central government SSA guideline. For example, in 1992-93 the city council spent £60 million less on education than the government allowed for in the SSA calculation (12.4 per cent below the government guidelines).

Political change in Birmingham: a new approach to prestige projects in the mid-1990s?

In 1993, the long-standing political consensus in the city (which supported the development and promotion of the ICC and NIA, the expansion of the NEC and the focusing of significant public-sector investment in the city centre) began to fracture with the election of the veteran left wing Councillor Theresa Stewart as deputy leader of the Labour ruling group of the city council. Her election followed a period of intense local and national debate about the social and economic impact of the city council's focus on the development of flagship projects and city-centre redevelopment. Following her election, Theresa Stewart noted that in respect of the ICC and NIA:

> "...had I been in the position to determine whether we'd had them or not I'd have left them out, preferring to go for better social services and more stable school roofs. Now they're in place though let's market them within strict boundaries ...... local government, of which I think the world, has strayed from providing the services it was established to provide .... what some call 'putting Birmingham on the map' has become a priority. I think that's wrong. The priority must be employment housing, social services and so on." (Messent, 1993).

Within a year of being elected deputy leader, Theresa Stewart was elected leader of the city council, replacing Sir Richard Knowles, a longstanding ardent supporter of the city's investment in prestige developments. The 1994-95 city council budget reflected the shift in political priority under the new leader: with the council's NEC/ICC Committee allocated a £2.6 million cut in budget, while the Education Committee received an additional £40 million of capital and revenue resources.

Whilst the new political leadership in Birmingham has sought to shift the emphasis of city-council policy and resources away from prestige developments, towards neighbourhood regeneration, and strategies to address educational and housing need, the city council's ambitions of developing the city centre and Birmingham's international reputation through the development of flagship projects have not been totally abandoned. During 1995, the city council (along with other cities such as London, Manchester and Sheffield) entered a national competition to secure National Lottery and Sports Council funding for a new 80,000 seat National Sports Stadium adjacent to the NEC site. The bid however, was unsuccessful. Similarly, the city council has forwarded a £100m scheme to develop the Digbeth area (which is located adjacent to the city centre) for funding from the Millennium Commission. This scheme seeks to facilitate the expansion of the city centre and encourage the redevelopment of the Bull Ring shopping centre. The significance of the change of political leadership is that for schemes such as these to proceed, funding will have to be forthcoming from the National Lottery or Millennium Commission, thus (in comparison to the ICC and NIA) reducing the amount of direct financial support necessary from the city council's own limited resources.

Conclusion

Birmingham has embarked upon an ambitious programme of prestige developments aimed at regenerating the city's local economy. In the wake of the collapse of its industrial base in the 1970s and 1980s, and in a climate of cuts in local government expenditure, the city council's decision to invest a huge amount of public resources in prestige projects and its CBD, was a bold one. During the late 1980s and early 1990s, nearly £276 million has been spent by the city council on capital work associated with city-centre developments. This expenditure has resulted in an impressive physical transformation of the city centre and is claimed by the city council to have boosted business confidence in the city and raised its international profile and image. However, there are substantial opportunity costs associated with such developments which did not (until recently) receive the same level of publicity and open debate.

The proponents of models of regeneration, which emphasise civic boosterism activities and the development of flagship developments, argue that costs associated with such initiatives are offset by the generation of increases in wealth, employment and investment opportunities. However, the evidence from Birmingham suggests that the projected employment impact of such schemes are often exaggerated by proponents, with little sign of large increases in inward investment directly related to such schemes. Research also suggests that employment opportunities directly generated by the ICC and NIA have been largely concentrated in low-paid, low-status and part-time jobs, with ethnic minority groups, in particular, largely failing to benefit from access to quality employment.

Birmingham's approach of generating economic growth through the development of prestige projects is coming under increasing pressure as other British cities develop similar and competing facilities. For example, Edinburgh opened a new International Convention Centre in 1995, while Manchester, Newcastle, and Sheffield have developed new indoor sports arenas in the 1990s. The future prospects of Birmingham's profit-making National Exhibition Centre is also under threat from a longstanding proposal to develop a rival exhibition centre in London. If this London centre is developed, then Birmingham City Council's present financial difficulties, which are being aggravated by the financial deficits of the ICC and NIA, will be further exacerbated.

The appeal of the model of regeneration based around prestige developments is that it is deemed to achieve instant and visible physical renewal; lever in private-sector resources; improve business confidence; create much-needed jobs; and ties in with enhancing a city's image and profile. Nevertheless, this strategic model of regeneration fails to address issues of social equity and the distribution of benefits and costs which accrue from such a strategy. Whilst CBD-focused regeneration strategies, which are premised on prestige developments may achieve the physical regeneration of the central business districts (as in the case of Birmingham), this may occur at the expense of needs of the disadvantaged groups.

In the context of massive cuts in central-government financial support for the local authorities, Birmingham City Council has demonstrated considerable skill in increasing its capital programme by tapping alternative sources of funding as a means of financing its prestige projects and boosterism initiatives. Evidence presented in this chapter, however, demonstrates that during the 1980s the scale of capital expenditure on Birmingham's CBD-focused regeneration strategy has led to the diversion of city council expenditure away from essential public services, such as public housing and education. In doing so, the city council has also undermined its own wider contribution to long-term urban regeneration and economic development - that is its role as a provider of social infrastructure and services such as education (Audit Commission, 1989; Keating, 1991).

In a climate of shrinking public resources, local authorities will always face stark political choices between approaches to urban regeneration, spending priorities, urban areas and public services. However, such political choices relating to urban regeneration initiatives, should follow full consideration, and public debate of, the wider costs as well as the benefits of such initiatives and their distributional consequences. In Birmingham, this public debate was not forthcoming until after its prestige projects had been constructed and were operational. When the full extent of the costs, and the implications of pursuing the regeneration strategy adopted became apparent, a public debate ensued which contributed to a change in the political leadership of Birmingham City Council, and a shift in the expenditure priorities of the council towards basic services. It remains to be seen whether such a shift in policy will be politically sustainable in the longer-term.

References

Audit Commission 1989 *Urban regeneration and economic development: the local authority dimensions* HMSO, London

Birmingham City Council 1983 *International convention centre: feasibility study* Birmingham City Council, Birmingham

Birmingham City Council 1986 *1986 review of economic strategy* Birmingham City Council, Birmingham

Birmingham City Council 1990a *Birmingham integrated development operation 1990* Birmingham City Council, Birmingham

Birmingham City Council 1990b *International convention centre/national indoor arena, employment impact within the Broad Street corridor* Internal report to the NEC/ICC Committee 6 June

Birmingham City Council 1990c *Housing investment strategy statement 1990* Birmingham City Council, Birmingham

Birmingham City Council 1992a *City centre strategy* Birmingham City Council, Birmingham

Birmingham City Council 1992b *Housing investment programme strategy statement 1992* Birmingham City Council, Birmingham

Keating M 1991 *Comparative urban politics* Edward Elgar, Aldershot.

KPMG Peat Marwick 1992 *The 1992 survey of foreign-owned companies in the West Midlands* KPMG Peat Marwick, Birmingham

KPMG Peat Marwick 1993 *The economic impact of the international convention centre, the national indoor arena, symphony hall, and the national exhibition centre on Birmingham and the West Midlands. Main report,* KPMG Peat Marwick, Birmingham

Loftman P 1990 *A tale of two cities: Birmingham, the convention and unequal city* Faculty of the Built Environment Research Paper 6 Birmingham Polytechnic, Birmingham

Loftman P and Nevin B 1992 *Urban regeneration and social equity: a case study of Birmingham 1986-1992* Faculty of the Built Environment Research Paper No 8 University of Central England, Birmingham

Loftman P and Nevin B 1996 Going for growth: prestige projects - three British Cities *Urban Studies* 33 6. (forthcoming)

Messent M 1993 The sensible socialist *Birmingham Evening Mail* May 12 p14

Palmer W 1992 Pupil morale plunges as schools decay *Birmingham Metro News* February 14 p5

The Planner 1991 Award for planning achievement 1991 *The Planner* 77 40 v-vi

Planning 1991 Birmingham takes broader view in regeneration drive *Planning* 948 11

Tully L 1990 City needs £100m for Schools *Birmingham Evening Mail* September 22

CHAPTER 15

Retail change and retail planning in the West Midlands

Peter J. Larkham and Tim Westlake

Shopping forms a very significant factor in any measure of the quality of life in our consumerist age. Access to good shopping facilities offering competitive prices, a good range and choice of goods and a comfortable shopping environment, are important to people. Shops also form the major component of the built form of city, town, district and local centres, contributing to the character, identity and economy of the region. This chapter covers some aspects of retail development and planning in the West Midlands county during the post-war period. This first requires discussion of the context within which such large-scale planning takes place, and thus begins with a discussion of the post-war changes in British retailing, and of the British planning system. Locally, the retail pattern of the era of traditional planning is shown to suffer from competition from new retail forms - the edge- and out-of-town centres - particularly after the abolition of the West Midlands County Council in 1986. Although the town centres have fought back, the future pattern of retailing is still in flux.

National changes in retailing

> For more than a decade the distributive trader has formed an extremely dynamic sector of the economy and changes within the sector have manifested themselves into new forms of retail development. These have resulted not only in innovation within the business itself but also from new pressures from consumers and from technological innovation and political intervention (Rees, 1987; 3).

Numerous reviews of recent trends in British retailing (for example, McFadyen, 1987) confirm that, for most of this century, shopping has enjoyed a strong traditional association with the town centre. However, since the late 1960s there has been continued pressure for retail developments to be sited away from established centres. The two most important trends through the 1970s, 1980s and moving into the 1990s has been the decreasing number of shops (Table 15.1) and the increased dominance of multiple retailing, for example as shown by turnover (Table 15.2).

During the post-war period, the number of retail outlets has declined by 40 per cent; from 583,000 in 1950 to just 338,248 in 1988 and a majority of this fall has occurred since the 1960s. This decline has taken place against the background of an increase in the real volume of retail sales; from £40.6 billion in 1950 to £57.4 billion in 1982, when measured in constant 1980 prices. There have been two major results of this trend; first, a significant increase in the size of stores and second, a dramatic increase in the concentration of capital (Wrigley, 1988).

This general trend of retail concentration within the UK is well documented. For example, the Census of Distribution shows that large corporate chains (those operating ten or more branches) more than doubled their share of total retail sales from 22 per cent in 1950 to 56 per

Retail establishment	1950	1960	1970	1980	1988
Co-ops	25,544 (4%)	29,396 (5%)	5,413 (3%)	8,556 (2%)	4,270 (1%)
Multiples	53,949 (9%)	67,299 (12%)	66,785 (14%)	65,241 (19%)	63,900 (19%)
Independents	503,639 (87%)	480,612 (83%)	390,793 (83%)	274,808 (79%)	270,078 (80%)
TOTAL	583,132 (100%)	577,307 (100%)	472,991 (100%)	348,601 (100%)	338,248 (100%)

Sources: Gayler (1984, 12); *Business Monitor* (1988, 11-12)

Table 15.1 Changes in the number and percentage of retail establishments in the UK by organisation, 1950-1988

Retail establishment	1950 (£m)	1960 (£m)	1970 (£m)	1980 (£m)	1988 (£m)
Co-ops	572 (11%)	959 (11%)	1,108 (7%)	3,869 (7%)	4,919 (4%)
Multiples	1,093 (22%)	2,580 (29%)	6,083 (39%)	28,046 (48%)	69,737 (61%)
Independents	3,335 (67%)	5,379 (60%)	8,419 (54%)	26,569 (45%)	40,049 (35%)
TOTAL	5,000 (100%)	8,918 (100%)	15,610 (100%)	58,484 (100%)	114,705 (100%)

Sources: Gayler (1984, 12); *Business Monitor* (1988, 12)

Table 15.2 Changes in the turnover of retail establishments in the UK by organisation, 1950-1988

cent by 1982, and that the ten largest retail groups accounted for 22 per cent of total retail turnover in UK by 1982 (Wrigley, 1987). The 42 per cent decline in the total number of shops over a period of nearly forty years since the end of the Second World War has been a major feature of retailing (Table 15.1). These changes have affected all but one of the retail categories. Such changes reflect both the concentration of capital within retailing, with a trend towards larger stores, but also that, in many areas of the country, there has been an over-provision of stores in the past (Gayler, 1984).

One trend which has accompanied the concentration of capital in UK retailing has been the switching of capital away from traditional central shopping areas. In this respect, retailing has followed an early movement of population and employment out of the `urban core' areas of Britain. These movements have resulted in a major loss of retail demand from the urban core areas and the creation of large, relatively under-provided, concentration of demand in suburban, outer suburban and urban fringe areas. Moreover, outer-city locations have been in demand as car ownership has risen. Retail corporations have inevitably wanted to shift outward to meet this under-supplied demand and take advantage of newer, larger and more profitable forms of retail operation (Wrigley, 1987).

Three such 'waves' of decentralization have been identified. The first wave of retail decentralization was the movement out-of-town of grocery stores. The large supermarket companies sold their old town centre interests and opened large, free-standing stores in locations either on the edge of towns or completely outside them: the first hypermarkets and superstores had arrived (Schiller, 1987).

Subsequent waves of decentralization have involved the sale of non-food or comparison goods, and have produced such retailing innovations as retail warehouses selling primarily bulky goods. In recent years, the third wave of decentralization has taken place, with the movement of comparison goods out-of-town in the form of regional shopping centres and other smaller developments. In the 1990s, a possible `fourth wave' of decentralization became apparent, with the development of edge- and out-of-town `warehouse clubs'. In some cases it was argued that these member-only facilities, offering substantial discounts on bulk purchases, were an attempt to circumvent restrictive planning policies on retail location: it took a major court case "to clarify the planning status of such operations, placing them firmly within the ambit of retail planning policy" (Planning, 1993: 4).

Although the traditional town-centre high street is clearly changing as a result of these trends towards retail decentralization, there is some optimism that they may retain a key function, although the nature and shape of that function may be more directed towards leisure shopping, provision of personal and financial services, etc (eg Dawson, 1988). The fighting-back of town centres is perhaps most clearly seen in the rise of town-centre management schemes to rival the tight management and marketing of the out-of-town centres, and increasing investment in construction and refurbishment.

It is apparent that the development of new forms of retailing in recent years has bought material advantage to the broad mass of the population in terms of greater choice, comfort and cheapness in shopping. These benefits are most conspicuous in the case of superstores and hypermarkets. However, the size and scale of these new facilities has meant that they are not as widely distributed over the urban area as the smaller, traditional types of shops were. As a result different groups of people in different areas of a city have varying degrees of access to them. Since strong disparities already exist in levels of income and mobility between different groups, who tend to be spatially concentrated in certain areas of a city, concern has been expressed that there are growing inequalities in shopping opportunities for the poorer, minority sectors of the population (e.g. Bowlby, 1988).

Planning Policies and their Impacts

Traditionally, planners have resisted the concentration of retail activity into larger, decentralized units. Policies have tended to be conservative in nature, relying on out-dated central-place concepts in an effort to maintain existing hierarchies. This, it would seem, has been based on the rationale that the existing retail hierarchy is adequate in meeting the needs of consumers. Davies

(1986) argued that, for many years, central government had no policy towards retail planning. Local authorities work within a statutory framework of land-use controls, set up by the 1968, 1971 and 1990 Town and Country Planning Acts, namely development control; Structure and Local plans; with central government providing guidance through circulars and appeal decisions. Despite this, in a period of dramatic retail change, retail planning policies have been unclear and inconsistent.

Planning regulations related to retail decentralization were gradually softened in the late 1970s. Wrigley (1988) gives three reasons for this change of heart. First, out-of-town grocery stores have had less impact on existing stores then expected. Second, district shopping centre development has been exploited as a tool in positive infrastructure renewal. Third, in a period of severe recession, the decline in the manufacturing sector has been combated by new service industry investment providing employment crucial to metropolitan local authorities suffering extreme levels of unemployment.

Since 1979, planners have been under pressure to have a more relaxed attitude towards retailing in line with the central government's general view that planning should fulfil a supportive role towards the market. This is clearly reflected in policy statements such as the White Paper *Lifting the Burden* (Great Britain, 1985), in numerous planning appeal decisions, and in various changes in planning law.

However, with the development of the comprehensive and influential system of Planning Policy Guidance Notes (PPGs), central government has begun to develop a policy direction for retailing. From 1988, there was evident Ministerial concern over the impact of the new waves of retailing (eg Howard 1990). General guidance, in PPG6 (Department of the Environment [DOE], 1993) has turned strongly against any further out-of-town centres on the regional scale of Merry Hill (West Midlands), Meadowhall (Sheffield) or the Metro Centre (Gateshead), but

> local planning authorities should not refuse permission for new retail development outside town centres on the grounds of the effect on that town centre, unless there is clear evidence to suggest that the result would be to undermine the vitality and viability of that centre that would otherwise serve the community well (DoE, 1993: 1).

A further DoE research report has also reaffirmed the importance of the continued vitality and viability of town centres (DoE, 1994a), and a separate PPG has stressed the need to reduce pollution, for example from car-borne shopping trips (PPG13: DoE, 1994b).

The current and projected changes in retailing, Rees (1987) argued, are of critical importance to town planning because of their locational implications. Present trends have led to a marked erosion of the hierarchical arrangements of retail centres which planners have traditionally sought to defend. Planners have continued such a policy for a number of reasons, including the following.

- The desire to maximise social and territorial equity in the spatial distribution of shopping opportunities. This may be linked to the belief that central-place theory is associated with hierarchies (which are now of lesser importance owing to increased mobility and car ownership) and also linked to a fear of the effect of increased suburban development on existing shopping facilities.

- The desire to maximize the economic benefits of traditional town and city centres.
- The desire to co-ordinate the ancillary, publicly-financed infrastructure and services in the most cost-effective way.
- The tendency to view sporadic development as bad.
- Awareness of the social consequences of such development, including the production of a two-tier system of retailing. A large minority, who have been described as 'disadvantaged' consumers, have been unable to take advantage of economies of scale associated with superstores, owing to their low income levels, limited purchasing power and restricted mobility.

Birmingham and the West Midlands region

The structure plan era

The dominance of the urban and economic history of the region is clearly shown by examining the region's pattern of retailing, and policies to govern it, in the period covered by the County Structure Plan, up to the 1986 reorganisation of local government. The focus was on Birmingham, the major town, which had the greatest turnover (measured in millions of pounds) and retail floorspace. Wolverhampton was next, closely followed by Coventry, but these were definitely much further down the urban hierarchy. Other local town centres, namely Dudley, Walsall, West Bromwich, Solihull and Sutton Coldfield were again much further down the hierarchy. Within each centre there has been a major retail centre, the CBD; and a series of district and local shopping centres. In many cases, these have been formerly separate villages that have been engulfed into the urban sprawl, such as Moseley and Harborne.

This hierarchical framework of settlement size and retail provision was recognised in the Structure Plan (West Midlands County Council, 1980). The adoption of such a framework does not imply that all centres within a particular category, or level in the hierarchy, will have an identical range of facilities; or that particular categories of centre will not lose or gain functions over time. Indeed, it was considered important that some flexibility was retained, particularly in the lower levels of the hierarchy, so that shopping provision could respond to changes in population distribution, for example. Nevertheless, the primacy of Birmingham city centre has always been stressed. However, this policy hierarchy was useful in attempting to ensure that residents in all parts of the county had reasonable access to at least one centre in each level of the hierarchy, from local shops up to the regional centre, thus ensuring the availability of a range of goods, services and competition.

All of the main town centres are strongly oriented towards `comparison shopping' - where proximity of several similar retailers allows customers to draw comparisons between goods and prices - and these centres are strongly dominated by the multiple retailers and, latterly, franchises. The few independent retailers still remaining are confined mostly to specialist trades. All centres have enjoyed a substantial degree of post-war redevelopment, and their growth at the expense of smaller centres has been promoted by the provision of ring roads and substantial car-parking to improve access. This meant that, by the mid-1970s, the West Midlands was well provided with a good range of modern shopping facilities. In general, both retailers and customers were satisfied by this level of provision.

However, there were some problems. By 1980, it was felt that this very success was leading to difficulties. In comparison to the rest of the country, the West Midlands was 'over-shopped'. Rental levels tended to be low, and so, with only a limited growth in retail spending foreseen, developers were expected to take a very selective approach towards further investment in new retail facilities. Interest was likely to be confined to development schemes in the larger centres, and to the development of single large stores in key locations. Local deficiencies would not, therefore, be met by new shops, and poor environmental conditions of semi-derelict shops in town centres would no longer be overcome by major redevelopment schemes.

In such a situation, the new shopping developments that did occur tended to be at the expense of existing shopping facilities, leading inevitably to an increased concentration of facilities. This was already occurring from the late 1960s owing to the extensive new shopping developments such as Wolverhampton's Mander Centre (of 1968), the increasing domination of retailing by chain stores at the expense of independent local traders, and the tendency of these multiple stores to operate through fewer and larger outlets. Smaller local shops, serving localised needs, have tended to remain viable, and thus the impact of these changing trends in retailing has fallen on the middle of the retail hierarchy, the district and local shopping centres. In this region, these problems are exacerbated by local population decline and a decaying physical fabric.

An associated problem is that, in the older urban areas, there are large numbers of old shops that are unsuited to modern retailing requirements. These have, therefore, suffered greatly from a loss of trade in recent years. Such areas are usually found on the fringes of central retail areas, or in suburban centres such as Selly Oak. Where a high proportion of shops have fallen vacant, this contributes greatly to the creation of a run-down image, which will not aid new investment. Indeed, the over-provision of facilities in the central areas detracts from investment in these fringe districts.

The trend towards the establishment of large new stores - hypermarkets, superstores and retail warehouses - became widespread through the 1970s and gave cause for concern in this region. Such developments have sometimes been located in established centres, but more typically they have sought free-standing sites where an extensive single-storey building and car parking, often for 400-plus vehicles, can be accommodated. In the West Midlands, such sites have often been on formerly derelict industrial land, such as `Battery Park' in Selly Oak with its adjoining J. Sainsbury superstore (Fig. 15.1) and IKEA in Wednesbury. Although providing attractive retail facilities, for car-borne customers at least, such developments divert trade from the district and local centres, particularly where retail supermarkets are concerned. At the same time, retail warehouses selling consumer durable goods and DIY materials can threaten the vitality of some retailing activities in the major town centres.

Having identified these problems, the County Structure Plan (particularly the 1980 revised version) sought to improve matters by concentrating attention on the major town centres, district centres and local centres. Investment in retailing facilities would normally be directed to the enhancement of existing centres and, in consequence, additional shopping developments were to be concentrated in the regional, sub-regional and other main town centres. The concentration of shopping within existing centres, together with other services such as administrative, entertainment and cultural facilities, were justified as conferring a number of practical benefits, including:

Fig. 15.1 J. Sainsbury superstore, Selly Oak, Birmingham: in existing suburban centre, built on a long-derelict site and with over 400 car parking spaces (photo Peter Larkham)

- assistance to the consumer by providing opportunities for competition and choice, and the convenience of making a variety of purchases and using non-retail facilities in a single trip;
- centres are generally accessible both to shoppers using a car and those using public transport;
- the concentration of activities within a centre assists transport by focusing demand at a limited number of locations where it can be efficiently served by public transport;
- centres represent, in general, a massive historical investment in infrastructure that should be used to the maximum;
- centres also contain the main buildings and areas of historical and architectural interest and, if these are to be conserved, it is necessary to retain commercial viability (West Midlands County Council, 1980: 112).

Elsewhere, according to the Structure Plan, new shopping development was normally to be confined to the replacement of existing floorspace or small shops required mainly to meet the everyday requirements of people living within walking distance. Policies for large new stores were concerned mainly with guiding location decisions so that they could contribute most effectively to the strategy for enhancing the existing centres.

In detail, policies were determined to maintain, indeed enhance, the existing retail hierarchy. Birmingham city centre was to remain dominant. Some development was envisaged in Coventry and Wolverhampton town centres, the "sub-regional shopping centres". Other town centres were strictly controlled. All such restrictions were to preserve the primacy of Birmingham. The justification for restrictions on Stourbridge, for example, was that one substantial development had been completed since 1970, a further one was in progress in the late 1970s and, while this included a large food store previously lacking in the area, the scale of development gave some cause for concern. Therefore, no further shopping development would be permitted.

In general, the County Structure Plan was successful up to 1986 in resisting much pressure for retail decentralization. Although some edge-of-town stores were developed, most effort and investment remained concentrated in the existing town centres. Even the new Sainsbury's superstore in Wolverhampton, for example, was still within the inner ring road, although at a small distance from the traditional core retail district.

The post-abolition experience

Following the abolition of the county council, its planning functions devolved to the newly-independent metropolitan boroughs, each of which had to formulate plans for its own area. These were initially based on the structure plan, which was, however, fast becoming outdated, being overtaken by a number of events.

One such was the Dudley Enterprise Zone, established between Brierley Hill and Dudley on the site of the former Round Oak steelworks. The intention was to encourage industrial regeneration by, amongst other things, offering developers 10 years free of commercial rates. The planning scheme for this 51.4 ha site restricted the retail sale of food, drink or clothing to no more than 2,508m^2 of the floorspace of any new or existing shop, but there was no restriction upon any other retailing. In 1981 and 1984, the time of designation, these limits were seen as being adequate to protect the existing shopping centres in the borough, and in particular in the adjacent local shopping centre of Brierley Hill.

Prior to 1984, a limited amount of retail floorspace was constructed, but the main emphasis was on industrial development. However, in 1984 a start was made on the construction of a major store for MFI and a block of retail warehouse units. This was followed by a second phase

Fig. 15.2 Early phase of the Merry Hill Centre, Dudley, developed in an Enterprise Zone

including a large superstore and covered shopping mall (Fig.15. 2). It became clear that Merry Hill, then entirely owned by Richardson Developments Ltd, a local development company, was beginning to take on the form of a single shopping centre providing a wide choice of products, and which would be in direct competition with existing local centres. In 1985, work continued on the construction of over 46,000m2 of floorspace, and Richardson Developments compounded the problem by submitting a planning application for a further 111,480m2 of retail and leisure development on the remainder of the site. The local authority considered the implications that such a development would have on local retailing, and believed that more would be gained from supporting such a scheme than in attempting to fight it. When completed, the Merry Hill Centre provided some 167,220m^2 of retail floorspace and leisure facilities, with over 9,500 car parking spaces and some public transport facilities. With completion of its Phase 5 it was (briefly) the largest retail development in Europe. In the mid-1990s there were plans for further large-scale expansion of the retail section of the Merry Hill site, but no decision had been reached on this proposal by early 1996.

Obviously, this major retail facility represented a considerable departure from the existing urban and retailing hierarchy that the Structure Plan had been at great pains to reinforce. It was not something that the County Council (before 1986) or local authorities could resist, the Enterprise Zone being a central government initiative. The retail development, exploiting a legal loophole, has had a notable effect upon the major centres of the county, and a very much larger effect upon the local town centre of Brierley Hill, only some 200m from Merry Hill. It has taken over a decade from the opening of the first retail warehouses for this town centre to show signs of recovery; and the shops opening are not the small, local shops that were driven out of business by the competition from Merry Hill. A Department of the Environment report suggested that Dudley itself had experienced a 70 per cent reduction in the market share of comparison shopping (excluding bulk durable goods). Stourbridge, also close to Merry Hill itself, suffered a 4 per cent reduction; while Birmingham and Wolverhampton lost between 10 and 20 per cent. Only Solihull and Worcester showed increases in comparison shopping market shares (Tym & Partners, 1993: 85).

Yet Merry Hill is only one aspect of major changes in retailing that have occurred throughout the 1980s. Between 1979 and 1989 the annual provision of new retail floorspace has risen by 500 per cent; there are constant changes in ownership of both major and minor retailers; the established hierarchy of retail shopping centres has been abandoned; Enterprise Zones now allow retail development in unusual places; and about 80 superstores, each over 100,000 square feet of floorspace, are being built each year in the UK. Developers have been quick to respond to the needs of retailers for new large stores, and this has resulted in the sudden rise of applications submitted to local planning authorities (in this case, the seven metropolitan district councils making up the county) from c. 1986, many of which have received planning permission. These applications proposed both major free-standing schemes and smaller developments that would, in restricted areas, acquire the characteristics of regional centres.

The sudden rise of applications for major retail schemes, commonly at edge-of-town locations, but in the West Midlands context also re-using derelict industrial sites, has led to a situation with which the then-current policy based on the Structure Plan was manifestly unable to cope (Larkham and Pompa, 1989). Some applications, for example, proposed over 93,000m^2 of retail floorspace on a single site. It was realised in late 1986 that some schemes have effects far beyond the boundaries of an individual district council or even a county council, and in many cases local authorities were finding difficulties in dealing with then. Arguably, this situation is worse in the metropolitan counties where there is no co-ordinating county council to mediate between the metropolitan districts. In the West Midlands, in addition to the giant Merry Hill centre, six major retail developments were proposed during 1987 (Larkham and Pompa, 1989) These include Fort Dunlop, F.H. Lloyd, Sandwell Mall and Walsall power station, all re-using derelict industrial sites; Monkspath near Solihull, a combination of several smaller applications close to a new motorway junction, and Lynton Square, in suburban Birmingham, a redevelopment of an existing retail site. Of these, Sandwell Mall and Fort Dunlop are worthy of closer study.

The first of these proposals to receive outline planning permission was the Sandwell Mall scheme, a £500 million entertainment and shopping complex comprising over 800 shops in several malls together with a 2ha water park on derelict industrial land. The outline permission was granted in 1986. This application was approved relatively quickly, and consultations with other planning authorities were limited. Walsall Borough Council estimated that this centre would cause a 10 per cent - 15 per cent drop in trade in the existing town centres - a rather larger impact than the developer's own estimate. It appears that Sandwell Borough Council, aware of the economic benefits of this scheme to the borough, and of the limited number of such schemes that would be viable within the conurbation, were staking their claim first. However, a revised proposal in 1987 substantially reduced the proposed floorspace to 130,000m^2, and the number of shops to 300. Construction was postponed until the 1990s by the decision to extract coal from part of the site, but the retail slump has recently led to a shelving of the entire project. The area is now likely to be developed for industrial use, perhaps as a vehicle spares and recycling centre.

The case of the Fort Dunlop scheme differs from Sandwell Mall in that it was not actively supported by the local planning authority. A speculative outline planning application was submitted for a shopping complex with a gross retail floorspace of over 116,000m^2. A range of retail impact and traffic studies were carried out. Other factors for consideration were the likely economic, employment, investment and traffic impacts, in addition to the loss of an existing and potential industrial site. There was considerable local political opposition to this scheme. Overall, the local authority appeared to be against the proposal for planning and political reasons. A revised scheme was later submitted, proposing a reduction to 77,000m^2 of retailing floorspace, to include supermarkets, a food court and 130 shop units, together with an hotel, museum, 10,000 car-parking spaces and a new railway station. Discussions are still under way for this site and no development has occurred by 1995.

Town centres fighting back

The main problem caused by these large proposals is that they would have caused great damage to the existing retail hierarchy of the town centres, as enshrined in the Structure Plan; although estimates of these impacts by the developers and local authorities have been at considerable variance. The impact study of the Merry Hill development suggested that the larger town centres lost between 10 per cent and 20 per cent of the comparison shopping trade. In a period of general retail slump, key stores such as Lewis's in Birmingham closed. Noting the changing type of town-centre shops, a key property journal suggested that "despite promoting itself as a city of culture, Birmingham's retail centre is geared towards bargain hunters with limited taste" (Goodchild, 1994: 47). In 1994, Birmingham's Corporation Street was dropped from the key property profession list of five highest-performing retail trading locations, while Merry Hill rose from tenth to third place in the national ranking of most profitable locations (DTZ Debenham Thorpe, 1995: 20).

Fig. 15.3 Interior of the Pallasades shopping centre (photo; Geoff Dowling)

Town centre retailers and property owners have attempted to counter the potential loss of trade that any of these schemes would cause, as is suggested by the completion of several major refurbishment schemes in the late 1980s, including the Mander Centre in Wolverhampton, of 37,000m^2, and Norwich Union's Birmingham Shopping Centre of 21,000m^2, renamed The Pallasades after its 1980s' refit and, in 1995-6, undergoing further refurbishment (Fig. 15.3). A considerable amount of new construction has also been evident in Birmingham city centre. This began with The Pavilions, a multi-level redevelopment on High Street, linking directly with the existing Marks and Spencer store (Fig. 15.4), and the City Plaza, a retail development with office tower above, opened in 1988. There have been problems with these projects, as pedestrian flow has not been as high as was planned, trade is down, retailers in the Pavilions negotiated a thirty per cent rent drop because of this, and not all shop units in City Plaza are yet leased.

Nevertheless, there is considerable demand for prime retail floorspace in the city centre from national multiple retailers, and redevelopment and refurbishment schemes current in 1995 proposed over 16,000m^2 of retail space (DTZ Debenham Thorpe, 1995: 20). These schemes are concentrated in New Street, in particular at Queen's Corner and the Midland Hotel. They are occurring just after completion of the major pedestrianization scheme, which has considerably increased the attractiveness of this area for the visitor and shopper on foot (Fig. 15.5).

For nearly a decade, discussions have focused on the future of the 32,500m^2 Bull Ring shopping centre of the 1960s (Fig. 15.6). This, Europe's first major covered shopping centre, was purchased in 1987 by a property developer, the London and Edinburgh Trust. A comprehensive area redevelopment was proposed, initially to consist of one major building stretching from New Street to Moor Street railway stations, and including 174 shops, four large stores and a four-floor department store; together with offices and car-parking (Fig. 15.7). This proposal gave 110,000m^2 of retail floorspace, at an estimated cost of some £250 million. This is of the same

Fig. 15.4 Interior of The Pavillions shopping centre. This multi-level centre has a food court on the topmost level and all floors link in to the pre-existing Marks and Spencer store. The banners reflect Birmingham's attempt to position itself as a European city (photo Geoff Dowling)

Fig. 15.5 New Street and the Midland Hotel refurbishment. Pedestrianization, tree planting and new street furniture has encouraged developers to refurbish the Midland Hotel and the ground floor shops. The banner illustrates a major factor in the reduction of street crime: the introduction of CCTV (photo: Geoff Dowling)

Fig. 15.6 The Bull Ring Centre, Rotunda office building and retail market (photo: Geoff Dowling)

Fig. 15.7 Model of LET'S original proposed shopping mall and office tower, Birmingham Bull Ring: from 1987 publicity brochure.

scale as some of the out-of-town proposals. Detailed discussions on this scheme are still progressing and, influenced by a local pressure group and the general retail slump, proposals current in 1995 suggest a smaller phased development in several blocks, aiming to recreate something of the medieval street pattern (Holyoak, 1995).

A 17,000m^2 redevelopment in Coventry city centre was completed in the early 1990s and Solihull, although targeted by the Structure Plan for minimal new retailing, is to have a major new shopping area adjoining the High Street, along with refurbishment of its Mell Square development of the 1960s.

Planning issues and conclusions

The events of the post-1986 period suggest a number of issues arising in retail planning in the West Midlands county. First, the demise of the county council has made the consideration of the impact of these schemes on the retail structure of the conurbation as a whole much more difficult. There is evidence that some of the large-scale applications were dealt with in an ad hoc manner, and that any 'policy' was essentially local and even informal, particularly immediately following the 1986 reorganisation. The case of the Sandwell Mall decision, for example, supports this view. A regional approach is clearly required in order to prevent this type of decision-making, but this still seems an unpopular concept in UK planning.

Secondly, if the forces of supply and demand are left to regulate these proposals at the regional level, it is possible that there will be a considerable regional over-provision of retail floorspace. As a consequence, it would probably be the existing town centres and suburban shopping centres that would suffer, as a result of relocations of retail outlets to the new shopping centres. This is clearly illustrated by the concern of Birmingham council over the Fort Dunlop proposal. Here, one can compare the likely impact on the retail floorspace of the entire city centre of Birmingham (177,000m^2) of the original Fort Dunlop proposal (116,000m^2), located just six kilometres away.

This proposal would actually be less significant if there were scope for a considerable growth in the retail floorspace of the region. In order to try to ascertain the potential for growth, the seven planning authorities making up the West Midlands county set up joint working arrangements following abolition of the county council, and commissioned a report from the chartered surveyors Drivers Jonas. This concluded that there is only scope for a total of 60,400m^2 of out-of-town retail development up to the early 1990s (pers. comm., Birmingham planning officers; the survey is unpublished). The six sites already mentioned have a total maximum proposed floorspace of approximately 465,000m^2; a considerable contrast to the conclusions of the Drivers Jonas survey.

It appears that the experience of retail planning in the West Midlands county is quite typical of the remainder of the country. A structure plan justified, and placed great reliance upon, retention and augmentation of the existing pattern of shopping provision, itself conditioned by the historical urban hierarchy of the region. Local authorities then saw a sharp upturn in the numbers of applications for major out- or edge-of-town shopping centres from 1986 onwards, and the scale of these proposals is far greater than previously seen in the UK. However, the new planning system in the metropolitan counties contains little provision for making decisions on a regional basis. There is, in contrast, some indication that individual local authorities may act alone, granting applications without regard for the surrounding area, to the benefit of their own local economies and employment. The large scale of some current town centre proposals should also be considered.

The great pressure for the development of these large retail facilities, and the apparent shortcomings of the development control and strategic planning systems in the metropolitan counties, will have a significant impact upon the existing town centres of the west midlands conurbation. Unfortunately, little work has been carried out to ascertain the nature and scale of this impact, but it seems obvious that the existing retail hierarchy could undergo marked change. The inter-urban hierarchy will become distorted by new edge- or out-of-town developments, while intra-urban change may occur by, for example, new, large-scale town-centre development drawing traders and customers away from the existing central retail areas. The impact of the new retail clubs and new concepts such as teleshopping have been limited so far, but could develop rapidly. The next decade could be one of significant change in the pattern of retailing.

References

Bowlby S 1988 From corner shop to hypermarket: women and food retailing in **Little J Peake L and Richardson P** (eds) *Women in cities: gender and the urban environment* Macmillan, London
Business Monitor 1988 *Retailing* Central Statistical Office HMSO, London
Davies R 1986 Retail planning in disarray *The Planner* 72: 20-2
Dawson J A 1988 Futures for the high street *Geographical Journal* 154: 1-12
Department of the Environment 1993 *Town centres and retail development* Planning Policy Guidance Note 6 (revised) HMSO, London
Department of the Environment 1994a *Vitality and viability* HMSO, London
Department of the Environment 1994b *Transport* Planning Policy Guidance Note 13 HMSO, London
DTZ Debenham Thorpe 1995 *West Midlands Annual Property Review 1994* DTZ Debenham Thorpe, Birmingham
Gayler H 1984 *Retail innovation in Britain: problems of out of town shopping centre development* Geo Books, Norwich
Goodchild S 1994 Centrefolio West Midlands: the market *Property Week* 47: 46-50
Great Britain 1985 *Lifting the burden* White Paper Cmnd 9571 HMSO, London
Holyoak J 1995 The new Bull Ring proposal *Birmingham for People Newsletter* May: 1
Howard M 1990 Britain in 2010: future patterns of shopping. Out of town shopping: is the revolution over? *Royal Society of Arts Journal* CXXXVIII: 162-71
Larkham P J and Pompa N D 1989 Planning problems of large retail centres: the West Midlands County in 1987 *Cities* 7: 309-16
McFadyen (ed) 1987 *The changing face of British retailing* Newman Books, London.
Planning 1993 Costco ruling puts warehouse clubs under retail policy head Planning 1043: 4
Rees J 1987 Perspectives on planning issues *Planning Practice and Research* 2: 3-8
Schiller R 1987 Out of town exodus in **McFadyen E** (ed) *The changing face of British retailing* Newman Books, London
Tym R and Partners in association with Colquhoun Transportation Planning 1993 *Merry Hill impact study* HMSO, London
West Midlands County Council 1980 *West Midlands County Structure Plan* (revised edition) WMCC, Birmingham
Wrigley N 1987 The concentration of capital in U.K. grocery retailing *Environment and Planning A* 19: 1283-8
Wrigley N 1988 Retail restructuring and retail analysis in **Wrigley N** (ed.) *Store choice, store location and market analysis* Routledge and Kegan Paul, Andover

CHAPTER 16

Urban Regeneration Policy as a Beauty Contest: Competition and The City Challenge Initiative in The West Midlands

Mike Beazley

City Challenge commits £1bn of government money to regenerating disadvantaged urban areas in England. It was launched in 1991 by then Environment Secretary Michael Heseltine, who invited local authorities to compete for funds to help economic, social and physical regeneration in urban areas. Since its launch, 31 partnerships have been created and are well into their five year regeneration plans (DoE, 1994).

Like watching Miss World and wondering which of the contestants is going to win, urban regeneration policy in the UK entered the beauty contest business with the introduction of the City Challenge programme. Local authority bidders had to parade themselves in front of a "panel of judges" at the Department of the Environment (DoE) to see if they were going to be lucky enough to secure "the crown" and the resources that go with it (£37.5 million over five years). It is in this sense that the arrival of City Challenge marked a significant change in the development and delivery of urban regeneration policy in England (there are no City Challenges in Wales or Scotland).

City Challenge was officially launched on 23 May 1991 by Michael Heseltine, soon after his return to the DoE. It was heralded as a new and innovative approach to the allocation of urban regeneration resources. It was said to be the most interesting change in government urban policy since the 1977 White Paper *Policy for the Inner Cities* (Mabbott 1993). According to the DoE, the aims of City Challenge were to be linked into strategies to assist disadvantaged urban areas to attract investment, stimulate wealth creation, widen social provision and create good quality environments and enterprise cultures, and thereby attract people to live and work in these areas (DoE 1994). Basically, City Challenge was said to be about improving the quality of local residents' lives and the creation of economically viable communities that could sustain themselves once City Challenge had ceased. The intention was to continue the process established during the 1980s of trying to lever in as much private-sector investment as possible, but to broaden out those who were involved in the process.

The key factor in the new approach was the decision to allocate funds on a competitive basis. Competition was seen as a means of encouraging potential bidders to become entrepreneurial in their approach. Moreover, Heseltine believed that competition was an essential ingredient of releasing "local creativity" in the development of City Challenge strategies (Atkinson and Moon 1994). The downside of this, however, is that like a beauty contest it has the potential to lead to a situation where "looks" and "presentation" can affect the outcome of the selection process as opposed to the decision being reached on the basis of a rational process based in some way on need. The Government remains committed to the concept of competition and it was used as the basis for determining the recent Single Regeneration Budget (SRB) allocations. The November 1995 budget statement announced a major expansion of the Challenge Funding approach which allocates public resources through competitive processes (HM Treasury 1995).

This chapter looks at the City Challenge programmes in the West Midlands and, at a broader level, explores the competitive dimension of City Challenge and raises some questions about the suitability of this approach for determining access to much-needed urban regeneration resources. It is argued that urban areas generally do not benefit from competition. In fact, the impact can potentially be damaging to both the resource base and psyche of the bidders, in much the same way as the failure to win Miss World can affect the tearful participants left backstage. It argues for a return to a system of public funds being allocated to those urban areas with the greatest need.

The City Challenge Approach

In preparing the competitive bids and action programmes for City Challenge funds, the DoE saw local authorities as taking the lead. This was in marked contrast to the policy initiatives of the eighties, when the role of local government was to a large extent marginalized. They were given the brief to establish broad-based partnerships in both the drawing up and delivery of the programme bids involving the public, private and the voluntary/community sectors.

In the first round eleven bids were chosen out of the fifteen Urban Priority Area (UPA) authorities that were invited to bid. These became known as the pacemaker authorities and included only one authority from the West Midlands, Wolverhampton MBC. In 1992, all 57 UPA authorities were invited to bid, out of which 20 were chosen, making a total over the two rounds of 31 City Challenges. The second round winners included three from the West Midlands: Birmingham (Newtown/south Aston), Sandwell (Tipton) and Walsall.

Bidders had to operate on a tight timescale; they only had about eight weeks to prepare and submit their bids. Each successful City Challenge then had to prepare and implement a five-year Action Plan. These Action Plans were required to identify a vision and specify clear targets which the City Challenge programme had to attain within the five years. In addition, these plans had to include specific measures to link the economic and physical regeneration of areas to improving the circumstances of disadvantaged residents and communities (DoE 1991). The 11 pacemaker authorities were required to have their Action Plans approved early in 1992 and had to be in operation by April 1992. Second round City Challenges had to be in a position to start by April 1993 (Bailey 1995).

The expected third round of City Challenge was suspended following the government's 1992 Autumn budget statement which announced the end of the Urban Programme and the introduction of the Private Finance Initiative (PFI), a scheme where the private sector was to be encouraged to invest in capital projects that otherwise would have been completely publicly funded (Bailey 1995). In November 1993, City Challenge was replaced by the SRB (Robson, 1994).

The West Midland City Challenge Areas

The West Midlands secured four City Challenge areas over the two rounds. Details of the nature of these areas are given in Table 16.1. It can be seen that all the areas experience significant levels of deprivation. A funding breakdown of how the spending profiles are allocated is given in Table 16.2. It can be seen that all the City Challenges have secured leverage resources to increase and support the £37.5 million City Challenge allocation.

All information taken from 1991 census	Total no of households	%Households with dependant children	%Households one parent families	%Households with no car	%Over crowding (2+ persons per room)	Tenure % owner occupied	Tenure % private rented	Tenure % housing association rented	Tenure % Local authority rented
Wolverhampton City Challenge Area	7,856	38.8	10.6	55.5	1.3	34.7	6.3	6.8	50.9
Wolverhampton	93,841	29.4	5.4	41.3	0.5	57.7	4.6	2.8	33.7
Walsall City Challenge Area	5,330	38.3	14.5	55.3	8.4	36.2	8.9	7.7	47.1
Walsall	97,700	32.0	3.5	36.3	3.1	60.6	4.6	2.8	32.0
Tipton City Challenge Area	9,223	30.1	4.2	53.9	4.0	33.3	1.8	2.8	60.3
Sandwell MBC	113,223	28.5	3.9	45.0	3.2	54.4	3.4	2.8	38.2
Newtown/south Aston City Challenge Area	4,425	31.4	14.3	80.6	6.0	11.8	1.5	6.8	78.2
Birmingham	374,079	29.2	5.4	45.0	4.0	60.1	6.6	5.6	26.4

Source: Essex, 1995

Table 16.1 West Midland City Challenge Areas: Deprivation Indices

	Wolverhampton	Walsall	Tipton	Newton/S.Aston
CCF	36,100	36,099	35,776	35,887
Private Funds	95,334	117,915	60,356	96,884
Other Public Funds	22,687	33,321	46,443	97,057
Total	155,521	188,736	144,301	231,441

CCF = City Challenge Funds
Total City Challenge Funds do not include amounts for administration overheads which bring the total to £37.5 million, for
Wolverhampton add £1400k
Walsall add £1400k
Tipton add £1722k
Newtown add £1613k

Source: Essex, 1995

Table 16.2 West Midland City Challenge Areas: Funding Breakdown

The Wolverhampton City Challenge area lies to the north of Wolverhampton town centre and has a total population of 21,879. The area consists of two wards, St. Peter's and Low Hill, which contain some of the highest levels of unemployment and social deprivation in the borough. The area also contains some important development opportunities and existing businesses. A major theme to run through the subsequent City Challenge proposals for the area is the development and expansion of sports facilities in the area into regional and national attractions, including the Wolverhampton Wanderers football ground at Molineux, the Dunstall racecourse, and a 17.4 ha sports facility at Aldersley (Essex, 1995). Money was to be levered in from the private sector and other public-sector sources to support these projects and undertake other initiatives including business development, derelict land reclamation, the development of housing, education and training, and environmental improvements.

The City Challenge area in Birmingham covered the Newtown/south Aston area of the city. It contains a population of 10,642 that live in an extremely poor environment beset with severe social and economic problems. The levels of deprivation in the area are probably the highest of all the City Challenge areas in the West Midlands. Unemployment, numbers of households without a car, lone parents, incidence of ill-health, and other deprivation indices are well over city and regional averages. It is a difficult area to regenerate given the time restraints and resource levels of a City Challenge programme. Part of the strategy for regeneration concentrates on three flagship projects: the redevelopment of a former landmark - the Lucas works site - into a mixed commercial, residential and open space development and it is to be the location for a new European Clothing and Fashion Centre; the redevelopment of the rundown Newtown shopping centre; and the reclamation of the King Edward's Trust land (an area of former industry). The proposals also contain a local labour strategy, a housing development programme, and health promotion and crime prevention measures. Overall, there are 200 individual projects identified within the Action Plan (Essex, 1995).

Tipton City Challenge is located in the Metropolitan Borough of Sandwell. At 23,814 residents it has the largest population of the four City Challenge areas in the West Midlands, but like its counterparts it exhibits a number of the same problems. Tipton is regarded as one of the most deprived areas in the borough. The approach of Tipton City Challenge to deal with these problems is different from the other City Challenge projects. There are no flagship schemes, but rather a large number of smaller-scale projects aimed at improving the environment, providing new housing development, business development, and projects directed toward improving health and reducing crime. Housing has been the main focus of Tipton City Challenge and it has spent the largest proportion of its funds on housing (nearly 33 per cent), which is the highest proportion of all the West Midland City Challenge areas. Tipton City Challenge also prides itself on the degree of community involvement in the process.

The Walsall City Challenge area incorporates three major parts of the borough, two major residential areas (Caldmore/Palfrey area and Beechdale), and part of the town centre around the canal basin. The total population of the area is 15,440 and again similar levels of deprivation to the other City Challenge areas are to be found. The Action Plan is premised on three major projects: the redevelopment of the former Reedswood power station, the development of the Town Wharf site in the city centre, and the redevelopment of the Pleck gas works into a low-tech industrial park.

Competition and Partnership

Competition and partnership are the two key themes that underpin the City Challenge approach. Competition was seen by central government as a positive and innovative means of allocating resources, but also as a means of challenging the complacency central government thought had developed within local government. The central government perception was that local authorities had lost their cutting edge (Oatley and Lambert 1995).

Competition was seen as a means of transforming the way in which local authorities and their partners approached the task of urban regeneration. It was to encourage the development of new and creative responses to the regeneration challenge. Recent government statements indicate that they remain convinced about the benefits of such an approach, the principle of competition is now being extended through the expansion of the Challenge Fund (HM Treasury 1995).

Moreover, City Challenge was seen as a means to develop new three-way partnerships between the public, private and voluntary/community sectors. This would then be used as a mechanism for encouraging the development of a broad consensus around the new approach to urban regeneration. These partnerships are in evidence to varying degrees within the West Midland City Challenge areas. All have secured the involvement of the private sector and private-sector investment (see Table 16.2). The degree, however, to which the voluntary and community sectors have effectively been brought on board is less clear.

The imposition of competition for regeneration funds has a number of significant implications for the operation of a regeneration strategy like City Challenge. First, it creates a scenario where there are winners and losers and raises important questions as to what happens to the unsuccessful bidders and their areas. Unsuccessful bidders lose out on a number of fronts. They lose out in terms of failing to secure the prize, that is the £37.5 million of government money, as opposed to the Miss World crown and the holiday in the Caribbean. They lose out in terms of the funds they would otherwise have received through the Urban Programme. They lose out in terms of the huge investment made to put the bid in. Money, time and effort that could have been put to different uses. It is difficult to estimate accurately the cost of the bidding process for local authorities, but the costs are substantial (Oatley and Lambert 1995). Dudley, for example, is a West Midland local authority that invested considerable effort and resources into mounting its City Challenge bid only to fail.

Unsuccessful bidders can also suffer from raising the expectations of all those involved in their respective communities. This leads to disillusionment which can be difficult to recover. Out of the 57 Urban Priority Areas, 32 secured funding, leaving 25 out in the cold and wondering where resources were going to come from to support future regeneration activity. As Oatley and Lambert (1995) point out losers are much worse off than before due first to the cost of the bid process itself and, secondly, due to the fact that the DoE top-sliced its other budgets for which they might be eligible.

Moreover, for the winners there is the realization that they have won at the expense of someone else and, tied into this, is the feeling that winners are also probably not too keen to publicize the secret of their success for fear of losing out next time. In this sense it can make bidders inward-looking and secretive about what they do, which is hardly in the spirit of openness and collaboration which is possibly the best way to attack problems of disadvantage. In addition, these attitudes could threaten any joint working relationships that might be in place at the time that might have worked well prior to the competitive climate. There is also the point that success can be self-reinforcing in that the confidence and knowledge gained through winning can ensure further success. The unfortunate corollary of that of course, is that losing breeds losing.

Secondly, it promotes the establishment of an enterprise culture and its attendant characteristics like the "survival of the fittest". Those local authorities with the resources to compete tend to have the advantage over those local authorities that do not. City Challenge as a beauty contest means that rewards can be related to the quality of the presentation rather than the quality of the case. This has the potential of developing into a "packaging over substance" scenario. The criteria for the winning selection were never made explicit by the DoE. A number of unsuccessful local authorities felt that their bids had been every bit as good as, if not better than, some of those that had won. It was said that there was a lack of clear and convincing feedback on the decisions (Oatley and Lambert 1995). In such circumstances the Government is clearly open to accusations of political favouritism and patronage.

Thirdly, competition puts local government in a difficult position, forcing them to gamble with scarce resources and to see each other as competitors for resources rather than allies in the regeneration process. Due to the levels of need within areas many authorities have to go all out to win resources, particularly when faced with the loss of other resources like Urban Programme funds. Competition can therefore be a divisive force and can mitigate against any form of strategic approach to the challenge of urban regeneration.

Fourthly, competitive bidding can be used to select priority areas and as a mechanism for reducing the number of areas receiving assistance and the total amount of money available for urban regeneration (Mabbott 1993). City Challenge and the SRB have been introduced in a period of significant resource cutbacks for urban regeneration:

> The Government's approach to urban areas since 1979 can be summarized crudely as involving a general reduction in State activity and Government investment on the one hand, whilst on the other, the targeting of special urban initiatives intended to open up market opportunities for the private sector in distressed towns and cities. This approach has necessitated the creation of specific budgets administered increasingly by unelected bodies, and a succession of policy initiatives such as Action for Cities and City Challenge which have been unsupported by any significant additional Central Government resources (Nevin and Shiner 1994 1).

Fifthly, competition creates a situation which sees bidders as clients resulting in a centrally-controlled system that involves complex project appraisal and monitoring procedures. As noted earlier, each successful City Challenge had to produce an Action Plan, which sets out in detail the five-year plan in terms of the proposed projects and schemes broken down into strategic objectives. These plans are subject to the approval of the respective DoE Government Office for the region. Only approved schemes are allowed to be included, and the City Challenges are also subject to both mid-year and annual reviews by the Government Office.

Awarders of the prize have to retain control to ensure winners act properly and responsibly, and do not, like some Miss Worlds, have affairs with famous footballers! The DoE acts as judge and executioner, it sets the rules, and has the power to chastise mischievous or under-performing City Challenges. If individual City Challenge partnerships did not spend their annual allocation of £7.5 million, they were liable to lose the unspent element to the more active or overspent programmes. This put pressure on the partnerships to spend quickly and, some commentators would argue, resulted in some money being used unwisely.

The DoE state that City Challenge is an output-led programme. There are identifiable Key Outputs which is a short list of standard quantifiable outputs used to provide summary reports on progress to ministers. These include figures on amounts of private-sector leverage, numbers of houses built, or numbers of jobs created, the amount of land improved or brought back into use, the number of business start-ups and so on. These are fleshed out by a longer list of Core Outputs which are again a standard list of quantifiable outputs and definitions for use in managing the City Challenge programmes themselves (DoE 1994). Targets for each City Challenge partnership are drawn from their Action Plans. Most City Challenges commissioned consultants or academic institutions to provide an outside view of their achievements through data gathering and surveys. Most produced baseline audits which could be revisited at stages throughout the life of the City Challenge programme to check on progress towards identified targets.

Sixthly, competition makes reliable and realistic monitoring difficult. Burton and Boddy (1995) make the valid point that the competitive climate encourages a situation where bidders are likely to make bold strategies and bold claims about the likely chances of success. This makes the collection of good quality data to assess the true performance of the City Challenge bodies, and to use this to influence the future direction of urban regeneration policy, difficult. The SRB continued the competitive element of urban policy without any proper evaluation of the suitability of this approach.

There are then a number of negative aspects to the process of competing for much-needed urban regeneration resources. It means that Urban Priority Area authorities now have to compete for resources they would have secured anyway under the former Urban Programme. It means having to put energy and resources into a speculative process with no guarantee of success, made worse by the lack of clarity or guidance about what was required. It creates uncertainty and threatens any long-term planning for the regeneration of urban areas. Moreover, many of the already existing programmes were placed under threat by the ending of the Urban Programme. There is a strong argument in the contention that urban problems are too serious to leave to the vagaries of a competitive process. It is more appropriate that resources should be allocated on the basis of need to ensure that such problems are addressed on a fair and comprehensive front.

Conclusions

City Challenge was heralded as a bold and imaginative innovation to the development of urban regeneration policy in England. The central theme of the process was the introduction of competition as a means to determine who gains access to resources. This theme is set to continue for the foreseeable future.

City Challenge marked a significant break with previous urban regeneration policy. On one level it facilitated a revived role for local authorities. On another it placed competition central stage in an attempt to transform the way local authorities and their partners approached the task of regeneration. It was seen also as a mechanism to develop new all-purpose and all-encompassing partnerships.

This chapter has looked at the City Challenge projects in the West Midlands and attempted to raise some questions as to the validity of such an approach by highlighting some of the difficulties and problems that competition brings to the bidders. It creates a scenario of winners and losers that impacts negatively on those authorities that are not successful in the bidding process. They suffer a serious loss of resources as well as potential disillusionment and detachment from the regenerative process. There is the danger that success will become self-reinforcing, further disadvantaging the losers. It is a process that promotes the culture of the survival of the fittest.

The City Challenge process on the one hand creates a more significant role for local authorities, but on the other facilitates considerable central control over the whole process. The detailed monitoring and evaluation requirements results in a complex and bureaucratic system. The whole process is politically sensitive in that it is open to accusations of political patronage and bias. The local authority perception of the process was that it was a highly politicized process with seemingly little relationship to levels of need.

In short, competition is potentially divisive and, in the long term, unproductive. Moreover, it detracts from the fact that all former Urban Priority Areas continue to need money, along with new areas experiencing problems of deprivation (like the former coalfield areas), and that the allocation of funds should not be determined by the merits or otherwise of a bid document. We do not need more beauty contests, but we do need sustained and sufficient resources to support a co-ordinated and effective attack on the whole range of economic, social and physical problems that continue to pervade our urban environment.

References

Atkinson R and Moon G 1994 *Urban Policy in Britain: The City, the State and the Market* Macmillan, Basingstoke

Bailey N 1995 *Partnership Agencies in British Urban Planning* UCL Press, London

Burton P and Boddy M 1995 The Changing Context for British Urban Policy in **Hambleton R and Thomas H** eds *Urban Policy Evaluation: Challenge and Change* Paul Chapman Publishing Ltd., London 23-36

Davoudi S and Healey P 1995 City Challenge - A Sustainable Mechanism of Temporary Gesture? in **Hambleton R and Thomas H** eds *Urban Policy Evaluation: Challenge and Change* Paul Chapman Publishing Ltd., London 158-174

De Groot L 1992 City Challenge: Competing in the Urban Regeneration Game *Local Economy* 7.3 196-203

DoE 1991 *City Challenge: A New Approach for Inner Cities* Government Guidance Department of the Environment

DoE 1994 *City Challenge: Partnerships regenerating England's urban areas* Department of the Environment

Essex J 1995 *City Challenge and the Underclass* Unpublished M.Soc.Sc. thesis, University of Birmingham

HM Treasury 1995 Major Expansion of Challenge Funding *HM Treasury Press Release* 28 November 1995

Mabbott J 1993 City Challenge - faith, hope and charities *Town and Country Planning* 62.6 137-138

Mabbott J and MacFarlane R 1993 *Local Authority Funding for Voluntary Organizations and City Challenge: Involving the Community* NCVO, London

Nevin B and Shiner P 1994 Behind the Chimera of Urban Funding *Local Work* No. 52 June

Oatley N and Lambert C 1995 Evaluating Competitive Urban Policy: the City Challenge Initiative in **Hambleton R and Thomas H** eds *Urban Policy Evaluation: Challenge and Change* Paul Chapman Publishing Ltd., London 141-157

Oatley N 1995 Competitive urban policy and the regeneration game *Town Planning Review* 66.1 1-14

Robson B 1994 No City, no civilization *Transactions Institute of British Geographers* NS 19.2 131-141

III
MANAGING THE BUILT ENVIRONMENT

CHAPTER 17

Making sense of Birmingham's townscapes

J W R Whitehand

Birmingham as a physical entity has been created by a series of growth pulses. Its physical make-up may be likened to the growth rings of a tree, in that it is the product of alternating periods of rapid and slow growth. The most important underlying causes of Birmingham's long-term growth have been increases in its manufacturing and service activities. But the relationship between these activities and the distinct phasing of the city's physical growth has not been one of simple cause and effect. There have been other factors involved in the translation of the functions performed by the city into the pattern of physical structures on the ground. This is particularly apparent in the case of the creation of its residential area, which in physical extent forms the most important single constituent of the city.

Development cycles

The great variations over time in the speed of growth of Birmingham's residential area reflect in large part the changing fortunes of the local house-building industry, which has in turn been influenced by a number of local and national factors. Particularly important has been the availability of finance for the building and purchase of houses. This has by no means equated with the growth in local employment or the number of households seeking accommodation. Thus, although the long-term growth of Birmingham as a physical entity can be seen as a product of the growth in the functions that the city has performed, the growth pulses that are deeply

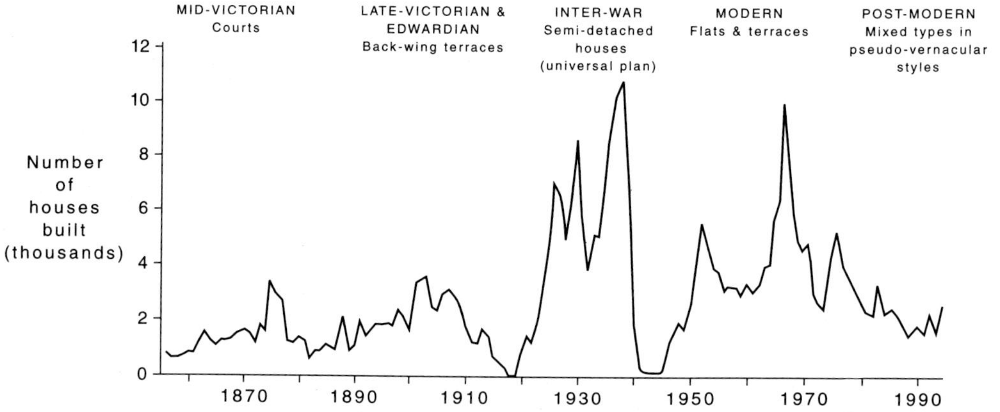

Fig. 17.1. House-building fluctuations and predominant house types in Birmingham, 1856-1994. Sources: Broaderwick, 1981, Fig. 3.2; Birmingham City Council, Department of Planning and Architecture (Computerised Land Information and Monitoring in Birmingham).

etched into its townscapes are to a considerable extent the products of other, especially economic, factors.

Figure 17.1 shows the enormous fluctuations in the amount of house building that has occurred in Birmingham in the last century and a half. Earlier fluctuations have also been documented (Broaderwick 1981, 51-6). Bearing in mind that, with the exception of recent decades, the large majority of houses were built at the edge of the city's built-up area as it extended outward into the surrounding countryside, these fluctuations emphasize the pulsating nature of Birmingham's outward growth, sometimes extending its residential area rapidly but at other times remaining almost stationary.

It was not only the residential area that grew outward in a spasmodic manner. Other forms of development progressed at an uneven pace, sometimes continuing during slumps in house building. Consequently house-building slumps were not necessarily characterized only by slower outward growth but also by outward growth of a different kind. For example, many public parks and golf courses were created at the urban fringe in the 1890s and there was a boom in the creation of public parks just before the First World War; both were times when house building was at a relatively low level (Broaderwick 1981, Figs 4.3, 4.7; Whitehand 1981, 135). It has been observed in other towns and cities that the development of urban fringe sites for these and other land-extensive purposes, particularly those of an institutional character, often continued during relative standstills in the outward growth of the residential area. In these conditions such land uses have had a tendency to form a zone around the edge of a built-up area, to which the term 'fringe belt' has been applied (Conzen, 1960, 58). Such belts generally survive long after renewed residential growth has embedded them within the built-up area.

Fringe belts

One such fringe belt in Birmingham comprises a zone marking the approximate edge of the built-up area at the time of the house-building slump that lasted from about 1910 until the early 1920s. Referred to as an Edwardian fringe belt, it is particularly evident in south-west Birmingham (Fig. 17.2), where it is still continuous between the Botanical Gardens and Cannon Hill Park. It includes, for example, the Warwickshire County Cricket Ground, the Nature Centre, Edgbaston Golf Club, Priory Lawn Tennis Club, the University of Birmingham and the Queen Elizabeth Hospital. Although some of the land uses have changed since these sites were actually at the urban fringe, this part of this fringe belt still retains some of its urban fringe character despite being deeply embedded within the built-up area, in places less than 3 km from the city centre (Fig. 17.3).

Several factors have contributed to the development of such fringe belts. These include barriers to residential development, for example the existence of poorly drained land, conditions of landownership that have not been conducive of residential development, and the influence on the types of land use attracted to a particular part of the urban fringe by the first urban land uses to locate there. Among the economic factors that have played a part have been the falls in land values that occurred during slumps in house building. Such falls in land values are particularly advantageous to firms, organizations and individuals that use large amounts of land relative to the amount of building they do on that land. Golf clubs, sports grounds, waterworks, houses in large grounds and many types of institution, especially where they include playing fields, are examples.

The fringe belt at Birmingham's current urban fringe was strongly influenced by the city's

Fig. 17.2 Part of Birmingham's Edwardian fringe belt, looking north east towards the city centre. In the foreground are some of the buildings and grounds of the University of Birmingham. In the middle ground are Edgbaston Golf Club and the grounds of several institutions. In the background (the area containing many tower blocks) are an inner zone of housing and the city centre. (Photograph by permission of the Calthorpe Estate).

adoption of a green-belt policy. Particularly important was the creation of a charitable trust in 1935 by Cadbury Brothers to permit the purchase of land on the fringe of the city that could be preserved as a green belt. By the time of the Second World War several thousand acres, mainly to the south and south west of the city had already been reserved for this purpose (Cherry 1994, 193). In the post-war period the idea of a sharp demarcation between city and countryside assumed a powerful influence in the city's planning (Cherry 1994, 152). The successful implementation of this policy is especially evident to the south and south west of the city, for example in the vicinity of Moundsley Hall, Wast Hills and Lickey Hills. Here, residential growth of the 1930s and the early post-war years ends abruptly at, or close to, the city's administrative boundary, and beyond it Country Parks, reservoirs, golf courses, sports grounds and other recreational uses are interspersed with institutions and farmland to provide an outer fringe belt of quasi-rural appearance. To the east of the city, the outer fringe belt is more heterogeneous and includes several golf courses, hospitals, reservoirs and sewage works, a power station, a waterworks, a deer park, several country houses in large grounds, the National Exhibition Centre, Birmingham International Airport and several motorway intersections (Fig. 17.4). To the west,

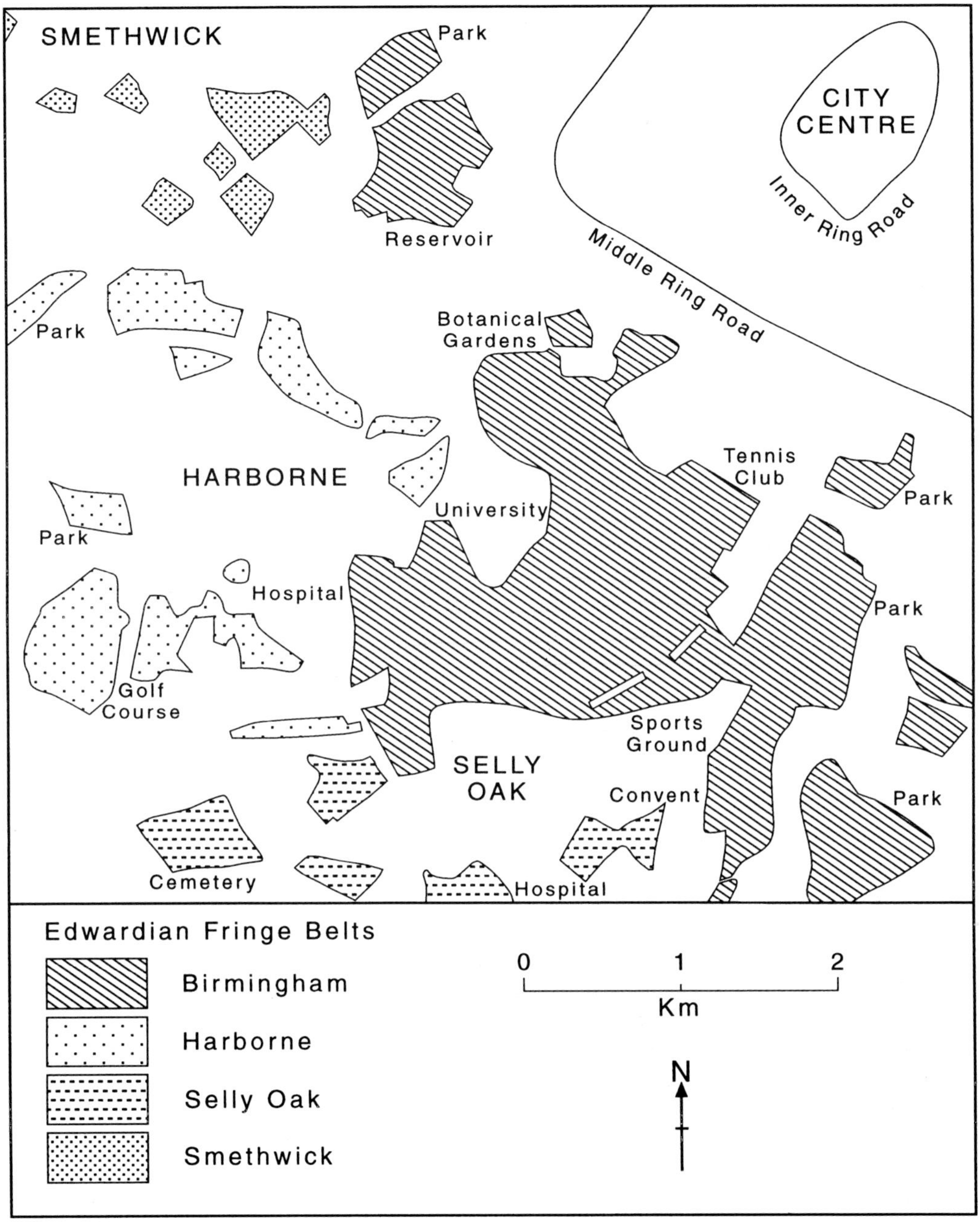

Fig. 17.3 Edwardian fringe belts in south-west Birmingham.

Fig. 17.4. Part of the eastern section of Birmingham's outer fringe belt, looking southwest. In the foreground is the intersection of the M6 and M42 motorways. In the background are the National Exhibition Centre and Birmingham International Airport. (Photograph 1989, by permission of Aerofilms).

the city's residential area had already to a large extent merged with the built-up areas of the Black Country in the inter-war period, if not earlier, and here the counterpart of the outer fringe belt to the south, east and north of the city consists of little more than a few residual open spaces in the vicinity of the M5 Motorway, the most extensive being occupied principally by Sandwell Valley Country Park and a number of other public open spaces.

Residential growth zones

These markers of the city's present and former fringes tend to form boundaries to the main residential zones of the city. The residential zones themselves differ from one another in their physical appearance. A major reason for this is that each house-building boom has been

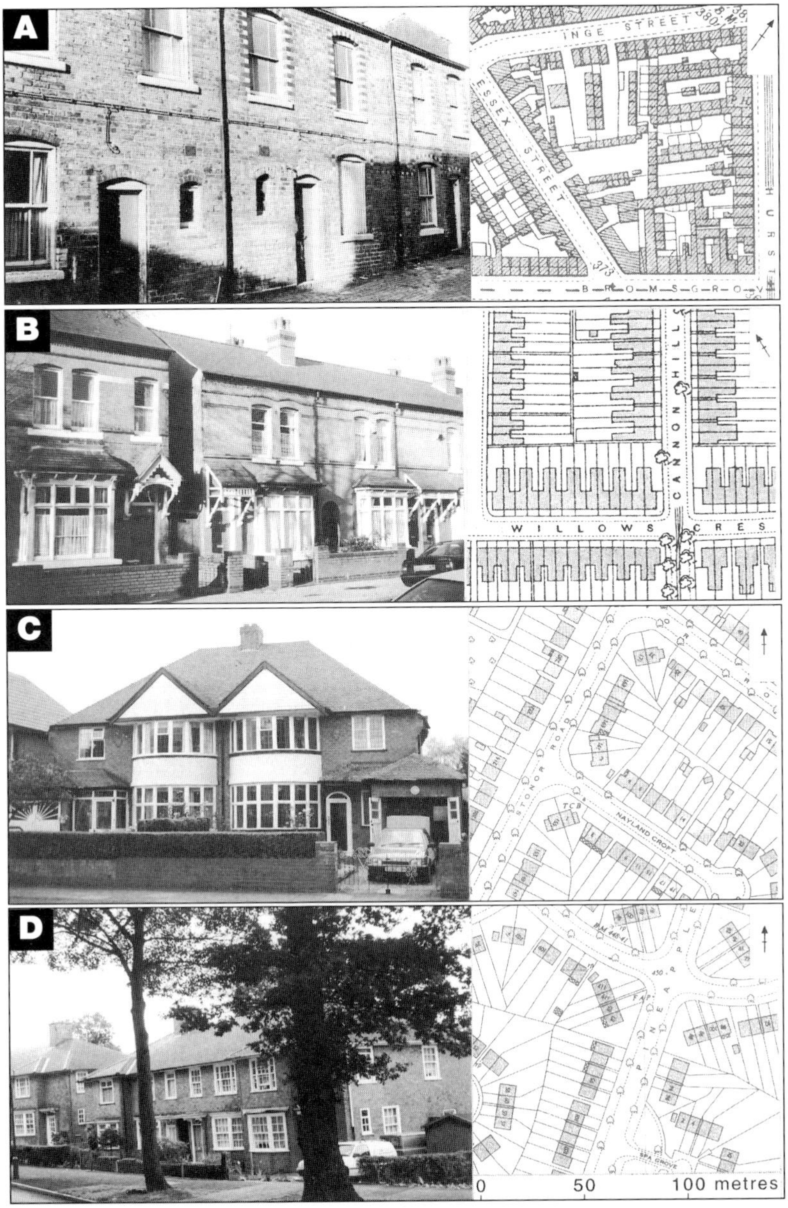

Fig. 17.5 Victorian and inter-war house types and associated town plans in Birmingham. (A) Mid-Victorian court dwellings (photograph of a court interior by permission of Jennifer Tann; plan reproduced from the Ordnance Survey 25 Inch Plan, revised 1902). (B) Late-Victorian, back-wing terraced houses (photograph 1995; plan reproduced from the Ordnance Survey 25 Inch Plan, revised 1914). (C) Inter-war semi-detached houses built by private enterprise (photograph 1990; plan reproduced from the Ordnance Survey 1:2500 Plan, revised 1954 Crown Copyright). (D) Inter-war, neo-Georgian, cottage-style terraced houses built by the Council (photograph 1992; plan reproduced from the Ordnance Survey 1:2500 Plan, revised 1955 Crown Copyright).

associated with the creation of forms in the townscape that are to some extent peculiar to itself (Fig. 17.1). This reflects the tendency for the innovations that have, over time, affected the physical form of cities, such as innovations in transport, building types, street layouts and architectural styles, to have been adopted in clusters during a particular house-building boom (Whitehand 1987, 65). Thus particular kinds of townscapes are associated with particular residential growth zones. For example, during the early- and mid-Victorian period, back-to-back houses and other forms of court dwelling, interspersed with workshops, formed a zone of very high density around the city's historical and commercial core (Fig. 17.5A). In contrast, the growth zone created during the late-Victorian and Edwardian house-building boom was characterized by terraced houses with back wings (often referred to as tunnel-back houses - Fig. 17.5B). This zone was laid out in conformity with local bye laws which gave effect to national legislation that reflected contemporary concerns over sanitation and the slums that had become widespread in the inner residential zones of cities (Tomlinson, 1964, 53-6). The enhanced access provided by the electrification of the tramcar from 1901 onward (Cherry 1994, 105) gave the speculative builders of the 'bye-law' terraced houses opportunities to build at greater distances from the city centre.

The 'bye-law' terraced houses and associated mechanistic, rectilinear street patterns were abruptly superseded in the inter-war period by garden suburbs (Fig. 17.5C) in which the semi-detached house with its 'universal plan' and front and back garden was the predominant building type (see chapter 20). These residential 'landscapes', in contrast to the 'streetscapes' that had previously dominated, were made possible on a large scale by another crucial innovation, namely the motor bus, which gave access to a swathe of garden suburbs around Birmingham that, within the United Kingdom, was exceeded in extent only by that around London. Though mainly constructed by private, speculative builders, they also included extensive council-built estates, in which short terraces and semi-detached houses were frequently inter-mixed and neo-Georgian 'cottage' styles predominated (Fig. 17.5D). Both private and council developments were strongly influenced by the Tudor Walters Report of 1918 which was itself influenced a great deal by nineteenth-century experiments in garden suburbs, such as that at Bournville (see chapter 19), which was beyond Birmingham's southern fringe when it began in 1879.

The post-war period brought further distinct additions to the residential townscape, but they were contained by a circumscribing green belt that represented a strong reaction to the largely uninhibited residential growth of the inter-war years. The increase in land values as the post-war boom gathered momentum in the late 1950s and 1960s was translated on the ground into smaller gardens. The 'cottage' styles and historical references that characterized the designs of the inter-war years were superseded by plain, Modern terraces and tower blocks in the council estates (Fig. 17.6A). In the case of houses built by private enterprise, Modernism frequently took the Anglo-Scandinavian style (Fig. 17.6B).

By the mid-1970s, Modernism too was passé. It had been superseded by Post-Modernism. The constraint of high land values was, if anything, even more evident in still smaller garden sizes, but the dominating feature was the return to quasi-historical styles. Many of them were versions of styles that had been common in the inter-war and Victorian periods (Fig. 17.6C). But there was nothing on the scale of the wide residential zone of the inter-war period. By the time that Post-Modern styles had become fashionable there were few 'greenfield' sites remaining, except beyond the green belt in a ring that included a number of free-standing towns such as Redditch, Tamworth and Warwick. The Post-Modern period has been characterized by the filling in of pockets of land left undeveloped in previous periods (Fig. 17.6D) or, more often, sites that

Fig. 17.6 Post-war house types in Birmingham.
(A) Council houses and flats built in the 1960s (photograph 1995). (B) Terraced houses built by private enterprise in the 1960s in the Anglo-Scandinavian style (photograph 1992). (C) Post-Modern terraced houses, built by private enterprise in the 1990s (photograph 1995). (D) Post-Modern detached houses, built by private enterprise in the 1990s on vacant land within an existing residential area (photograph 1995).

had become surplus to the requirements of other users, such as vacant industrial sites or disused railway sidings, or older, low-density residential areas that had become more valuable for redevelopment than to be retained in their existing use.

Thus the tree-ring city had run its course. Indeed, developments much earlier in the twentieth century reveal that, in the case of Birmingham, the notion of unicentric growth is too simple. Even during the Edwardian building boom the city's then outer zone was in places merging with those of other urban settlements - most obviously Smethwick to the west - and, as it had done in the later nineteenth century, it was engulfing numerous smaller settlements, such as Selly Oak and Harborne to the south west. This process of physical absorption is reflected in the incorporation of a number of previously separate administrative areas within Birmingham at this time. In the townscape these formerly discrete settlements still form nuclei of older development within a younger matrix, reflecting a process that was to become even more widespread during the inter-war period.

A model of concentric residential growth zones separated to varying degrees by fringe belts thus needs to be amplified to take account of the process whereby neighbouring settlements, some of which have their own residential zones and fringe belts, have been incorporated within the larger city (Fig. 17.3).

Internal change

A further consideration has become crucial as Birmingham has grown and aged. Simultaneously with outward growth, there has been internal change. This has been particularly evident in the older, inner parts of the city. In the course of the last 150 years, Birmingham's city centre has undergone a number of radical changes. However, they have been heavily constrained by an old-established street system. Much of this street system, including the Bull Ring (the main market place), High Street, Digbeth, New Street, Dale End and Bull Street, was laid out in the medieval period (Fig. 17.7). Other important streets, such as Great Charles Street and Suffolk Street, were added in the eighteenth century. Changes to the commercial core that developed within the physical framework of these mainly medieval and eighteenth-century streets were of four main types: changes to existing buildings (notably extensions and façade alterations), the replacement

Fig.17.7 The south end of High Street and the Bull Ring, Birmingham's main medieval market, in 1827, in a drawing by David Cox. (Photograph from the John Whybrow Collection).

of individual buildings within existing plots, redevelopments of two or more sites within existing street blocks, and more extensive redevelopments entailing changes to the street system. Like the outward growth of the built-up area, all of these have occurred at greatly differing speeds over time. Until the middle of the nineteenth century, change was largely of the first two types. The construction of New Street Railway Station in the early 1850s (subsequently extended in the 1880s), close to the core of the city centre, was the first instance of a redevelopment scheme entailing large-scale demolition and significant change to the street system. However, by far the

Fig. 17.8 The south end of Corporation Street from New Street in 1920. (Photograph from the John Whybrow Collection).

most extensive central redevelopment scheme before the Second World War was that initiated in 1878 by the city itself (Tann, 1978). Taking over a quarter of a century to complete, it entailed massive clearance of buildings to the north east of New Street and the construction of the major thoroughfare of Corporation Street and a number of streets linking it to existing streets (Fig. 17.8). Most of the sites were eventually leased to private developers and the large majority of buildings constructed along these new streets were exclusively for commercial purposes.

The inter-war period within the city centre was dominated by the replacement of individual buildings and shop-front replacements within the main shopping streets, High Street, New Street and Corporation Street. It was not until after the Second World War that a second phase of large-scale redevelopment began. This included the construction of an inner ring road, with an extensive system of underpasses and pedestrian subways, and comprehensive redevelopment of New Street Station and the Bull Ring (Fig. 17.9A). A major feature of this scheme was two large covered shopping centres. Further substantial redevelopments took place on part of the east side of Corporation Street, which destroyed much of the character of this street as a late-Victorian commercial thoroughfare (Cherry, 1994, 211-14). All the redevelopments at this time were Modern in style and gave high priority to private motor car access to, and within, the city centre. Glass and concrete were in abundance and emphasis within building façades was on horizontal lines, in contrast to the previous vertical emphasis (Fig. 17.9B). As in other British city centres that underwent wholesale modernization in the 1960s, many specialized retailers that previously

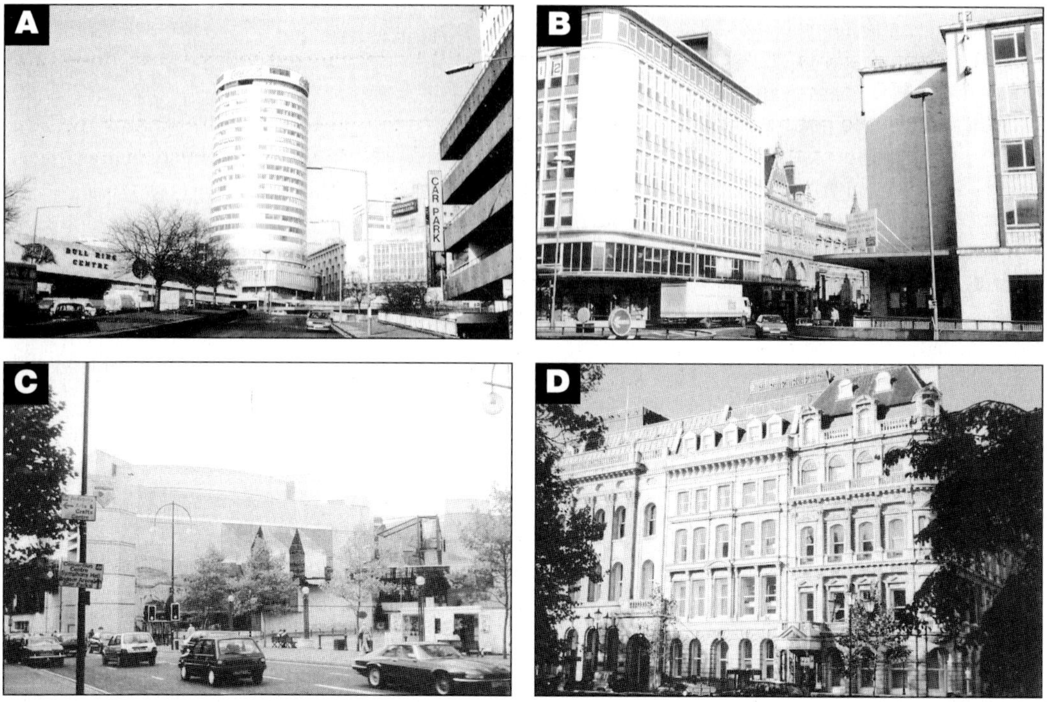

Fig. 17.9 Redevelopment in central Birmingham. (A) The Bull Ring Centre and the Rotunda (photograph 1992). (B) Corporation Street, at its junction with Priory Queensway, showing the contrast between the façades of buildings constructed in the 1960s (nearest to the camera) and those of Victorian buildings (photograph 1992). (C) The International Convention Centre (photograph 1995). (D) New buildings in Colmore Row, retaining the façades of mid-nineteenth century office buildings (photograph 1995).

occupied old premises were unable to afford the high rents in the new buildings and the tenants replacing them tended to comprise a higher proportion of shops selling high-turnover goods. Small traders were displaced and the socio-cultural role of the city centre was diminished.

In contrast, in the late-1980s and 1990s, in accord with the prevailing Post-Modern ethos and following similar developments in North American cities, there was a major attempt by the City Council to re-establish the city centre as a focus of social and community life. Strenuous attempts were made to promote the city centre as a place for conventions and leisure, notably by refurbishing old buildings and features of significance in the historical development of the city, such as the canals, introducing 'historical' street furniture, investing in sculptures at foci of pedestrian movement, and, not least, building an International Convention Centre (Fig. 17.9C). Decoration rapidly became almost a sine qua non for shopping centres, as did historical styles, notably neo-Victorian, for new office buildings. Part of the inner ring road was converted into a boulevard with pedestrian crossings at street level, and vehicular access to certain streets was precluded or severely restricted.

Remarkable though the two successive post-war transformations of the city centre have been, much of the street pattern and many of the buildings survive from the nineteenth century, albeit that some of the buildings are actually nineteenth-century façades disguising new structures, as in the case of substantial parts of the north-west sides of Colmore Row and Waterloo Street (Fig. 17.9D). Thus major parts of the city centre would still be recognized today by an observant visitor from 100 years ago.

The same could not be said, however, of much of the zone immediately surrounding the city centre. At the end of the Second World War the economic return on the renewal of the huge, largely rented, housing stock in this zone, whether by refurbishment or redevelopment, was generally perceived to be small in comparison with that on alternative investments, even where units of property ownership were sufficiently extensive for large-scale redevelopment to be practicable. In the majority of cases it was in the economic interests of landlords to undertake minimum maintenance. Increasing concern over the poor housing conditions associated with this physical deterioration led to a sharp increase in the acquisition of property by the City Council. This was followed by comprehensive redevelopment during the 1950s and 1960s at the same time that the city centre was undergoing its first post-war transformation. Virtually all the houses, most of them court dwellings and nearly all of them built before 1876 when the city adopted model bye laws, were demolished. Many of the numerous obsolescent industrial buildings in this same zone, most of them workshops, were also cleared. The present townscape is dominated by terraced houses and, in particular, multi-storey flats separated by open greenswards. Nineteenth-century buildings of predominantly local brick have been replaced by buildings in Modern styles, often having large surfaces of concrete, glass and other materials that are largely foreign to the local environment (Cherry, 1994, 168-74; Chinn, 1991, 107-19). The contrast with the domestic scale of the court dwellings that were demolished could hardly have been sharper and was emphasized by the multiple-lane middle ring road that was simultaneously constructed (Fig. 17.10A). Although careful study of old Ordnance Survey plans allows detection of the influence of old street lines on present streets, in many cases even that underlying relationship with the past cannot be discerned in this zone.

The fashion for comprehensive redevelopment had run its course by the early 1970s. The large majority of houses in the next zone outward, the 'bye-law' terraced houses, had not been reached by the demolition gangs when a marked change took place in attitudes towards redevelopment. Middle-class residents were demonstrating the feasibility in the Lea Bank area of refurbishing nineteenth-century dwellings, as had their counterparts in London. At the same time social problems associated with life in high-rise flats were becoming evident countrywide. Comprehensive redevelopment rapidly became unfashionable in Birmingham, as elsewhere within the UK, and in the 1980s the city embarked on the large-scale refurbishment of the exteriors of 'bye-law' terraced houses in selected areas. Although these houses were mostly privately owned, the work of 'enveloping', as it was called, was largely undertaken at the expense of the City Council (Chinn, 1993, 31-2). The use of standard materials compatible with the styles of the houses sometimes gave areas a greater unity than they had ever had, individual streets often having originally been built-up piecemeal by a number of small builders (Fig. 17.10B).

Change has by no means been confined to the older areas of the city. Virtually every street that is more than a few years old has had some change. Some of this change consists of extensions to and modifications of the inter-war, semi-detached houses that occupy much of the outer city and is discussed in chapter 20. Most of the changes to the large stock of council houses of this and later periods, notably changes to front doors, windows and porches, but also including extensions, have followed the sale of houses to their tenants since the late 1960s (Fig. 17.10C).

The greatest change outside the inner zone has occurred in areas of detached houses in large gardens. Whereas in areas of terraced houses and semi-detached houses the small size of the

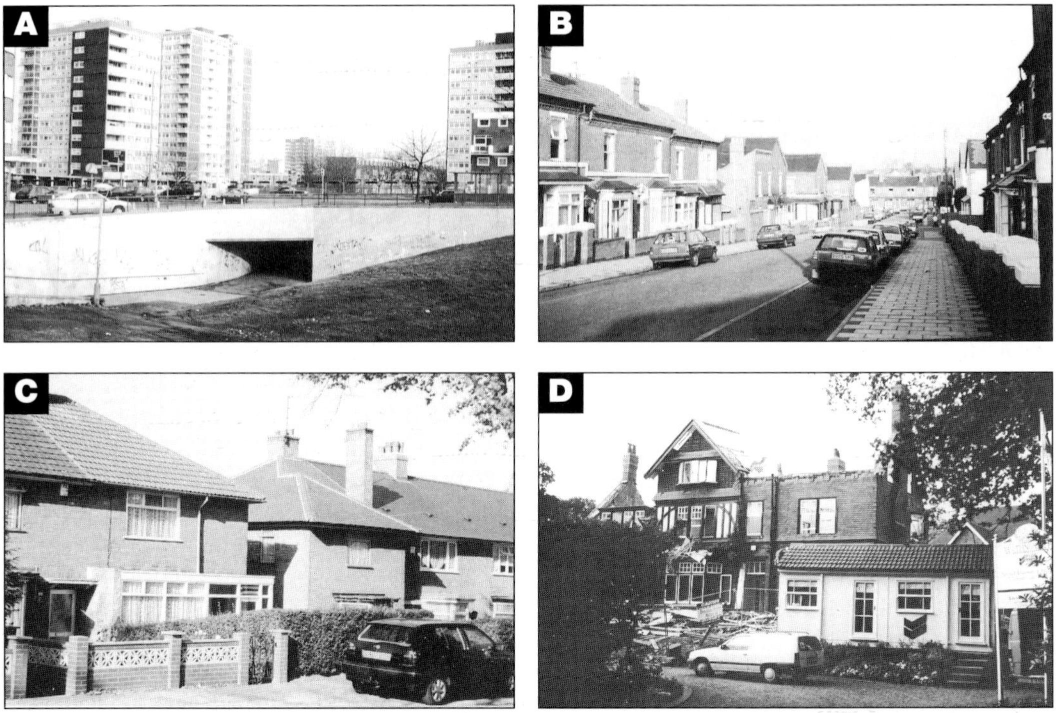

Fig. 17.10 Adaptation and redevelopment of Birmingham's residential area. (A) Comprehensive redevelopment of part of the inner residential zone in the 1960s (photograph 1992). (B) 'Enveloped', late-Victorian, back-wing terraced houses (photograph 1992). (C) Alterations to inter-war council houses (photograph 1995). (D) Demolition of large detached house in progress: the sales office for the four detached houses that are in the process of construction on its plot is already in place in the foreground (photograph 1995).

plots makes it difficult for either redevelopment or the building of additional dwellings to be undertaken without the compulsory purchase of land by the Council, where plots are large the garden of a single house may provide sufficient space for the construction of additional dwellings with or without demolition of the original house and with or without the amalgamation of plots (Whitehand et al., 1992). Indeed, such piecemeal increases in dwelling densities have been widespread, particularly in areas originally laid out with plots of predominantly over 0.2 ha, notably in Edgbaston, Four Oaks and Handsworth Wood, and beyond the city boundary in Barnt Green (Fig. 17.10D) and Little Aston. A major factor affecting the way in which additional dwellings are incorporated is the plot pattern and street system of the initial development. Deep plots lend themselves to the filling-in of plot tails, access being gained by culs-de-sac from existing roads. Wide, shallow plots are more suitable for the lengthways division of each plot and the insertion of an additional house alongside of the original house (Whitehand et al., 1992, 233).

Townscapes as object lessons

Birmingham has stopped growing outward, unless of course surrounding towns beyond the green belt are regarded as part of the city. Even if the present green belt were to be completely abandoned, which seems most unlikely in the near future, the impress of this latest fringe belt on the landscape will remain for a very long time if past patterns of urban development are indicative. The most likely scenario is that in the twenty-first century, unlike during most of the two preceding centuries, Birmingham's physical development will largely entail change to the existing urban area. An important task of urban planning will thus concern the physical reshaping of the areas described in this chapter. But before the nature of this task can be clarified and specific policies formulated, there is the need to make a comprehensive assessment of the significance and character of the existing townscape. This requires an understanding of the way in which the townscape has developed and is developing, of which the scenario presented in this chapter can only be a sketch. The value of this understanding for the purposes of planning stems from the importance of the townscape as a source of knowledge and experience. Past successes and failures that are embodied in the physical environment in which we pursue our daily lives provide particularly effective object lessons. These can benefit future decisions about the replacement, modification and conservation of the existing townscape.

Two particularly significant governmental interventions in the essentially economic process whereby land uses and built forms find a place in the townscape illustrate this point: the first is green-belt policy and the second is the major part played by the city in the comprehensive redevelopment of inner areas, including parts of the city centre, in the early post-war decades.

The green belt maintains a fringe-belt tradition that has deep historical roots in several different cultures. The fortification zones around medieval European towns and cities are one of the most powerful types of fringe belt to originate in pre-industrial cities, and green belts themselves have antecedents in the nineteenth century, if not earlier (Thomas, 1963). Such belts not only provide practical, geographical orientation at the simple level of providing a sense of position within or on the edge of a city, but they provide a historico-geographical frame of reference that allows the growth phases and surviving physical forms of previous societies to be related to the physical configurations of present cities. The West Midlands Green Belt - much of it Birmingham's outer fringe belt - already helps to provide that frame of reference. Containing within it a large number of country houses, many of them adapted for institutional and other purposes, reservoirs, landscape parks, lakes, woodlands, recreational areas and other sites of historic and scenic value, it already contributes to the historicity of the city and for this reason, if no other, merits consideration in assessing conservation priorities (cf. Conzen, 1975).

In contrast, the almost indiscriminate comprehensive redevelopment of the early post-war years which had its most extreme manifestations in the zone previously occupied by court dwellings, was an object lesson in inappropriate townscape planning. The city, like virtually all other large cities in the UK, severed its historical roots in a frenzy of devastation that made the efforts of the *Luftwaffe* seem puny by comparison. In place of the essentially domestic scale of the inner city were created, at great cost, tower blocks, vehicle-dominated thoroughfares, and unfriendly pedestrian subways, and near the edge of the city centre unsightly rear views of nineteenth-century buildings were opened up that had never been intended by their builders. Although most of the inhabitants had dwellings that were much more hygienic than those in which they had previously lived, they faced alien townscapes. The spirit of the place had been destroyed. The consequent physical disorientation was serious enough, but the severance of historically-rooted ties to home and community and the destruction of the objectivations of these ties in the townscape had social consequences that were incalculable.

With the hindsight of a quarter of a century, the early post-war period of comprehensive redevelopment appears to be a deviation from a pattern of historical evolution in which internal change has been strongly constrained by existing forms. Quite apart from any wish to conserve, existing frameworks of streets and, to a lesser extent, plots, buildings and land-use patterns have ensured that change has generally been conservative, taking place at a pace and in a manner that has preserved a degree, sometimes a large degree, of continuity with the past. In the 1980s and the first half of the 1990s there has in some respects been a return to this scale and type of change, although as in the past this has been no guarantee that the new has been compatible with the old. With the virtual cessation of Birmingham's outward growth as a continuous physical entity, decisions about the manner in which internal change is to be achieved, in particular concerning the choices that need to be made between conservation and redevelopment, have become the main issues for townscape planning. Understanding the significance, especially the historical significance, of what is being changed is therefore of paramount importance. Birmingham's townscape is full of object lessons, if only we can recognize them and heed them.

References

Broaderwick R F 1981 An investigation into the location of institutional land use in Birmingham Unpubl. PhD thesis Department of Geography, University of Birmingham

Cherry G E 1994 *Birmingham: a study in geography, history and planning* Wiley, Chichester

Chinn C 1991 *Homes for people: 100 years of council housing in Birmingham* Wheaton, Exeter

Chinn C 1993 *Keeping the city alive: twenty-one years of urban renewal in Birmingham 1972-1993* Birmingham City Council, Birmingham

Conzen M R G 1960 *Alnwick, Northumberland: a study in town-plan analysis* Institute of British Geographers Publication No. 27, George Philip, London

Conzen M R G 1975 Geography and townscape conservation in Uhlig H and Lienau C eds *Anglo-German Symposium in Applied Geography, Giessen-Würzburg-München* Lenz, Giessen 95-102

Tann J 1978 *Joseph's dream: Joseph Chamberlain and Birmingham's improvement* University of Aston in Birmingham, Birmingham

Thomas D 1963 London's Green Belt: the evolution of an idea *Geographical Journal* 129 14-24

Tomlinson M 1964 The city of Birmingham: secular architecture in Stephens, W B ed *A History of the County of Warwick* Vol. 7, Oxford University Press, London 43-57

Whitehand J W R 1981 Fluctuations in the land-use composition of urban development during the industrial era *Erdkunde* 35 129-40

Whitehand J W R 1987 *The changing face of cities: a study of development cycles and urban form* Institute of British Geographers Special Publication No. 13, Blackwell, Oxford

Whitehand J W R Larkham P J and Jones A N 1992 The changing suburban landscape in post-war England in Whitehand J W R and Larkham P J eds *Urban landscapes: international perspectives* Routledge, London 227-65

CHAPTER 18

Whose heritage?

Conserving historical townscapes in Birmingham

T. R. Slater and Peter J. Larkham

Birmingham is the archetype mid-twentieth century Modernist British city. It grew very rapidly through the inter-war period, largely on the basis of its motor-car and motor-cycle industries; its suburban townscape of that period was extremely well-planned; and its inner-city slums and city centre were redeveloped through the 1950s and 1960s comprehensively and efficiently - but without soul (Birmingham City Council, 1989). Birmingham has an image problem. People perceive it to be a place of industrial ugliness, urban motorways and system-built tower blocks, and there can be little argument that this is so.

But the city's economy and townscape have undergone a partial transformation in the 1980s and 1990s, owing to vigorous local government action allied with national and, more significantly, European Union finance (Cherry 1994). The service sector has been encouraged and the city image is being transformed through policies which encourage the arts and sport, and by a second city-centre refurbishment characterized by heritage management, pedestrianization and the most substantive public art policy of any city in Britain (Miles, 1995). That policy has been concentrated in the city centre and has proceeded furthest in the civic areas of Victoria and Centenary Squares, and in the Jewellery Quarter.

Modernism had little truck with the conservation of buildings or townscapes, and so it is unsurprising that the city was slow off the mark in designating conservation areas under the provisions of the 1967 Civic Amenities Act. However, the need to provide a new city image appropriate to the attraction of service industries and business tourism has involved a rapid development of heritage resources and urban conservation. The 1992 Conservation Strategy for the city (Birmingham City Council, 1992a) had ten objectives:

- to secure more statutory protection for the historic infrastructure of Birmingham;
- to provide better guidance and advice to the owners of historic buildings regarding maintenance and alterations;
- to prepare an audit of the listed buildings in the city;
- to enforce protective maintenance on buildings at risk;
- to encourage preservation trusts and voluntary sector assistance in urban conservation;
- to stimulate interest in conservation in schools in the city;

- to secure more funds for conservation from grant-awarding bodies;

- to encourage research on Birmingham's building history and liaise with higher education establishments to encourage such research;

- to develop a comprehensive policy for planning control; and

- to adopt a more positive role in archaeology in the city through appointing a field archaeologist.

Today, Birmingham has a wide range of designated conservation areas and listed buildings. The city demonstrates well the development of tastes and trends in valuing historic buildings. First, the number of listed buildings increased immensely in the 1970s and 1980s as Victorian and industrial buildings became accepted and valued — and as the nation-wide re-survey of the statutory list of buildings of historic and/or architectural merit was speeded up (c.f. Robertson, 1993).

Secondly, since the 1967 Civic Amenities Act, protection has been extended from individual buildings to zones felt to be "areas of special architectural or historic interest, the character or appearance of which it is desirable to preserve or enhance". Unlike the listing of individual buildings, which remains in the hands of the Secretary of State for National Heritage (albeit advised by experts from English Heritage), the designation of conservation areas is a simple process carried out by the local authority. However, a recent study carried out for the Royal Town Planning Institute showed that the reasons for designation are varied, as is the success of these tools of conservation management. Many designations are motivated by political concerns including public pressure, or by the desire to increase planning controls especially over the demolition of buildings. Many authorities do not regularly review their designated areas and nor have they carried out appraisals of area character as required, whilst their conservation budgets are small or non-existent (Jones and Larkham, 1993).

Listed Buildings

The current statutory list for Birmingham was issued in 1982 and that for Sutton Coldfield in 1976. Together, they contain 1,716 buildings listed for their architectural or historic importance. It is no surprise to find that the `Old Crown' inn, in Digbeth (Birmingham's oldest building, dating probably to the late 1400s) is listed, or that Aston Hall, one of the greatest Jacobean mansions in Britain, has the highest level of protection (Grade I). However, equally significant in Birmingham's townscape are the florid late-Victorian and Edwardian shops, offices and pubs faced with pale orange terra-cotta, and the intricate deep red terra-cotta found on schools, hospitals, libraries and other institutional buildings built by the architectural practice of Chamberlain and Martin. The Grade I listed School of Art in Margaret Street was one of the last commissions of this firm (Fig. 18.1A).

Industrial buildings are well represented in the lists as befits an industrial city, but much of this heritage is small-scale and unspectacular. The recently-listed Abingdon Works in the Gun Quarter and the Albert Works (Fig. 18.10A) in the Jewellery Quarter are amongst the largest industrial buildings. As the 'Workshop of the World', most of Birmingham's 1,001 products were made in workshops, not grand factories. The recent rediscovery of the works in Broad Street

Fig. 18.1 A) The School of Art, Margaret Street by Chamberlain and Martin, Listed Grade I (photo: Terry Slater)
Fig. 18.1 B) The New Street Station signal box, recently Listed Grade II (photo: Geoff Dowling)

where William Murdoch put into practice his discoveries of gas lighting, and the unearthing of the remains of Matthew Boulton's Soho Mint demonstrate that there is still some way to go in the identification, protection and conservation of the industrial heritage.

Birmingham's protected housing is dominated by houses designed by architects prominent in the Arts and Crafts movement of the 1880-1914 period. W.H. Bidlake, C.E. Bateman and W.A. Harvey are perhaps the most prominent. Harvey designed many of the first houses at Bournville (see chapter 19), while fine houses by Bidlake and Bateman are found on the Four Oaks estate at Sutton Coldfield, and in Edgbaston. The city is also well-represented in the lists with its post-war buildings. The thematic listing campaign for educational buildings produced several listings of 1950s' and 1960s' buildings on the University of Birmingham campus, and the first set of nominations upon which public views were invited resulted, in November 1995, in the listing of the New Street Station signal box, with its uncompromising Brutalist modern architecture (Fig. 18.1B).

Besides the statutory listing of structures by the Secretary of State for National Heritage, the City Council Planning Committee maintains a Local List of Buildings of Architectural or Historic Interest. Since 1987, some 160 buildings have been placed on this list, some of which have subsequently been statutorily listed. Most recently, in January 1996, this has happened with the 17 well-preserved 'pre-fabs' in Wake Green Road, Moseley; the last survivors of over 6,000 built immediately after the war (Fig. 18.2).

The protection of buildings through the processes of national and local government is, of course, a contested process. The demolition of much of Birmingham's high Victorian city-centre

Fig. 18.2 Prefabs, recently Listed Grade II in Wake Green Road, Moseley (photo: Geoff Dowling)

fabric by commercial developers and the city planners alike, working hand-in-hand, led to an enormous loss of sense of place on the part of ordinary people in the city. This was articulated through élite preservation societies such as the Birmingham branch of the Victorian Society. The battleground which can be seen, in retrospect, to have been the turning-point in the retreat from Modernist reconstruction to adaptive re-use was the central Post Office in Victoria Square. Built in 1891, its smoke-blackened structure was, as Pevsner reported laconically, 'to be demolished' (Pevsner and Wedgwood, 1966). However, it survived, was cleaned, became a valued building and was eventually listed for preservation. Ironically, it is now the prestigious entrance to the TSB headquarters offices; where once thousands of Brummies could buy their stamps and post their parcels under finely-wrought plaster ceilings in a setting of considerable grandeur, now, only a few highly-paid executives pass through, and the Post Office has been banished to a cellar below. The building has been saved, but it has been appropriated, and the people of the city have lost this fine room as effectively as if it had been demolished. On the other hand, the cleaning and adapting of the former Midland Bank headquarters building of 1869, in New Street, has opened a similarly ornate building to everyone. Many original decorative features have been retained or reinstated in the refurbishment of 1993 - cornices, panelling, and the stained-glass domed roof; and these are now accessible to the public through conversion to a Dillons bookstore.

Conservation Areas

The city council published a conservation strategy in 1986 (Birmingham City Council, 1986), which was a useful attempt to provide a local interpretation of government policy and guidance, setting local policies and targets, although the format remained that of an official report: rather user-unfriendly. Nevertheless, it explicitly recognised that

> there are three distinct aspects to the conservation area programme in Birmingham. There is the care and control of existing designated conservation areas largely through development control procedures. There is the question of conservation area and environmental improvement programmes, and there is the consideration of the future conservation area designation programme (Birmingham City Council, 1986: 1).

In the early 1990s the city was moving towards adoption of its new Unitary Development Plan (UDP). The early drafts contained little conservation-relevant material and it took the substantial involvement of English Heritage to bring the conservation section up to what was considered an acceptable standard (pers. comm., senior English Heritage planning staff). The new UDP policies were inserted into a reworked *Conservation Strategy for Birmingham* (Birmingham City Council, 1992a), which was launched by the Chief Executive of English Heritage and was a much more publicly-accessible document. However, it seems now a rather bland document, containing relatively little detail; and the UDP policies which it repeats are, along with those of many other planning authorities, aspirations closely based on the wording of national legislation and guidance.

Since the late 1980s, the arrival of a new chief planning officer has coincided with a series of urban design initiatives (Tibbalds *et al.*, 1990). These have been concentrated in the city centre (that is, the area within the middle ring road), and have proceeded furthest in the civic area of Victoria and Centenary Squares, where prize-winning urban design schemes allied with displays of public art have been carried out (Wright and Blakemore, 1995) and the Gun Quarter, Digbeth and the Jewellery Quarter, for which further detailed design studies have been published (Llewelyn-Davies, 1993; Tibbalds *et al.*, 1993; Birmingham City Council, 1995).

Although much urban design work has been carried on within the city-centre conservation area, including the pedestrianization of New Street and traffic limitation along Corporation Street, the degree to which these schemes actually do preserve or enhance the character or appearance of the designated area (in the words of the legislative definition) must be questioned. In the majority of pedestrianization schemes, 'where the highway authority is investing in "improvements" they usually only relate to safety, parking and traffic flows; often at the expense of visual character' (Jones and Larkham, 1993: 98); while 'solving the problem of unsuccessful public places by eliminating traffic is not the answer' (Falk, 1995: note that Falk acted as a consultant in the regeneration of the Jewellery Quarter, see below). Additionally, in Birmingham, there have been protests that the design of the pedestrianized area is unfriendly to disabled users. Likewise, the effectiveness of local policies in resisting the demolition of listed buildings within the central conservation area and the construction of new structures behind retained older façades must be questioned. A large number of such developments have been and are still being carried out, and the additional lettable floorspace built into the roof of some buildings, for example on Colmore Row, is particularly intrusive in the townscape. Local policies seem powerless to resist these developments: although some planning applications have been refused, appeals to the Secretary of State have been successful, again as was the case with Colmore Row (c.f. Barrett and Larkham, 1994).

Birmingham City Council has designated 25 conservation areas, and a further 15 or so have been under investigation in the mid-1990s with a view to making further designations. These 25 areas range from much of the city centre and the cores of several of the pre-urban villages such as Moseley and Harborne, to the industrial Jewellery Quarter and the innovative designation of an area of 1930s' houses in Hall Green. The remainder of this chapter examines the latter two areas in assessing the protection of the wider historic urban landscape. A case study of the Jewellery Quarter demonstrates how a neglected industrial area can be revitalised through

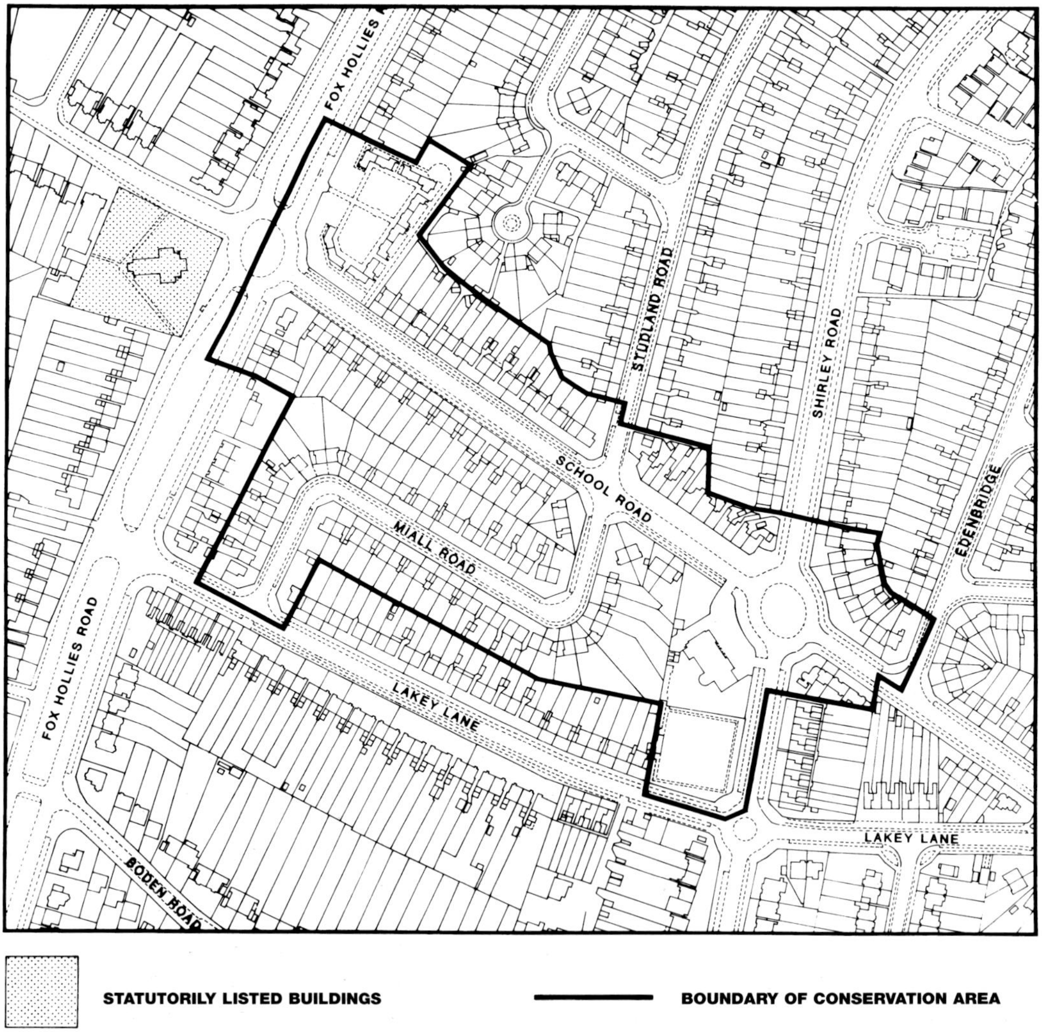

Fig. 18.3 The School Road, Hall Green, Conservation Area. Reproduced from the Ordnance Survey 1:2500 Plan. Crown Copyright.

conservation and industrial regeneration policies, although the regeneration and its associated tourism have both markedly changed the area's character and appearance. Conservation areas can also be controversial, as is the case of the Hall Green inter-war street of semi-detached houses, which many have seen as an inappropriate designation, 'debasing the coinage' of the concept of the conservation area. Although plainly reflecting national trends in conservation, Birmingham is evidently more advanced in some aspects of its activities.

Designation and management: School Road, Hall Green

In the late 1980s and into the 1990s there has been a rising concern in the professional press (summarized in Larkham and Jones, 1993: 24-6) that too many conservation areas, of the wrong sort, were being designated, for the wrong reasons. Morton (1991), for example, questioned the rise in numbers and discussed the concept of `debasing the coinage', while Reade (1991) critically discussed the management (or lack of it) of one particular area. In this respect, at a time when unusual designations such as the Settle-Carlisle Railway, many miles of rural canal, and various derelict industrial areas were being designated, Birmingham City Council took the brave step of designating an area of apparently unremarkable speculatively-developed semi-detached suburban houses in Hall Green (Fig. 18.3).

School Road, part of a large expanse of inter-war suburbia in south-east Birmingham, was designated in November 1988. At the time it was one of *the* first, if not the first, 1930s' suburban conservation areas in the country. The issues surrounding this designation even led to a feature article in *The Times*:

> Birmingham's aim is to wrap this arcadia in aspic by means of a conservation order, and all the signs are that it will manage to do so ... If it does, then this may be the very first development of the period to be thus protected in this country. In practical terms it would mean that nothing in the designated area of about 150 homes could be added to or altered unless strictly in the style of the original. ... One immediate result of that would be to prevent any more of the bay windows disappearing as the softwood rots and the owners look for a cheaper replacement. ... School Road happens to be an excellent example of the *genus*, and the whole city has become so sensitive about conserving what is good that it is now doing so long before a desperate rearguard action is required (Franks, 1988: 11).

School Road is similar to its neighbouring areas of Acocks Green and Kings Heath. School Road itself was constructed mainly by a single developer and consists of residential properties, a public house, a parade of shops and a group of almshouses (Fig. 18.4A). The houses have a distinct period character with bay windows and wooden Tudor-style gables (Fig. 18.5); there are also some Moderne-style detailing such as 'sunburst' patterns in gates and doors, and a few curving bay windows. Although all of the housing is semi-detached, there are, according to Birmingham City Council (1992b), four variations of size and design. The parade of shops is still at the centre of the community. The upper floors of these premises retain their mock-Tudor style, whilst the ground floors have modern fascia signs and advertisements (Fig. 18.4B).

A certain amount of public and professional unease has been evident at this designation. If this is a 'typical' 1930s' suburb, why should it (and not another area) be designated? What is, in the statutory definition, `special' about this area? How might it be managed to retain whatever

Fig. 18.4 A) The almshouses B) The shopping parade in the School Road Conservation Area (photos: Terry Slater)

special characteristics were identified? The response of the city council conservation staff (in conversations with the authors) has consistently been that their studies suggested that School Road was unusual in that there had been relatively few alterations and extensions which had changed the character or appearance of the original buildings and street views. Although it was typical of its period, its survival in relatively untouched state was sufficiently special to merit designation.

The question of management had also been considered by the planners. Here, the threat was not of demolition and redevelopment, but of continued relatively small-scale incremental change. At the time of the designation, additional powers were envisaged to control permitted development rights (ie minor changes which do not normally need planning permission) in the area. In September 1992, the city council made a Direction under Article 4 of the General Development Order which took effect immediately for a period of six months. This removed permitted development rights and did not require the Secretary of State's consent (The Article 4 system is dealt with in detail in Chapman *et al.*, 1995.). In seeking an Article 4 Direction, Birmingham City Council stated that

> although School Road has to a large extent retained its intrinsic character, some changes have taken place with the addition of storm porches, garages and the replacement of windows with metal or uPVC double glazing. Many of the shops have acquired large, garish and unsightly fascia signs (Birmingham City Council, 1992b: 1) (Figs. 18.4B, 18.5).

Fig. 18.5 A pair of 1930s' semi-detached houses in School Road. The house on the right has had its windows replaced and a porch door added (photo: Terry Slater)

As School Road is such an excellent example of 1930s' 'arcadia', the city council believed that it was necessary to remove permitted development rights in order to control small-scale alterations and to safeguard the original character and appearance of the area. The area covered by the Direction encompassed the entire conservation area including all of the houses and shops. In making the Direction the city council's planning department distributed to residents an explanatory leaflet detailing the type of work needing planning permission.

However, the Secretary of State refused to confirm the Direction as he was `not satisfied that a special case has been made for the withdrawal of permitted development rights' (DoE decision letter dated 8.12.92), and the Direction lapsed in May 1993. No substantial explanation was given for the refusal, but the following points should be raised. First, the application for the Direction covered the whole of Hall Green Conservation Area; yet guidelines issued by the DoE state that the boundary should be drawn selectively. Secondly, Hall Green contains a parade of shops. Advice given in circulars on policy for conservation areas repeatedly emphasises the need for local authorities to preserve thriving commercial centres. It could be judged that, by placing an Article 4 Direction on these premises, traders would be adversely financially affected. It is possible for the local authority to apply instead for an order controlling fascia signs and advertisements. Finally, the city council did not mention any specific threat currently or potentially recognised. Indeed, the justification was extremely thin, as was the description of the area's character and/or appearance which were threatened.

This example well illustrates the contestations inherent in conservation. First is the conflict between the city and the state planning authorities. Secondly, the desire for additional control is an élite one, and there was no evidence that the local residents unanimously supported it. On the contrary, in attempting to modernize their homes and incorporate modern conveniences, they were clearly acting against strict notions of conservation: arguments of self-interest, rather than the nebulous concept of protection for the public good, prevailed. Lastly, there is the common conflict of conservation and business use. To retain buildings in use, shops and businesses have to be competitive and advertize; these requirements again conflict with conservation ideals.

Ironically, a revision of the Article 4 regulations in June 1995 means that the city council could now put in place a permanent Direction, without the previous requirement for specific consent from the Secretary of State. Yet the delay has meant that a number of minor changes have been carried out; and the replacement of timber window-frames with uPVC, for example, which has occurred in several properties, can materially affect the character and appearance of this type of conservation area (EHTF 1992).

Practice examined: the Jewellery Quarter

The Jewellery Quarter forms another useful case study with which to examine recent practice in Birmingham, since it contains three separate conservation areas of rather different character (Fig. 18.9). It is also notable because it reflects neither civic splendour, ancient history or upper/middle class housing, which are the usual bases of British conservation areas; rather, it is an area of classic, early-modern, small-scale industrial enterprise — part of the metal-bashing historical image from which Birmingham is trying hard to escape. It is, therefore, an interesting area in which to pose the question as to whose heritage is being preserved, polished, bejewelled and re-presented, and whose is being repressed and hidden: since this, too, is certainly a contested landscape.

The Jewellery Quarter lies just to the north-west of the city centre (Fig. 18.6). It has been one of the principal jewellery manufacturing districts of Britain since the middle of the eighteenth century. The industry began at a domestic scale of operation but, by the 1860s, had been transformed into a workshop industry. It was marked by a very high degree of specialization and by sub-division of labour so that a closely-integrated spatial location of firms was essential (Vance, 1967). The resultant townscape was a densely-built mass of small factories, workshops, slum housing, service buildings and institutions, rarely more than three storeys high, brick built, and primarily nineteenth-century in character (Skipp, 1983).

By the beginning of the twentieth century, jewellery manufacture was Birmingham's second largest industry, employing some 50,000 people, and the industry had expanded spatially into former residential properties (West Midlands Group, 1948). Additional workshops were built in back gardens and a single house could contain as many as six or seven different businesses, the majority of which were one-person operations. At the other end of the scale, there were purpose-built factories for steel and gold pen manufacture, rolling mills, wire works, brass manufacturers, and a button factory.

The Jewellery Quarter contains a number of distinctive *plan units* (Conzen 1969). As is often the case in British industrial cities, these are closely related to the pattern of land ownership at the time at which the land was first released for development. Most distinctive is the northern part of the New Hall estate of the Colmore family, which was laid out in the building boom of the 1770s (Chalklin, 1974: 81-89). The plan was a rectangular grid of streets, with an open square towards the centre, in which a new parish church was to be built. The street blocks were sub-divided into regular-sized plots which were advertised to builders for leasehold development. Most untypically for Britain, the landowners exerted little further control.

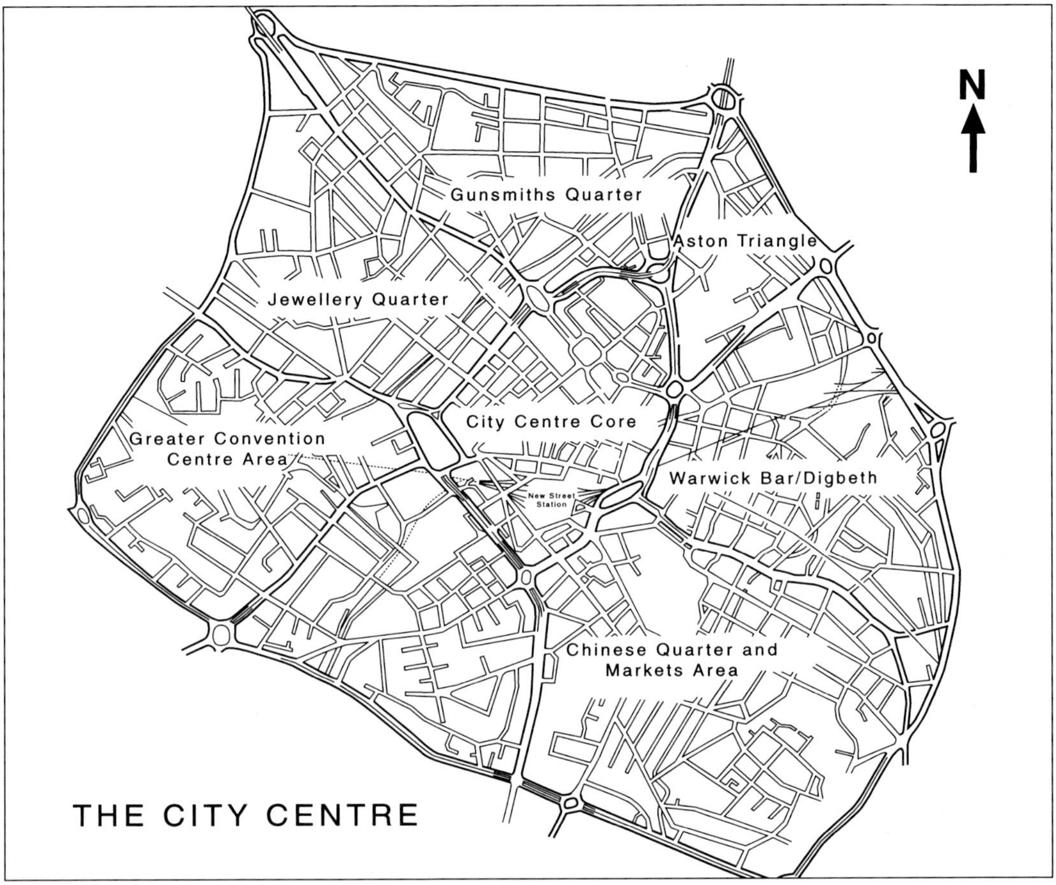

Fig. 18.6 Location of the Jewellery Quarter

To the north-west of the Colmore estate, five further plan-units are recognisable. This area was divided between four separate landowners, and the majority was not laid out for building until the second half of the nineteenth century. The Inge estate replicated the courtyard back-to-back slum housing of the northern edge of the Colmore estate and like that area, was redeveloped in the 1930s or 1950s. It is now characterized by factories, car parks, and still-derelict land. Westwards, along Frederick Street, land is owned by the King Edward's School Foundation. Here, neo-classical semi-detached villas of the 1840s to 1860s were built on generous plots, most of them occupied by Jewish jewellers and goldsmiths. Some still survive, though adapted for industrial use. They form another distinctive plan unit. Surrounding this street of villas is the main area developed as purpose-built small factories in the 1850-1914 period. They have an enormous architectural variety, but most are brick built and are rarely more than four storeys high (Fig.18.7) (Victorian Society, 1977).

Northwards, again, beyond Warstone Lane, is the fourth plan unit. Here the Vyse estate was developed after 1850 as a residential district. This was a townscape regulated by the municipal bye-laws with standard-width streets and long, rectangular street blocks, except where the geometry of estate boundaries demanded triangles. Each street block was divided medially, and

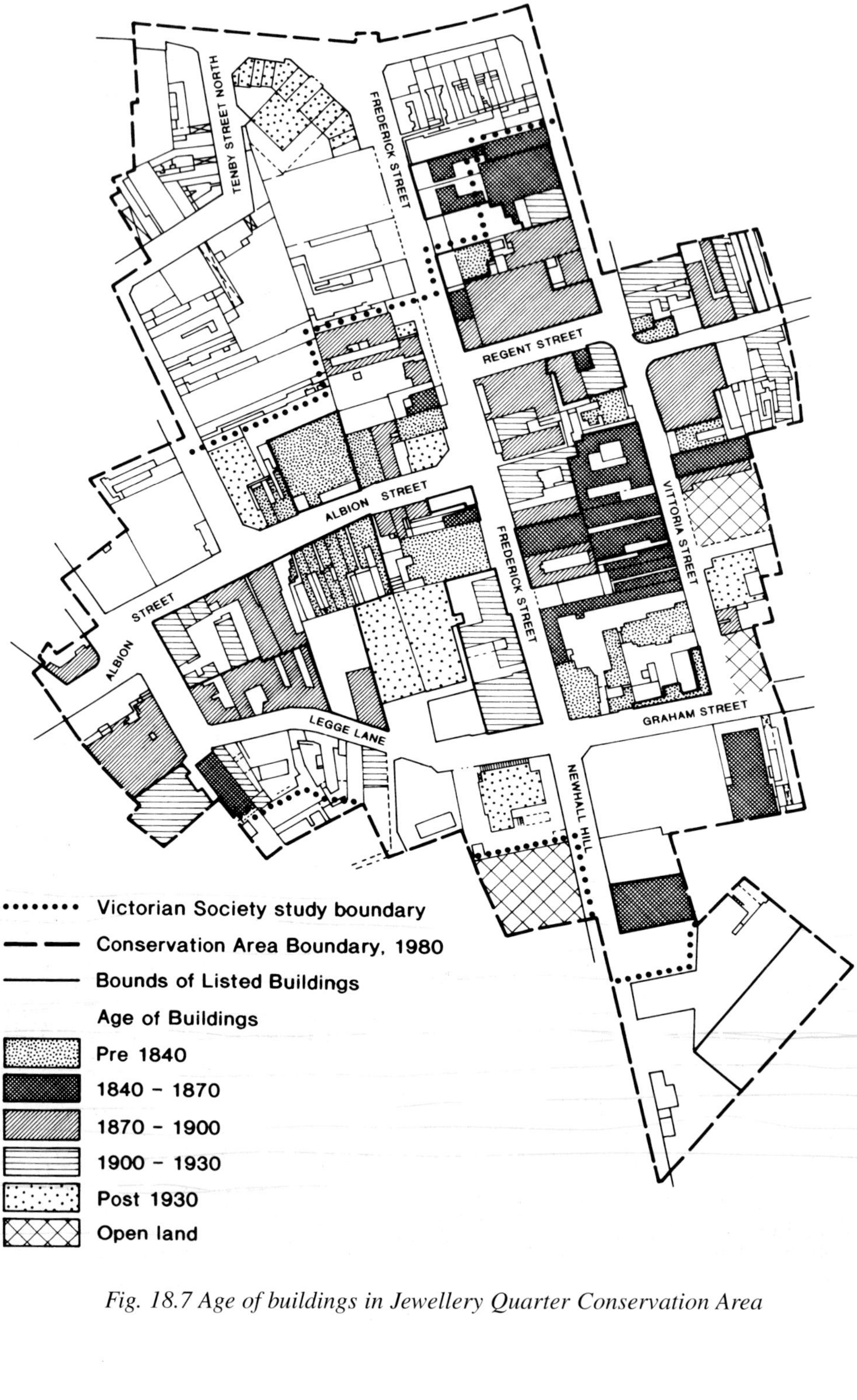

Fig. 18.7 Age of buildings in Jewellery Quarter Conservation Area

each house plot was of equal width. The houses were of two or three storeys, red-brick terraced dwellings, often with bay windows, small front gardens, and kitchen and scullery in the rear wing (Fig. 18.10B). However, as the jewellery industry expanded in the late-nineteenth century, it colonized this plan-unit too. Workshops were added to back gardens, houses were sub-divided, bays were enlarged over front yards, and the area became the core district of the one- or two-person jewellery firm (Wise, 1949). The final plan unit consists of two of Birmingham's mid-nineteenth century cemeteries, which mark the western boundary of the district.

This brief description gives an impression of an extensive and very distinctive urban region and of its mixed residential and industrial land uses. Notable, too, is the fact that the small scale of manufacturing units and the close admixture of living and working produced a cohesive working-class community which survived intact until the 1950s (Dayus, 1982).

Contesting groups

The key players in this contested landscape must next be examined. The perspective of five groups: city planners, jewellery manufacturers; the academy; developers and tourists, will briefly be noted. The attitudes of the first of these, the planners, can most clearly be documented.

In the post-war decades, to the unashamedly Modernist planning department of the city, and to the politicians of the city council, the area was a problem. The first half of the twentieth century had been a period of long, slow decline for the Jewellery Quarter. Wartime bomb damage and post-war municipal slum clearance of back-to-back housing had left extensive areas of derelict land (Bournville Village Trust, 1941). The factories and workshops failed to meet

Fig. 18.8 The Hockley Centre. This flatted factory has only recently been fully occupied (photo: Terry Slater)

modern health and safety-at-work regulations and many of them, too, stood condemned by 1960. The Modernist solution was comprehensive clearance and rebuilding — new factories for a new, reborn industry (City of Birmingham, 1952). It was intended to be reborn since, even in 1965, 900 jewellery firms in the area still provided employment for over 8,000 people. It was a brave new world for the planners and it demanded a new townscape for the late-twentieth century. A start was made at the end of the 1960s with the clearance of an area at the heart of the jewellery manufacturing district at the junction of Vyse Street and Warstone Lane, which the council had acquired in 1963. More than 150 businesses were affected by this clearance.

The built form intended to replace this dereliction was the flatted factory - small workshop units within a multi-storey block - clean, efficient and properly serviced. The first of these, the eight-storey Hockley Centre (Fig. 18.8), was opened in 1971 as a model for this Modernist, planned view of the future, since other blocks were intended to line Vyse Street as clearance progressed. It dominates the district with its physical bulk. However, no-one had thought to ask the jewellers. For them, crucially, the rents proved to be too high, and most either closed down altogether as their premises were demolished, or they moved to other older properties elsewhere in the district (Sagal *et al.*, 1987). The Hockley Centre remained under-utilised throughout the 1970s and 1980s. It quickly became clear that the vision of the 1940s' brave-new-world Modernism was not able to resolve the very real problems of this distinctive and historic townscape region.

Secondly, there were the jewellery manufacturers. For most of the period since 1945, they have been beset by problems of adapting to a rapidly-changing world of industrial production. The extreme sub-division of skills in the industry, and the consequent high degree of interaction between firms, developed a well-integrated community. However, these same forces meant that it was a conservative community, unresponsive to the changing context of a high-wage mass-production economy and, consequently, an ageing workforce continued to produce artefacts which did not reflect changing fashion in jewellery (Smith, 1989). None the less, that community also produced a response to the threat of comprehensive redevelopment by forming associations of jewellers which could both negotiate with the city council from a position of greater strength, and encourage discussion between manufacturers about product innovation and marketing. They also began training young people in the skills of the many facets of jewellery manufacture. Given the low capitalization within the industry, however, they could do little for the buildings which reflected the past heritage of jewellery manufacture. Yet there was an increasing realization that, if the industry was to survive, the refurbishment of workshops to meet health and safety legislation was a bare minimum.

Thirdly there was the academy. Some of the younger teachers in the many higher education institutions in the city were prominent members of the Birmingham Group of the Victorian Society. They campaigned vigorously for the preservation of the city's rich heritage of Victorian pubs and schools, surviving city-centre buildings of the period, art-deco cinemas, and for the factories and workshops of the Jewellery Quarter. In 1977, they prepared a carefully-documented report on the buildings of the factory-dominated plan unit centred on Frederick and Vittoria Streets (Victorian Society, 1977). They proposed the creation of a conservation area for the district, and campaigned actively with both national government for key buildings to be listed, and with the city council for the conservation area designation. They also liaised with the jewellery manufacturers, since they were aware that the implementation of the strict planning controls of conservation area status was unlikely to be sufficient of itself to halt the physical decline of the area: it could slow demolitions and redevelopment, but it would not encourage

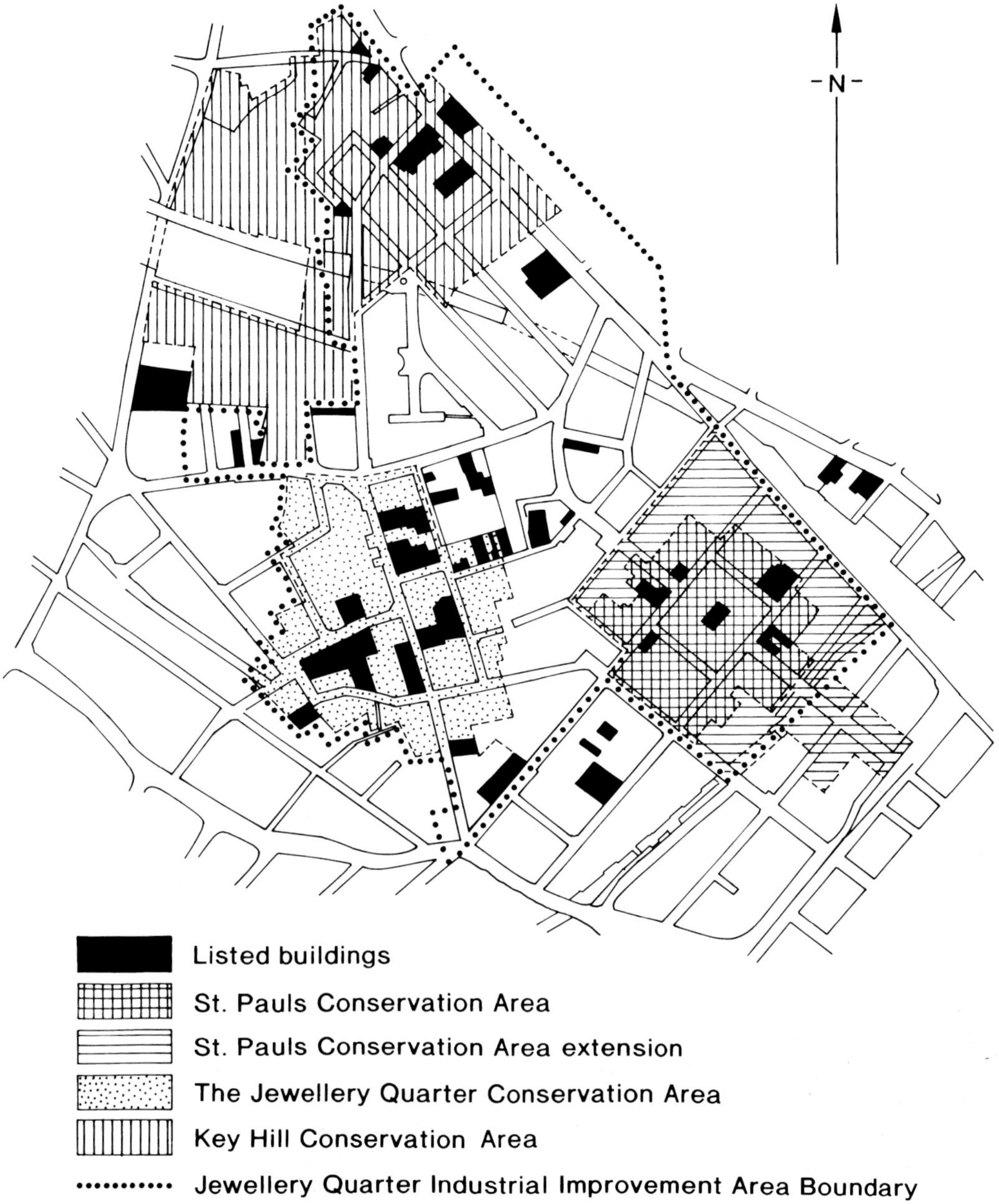

Fig. 18.9 Conservation areas in the Jewellery Quarter

refurbishment and enhancement.

There was another facet to their interaction and influence with central and local government which was even more significant. They suggested that the newly-announced availability of grants for Industrial Improvement Areas might fruitfully be combined with conservation area policy in a more proactive way. This involved combining policy areas administered by two separate local authority departments, but such an initiative was indeed established in 1980. Two new conservation areas were established in the Jewellery Quarter to add to the older area around St Paul's Square, which was one of the city's earliest-established conservation areas (Fig. 18.9). At almost the same time, the DoE was persuaded to review its schedule of listed buildings for the Quarter, and more than 180 additional structures were listed; ranging from large factory buildings to a cast-iron urinal in Vyse Street (Sagal *et al.*, 1987). Thirdly, an Industrial Improvement Area, covering the whole Jewellery Quarter, was declared (Fig. 18.9). Under the 1978 Inner Urban Areas Act, grants of up to £50,000 could now be made available to meet up to 50 per cent of property refurbishment costs for industrial premises. In the decade 1980-1990, some £1.5 million has been used to finance some 370 different projects in the Industrial Improvement Area, stimulating in turn some £4.5 million of private-sector investment. There can be little doubt that this has made a significant positive economic impact in the area (Sagal *et al.*, 1987).

This leads to a consideration of the developers since it was they, not the jewellery

Fig. 18.10 Factory and workshops in the Jewellery Quarter. A. The Albert works is one of the most spectacular factories in the Quarter. It was built in 1862-3 for W.E. Wiley, pencil and gold pen manufacturer. B. Workshops in Hylton Street converted from bye-law housing. Note the security bars on the windows and the additional workshops added in the roof space (photos: Terry Slater)

manufacturers, who have been responsible for this turnaround. The largest single investor in the future of the Quarter has been the Duchy of Cornwall, as part of the Prince of Wales's practical interest in inner-city regeneration. Some £2.5 million was invested by the Duchy in the Jewellery Business Centre to provide workshops, offices and exhibition space. Other developers have invested in the transformation of some of the large factories — key buildings in the townscape — in the form of mixed-use developments of workshops, studios, offices, retail units and high-status loft apartments. These were outsiders, but many smaller firms already functioning in the area took advantage of the grants available to transform the working conditions in factories and workshops, and the outward appearance of buildings (Falk 1993).

Finally, there are the tourists to consider. One of the key city council policies in promoting Birmingham's economic revitalization has been the development of business tourism and the conference and exhibition trade. The Jewellery Quarter provides two strands in the city's promotional strategy: on the one hand is the emphasis on an interesting and historic environment that forms part of the tourist experience of Birmingham. This emphasizes the built environment; the walking and bus tours to experience that environment; the museums, including the newly-developed Jewellery Quarter Discovery Centre, which utilizes the 'time capsule' of the Smith and Pepper factory, abandoned with all its fixtures and fittings in the early 1970s (Birmingham Museums and Art Gallery, 1992), and the opening of a new local railway station in 1995 to reach the heart of the area. The second strand emphasizes retail experience, since one of the major transformations of the 1980s was the rapid development of a jewellery retailing function to match the jewellery manufacturing function, often on the part of manufacturers themselves expanding their business by direct sale ventures (Falk, 1993).

Winners and losers

Whose heritage has survived this unremitting struggle against economic decline over the past half century, and the uneasy relationships between planners, manufacturers and developers? Quite clearly, the experience that has been most effectively eradicated from the Jewellery Quarter is that of working-class residence. Neither the townscape, the museums, or the tourist literature reflect the thousands of inhabitants who lived here until the late 1950s. The slum courtyards of back-to-back houses have been eliminated, except for a single 'front house'. Former residents now live in tower blocks and peripheral estates. Yet this is the experience that has been most effectively recreated through the autobiographical writings of Kathleen Dayus, who lived and worked here for most of her long life (Dayus, 1982; 1986; 1988). The school which she attended, the public houses in which adults drowned their sorrows or celebrated family occasions, the churches and chapels which provided charity, and many of the businesses in which they worked, still survive. This is one representation of the past of which visitors see, hear or read little, unless they have read Dayus's three books. Gentrified residents have now begun to return to the Jewellery Quarter, but living in the district is discussed hardly at all in the literature that presents this area to resident and visitor alike. Yet there are still thousands of people in the city - and elsewhere - who have direct experience of living and working here. To give but one example, the Quarter was mentioned in a conversation one of the authors had recently with the economic historian Professor Maurice Beresford. He immediately became animated, remembering taking his grandfather's lunch to his Hockley jeweller's workshop as a 10-year-old; climbing the narrow stairs to the place where he had his bench; the heat and aroma of the gas flame and the metal. A greater willingness to capture this oral history - a vanishing resource - and to present it effectively would broaden the heritage experience of the Jewellery Quarter immeasurably.

Fig. 18.11 Georgian buildings in St Paul's Square. A. In 1971 the house was occupied by Pitt and Swatkins Ltd; note the yard entrance arch. B. By 1995 the factory had been refurbished as prestige office premises with car park in the yard (photos: Terry Slater)

In this respect, the academy has failed the Quarter. With the notable exception of the city's community historian, Dr Carl Chinn (Chinn, 1994), academic expertise and planning control have concentrated on the buildings. Yet, even here, there is a missing heritage. This is most apparent in the St Paul's Square conservation area, where the gentrification process is furthest advanced. The Grade I listed St Paul's Church has been cleaned and the churchyard landscaped and the square is now surrounded by offices, exclusive apartments, trendy and expensive restaurants and prestige company headquarters (Fig. 18.11B). It is represented in the heritage guides as Birmingham's archetypal Georgian square. This may have been the intent of the Colmore family 200 years ago, but the reality was of craftsmen manufacturers living on the upper floors with a front office and a wide entry leading to the workshops behind (Fig. 18.11A). That reality survived until the 1970s, but it is now already being forgotten by today's generation of Birmingham residents.

Conclusion

Conservation of the historic urban landscape remains as problematic in Birmingham as for the majority of other planning authorities. The Jewellery Quarter case shows that, as various policies change over time, so the protection afforded to an urban landscape changes. The industrial improvement and clearance schemes were replaced by conservation area designations, later extended; but the extent to which the urban landscape is preserved or enhanced remains questionable. The morphological analysis demonstrates clearly the amount of retained features (streets, plots and buildings); yet the nature and design of recent developments has challenged the general interpretation of 'preserve or enhance'.

School Road was a brave designation, made in the face of some scepticism as to the designation-worthiness of this 'ordinary' area. Although the planners did have a management tool in mind from the date of designation onwards, its deployment required permission from central government which was not forthcoming. This example demonstrates the clear problems of dividing management power between central and local government: the negative decision calling into question the locally-based policies and applications, even though they had some support from local people. Conflicts also still arise between the interests of some local inhabitants and businesses, and those of conservation. There is an issue of whose heritage is being preserved and for whom, even though this is a small, quiet, residential backwater, far from the tourist routes.

Birmingham has been particularly adventurous in commissioning large-scale area-based urban design studies, which have recognised the conservation-related characteristics of their areas. Yet the designs of various implemented 'urban design' or 'improvement' schemes do not necessarily 'preserve' parts of the central conservation area. Whether they 'enhance' them is also arguable, given the strength of local feeling towards some of the architecture and public art.

Birmingham thus demonstrates the key conflicts and dilemmas of contemporary conservation in Britain. Conservation is a process of legal definitions and managerial approaches, with conflicts between the central and local managerial regimes. Locally, however, the implementation of managerial solutions leads to contestation. Notions of heritage management and interpretation may lead to conflicts between residents and tourists. Reality is sanitised to produce heritage, and memories of industrial 'nastiness' suppressed. Yet, as Chinn's work shows, the burgeoning interest in local and oral history may go some way to redressing this imbalance.

Nevertheless, from a city which, in the 1970s, demolished solid Victorian buildings to construct the infamous Brutalist public library likened by Prince Charles to an incinerator for burning books, significant steps forward have been taken. Adventurous decisions have been made and implemented, and policies developed; although these have not always been upheld at national level. Many of the physical changes are, in fact, reversible. New Street could be returned to vehicular traffic if desired, thus restoring something of its former character and appearance. But the city has positively attempted to balance the retention of certain features and areas with economic development: a necessary step if the city is to grow rather than to stagnate.

References

Barrett H and Larkham P J 1994 *Disguising development: façadism in city centres* Research Paper 11 Faculty of the Built Environment University of Central England, Birmingham

Birmingham City Council 1986 *Conservation Strategy for Birmingham* City Council, Birmingham

Birmingham City Council 1989 *Developing Birmingham 1889 to 1989, 100 years of City Planning* City Council, Birmingham

Birmingham City Council 1992a *Conservation Strategy for Birmingham* (2nd edition) City Council, Birmingham

Birmingham City Council 1992b *Article 4 Direction: School Road conservation area, Hall Green: reasons for making the direction* Department of Planning and Architecture, City Council, Birmingham

Birmingham City Council 1995 *Digbeth Millennium Quarter: planning and urban design for the future* Consultation draft City Council, Birmingham

Birmingham Museums and Art Gallery 1992 *Jewellery Quarter Discovery Centre* City Council, Birmingham

Bournville Village Trust 1941 *When we Build Again* Allen and Unwin, London

Chalklin C W 1974 *The Provincial Towns of Georgian England* Arnold, London

Chapman D W Larkham P J and Street A 1995 *The use of Article 4 Directions in planning control* Research Paper 15, Faculty of the Built Environment University of Central England, Birmingham.

Cherry G E 1994 *Birmingham: a study in geography, history and planning* Wiley, London

Chinn C 1994 Birmingham: the great working city City Council, Birmingham

City of Birmingham 1952 *Report on the Survey carried out under Section 5 of the Town & Country Planning Act, 1947: Written Analysis* City Council, Birmingham

Conzen M R G 1969 *Alnwick, Northumberland, A study in Town Plan Analysis* Publication 27 (2nd edition) Institute of British Geographers, London

Dayus K 1982 *Her People* Virago, London

Dayus K 1986 *Where there's Life* Virago, London

Dayus K 1988 *All my Days* Virago, London

English Historic Towns Forum 1992 *Townscape in Trouble* EHTF, Bath

Falk N 1993 Regeneration and sustainable development in **McCreal S** (ed.) *Urban Regeneration Today* Spon, London

Falk N 1995 Successful public places: going from vision to results *Report 4*: 16-18

Franks A 1988 The street they froze in time *The Times* July 15, 11

Jones A N and Larkham P J 1993 *The character of conservation areas* Royal Town Planning Institute, London

Llewelyn-Davies 1993 *The Gun Quarter: planning and urban design framework* Llewelyn-Davies, London

Miles M 1995 Art and urban regeneration *Urban History* 22: 238-52

Morton D 1991 Conservation areas: has saturation point been reached? *The Planner* 77, 5-8

Pevsner N and Wedgewood 1966 *The buildings of England, Warwickshire* Penguin, London

Reade E 1991 The little world of Upper Bangor: how many conservation areas are slums? *Town and Country Planning* 60, 340-3

Robertson (ed.) 1993 Listed buildings: the national resurvey of England *Transactions of the Ancient Monuments Society* 37, 21-94

Sagal Quince Wicksteed 1987 *Jewellery Industry and Jewellery Quarter Development Study* Sagal Quince Wicksteed, Birmingham

Skipp V 1983 *The Making of Victorian Birmingham* Studio Press, Birmingham

Smith B M D 1989 The Birmingham Jewellery Quarter: a civic problem that has become an opportunity in the 19809s in **Tilson B** (ed.) *Made in Birmingham: design and Industry, 1889-1989* Brewin, Studley

Tibbalds Colbourne Karski Williams Monro 1990 *City of Birmingham City Centre Design Strategy* City Council, Birmingham

Tibbalds Colbourne Karski Williams Monro 1993 *Urban Design Framework, Area 1 St Pauls and Environs* City Council, Birmingham

Vance J E Jr 1967 Housing the Worker: Determinative and Contingent Ties in Nineteenth Century Birmingham *Economic Geography* 43, 95-127

Victorian Society (Birmingham Group) 1977 *Proposals for Conservation in Birmingham's Jewellery Quarter* Victorian Society, Birmingham

West Midlands Group 1948 *Conurbation: a Survey of Birmingham and the Black Country* Architectural Press, London

Wise M J 1949 On the evolution of the Jewellery and Gun Quarters in Birmingham *Transactions of the Institute British Geographers* 15, 59-72

Wright G and Blakemore J 1995 Victoria Square, Birmingham *Urban Design Quarterly* 54: 21-4

CHAPTER 19

Bournville :

A hundred years of social housing in a model village

J.R. Bryson and P.A. Lowe

The rapid growth of cities, and particularly the industrial towns of the midlands and the north, was one of the most dramatic and visible social transformations of the industrial revolution. The resulting expansion of urban areas was unplanned, producing organic urban development as small speculative developers maximized the returns on their capital by economizing on land and achieving the highest possible density per acre (Burnett, 1986). Overcrowding and inadequate sanitation resulted in slum conditions and high mortality rates.

Outside the central areas of the midland towns, working-class housing was typically high-density, terraced housing, often back-to-back, or forming courts, with either minimal or non-existent open spaces and gardens (see chapter 17). Engels, writing in 1844, estimated that Birmingham contained about 2000 courts which housed a high proportion of the working-class population. 'These courts are usually narrow, muddy, badly ventilated, ill-drained, and lined with eight to twenty houses, which by reason of having their rear walls in common, can usually be ventilated from one side only. In the background . . . there is usually an ash heap or something of the kind, the filth of which cannot be described' (Engels, 1984 :70).

Towards the end of the nineteenth century a small group of industrialists considered that the housing problem of the central city, insanitary conditions, and land shortage were having a detrimental impact on the working population. Disraeli describing a model factory and village in his novel *Sybil* suggested that ties other than wages should exist between factory owners and their employees. In 1849, Sir Titus Salt decided to relocate his alpaca wool factories away from the polluted air and water of Bradford to a valley site on the river Aire, four miles north of Bradford. Salt stated that the new location would 'draw around me a well-fed, contented and happy body of operatives' (Holroyd, quoted in Bell and Bell, 1972). Similarly, in 1888, William Hesketh Lever relocated his soap factory to the banks of the River Mersey after his plans to expand in Warrington were frustrated. He took the opportunity to build Port Sunlight, a model community for his employees, where 'Our workpeople will be able to live and be comfortable - semi-detached houses with gardens back and front in which they will be able to know more about the science of life than they can in a back-to-back slum' (Lever, quoted in Darley, 1975). Both of these model communities, however, were factory settlements, with the occupation of housing dependent on employment in the factory.

In 1895, a significant development in the provision of model housing by manufacturers occurred with the commencement of the first model village which provided low-density housing not restricted to factory employees. This was the development by George Cadbury of the *Bournville Building Estate*, located four miles outside Birmingham. In a letter to Lloyd George, Cadbury stated that 'I have never kept the village to our workpeople, otherwise as an experiment, it would have been of comparatively little value' [1]. This was also the first attempt to persuade speculative builders that the construction of model low-density housing could be a profitable activity. Bournville played an important part in the development of the garden city movement. Dame Henrietta Barnett, founder of the Hampstead Garden Suburb, acknowledged that Bournville was 'the parent of the whole [garden city] movement' (Gardiner, 1923). The Bournville experiment attracted considerable international interest from a wide audience and encouraged the development of a series of model settlements, for example, Forest Hills Gardens, New York City (Stilgoe, 1988).

A brief description of this model community is to be found in most planning histories and text books. Most of these published accounts are based on a variety of secondary sources, and many of them contain significant factual errors. One of the problems with previous accounts of Bournville is a confusion between the activities of the Bournville Building Estate (1895-1900), Bournville Village Trust (1901-), and the philosophy of George Cadbury (see for example, Dellheim, 1990).This chapter examines the development of Bournville using the minute books and quarterly reports of the Bournville Village Trust, and additional archive material.

Bournville's beginnings

The Quaker family firm of Cadbury Brothers began trading in Birmingham in 1824. In 1861, Richard and George Cadbury took over an ailing firm and concentrated on producing 'pure' cocoa. By 1878, the firm of Cadbury Brothers had outgrown its Bridge Street site in the centre of Birmingham. Over the preceding 18 years the number of employees had increased tenfold (Williams, 1931) and no city-centre site would provide sufficient space for future expansion. In 1866, the factory introduced 'Pure Cocoa' with the slogan 'Absolutely Pure, Therefore Best' (Dellheim, 1987). Living and working conditions in central Birmingham were increasingly becoming unsuitable for food production and for the constructed image of the purity of the company's products.

From the age of 20, George Cadbury acquired direct experience of the difficulties facing men living in small, overcrowded houses through his involvement with the Adult School movement (Gardiner, 1923). He came to believe that such an environment would result in a deterioration in physical ability and a 'diminished power to resist temptations to intemperance and to other vices' (Barrow, 1908, 137). Cadbury visited the members of his adult class in their homes and stated that it was 'largely through my experience among the back streets of Birmingham [that] I have been brought to the conclusion that it is impossible to raise a nation, morally, physically, and spiritually, in such surroundings, and that the only effective way is to bring men out of the cities into the country and to give to every man his garden where he can come into touch with nature' (Cadbury, quoted in Wood, 1933). It is from this experience that many of the ideas incorporated into the Bournville experiment may originate.

The factory's move from Bridge Street was, however, driven by commercial rather than philanthropic reasons. In 1878, a 5.87 ha greenfield site was purchased situated between the villages of Stirchley, Kings Norton and Selly Oak, adjacent to the Birmingham West Suburban Railway and the Worcester and Birmingham Canal. This site would also allow Cadbury Brothers to promote its image of pure products produced in a healthy environment. A reporter from the 'Midland Echo' visited Bournville in 1884 and described the factory as 'Standing far enough out of Birmingham to be clear of the smoke, in the midst of green fields, with the ripple of the brook-like Bourne, whose limpid waters are famous for the lively trout, and on whose banks the kingfisher and the moorhen find a home', Bournville 'forms the central figure of a natural picture as refreshing to the senses as a sup of cocoa manufactured there to the weary traveller' (quoted in Crosfield, 1985). Cadbury's marketing department emphasised the advantages of producing confectionery in a rural idyll, continually reissuing a promotional pamphlet entitled 'The factory in a garden', and even piloting a brand of chocolates to be known as 'Cadbury's Garden City Cremes' (Hardy, 1992).

In Bournville the company expanded rapidly, employment growing by 109 per cent between 1876 and 1899 to 2,685, of which only 601 were men (Crosfield, 1985). The new factory layout was designed by George Cadbury covering 1.2 ha of land, and was designed to meet the expansion needs of the firm over the next twenty years. However, after only four years the demand for the factory's products had doubled, forcing Cadbury Brothers to expand. The relocation of the company into the countryside was considered by contemporaries to be a high-risk strategy as Cadburys was one of first British companies to undertake such a move (Gardiner, 1923).

The Bournville site had one major disadvantage in that all employees, except for a few favoured foremen, had to commute from central Birmingham. Fifteen houses were built adjacent to the factory for senior foremen. These houses, designed by George Gadd, were typical semi-detached houses of the period, constructed in brick with terracotta dressings and gables (Pevsner and Wedgwood, 1966). Cadburys did not have the financial resources to provide housing for all its employees, but negotiated cheap fares with the railway company. However, the trains did not always run at a convenient time. Before Christmas one year the factory had to open at 6 am to meet increased demand, but there was no train service timetabled, thus requiring employees to walk the four miles from Birmingham. Accommodation was found for some of the Birmingham employees in lodgings in the nearby villages, and initially two dozen girls slept in temporary cubicles in a room in the factory, returning home only at weekends (Williams, 1931).

The new location dramatically improved working conditions in the factory, and provided Cadbury Brothers with sufficient room for expansion, but it did not affect the living conditions of the majority of employees. In fact, it could be argued that the increased travelling time and expenditure on rail fares was detrimental to the quality of life of many of its employees. The difficulties of the new location were only partially ameliorated by the provision of cooking facilities, as well as a cricket and football field for the men and a garden and playground for the girls (Crosfield, 1985).

The initial development of the model village

By 1889, the original area of the factory building had doubled, and trebled by 1899. Part of this increased demand for chocolate is explained by the 80 per cent rise in average real wages that occurred in the UK between 1850 and 1900 (Mitchell and Deane, 1962). In 1895, the Bournbrook Hall estate adjacent to the factory was purchased to enable further expansion of the factory. This purchase also provided land for the expansion of the recreation grounds. 4.86 ha were laid out as the girls' recreation grounds and a further 4.86 ha site was provided for men and laid out as a fully-equipped sports ground. The continued success of the factory provided George Cadbury with a considerable personal fortune allowing him to pursue his philanthropic activities; by the time he died in 1922 this amounted to £1,071,000 (Corley, 1988).

To prevent the factory being surrounded by high-density speculative terraced housing, in 1893 George Cadbury purchased 48.56 ha adjoining its grounds. Between 1893 and 1895 he established the Bournville Building Estate, and appointed A.P.Walker as estate architect. The object of this undertaking according to the general prospectus was 'to make it easy for working men to own houses with large gardens secure from the danger of being spoilt either by the building of factories or by interference with the enjoyment of sun, light, and air', and 'the speculator will not find a footing' (Bournville Building Estate, undated). A fundamental contradiction existed between Cadbury's philanthropic interests and the initial development at Bournville. The prospectus specified that 'none of the houses must be below a given size or cost less than £150 as this will secure a superior class of quiet and respectable tenant'. Thus the first houses to be constructed by George Cadbury were not for artisans, but for the middle classes, and especially for the senior management staff of the factory. Consequently, William Tallis, Cadbury Brothers first works' foreman moved from one of the original Gadd houses to a house on the new Building Estate. Six other senior staff also purchased properties on the new estate.

Between 1885 and 1990, 138 houses were released by George Cadbury on 999-year leases. It was considered that long leases would 'maintain the rural appearance of the district and the comfort of the inhabitants' (Bournville Building Estate, undated), as Cadbury would retain a measure of control over the appearance of the houses and gardens. The houses were released at cost price plus a 4 per cent return, and Cadbury was prepared to supply up to £40,000 on mortgages at the rate of 2.5 per cent to purchasers who were prepared to pay half of the cost of the house, and 3 per cent to those able to pay a smaller deposit. Repayment was usually over twelve years. It was argued that the ground rent should be covered by the produce obtained from the garden, especially from keeping poultry. According to the prospectus 'a tenant renting the

Fig. 19.1 : A typical 'Bournville Style' house designed by W.A. Harvey (Photo: R.T. Lowe).

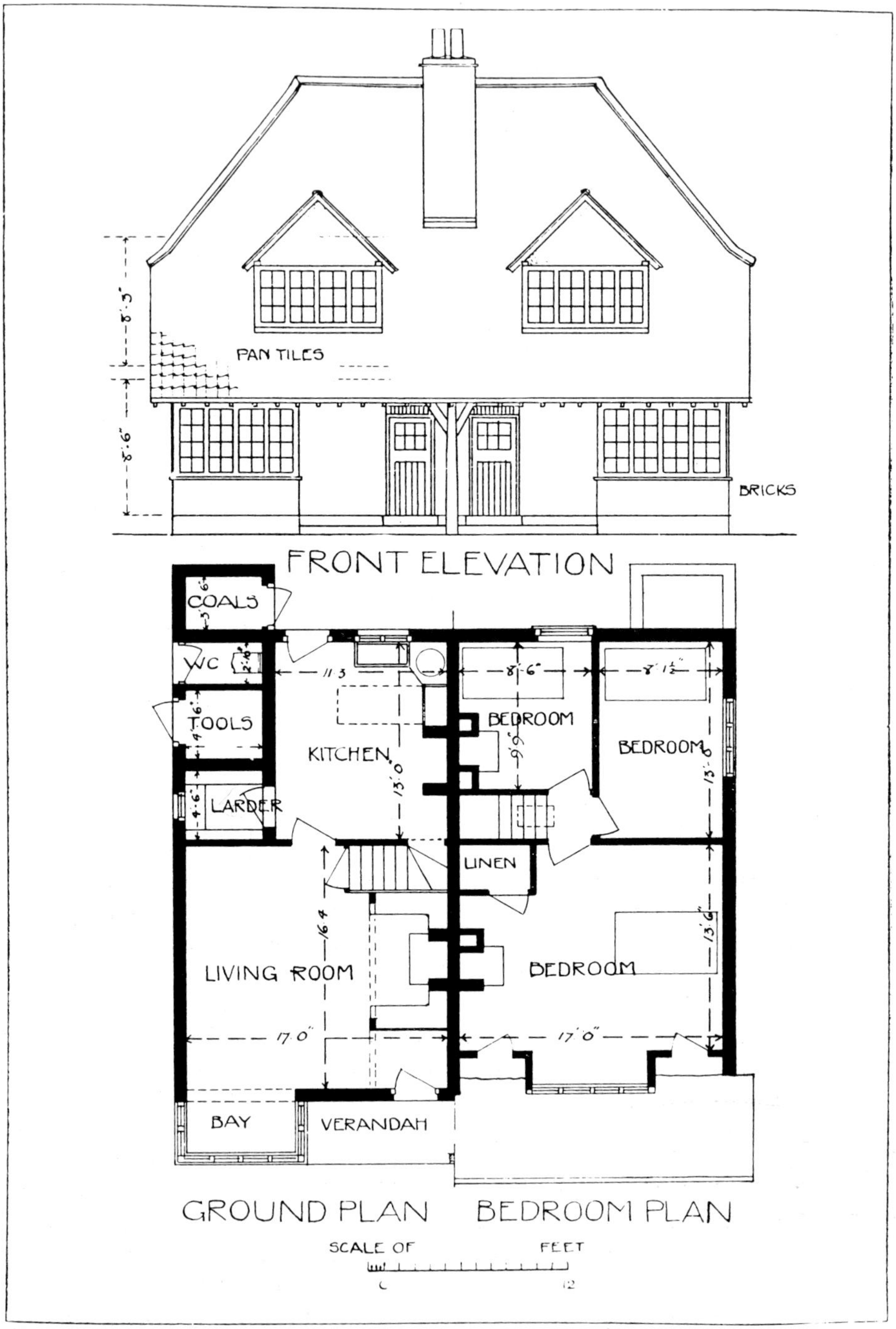

Fig. 19.2 : A typical 'Bournville Style' house, plan by W.A. Harvey, 1906

house for fifteen-years almost pays for it and not a brick of the house is his own, while by purchasing lives in it rent free, and owns a house worth probably more than £200 at the end of the time' (Bournville Buildings Estate, undated). The interest and repayment together for a £200 house came to £236 over a fifteen-year period, compared to £234 rent. The area of the village was doubled in 1898. Cadbury realised that all artisans were unable or did not wish to purchase property, and constructed 227 smaller houses, in groups of two, three or four, for weekly rent. Houses were let at rentals of 4s.6d and 5s.6d weekly, so that they could be afforded by thrifty artisans (Whitehouse, 1902).

In 1895, George Cadbury appointed as principal house designer and estate architect, William Alexander Harvey (1875-1951), an aspiring twenty-year-old Birmingham architect. Harvey was responsible for most of the houses constructed by the Bournville Building Estate, and developed what has come to be known as the 'Bournville Style'. Houses were built at a density of six to the acre, in a variety of styles. Monotony of style and composition was avoided through the use of porches, bay windows, gables, buttresses, roofing materials, roughcast, brick detailing and an irregular building line, but exposed eaves, and casement windows frequently positioned under the eaves, provided a continuity of style (Figs. 19.1; 19.2). Harvey concurred with the views of William Morris, 'beauty is based on utility', and condemned 'plebeian and vulgar tastes for shoddy display', considering 'that the jerry-builder introduced considerable ornament in detail . . . [which is] neither necessary nor beautiful' (Harvey, 1904). The diversity of styles and sizes of houses is reflected in prices which ranged from £184 to £527.

It is difficult to attribute Bournville design components to either Cadbury or Harvey. Cadbury always claimed that he was totally responsible for Bournville and all planning innovations. However, Harvey in his 1906 book, 'The Model Village and its Cottages: Bournville', attributes the development of low-density housing to Cadbury, but the articulation of this idea and its realization was Harvey's responsibility. In a vote of thanks to Harvey at the end of a lecture given to the Architectural Association in 1904, it was stated that 'it was most interesting to see what could be done with [cottage homes] . . .when left in the hands of a capable architect, and it was quite certain that Mr Harvey had not been hampered by a lot of restrictions or by a fussy client' (Harvey, 1904). Harvey's role in the Bournville experiment should not be understated as even after his resignation as estate architect in December 1903, he was retained as consultant architect. The Trust also reused his existing plans rather than commissioning new ones as it was considered that this would increase both efficiency and economy [2].

An important new planning principle was written into the leases. This introduced the requirement that houses should not cover more than one-fifth of the land as Cadbury strongly believed that a man may work in a factory 'if he has a garden and in no way deteriorate physically or mentally'[3]. Gardens and open spaces were the central component of George Cadbury's philosophy (Fig. 19.3). As a Quaker, Cadbury was firmly committed to the temperance movement and fully believed that alcohol was 'the most dangerous agent of destruction of labouring power' (Gramsci, 1971). No alcohol was permitted to be sold on the estate. Cadbury believed that the benefits of gardening were both spiritual and financial. These benefits are highlighted by a tenant who claimed in 1903 that ' before coming to the village, now nearly two years ago, he was a hard drinker: but last Christmas he stated to a friend that he was better off than he had been before, having actually two suits of clothes, and this he definitely attributed to the keen interest he had taken in his garden. It had occupied his leisure and kept him out of temptation' [4].

Fig. 19.3 : Semi-detached houses in the 'Bournville Style' designed to look like a large detached dwelling. Architect : W.A. Harvey (Photograph: R.T. Lowe).

Foundation of Bournville Village Trust

Three years after the successful establishment of the village, Cadbury became concerned over its long-term development. He sent a 'clever young lawyer' to Saltaire and to the Peabody Trust and discovered that nothing had been done to secure their future[5]. Cadbury feared that on his death Bournville would succumb to speculative builders. To prevent this occurrence in December 1900 he transferred ownership of the estate to a charitable trust to be known as *Bournville Village Trust* (BVT), of which he was chairman. The objective of the trust was the 'amelioration of the condition of the working class and labouring populations, in and around Birmingham, and elsewhere in Great Britain, by the provision of improved dwellings, with gardens and open spaces', and 'of securing to the workers in factories some of the advantages of outdoor village life'. One tenth of the village's total area was to be reserved for parks, recreation grounds and other open spaces. An essential aim of the deed of foundation was to preserve the rural character of the village, and provide a healthy environment for its inhabitants. The establishment of the Trust allowed the founder to retain considerable personal control over the estate, without appearing to be a twentieth-century feudal lord. The term 'Trust' had an especial significance for Cadbury as a Quaker as it implied stewardship of God's gifts by the privileged. It was the creation of the BVT that transformed the Bournville Building Estate into a model village.

The donation of 313 houses on 133.6 ha was valued at £172,724 at the time of the formation of the Trust. George Cadbury's generosity did not go unnoticed; both Birmingham City Council and Kings Norton and Northfield Urban District Councils recorded their appreciation of 'the erection of sanitary and healthful dwellings for the working classes and labouring population'[6]. The Trustees released details of the Deed of Foundation to the press, resulting in widespread positive publicity and numerous visitors to Bournville. In September 1901, the first *Garden City Association* conference was held at Bournville and, in 1902, a fully-furnished cottage was made available as a show cottage to satisfy the demand of visitors.

Fig. 19.4 : The first group of houses constructed by the Bournville Village Trust. Architect : W.A. Harvey (Photograph: R.T. Lowe).

Plans were made for the development of smaller cottages with two bedrooms which could be let at a lower rent to encourage greater social diversity (Fig. 19.4). This proposal did not meet with a favourable response from the leaseholders of 999 year leases purchased at the time of the Bournville Building Estate 'several expressed decided opposition to the policy of building small cottages, their reason being that it will tend to devalue leaseholders' property . . . and that to build small cottages in close proximity to houses of greater value would be an infringement of the spirit, if not, of the letter of the leases.'[7] The Trust's response was that the estate was 'from the very first intended for working men'[8] a response which appears to be at odds with the initial prospectus for the Bournville Building Estate.

Further areas of early dissatisfaction with the estate included the absence of schools, children's playgrounds and shopping facilities. However, when 'incoherent and mutually contradictory'[9] letters were published in the Birmingham Daily Mail many tenants and others also wrote 'firmly defending the village and its founder'[10]. An unusual complaint from a tenant was 'that the walls of his house were covered with blue-bottle flies, for which visitation he seemed to consider the estate architect was responsible' [11].

Associated with the development of the Building Estate was the establishment of a brick works on land leased from George Cadbury between Elm Road and the railway. The existence of this brickworks was contrary to the ideals of a healthy rural environment, free from smoke, grime and industrial pollution. Evidence of the impact of this industry is to be found in the gardener's report for 1904 which notes that 'the yew hedge at the corner of Elm and Laburnum Roads looks very sickly and as yet has never looked well. This may in part be accounted for by its proximity to the brickworks'[12]. By 1906 the brickworks was closed and demolished and the site was used for building.

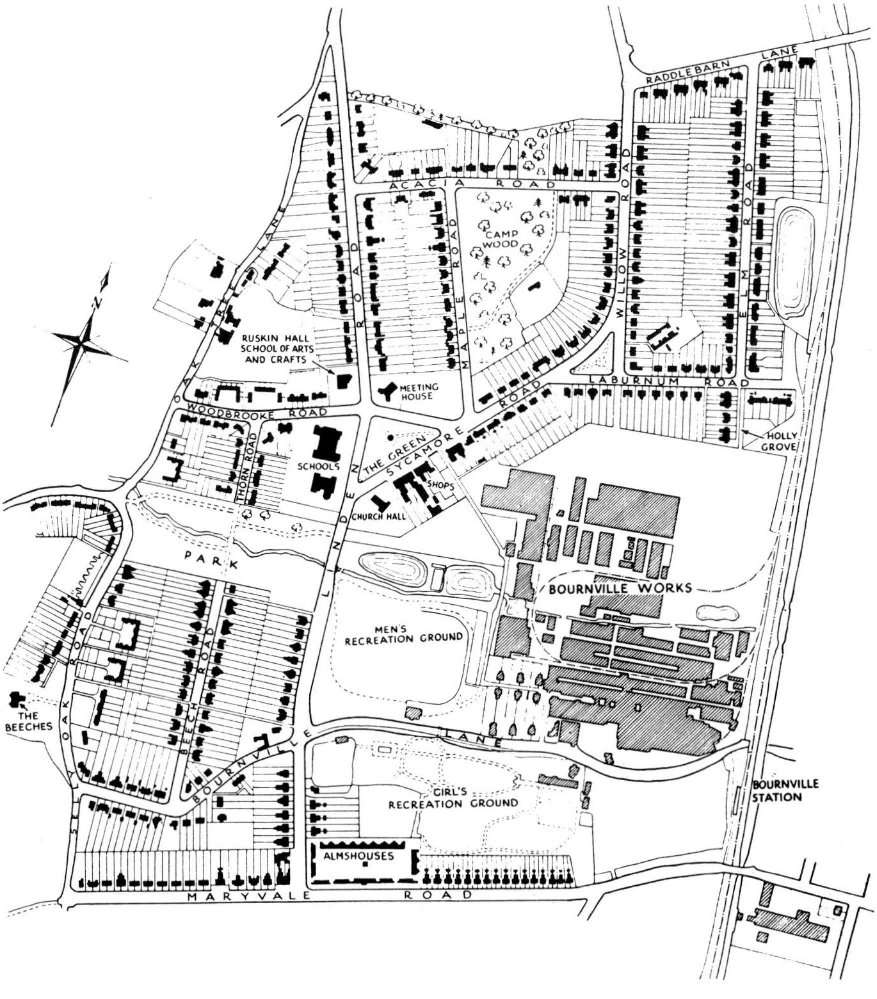

Fig. 19.5 : Bournville in 1915 (Source: Bournville Village Trust, 1955)

By 1902, Bournville was established as a community with a population of 1,925. Forty-four per cent of the heads of households worked in the Cadbury factory and 52 per cent worked in Birmingham and Selly Oak [13]. The first properties built by the Bournville Village Trust from excess funds were let immediately upon completion in 1902 at rents of less than 5/- a week (Fig. 19.4). Upon completion of building works all the cottage gardens were laid out with gravel paths, fruit trees and bushes and the ground was dug over, to encourage gardening activities. During the 1901 planting season, 1050 fruit trees, 2000 gooseberries and currants, 600 road trees and 300 forest trees were planted, as well as 15,000 hawthorn and 1,000 privet hedging plants. The small size of these cottages constructed for the working class prompted a series of criticisms from the judges of the 1905 *Cheap Cottages Exhibition* held at Letchworth. The judges considered that the BVT entry could be improved by having 'larger bedrooms, easier stairs and additional cupboards', and the Trust was not awarded a prize[14]. Despite these apparent defects, 'the demand for houses continues unabated, and it seems as though an almost unlimited number of the cheaper houses can be let' [15].

The transfer of the Building Estate to the BVT saw the demise of 999-year leases for two reasons. First, the Trust wanted to retain ownership and control over its assets, and secondly, speculation was beginning to occur as a result of the houses being released at cost price plus four per cent. By 1906, 30 of the original 134 houses on 999-year leaseholds had changed hands at least once and 'in almost every case the original owner had been able to sell at a profit, sometimes a large one, and usually the second vendor has also done well' [16]. One George Exell bought a semi-detached pair, 104-106 Linden Road, in 1896 for the sum of £700. By 1906, he had sold 106 for £450 and in 1917 he sold 104 for £385.

Houses outside the estate	10%
999 year leases on estate	10%
99 year leases on estate	6.25%
Property not owned by Trust, but rents paid to it	6.25%

Source : Minutes of Bournville Village Trust, minute 36, January 1902

Table 19.1: Scales of Building Commission for Repairs by BVT

One indication of the BVTs attitude to 999 leases is to be found in their scales of building commission (Table 19.1). Long leaseholds were charged for building repairs at a significantly higher profit margin than short-term leaseholds. Initially the Trust purchased houses held on 999-year leases as they came up for sale, but altered this policy by 1904 because it was considered better to use available resources for building as opposed to buying back houses. Until 1906, all 115 houses built by the Trust were rented on weekly tenancies. In September, it was decided that due to indebtedness to the chairman and the frequent requests to purchase houses on the estate, the Trust would construct houses for sale on 99-year leases, and 'thus by turning over the money allow a steady advance in the development of the estate' [17]. The history of BVT is, thus, one of an institution constantly responding to internal and external pressures, and having to alter parts of its fundamental philosophy.

Bournville's development

Since 1900, the Trust has steadily expanded its activities. By 1995, the estate consisted of 404.7 ha, 7,687 houses, of which 3,861 were tenanted dwellings. After the initial establishment of BVT, George Cadbury continued to supply capital and to purchase land, both to protect the rural character of the estate, and to permit future expansion. The size of the estate meant that it would be impossible for BVT to develop it completely using its own resources. The expansion in housing that occurred from 1907 was the consequence of a mosaic of development by the Trust in conjunction with public utility societies, self-build housing associations, and private developers. The Trust released land periodically on leases which stipulated housing densities and the provision of open spaces.

The first development outside the original village was a co-partnership housing scheme known as *Bournville Tenants Ltd*. Co-partnership housing has its origins in the Co-operative Movement of 1855. Individuals subscribed to shares in the housing society, and acquired the right to rent a house, but were not obligated to do so. Houses were let to society members at ordinary market rates so as to provide interest on the capital loans. Any surplus profit was divided amongst the tenant holders of shares in the society (Skilleter, 1993). Some of the Bournville housing societies were very innovative in their attempt to provide inexpensive, but modern accommodation. For example, in 1925 the Woodlands Housing Society Ltd built the first 'all electric house' in the area (Garden Cities and Town Planning, 1926).

The Bournville Tenants development was constructed on land held on 99-year leases from the Trust and was seen as a separate village to Bournville, possessing its own village hall and green. For every 10 acres leased from the Trust, the Tenants received one free acre for the provision of open spaces. By 1911, 261 members had subscribed £8,850, and the society had borrowed £20,680. The net profit for 1911 came to £321 which generated a 4 per cent return on borrowed capital (Bournville Village Trust, 1955). Bournville Tenants constructed 146 houses designed by the former Trust architect, W.A.Harvey. This resulted in Harvey's 'Bournville style' being replicated in this part of the estate.

Weoley Hill Ltd was formed as a housing society in 1914 to built houses on the north-west side of the main Bristol Road. This society built 500 houses, which were sold on 99-year leases. Four other societies operated on the estate providing another 500 dwellings. One of these societies constructed a building in 1920 (St. George's Court) to supply accommodation for 49 single business and professional women in self-contained flats and bed-sitting rooms.

A significant development occurred on the estate in 1902 when the Bournville Works Housing Society Ltd (BWHS) was established to provide accommodation solely for employees of Cadbury Brothers Ltd. Building continued after the First World War despite substantially increased labour and material costs. In an attempt to make the most efficient use of available capital, BWHS undertook an experiment in 1920 to investigate five alternative methods of construction. These were: a wooden bungalow, a brick bungalow with ash slabs inside, two pairs of concrete houses and a *pise-de-terre* bungalow (rammed earth). After reviewing the cost and difficulty of each construction method it was decided that brick was the most economical method of construction. This experiment was widely publicised, attracting over 3,000 visitors to the site during Easter 1920. The houses were let to specially-selected young married couples with one or two children who had lived in lodgings or with in-laws. A condition of the tenancy was that for one year tenants must permit visitors to view their homes, and for this inconvenience no rent was collected for the first year (Haynes, 1995). Of the five construction methods the *pise-de-terre* proved least successful. Building work had to cease during wet periods and the finished building was later demolished as it failed to withstand the British climate.

In 1950 the Trust was approached by a group of Cadbury factory workers who wanted to self-build a group of houses on the estate. As a result the *Hay Green Housing Society* was formed, and land was leased from the Trust for the construction of 24 bungalows. This development was followed by the *Self Build Housing Association*, formed by a group of employees of Joseph Lucas Ltd., to construct 48 houses. 28 self-build housing societies operated on land leased from the Trust, building a total of 400 houses. The societies ranged in size from 20 to 48 members, and usually consisted of factory workers organized and trained by a limited number of building workers. In two cases firemen banded together to construct houses under the tutelage of a master builder. The advantage of self-built as a form of construction is that the future occupier provides the labour and time. The labour-intensive nature of construction activity means that a high proportion of the value of a completed house is labour costs. The majority of self-built houses were of traditional construction, and all designs were approved by the Trust. In 1967 the last self-built housing development was completed. Each house cost the society between £1,650 and £2,016, but a similar commercially-constructed property would have cost £4,000.

The original village of Bournville was planned around gardens (64.8 per cent of land), open spaces (10 per cent), and houses (6.6 per cent) (Fig. 19.3). The low density of this development has been impossible to repeat due to constraints imposed on the Trust by the local planning authority which has insisted that developments constructed since the 1960s be developed at higher densities. Once again, this is an example of the Trust having to modify its activities as a consequence of an external constraint.

Conclusion : Bournville in the 1990s

An important feature of the development of Bournville is the constant adaptation made in response to both internal and external constraints. Unlike many of the early garden-city developments, Bournville Village Trust has continued to change to meet alterations in the demand for social housing. Because of this continual process of organizational change BVT remained an important provider of new social housing.

To continue the expansion of the Trust's activities it became a Housing Association to obtain access to Housing Corporation funding. As a housing association, BVT has to obtain a portion of its new tenants from the local authority housing list. In 1994, the Trust agreed to fill 50 per cent of its vacancies from this source. The consequence of this is that the social character of Bournville will alter over the next twenty years as its population comes to reflect that of Birmingham as a whole. In 1994, 59 per cent of new tenancies went to the homeless or those threatened with homelessness, and 73 per cent of new lettings went to tenants wholly supported by housing benefit.

Besides developing and refurbishing its housing stock held on the Bournville estate, BVT has begun to expand its activities into other locations. To obtain finance to support this activity, in 1993, BVT sold the last substantial building site on the Bournville estate for £1.9 million to the private house building company, George Wimpey Plc, which is developing it in conjunction with Berkeley Homes. The expansion of the Trust's activities outside Bournville is reflected in its acquisition of houses in Shropshire. For example, in Wellington the Trust acquired a scheme of 30 one and two bedroom flats from a private developer, and in Telford construction began on a £1 million development of 12 houses and 20 flats in 1995. In the centre of Birmingham the Trust has become involved with the regeneration of a declining inner city area as part of the Heartlands Development Corporation area. George Wimpey Plc is building 29 flats and four shops which will be acquired and managed by the Trust, which will also manage the local community centre.

The history of George Cadbury's Bournville Building Estate and of the BVT is one of constant evolution as these organisations responded to changing circumstances. This chapter has clarified some of the differences in the activities and philosophies used by each of these organisations and has identified some of the key adaptations and developments that have occurred.

Acknowledgements

The author would like to thank the Bournville Village Trust for the use of their archive.

Notes

1) Bournville Archive, Birmingham City Library, MS 1536, Box 5, letter to Lloyd George dated February 17, 1916.
2) Quarterly Report of the Bournville Village Trust, Secretary's Report, December, 1903
3) Bournville Archive, Birmingham City Library, MS 1536, Box 5, letter to Mr Runciman dated 28 April 1906.
4) Quarterly Report of the Bournville Village Trust, Secretary's Report, January 1903
5) Bournville Archive, Birmingham City Library, MS 1536, Box 5, letter to John Burn, dated 20 November 1899.
6) Minute 19 29th April 1901 Minutes of the Bournville Village Trust
7) Minute 24 29th April 1901 Minutes of the Bournville Village Trust
8) Minute 24 29th April 1901 Minutes of the Bournville Village Trust
9) Quarterly Report of the Bournville Village Trust, Secretary's Report, January 1902
10) Quarterly Report of the Bournville Village Trust, Secretary's Report, January 1902
11) Quarterly Report of the Bournville Village Trust, Secretary's Report, January 1903
12) Quarterly Report of the Bournville Village Trust, Gardeners' Report, September 1904
13) Quarterly Report of the Bournville Village Trust, Secretary's Report, April 1902
14) Quarterly Report of the Bournville Village Trust, Secretary's Report, September 1905
15) Quarterly Report of the Bournville Village Trust, Secretary's Report, January 1903
16) Quarterly Report of the Bournville Village Trust, Secretary's Report, September 1906
17) Quarterly Report of the Bournville Village Trust, Secretary's Report, September 1906

References

Atkins P 1989 The architecture of Bournville 1879-1914 in Tilson B ed *Made in Birmingham: Design and Industry 1889-1989* Brewin Books, Studley, Warwickshire pp 35-48

Barrow A 1908 Bournville Village in *Handbook of the Yearly Meeting of the Society of Friends* Birmingham pp 133-148

Bell C and Bell R 1972 *City Fathers : The early history of town planning in Britain* Penguin, Middlesex

Bournville Building Estate undated *General Particulars* Bournville, Birmingham

Bournville Village Trust 1955 *The Bournville Village Trust*, 1900-1955 BVT, Birmingham

Bournville Village Trust 1994 *Annual Report* BVT, Birmingham
Burnett J 1986 *A social history of housing : 1851-1985* Methuen, London
Corley T A B 1988 How Quakers coped with business success: Quaker industrialists 1860-1914 in Jeremy D J ed *Business and Religion in Britain* Gower, Aldershot pp 164-187
Crosfield J F C 1985 *A History of the Cadbury Family Vol. 2* University Press, Cambridge
Darley G 1978 *Villages of Vision* Paladin, London
Dellheim C 1987 The Creation of a Company Culture : Cadburys, 1861-1931, *The American Historical Review* 92.1: pp. 13-46
Dellheim C 1990 Utopia Ltd: Bournville and Port Sunlight in Fraser D ed *Cities, Class and Communication : Essays in honour of Asa Briggs* (Harvester, London) pp 44-57
Disraeli B 1982 *Sybil : or the two nations* Longman, London
Engels F 1984 *The conditions of the working class in England* Panther Books, London)
Garden Cities and Town Planning 1926 All-electric houses at Bournville *Garden Cities and Town Planning : A journal of housing, town planning and civic improvement*, February pp 39-40
Gramsci A 1971 *Selections form the Prison Notebooks* Lawrence and Wishart, London
Gardiner A G 1923 *Life of George Cadbury* Cassell and Co, London
Hardy D 1992 The Garden City Campaign: an overview in Ward S V ed *The Garden City: past present and future* E & FN Spon, London pp 187-209
Harvey W A 1904 Cottage Homes *The Builder*, Feb 13
Harvey W A 1906 *The Model Village and its Cottages : Bournville* Batsford, London
Haynes G L 1995 *An Epoch's Ending : A new home in a model village* B C S, Birmingham
Pevsner N and Wedgewood A 1966 *The Buildings of England : Warwickshire*, Penguin Books, Middlesex
Mitchell B R and Deane P 1962 *Abstract of British Historical Statistics* Cambridge University Press, Cambridge
Skilleter K J 1993 The role of public utility societies in early British town planning and housing reform, 1901-36 *Planning Perspectives* **8**:125-165
Stilgoe J R 1902 *Borderland: Origins of the American suburb 1820-1939* Yale University Press, Cambridge Massachusetts
Whitehouse J H 1902 Bournville : A study in housing reform *The Studio* 24: 162-172
Williams E 1984 *The story of Sunlight* Unilever, London
Wood H G 1933 George Cadbury in Martin H ed *Christian Social Reformers of the Nineteenth Century*, Student Christian Movement Press, London pp 185-202

CHAPTER 20

Birmingham's inter-war suburbs: origins, development and change

Christine M H Carr and J W R Whitehand

Even now, more than half a century since the Second World War brought to a dramatic end the great house-building boom of the 1930s, one-fifth of England's houses can be identified as having been built between the two world wars (Department of the Environment et al., 1993, Table 9.5, 132). The growth of suburbs during the inter-war period left a physical legacy that will continue to influence perceptions of British cities well into the next century. That legacy in Birmingham is as great as, if not greater than, that in any other British city outside London. In Birmingham more than 110,000 houses were built during the inter-war period (MacMorran, 1973, 174), creating a new suburban ring that in physical extent was greater than the entire city as it existed in 1918. However, suburban development was not a new phenomenon to the city; the story of suburbs in Birmingham can be traced back at least to the first half of the nineteenth century.

Early suburban development

The earliest of Birmingham's suburbs, as that term is now widely understood, began to develop in the early nineteenth century, at Edgbaston. This `aristocratic suburb' (Cannadine, 1980, 94-108), constructed on land belonging to the Calthorpe family, is characterized by large houses set in their own gardens. While most of the dwellings are detached, some semi-detached houses were built in the early nineteenth century, for example in Frederick Road (Fig. 20.1A), foreshadowing the great inter-war boom in `semis' by more than a century.

Later, more influential, developments were at the cheaper end of the housing market. These suburban developments, closely associated with the development of town planning as a discipline, took place during the late-nineteenth and early-twentieth centuries. During the nineteenth century, there was an increasing recognition that housing standards and health were linked, and various Public Health Acts were passed in an attempt to improve them. The most significant of these was the Public Health Act of 1875; this was a major attempt to eliminate the worst health problems by giving local authorities the power to enforce minimum housing standards through their bye-laws. However, reformist opinion suggested that these measures did not go far enough, and advocated decentralization of population from the inner areas of cities into lower-density developments, where fresh air, space and sunlight would be beneficial to the physical well-being of the residents. Such opinion found expression in the garden city movement, inspired by Ebenezer Howard, and the closely-related development of garden suburbs.

In Birmingham the most famous example of garden suburb development is Bournville Village, some 6 km south of the city centre. Begun by the Cadburys for the workers in their decentralized chocolate factory (see chapter 19), it was greatly enlarged from 1900 onward by

Fig. 20.1 Suburban houses built before 1918. (A) Early nineteenth century semi-detached houses in Edgbaston (photograph 1994). (B) Late-Victorian semi-detached houses in Bournville (photograph 1994). (C) `Bye-law' terraced houses in Selly Oak (photograph 1992). (D) Garden suburb development, Moor Pool Estate, Harborne (photograph 1995).

Bournville Village Trust, set up by George Cadbury. Developments at Bournville both influenced, and were influenced by, the garden city movement. The earliest workers' houses, built here in 1879, pre-dated the publication of Howard's (1898) treatise on garden cities, *Tomorrow: a peaceful path to real reform* by nearly twenty years. The importance of this estate in influencing the shape of later suburban growth nationwide was suggested by Neville Chamberlain in 1913 when he wrote, with reference to the growing importance of town planning, that 'garden cities, such as Hampstead, Letchworth, and Bournville, have sprung up to demonstrate its possibilities' (Chamberlain, 1913, 175). Bournville's tree-lined roads and picturesque houses, with front and back gardens (Fig. 20.1B), contrasted sharply with the high-density linear arrangements of `bye-law' terraced houses (Fig. 20.1C) that dominated the development of Birmingham and other major English cities in the few decades before the First World War (see chapter 17).

Another garden suburb, built during the early decades of the twentieth century, was Moor Pool Estate, some 4 km south west of the city centre. At one time there had been a proposal to build 'bye-law' terraced houses on the 22 ha site, but the land was subsequently acquired by Harborne Tenants who chose to develop it along garden suburb lines (Fig. 20.1D). Plans drawn up before the First World War proposed the construction of nearly five hundred houses (at an average density of about 23 houses per ha), shops, a club house, and a public house (Nettlefold, 1914, 98-9).

One of the people who was influential in shaping the suburban development of Birmingham in the early decades of the twentieth century was Councillor J. S. Nettlefold. Besides being Chairman of Harborne Tenants, he was an advocate of town planning generally, writing books on the subject (Nettlefold, 1908, 1914) and campaigning for the introduction of national legislation. Until the passage of the Housing and Town Planning Act 1909, local authorities had little control over the shape of development: town planning legislation, which concentrated on greenfield sites, was seen as the key to rectifying this. However, Birmingham had built up to its administrative boundaries, despite having increased its administrative area in 1891 and 1909, and therefore required a further extension of its boundaries before it could make much use of its new powers. Thus Nettlefold was also a supporter of a scheme to greatly expand the city's limits. This duly occurred in 1911, when the incorporation of surrounding districts into the city resulted in Birmingham's administrative area increasing more than threefold (Robertson, 1913, 164). Of the new land incorporated into the city, some 80 per cent was undeveloped (Chamberlain, 1913, 176), and therefore available for town planning. Although the 1909 Act encouraged local authorities to draw up town planning schemes, Birmingham proved unusual in its willingness to do so (Cherry, 1988, 72). Its first two schemes, the Quinton, Harborne and Edgbaston Scheme, and the East Birmingham Scheme, were approved before the outbreak of the First World War (Chamberlain, 1913, 176).

After the First World War, Birmingham continued drawing up schemes with more enthusiasm than most cities, prompting Wiltshire to write in 1927 that `it is interesting to observe that today, nearly twenty years since the Act of 1909 was passed, Birmingham is still the only large industrial cty that has actually town-planned its area to any appreciable extent' (Wiltshire, 1927, 30). These early town planning schemes typically made provision for the construction of new streets and the improvement of existing ones. They also contained statements of what were acceptable land uses and maximum housing densities. Later, the Birmingham South and the Birmingham South West Schemes, approved in 1925 and 1936 respectively, gave the local authority power of veto over building applications on grounds of aesthetics. The five schemes that were eventually approved (discounting amendments), were progressively larger and more ambitious. However, the Council's intention of producing schemes for the whole of the area surrounding the original nineteenth-century city (Wiltshire, 1927) did not come to pass, as the Second World War started before the North Birmingham Scheme was adopted.

Although the value of these schemes is debatable, since areas not covered by such controls often show similar characteristics, including housing densities, to those that were, and the powers that the cty had to enforce them were limited, they are significant for two reasons. The first is that the willingness with which the city drew them up is a mark of its spirit of innovation during the first half of this century. The second is that the planning practices that were codified in the schemes have undoubtedly left their mark on the townscape. Suburban dual carriageways and roundabouts indicate where road construction and improvement took place, just as wide greenswards and deep building lines often indicate where provision was made in town planning proposals for subsequent road widenings that did not take place. In some cases these proposals were abandoned, sometimes decades later.

The inter-war period

The majority of the 4 million dwellings built in England and Wales between the wars were constructed on the fringes of existing urban areas, and formed the vast areas of low-density housing - usually between 12 and 15 houses per acre (approximately 30 to 37 houses per ha) - that came to typify inter-war suburbia. One-quarter of these houses were built by local councils, a legacy of Lloyd George's `homes fit for heroes' campaign, launched in 1918. At the end of the First World War there was a great change in national housing policy as central government became involved in large-scale housing provision for the first time. The so-called Addison Act of 1919 made it obligatory for municipalities to build houses, and these were built according to `garden suburb' principles, as recommended by the Tudor Walters Report of 1918, and the Housing Manual of 1919.

Although council housing standards did decline slightly during the 1920s as the full cost of building to the specifications laid out at the start of the period became apparent, the shape of municipal suburbia had been set for the next thirty years. These municipal estates are well represented in Birmingham, where almost 50 per cent of the inter-war housing stock is comprised of council-built dwellings, a much higher proportion than the national average (Table 20.1). By the end of the 1930s, council houses covered one-eighth of the city's area, 5,380 acres (2,177 ha) and 200,000 people had been rehoused (Birmingham City Council, 1989, 54). This represents approximately one-fifth of the city's 1939 population of 995,039 (National Register, United Kingdom and Isle of Man, 1944, Table 1, 21).

	Council		Private		Total	
	Number	%	Number	%	Number	%
England and Wales [1]	1,111,700	27.81	2,886,000	72.19	3,997,700	100
Birmingham [2]	51,681	46.38	59,744	53.62	111,425	100

[1]Source: Bowley 1945, 271
[2]Source: MacMorran 1973, 174

Table 20.1: Numbers and proportions of houses built by private enterprise and local authorities between 1919 and 1939 in England and Wales, and in Birmingham

Although the numbers of council and privately-built houses constructed in Birmingham during the inter-war period were broadly similar, the phasing of the two was different. The 1920s were dominated by council house building, but the pace of this building fell sharply after the beginning of the 1930s. It was in the latter decade that the boom in speculative suburbia occurred, reaching a peak in 1938, when 7,804 houses were built by private enterprise within the city's boundaries (Fig. 20.2).

Suburban growth during the inter-war period is often associated with the increasing availability of white-collar employment, especially in south-east England where speculatively-built estates dominate. However, there are indications that this was not the case in Birmingham. That such a high percentage of inter-war housing was built by the local authority is one indication of the importance of blue-collar residents in housing demand. Another may be found in the occupational characteristics of the city's population during this period. The percentage of men

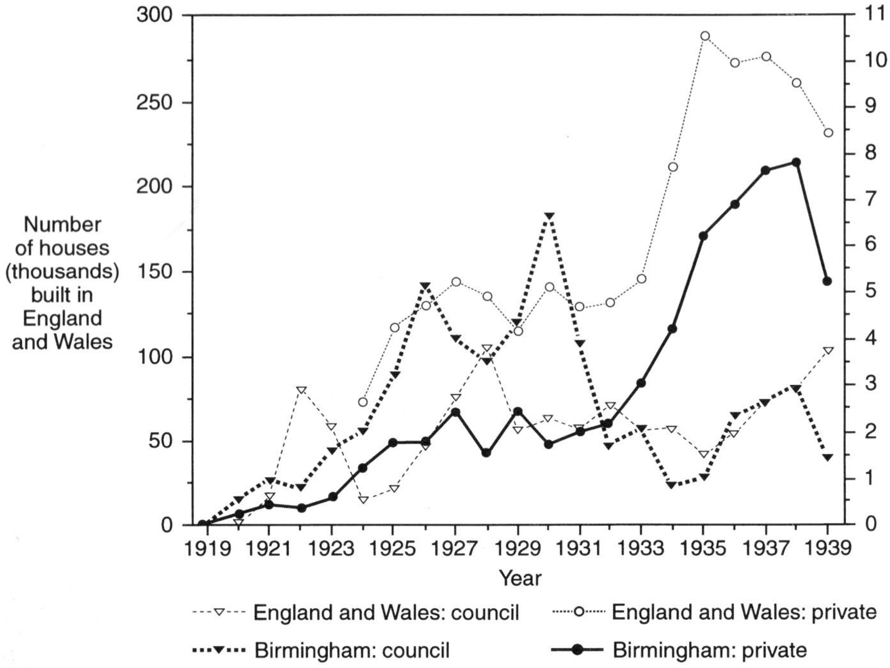

Fig. 20.2 Number of houses built in Birmingham and in England and Wales 1919-1939. Sources: Bowley, 1945, 271; MacMorran, 1973, 174.

of working age employed in professional occupations was 1.93 in 1921, 2.07 in 1931 and 4.41 in 1951. The corresponding percentages for employment in clerical and related jobs were 4.59, 5.98 and 3.37 (General Register Office, 1923, 1934, 1956). If white-collar employment as a whole had been rising in Birmingham, it might be reasonably assumed that it would have been reflected in these figures. But since it is not, the conclusion seems inescapable that Birmingham contributed little to the marked rise in non-manual occupations that took place in the country as a whole (Burnett, 1986, 251).

There are thus indications that Birmingham's inter-war housing stock in large part occupied the cheaper end of the suburban housing market. The houses with five or six bedrooms, including some with a `maid's room', that were built along Hamstead Hill, Handsworth Wood during the second half of the 1920s were very much the exceptions, as were the large, detached houses that were built in the inter-war period in Edgbaston.

Layouts and house types

Many of the municipal developments took the form of large estates, designed with strongly geometric road layouts, clearly identifiable from maps and from the air. The favoured house types were semi-detached or terraced. The terraces usually consisted of four houses, with a tunnel access to the rear of the middle dwellings (Fig. 20.3A). Occasionally two flats can be found masquerading as a semi-detached house, or as an end terrace. Generally, however, flats were not favoured by the local authority in the inter-war period, and only two municipal

Fig. 20.3 Contrasting architectural styles. (A) Neo-Georgian, cottage-style, council houses, Moor Green (photograph 1990). (B) Semi-detached houses with neo-Tudor gables, Hall Green (photograph 1995). (C) Picturesque houses influenced by the Arts and Crafts movement, Bournville (photograph 1995). (D) Modern, flat-roofed, houses, Selly Park (photograph 1995).

developments took place at this time that contained blocks of more than two storeys. These were the three-storey blocks at Garrison Lane, built in the 1920s, and the Emily Street flats, which were opened in 1939 (Birmingham City Council, 1989).

Residential developments by private enterprise ranged from bespoke designs for individual houses, through small speculative developments, to large estates conceived, designed and built by one builder. However, even where one builder was responsible for an entire estate, it was rarely as large as the municipal developments, and was often completed in several stages. For example, the Severne Estate, Hall Green - a development consisting of 12 shops and some 450 houses - built by H. Dare and Son in the 1930s, took about six years, and 16 separate building applications, to complete. Such developments are less startling when seen in plan than the council estates, perhaps partly because the generally smaller operations and sites of the private-enterprise builders made geometrical street layouts impracticable. House types are predominantly semi-detached and detached two-storey dwellings. Speculatively-built terraced houses are rare in Birmingham, and flats even more so.

The architectural style favoured at this time by municipalities, as well as the architectural profession generally, was unadorned neo-Georgian. However, occupiers of houses built by private enterprise during the same period liked their purchases to have styles that were distinct from those of council houses. Thus, not surprisingly, neo-Georgian house styles were not generally favoured by speculative builders, although they were by Bournville Village Trust. Also less favoured in Birmingham were the neo-Tudor styles that are so characteristic of speculative suburbia in London. The affixing of timber to walls, where it occurs, is often confined to gables (Fig. 20.3B).

Inter-war houses vary greatly, both in plan and elevation. While the stylistic antecedence of many can be traced back to the arts and crafts movement, with its emphasis on sweeping roofs and the picturesque (Fig. 20.3C), Birmingham also has examples of Modern architecture. Builders were encouraged by the architectural press to simplify the stylistic details of their houses, contrary to the wishes of purchasers: the plain lines of the Modern style were seen as being a compromise between the architects' preference for the simplicity of neo-Georgian and what were seen as the ornamental excesses of many private-enterprise developers. The perceptions of architects at this time are reflected in the comment of one of their number, a Fellow of the Royal Institute of British Architects, in the 1930s:

> If one looks through the advertisements in daily papers or in any publication concerned with the sale of small houses, it will be found that about 90 per cent. of the "desirable villas," "labour-saving houses," or "ideal homesteads" illustrated are devoid of taste and unsuitable to modern requirements. They are either vulgarly ostentatious with a riot of ill-proportioned gables and windows, or merely replicas of the pre-war suburban street. (Lloyd, n.d., 124)

Though not numerically significant in Birmingham, the Modern style has left its mark on the urban landscape. For example, there are flat-roofed houses in Kensington Road, Selly Park (Fig. 20.3D), and essentially Modern houses, albeit with hipped roofs, in Quinton Road and Ridgacre Lane, Quinton.

It is widely held that architects had little to do with suburban design during the inter-war period. Comments such as `few [suburban houses] are built under competent architectural supervision' (Bradshaw, 1939, 103) and `the majority of new houses were designed by the builders themselves, without the benefit of architects' (Burnett, 1986, 259) are not unusual. However, while there are many cases in which architects were not employed - the large Severne Estate in Hall Green was apparently not architect designed, since the builder appears to have been responsible for the building plans - there is evidence that architects were involved in suburban development at all levels in the market. Even many of the houses on the lower rungs of the suburban house market, which were thought to have been designed by speculative builders who chose to avoid architects' fees, were actually architect designed. However, the percentage of architect-designed houses varied greatly between different areas (Table 20.2). These figures, allied to the fact that houses built in the inter-war period are nearly all still standing, calls into question the widespread belief that these houses were `jerry-built', and would not last. This erroneous belief is graphically illustrated by the words of Taylor (1938, 759):

> They took the plunge into a small semi-detached hire-purchase villa on the wonderful new Everysuburb estate, adjacent to one of our great by-passes and only twenty minutes from the station. The estate was Mr. Jerrybuilder's fifth successful venture into the property market. By this time he had thoroughly mastered the technique of using the cheapest unseasoned timber, the lightest of breeze block, and the smartest of bathroom fittings.

Area	Number of houses in 25 hectare area	% designed by RIBA and/or BFCAA architects*
Quinton	498	87
Handsworth	434	50
Brandwood	314	20
Yardley	576	36

*RIBA: Royal Institute of British Architects
BFCAA: Birmingham and Five Counties Architectural Association

Table20.2: Percentage of houses in four areas of Birmingham designed by architects

Other developments

Suburban development was not confined to dwellings. Other notable features of the inter-war landscape included public houses, cinemas and petrol stations. The public houses were mostly large structures, usually sited on prominent street corners, and they lacked both the intimacy and the notoriety of older taverns found closer to the city centre. They often reflected an idealized vision of the past, in many cases using neo-Jacobean or neo-Tudor styles (Fig. 20.4A). The pubs therefore contrasted sharply with the newly-built cinemas which were frequently built using Art Deco styles (Fig. 20.4B).

Residential areas were generally laid out with little or no thought having been given to services. Shops were concentrated in a limited number of areas, in contrast to the individual corner shops that were characteristic of the majority of residential areas constructed before 1914. Residents of new estates - mainly wives who were left at home all day - often found themselves inconvenienced and isolated. This problem, by no means unique to Birmingham, was sufficiently common that the medical profession gave a name to the condition arising from it, the so-called 'suburban neurosis' (Taylor, 1938, 759).

Ironically, given that garden suburbs had been given the seal of approval by the Tudor Walters Report, concern grew throughout the inter-war period about urban sprawl. The Restriction of

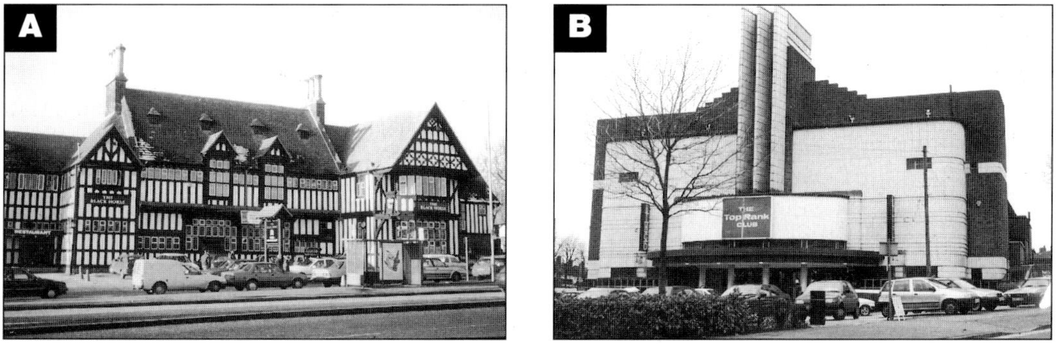

Fig. 20.4 Non-residential suburban buildings. (A) Public house in neo-Tudor style, Northfield (photograph 1995). (B) Cinema in Art Deco style, Kingstanding (photograph 1995).

Ribbon Development Act (1935) was an attempt to curtail the worst excesses of this, but it was the city's adoption of a green-belt policy, already under consideration in 1935, that eventually put a stop to unrestrained outward growth (see chapter 17).

The influence of pre-urban features

Despite, or perhaps because of, the scale and speed of suburban development in the inter-war period, the form of the earlier, rural landscape can often be discerned. It was common for roads previously in the country to be subsumed in the suburban landscape. Webb Lane, Hall Green (Fig. 20.5A) is a narrow country lane, edged by small bungalows, in contrast to the suburban dual carriageway of Highfield Road (Fig. 20.5B), into which it leads. Similarly, old hedgerows are

Fig. 20.5 Contrasting road types. (A) Incorporation of a country lane within suburban development, Hall Green (photograph 1995). (B) Dual carriageway, Hall Green (photograph 1995).

sometimes preserved in the inter-war landscape, and the edges of a development by a particular builder often correspond to field boundaries. Thus the landscape that existed before the outbreak of the First World War was influential in shaping the inter-war landscape.

Post-war change

Dramatic changes elsewhere in Birmingham have helped to encourage the notion that inter-war suburbs have undergone little change in the post-war period. Major development proposals that have attracted media attention have mostly been in and around the city centre or, occasionally, at the urban fringe. This has deflected attention away from the large number of piecemeal changes to inter-war suburbs that have cumulatively had a major impact on their appearance. Large-scale redevelopments, such as that of the council estate of Pype Hayes, are exceptional. Two factors in particular have had a bearing on these changes. First, there has been the containment of further outward growth associated with the adoption of a green-belt policy by local authorities surrounding Birmingham. In combination with a high demand for new houses after the Second World War this has led to both private developers and the council seeking sites within the existing urban area, many of them within the zone of inter-war suburbs. Secondly, there has been a variety of social and economic changes, including an increase in the number, and a diminution in the size, of households, and increases in female employment, personal mobility and household

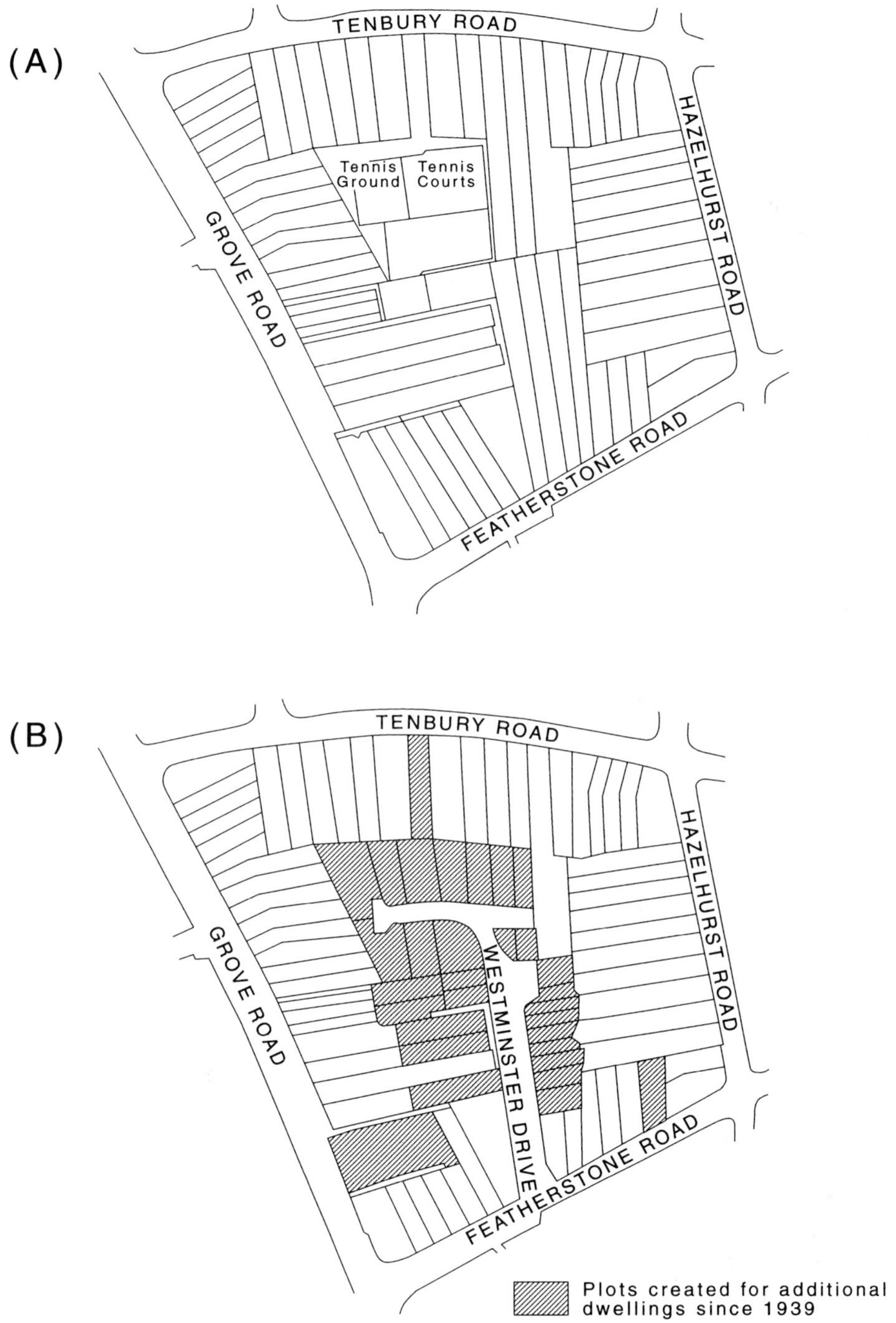

Fig. 20.6 Influence of original layout on the form of infill, Kings Heath. (A) Plot pattern in 1939. (B) Approximate plot pattern in 1995.

equipment. All of these have influenced physical change, but the form that this has taken has been greatly affected by the characteristics of existing suburban areas.

Areas most susceptible to the insertion of new dwellings have been those initially developed at very low densities. Here the large size of plots has meant that more intensive development is feasible largely within existing frameworks of plots and ownership units. In contrast, in the case of areas with average dwelling densities, such as those occupied by semi-detached houses, there is the need for the acquisition of several plots, each in different ownership, if a higher-density development is to be feasible. In these circumstances the likelihood of development is greatly reduced. Thus, ironically, areas containing the highest quality houses - large detached houses in large gardens - are the most susceptible to redevelopment.

An example of the influence of plot size and the layout of the original development on the insertion of additional houses is provided by a small area in King's Heath bounded by Tenbury Road, Hazelhurst Road, Featherstone Road and Grove Road (Fig. 20.6). The majority of the original development in this area occurred during the 1920s and 1930s, although all the roads were laid out before the First World War. The crucial factor creating scope for a considerable increase in the density of dwellings in the post-war period was the unusually long plots and the existence of a tennis club at the centre of the street block. During the 1960s the owners of four adjacent houses in Featherstone Road jointly initiated a series of planning applications that

Fig. 20.7 Post-war change. (A) Houses in Anglo-Scandinavian style inserted in back gardens, Kings Heath (photograph 1995). (B) Side extensions of adjacent semi-detached houses creating the effect of a terrace, Hall Green (photograph 1995). (C) Multiple changes to an inter-war house, Hall Green (photograph 1995). (D) Alterations to inter-war council houses, Warstock (photograph 1995).

involved the demolition of two of the houses to allow the insertion of a cul-de-sac. This new road was designed to create a new access to land made available by the truncation of gardens behind the houses left standing. Early planning applications sought permission to build flats, but the eventual development comprised eleven houses in the Anglo-Scandinavian style (Fig. 20.7a) and two bungalows, which were built on land that had previously been an orchard behind houses in Grove Road.

This new development had several side affects. Not only did the new cul-de-sac, Westminster Drive, enable access to be gained to the newly-built houses, it also provided a new access to the backs of plots fronting Grove Road. Three houses have been inserted into these plots, splitting the gardens of the original houses in half. The tennis club, to which access had originally been gained from Tenbury Road, was subject to proposals for development. Seven bungalows were built on an extension of Westminster Drive and a house was inserted fronting Tenbury Road, on the site of the access path. Finally, five smaller bungalows were built in the back gardens of houses fronting Tenbury Road, again using an extension to the Westminster Drive cul-de-sac.

Thus, over a period of thirty years, the number of dwellings in the street block increased from sixty-four to ninety-three (including a bungalow and house inserted in the backs of existing gardens separately from the developments just described). The new dwellings contrast sharply with those existing at the time of the Second World War.

The construction of additional dwellings within existing residential areas is just one aspect of the way in which inter-war suburbs are changing. In the large majority of areas, less striking individually, but more important cumulatively, are changes to existing buildings. Among the more evident of these are extensions to living space. Side extensions to adjacent semi-detached houses have sometimes created the effect of a terrace (Fig. 20.7B). During the 1960s many of these were constructed with flat roofs that were stark mismatches with the generally hipped roofs of the original houses. Over time these designs have fallen out of favour with development control officers, and less obtrusive extensions which extend the roof of the original house over the new rooms are now more common.

Other changes include the conversion of front gardens into areas for car parking, the replacement or alteration of porches, windows, doors and outbuildings, and the alteration or removal of chimneys (Fig. 20.7C). The re-roofing of houses in materials different from those originally used and the cladding of brick walls, for example by imitation stone, have in places been very obtrusive. Since council tenants have had the right to purchase their houses, council estates, too, have been susceptible to such changes; indeed the effects here have often been disproportionately large since consistency of design, which was one of the hallmarks of council estates, can be destroyed by change to a single house (Fig. 20.7D).

In the case of these changes to houses, the motivation for change is different from that in the case of the inserting of individual dwellings. Where additional dwellings are built, the purpose of the property owner is, in the large majority of cases, solely to enhance the sale value of the land. In the case of changes to individual houses, in contrast, the stimulus for change is primarily the desire of owner-occupiers to enhance their property for their own use; indeed the increase in market value is often not commensurate with the cost of those changes, although this may not be appreciated by those who initiate them.

Despite the widespread criticism of suburbs, especially among prominent architects and intellectuals in the 1920s and 1930s, there has in recent years been evidence of a reappraisal. In 1988 Birmingham City Council was one of the first local authorities to designate a conservation area, in the School Road - Miall Road area of Hall Green, comprised almost entirely of inter-war, semi-detached houses (see chapter 18).

Conclusion

The impress of inter-war suburbs on the configuration of Birmingham, in terms of streets, building forms and land utilization, is probably greater than on that of any other city in the UK outside London. The historical geography of the antecedence, creation and modification of these suburbs casts considerable light on British urban development in the twentieth century. The town planning movement was influenced to a major extent by early garden suburbs such as Bournville. The vast suburban sprawl that followed was in turn brought to an end by official recognition of the high cost, both in land consumption and urban efficiency, of a policy of garden suburbia for all. The creation of a green belt around Birmingham and neighbouring major urban areas has increased the interest of developers and owner-occupiers in the adaptation and more intensive use of existing suburban areas. But town planning has been slow to provide a coherent response to the challenges that this has presented. As a consequence a great deal of piecemeal change, including alterations to houses, the squeezing of new houses into existing gardens and small-scale redevelopment, has taken place in a manner that has often been in sharp contrast with the suburban landscapes that existed before the Second World War. The recent designation of suburban conservation areas would seem to reflect the recognition, albeit belatedly, of the importance of ordinary landscapes in the planning process. But, more generally, the appearance of Birmingham's inter-war suburbs is likely to continue to be primarily in the hands of its residents. Much of the piecemeal change that has so far been such a notable characteristic seems likely to remain outside the scope of planning legislation.

Acknowledgements

The research on which this chapter was based was funded by the Leverhulme Trust and the Economic and Social Research Council

References

Birmingham City Council 1989 *Developing Birmingham 1889 to 1989: 100 years of city planning* Birmingham City Council Development Department, Birmingham

Bowley M 1945 *Housing and the state 1914-1944* George Allen and Unwin, London

Bradshaw H C 1939 The suburban house in **Abercrombie P** ed. *The book of the modern house:a panoramic survey of contemporary domestic design* Hodder and Stoughton, London

Burnett J 1986 *A social history of housing 1815-1985* Methuen, London

Cannadine D 1980 *Lords and landlords: the aristocracy and the towns 1774-1967* Leicester University Press, Leicester

Chamberlain N 1913 Town planning in Birmingham in **Auden G A** ed. *A handbook for Birmingham and the neighbourhood prepared for the 83rd annual meeting of the British Association for the Advancement of Science* Cornish Brothers, Birmingham 175-82

Cherry G E 1988 *Cities and plans: the shaping of urban Britain in the nineteenth and twentieth centuries* Edward Arnold, London

Department of the Environment, Scottish Office Environment Department, Welsh Office n.d. *Housing and construction statistics 1983-1993: Great Britain* HMSO, London

General Register Office 1923 *Census of England and Wales 1921: County of Warwick* HMSO, London

General Register Office 1934 *Census of England and Wales 1932: Occupation Tables* HMSO, London

General Register Office 1956 *Census 1951 England and Wales: Occupation Tables* HMSO, London

Howard E 1898 *Tomorrow: a peaceful path to real reform* S Sonnenschein & Co, London

Lloyd T A n.d. The architect and housing by the speculative builder in Betham E ed. *House building 1934-1936* Federated Employers' Press, London

MacMorran J L 1973 *Municipal public works and planning in Birmingham* City of Birmingham Public Works Committee, Birmingham

National Register, United Kingdom and Isle of Man 1944 *Statistics of population on 29th September, 1939 by sex, age and marital condition: report and tables* HMSO, London

Nettlefold J S 1908 *Practical housing* Garden City Press, Letchworth

Nettlefold J S 1914 *Practical town planning* St Catherine Press, London

Robertson J 1913 The public health of Birmingham in **Auden G A** ed. *A handbook for Birmingham and the neighbourhood prepared for the 83rd annual meeting of the British Association for the Advancement of Science* Cornish Brothers, Birmingham 157-74

Taylor S 1938 The suburban neurosis *The Lancet* 234 759-61

Wiltshire F H C 1927 The Birmingham schemes and some problems of town and regional planning in *Report of proceedings: regional planning exhibition and conference 20-24th June 1927* Midland Joint Town Planning Advisory Council

CHAPTER 21

Creating recreational space for the City of Birmingham

Michael Tanner

Until the 1960s, the pattern of recreational space in Birmingham was a relatively simple one. Not only did it comprise readily identifiable recreational facilities and areas of open space, but these could be conveniently divided into those that had been created as a result of municipal enterprise and those that were provided by the private, mainly voluntary, sector. The former comprised the system of public parks, recreation grounds, golf courses and other open spaces that had been created since the second half of the nineteenth century, together with a number of municipal swimming pools and allotment sites. In addition, there was a separate system of school playing fields and gymnasia administered by the local education authority, which was sometimes made available to outside clubs on an ad hoc basis, but was mainly restricted to educational use. The private and voluntary sectors provided a rather different but overlapping range of mainly sports facilities. Many industrial and commercial concerns provided playing fields, and occasionally indoor sports facilities, for their workers, while private clubs often owned or controlled the sports grounds, golf courses, bowling greens and tennis courts that they used. Some indoor sports, like badminton and table tennis, also made use of church halls and similar buildings primarily provided for some other purpose.

Birmingham's recreational space in 1965

Municipal provision

Birmingham's municipally-provided recreational space is clearly described in its *Handbook to the Departments of the Corporation for 1965*, the last such handbook published by the city. This reflected the traditional committee structure of English local government, which in Birmingham dated back to 1851. The affairs of the council were administered by no fewer than 33 committees, three of which were directly concerned with the provision of recreational facilities through the departments which reported to them. Two of these had relatively straightforward responsibilities. The Smallholdings and Allotments Department provided a total of 11,160 allotments on 405 ha of land; 9100 of these allotments on 160 sites were held on a permanent basis. Similarly, the Baths Department managed 23 swimming pools, the earliest dating from 1851 and the most recent having been completed in 1962. These attracted nearly 3 million bathers each year, including organised school groups and some 50 clubs which were permitted to reserve evening sessions for competition and training. Twenty of the pools also provided washing baths, which were still used by nearly one million people a year, while there were suites of Russian and Turkish baths at four of the older establishments (Bradnock 1965).

The Parks Department had rather more diverse responsibilities. Like other industrial cities, Birmingham had acquired its first public parks during the second half of the nineteenth century through a combination of philanthropy and municipal enterprise. This process accelerated rapidly after 1900 with the addition not only of further parks but also of recreation grounds and smaller open spaces; the city also acquired 20 parks and recreation grounds created by other local authorities as a result of its boundary extension of 1911. Most of these early parks were established near the outer edge of the then built-up area and there were few open spaces in the inner city, apart from children's playgrounds and nine public gardens converted from old burial grounds between 1880 and 1915. The larger Victorian and Edwardian parks were carefully landscaped in accordance with the fashion of the time to resemble an idealized country estate within the city. Indeed, many of these early parks were created from the estates surrounding country houses. Their design was therefore based on a combination of flower beds, shrubberies, lawned areas and plantations of native and exotic trees, through which winding paths provided pleasant walks (Fig 21.1). These were often embellished with other attractions, including ornamental lakes, rockeries, bandstands, hothouses, bowling greens and tennis courts. Some also provided pitches for football, cricket and other team games. Because of this emphasis on creating what was essentially an artificial environment, the maintenance of such parks tended to be very labour-intensive.

Rather different kinds of recreational space were created during the inter-war years when rapid suburban expansion was accompanied by the acquisition of extensive areas of land in the outer parts of the city. Some of these were used to create new public parks, although these were usually less elaborate than the older ones, but the main emphasis was on the provision of recreation grounds and playing fields, both for public and schools use. It was during this period that the city also began to provide public golf courses in the outer suburbs. This process continued after the Second World War as slum clearance and central redevelopment led to a further massive transfer of population to new suburban estates, but priority was also given to the creation of new areas of open space in the redeveloped inner city.

The effect of this expansion was that, by 1965, the Parks Department was responsible for over 200 areas of open space extending to some 2268 ha, mainly comprising parks, recreation grounds and gardens, but also including six municipal golf courses and 170 ha of cemeteries. The city's recreational estate also included two areas outside its boundary which had been acquired because of threats to their high amenity value, Warley Woods and the Lickey Hills. The latter, which lie some 12 km to the south-west of the city centre, comprise the only range of hills readily accessible to the people of Birmingham, for whom they have acquired a symbolic value since the first part was donated to the city in 1889. Subsequent purchases and gifts from the Cadbury family meant that by 1965 the city owned 213 ha of the Lickey Hills, much of which is covered with woodland. These lay at the end of direct bus routes from the city centre and were heavily used, especially during summer weekends and bank holidays.

Like the swimming pools, the parks and open spaces also played an important role in providing facilities for both casual and organised sport. Municipal pitches were used by over 900 football and by nearly 100 cricket teams, as well as by smaller numbers of rugby, hockey and gaelic football teams. Similarly, many parks provided tennis courts, bowling greens and boating lakes, while more limited opportunities were available for fishing, sailing, rowing and model boating. As part of the city's policy of encouraging the use of its facilities, coaching schemes and competitions were organised for a number of sports, especially for young people. The parks were also used for various entertainments and special events which had, to a large extent, replaced the more traditional bandstand performances. These included bonfire night carnivals, the Birmingham Show, a Searchlight Tattoo and the Tulip Festival in Cannon Hill Park. As well as maintaining the flower beds, lawned areas, sports facilities and other amenities of its open spaces,

Fig. 21.1 Cannon Hill Park. Cannon Hill Park is a classic example of the Victorian landscaped park, with its trees and shrubberies, boating lake, winding paths and ornamental flower beds (photo: Geoff Dowling).

the Parks Department was responsible for the planting and maintenance of flowers and trees along the city's road system and hanging baskets in the city centre. Such importance was attached to these activities that the department had established its own Horticultural Training School in 1952. Expenditure on the parks and recreation grounds absorbed more than 5 per cent of the council's budget, excluding education, and the Parks Department employed over 1300 staff, about half that of the city police force (Bradnock 1965).

Private provision

It is more difficult to assess the extent of private recreational space in 1965, most of which comprised playing fields and other sports facilities. Apart from areas of disused and derelict land, which were often important locally for informal recreation, there were only two areas which performed a similar function to the public parks, and one of these was restricted to local residents who paid the appropriate annual subscription. This was Moseley Park which was created in 1899 to preserve part of the park of Moseley Hall threatened by development. The area, which extends to 6 ha, is still maintained as a private park and includes a lake and the remains of the former bluebell woods, as well as a tennis club. The other private area was the Birmingham Botanical Gardens, which opened in 1831 on a 6.5 ha site in Edgbaston just over 2 km from the city centre. Like Moseley Park, these were initially limited to the exclusive use of subscribers, but in 1844 it was decided to admit the working classes on two days each week at a cost of one penny and they have been open to the public on a day ticket basis ever since. Part of the site has also been occupied by one of the city's leading tennis clubs since 1881.

The only other large areas of private recreational space were the nine golf clubs, which covered a total area of 290 ha, and the facilities associated with the major spectator sports. These included the grounds of Birmingham's two leading football clubs, Aston Villa and Birmingham City, two dog tracks and the Warwickshire County Cricket Ground at Edgbaston, while the city's only racecourse at Bromford closed in 1965. In addition, there were a large number of playing fields and other facilities used by private sports clubs, most numerous of which were the 130 clubs affiliated to the Midlands Club Cricket Conference. A striking feature at this time was the extent to which such clubs were associated with industrial and commercial firms or other institutions, many of which provided high-quality facilities for use by their employees, and sometimes for outside members as well. These included a third of the 130 cricket clubs, half the 14 "leading hockey clubs" and 32 out of the 78 tennis clubs within the city affiliated to the Warwickshire Lawn Tennis Association. Similarly, 10 of the 32 rugby clubs affiliated to the North Midlands Football Union and eight of the 34 badminton clubs affiliated to the Birmingham and District League were associated with private firms or other institutions (Birmingham Post 1965).

Changes in the recreational planning environment since 1965

The period since 1965 has seen significant changes in the pattern of recreational space within the city, although these are reflected not so much in the amount of land devoted to such provision as in the type of facilities provided and the way in which these are managed. To some extent at least, such changes may be regarded as an outcome of the statutory planning process. Birmingham's first Development Plan was approved by the government in 1960 and provided the framework that has guided the subsequent provision of recreational space within the city. Conceptually, open space was regarded as a network of parks, playing fields and riverside walks that would link together the surrounding green belt countryside and new parkways to be created around the redeveloped inner city (City of Birmingham 1960). This Development Plan was superseded in 1973 by a new Structure Plan which, although presented in a new format, largely adopted the recreational policies proposed in the earlier plan. It also identified a serious deficiency in sports facilities, both indoor and outdoor, and emphasised the potential of the canal system for linking the city's network of open spaces (City of Birmingham 1973). Before these proposals could be implemented, planning responsibilities changed as a result of the 1974 reorganisation of local government under which the new West Midlands County Council became the Structure Plan Authority for the whole of the conurbation. The Structure Plan for West Midlands County was prepared by 1980 and, although covering a much wider area, broadly endorsed the proposals in Birmingham's plans (West Midlands County Council 1980). When the County Council was abolished in 1985, planning responsibility reverted to the City of Birmingham, which produced its Unitary Development Plan in 1993 (Birmingham City Council 1993).

Land-use planning and changes in recreational provision since 1965

The most important change that has accompanied this succession of plans is the adoption of an increasingly flexible approach to the provision of recreational space. Such provision is no longer conceived of primarily as the acquisition and management of discrete areas of land within clearly-defined administrative boundaries, but as part of the general process of environmental management. There are two aspects of this change. The first is the growing recognition that not only can many different kinds of resource provide recreational opportunities but that recreational resources themselves can make a valuable contribution to environmental quality. This new approach is clearly reflected in the city's 1993 Unitary Development Plan in which open space, together with playing fields, allotments and sports facilities, is included in the section on environment (Birmingham City Council 1993). The second is that recreational resources are now regarded as part of a regional or even national system that not only crosses administrative boundaries within the conurbation but also extends into the surrounding countryside. As a result, the urban region has become the primary framework for the planning of major facilities and the previously rigid distinction between urban and rural provision has become blurred. The adoption of a broader approach to recreational provision has also been facilitated by the publication of a series of regional strategies for sport and recreation by the West Midlands Sports Council.

The changing roles of local authorities and new sources of funding

Underlying this new approach are two more fundamental changes which mean that the provision of leisure and recreation facilities has developed a momentum of its own since the late 1960s that, to some extent at least, is independent of the statutory planning process of individual local authorities. The first is the changing role of local authorities, especially in terms of their budgetary freedom and their relationship with central government. Cities like Birmingham are now required to adopt a more entrepreneurial role in developing the economy and improving the environment of their area, while obtaining access to funding for anything other than the more basic local government services has become an increasingly competitive process (see chapter 16). The second is the availability of new sources of funding. The main initial source of such funding has been the central government, which has sought to encourage the provision of particular kinds of facilities in the interests of national policies, but it has also placed growing emphasis on the involvement of the private sector. This in turn has led to two important but inter-related changes in the way in which recreational facilities are provided. These are the fact that the capital needed for investment in new facilities does not have to be wholly generated within the area of an individual local authority and the encouragement given to collaborative ventures, both between different local authorities and between local authorities and other public and private sector agencies.

In some cases, central government funding has been specifically directed at improving opportunities for leisure and recreation in and around the city and is channelled through agencies which adopt a strategic approach to the allocation of resources. Grant-aid for the development of sport facilities has been available from the Sports Council since 1972, while the Countryside Commission has been able to fund initiatives for improving access to the countryside since 1968. Other sources of funding have become available through policies primarily directed at the regeneration of inner city areas under the government's urban programme, which began in the late 1960s. These policies are implemented at the local level by specially-appointed bodies and originally emphasised redevelopment projects, derelict land clearance and similar measures intended to make the area more attractive to industry. More recently, this approach has been extended to incorporate other forms of environmental improvement, including the provision of recreational facilities, which can contribute to the strengthening of the local economy.

The effect of these changes on the pattern of public recreational space in and around the City of Birmingham is reflected in both the provision of new facilities and the management of existing resources. Three kinds of new facilities have been provided since 1965, all of which have benefitted from the availability of central government funding. These are footpaths and country parks, which are intended to offer a rural recreation experience; leisure centres and specialist sports facilities, which are designed to improve opportunities for both indoor and outdoor sports; and the environmental improvements associated with urban regeneration, especially those affecting the canal system. Existing resources mainly comprise allotments and the various elements of the public parks system, all of which have been affected by budgetary constraints and changes in the way in which local authority services are delivered.

Footpaths and Country Parks

National funding to support certain kinds of recreational initiative at the local level was introduced by the *Countryside Act 1968*. This was primarily concerned with meeting the recreational needs of an increasingly car-borne public in a countryside that was perceived to be under growing pressure. Concern was particularly expressed about the effects of such pressures on the national parks and a new form of recreational facility, the country park, was proposed to provide a countryside recreation experience closer to the main centres of population. Such country parks would be designed to absorb high levels of use and grant-aid was available from the Countryside Commission, which encouraged their establishment in the urban fringe. The Commission also supported environmental improvement and recreational provision in such areas through locally-based management initiatives.

Although this grant-aid was initially only available outside the built-up area, it stimulated a number of developments around Birmingham. The city itself quickly secured the designation of the Lickey Hills as a country park in 1972, and three other country parks were established by Hereford and Worcester County Council along the line of hills that marks the south-west edge of

Fig. 21.2 Urban farm in the Woodgate Valley Country Park. This urban farm forms part of the Woodgate Valley Country park, which was established by the City of Birmingham in 1985 to protect one of the last green wedges penetrating into the city (photo: Geoff Dowling).

the conurbation, at Waseley Hills in 1971, Kingsford in 1972 and Clent Hills in 1974. Like the Lickeys, the Clent Hills had been a popular weekend destination for Birmingham people for a century or more, although they are less accessible. More recently, the city has designated two country parks within its boundaries. The first is the Woodgate Valley (Fig 21.2), which was established in 1985 and comprises some 180 ha of former farmland that forms a green wedge 3.5 km long penetrating into the south-western part of the city. It also includes an urban farm and a pony-trekking centre. The other is Sheldon Country Park, designated in 1986 and close to Birmingham International Airport to the east of the city, which extends to 97 ha and includes a working seventeenth-century farm.

To the north-west of Birmingham, 142 ha of Sandwell Valley, another green wedge penetrating into the heart of the conurbation, was similarly designated as a country park in 1983. This includes formal park areas, picnic sites, woodlands and two large pools, which provide facilities for a range of recreational activities, including walking, golf, sailing, windsurfing, horse-riding, fishing, cricket, tennis and bowls. Sandwell Valley Country Park is itself part of the much larger Beacon Regional Park which emerged from an initiative by the former West Midlands County Council and the Countryside Commission. Its management was then taken over by a partnership of Walsall, Sandwell and Birmingham councils, which were joined more recently by Lichfield Borough Council. The park comprises some 3250 ha of countryside interspersed with urban development which includes various kinds of open space, mainly owned by the participating authorities and linked by a network of footpaths, towpaths and bridleways. It also reflects the more informal approach which has characterized much recent provision of recreational space, for its boundaries are not clearly defined on the ground and its component parts are managed by the local authority which owns them, although these work together at officer level.

This informal approach is similarly reflected in the establishment of waymarked footpaths in and around the city. Some of these have been designated by the surrounding county councils and have been given distinctive regional names, like the North Worcestershire Path, which runs for 44 km along the southern fringe of the conurbation. This not only links four country parks but also two other major footpaths providing access to more distant recreational areas. These are the Worcestershire Way, which provides a 63km route southwards to the Malvern Hills, and the 153km Staffordshire Way, which runs along the western and northern fringes of the conurbation from Kinver Edge to Cannock Chase, where it turns northwards to Congleton on the edge of the Peak District National Park.

Within the conurbation, the Beacon Way runs for 27 km through the Beacon Regional Park and links Sandwell Valley Country Park with Chasewater, a canal feeder reservoir 25 km to the north of Birmingham, which is much used for water-based recreation. Birmingham itself has created the Harborne Walkway from 4 km of disused railway line only 4 km from the city centre, while walking along the extensive canal system within the city is encouraged by numerous towpath guides. The establishment of a riverside footpath is also a core feature of Project Kingfisher, a joint initiative by Birmingham and Solihull councils to improve the environment along 11 km of the valley of the River Cole, from Small Heath to Chelmsley Wood. The project formally began in 1985, although the preservation of the Cole valley as a green corridor had first been proposed in 1909 and a plan was prepared in the late 1940s. Some 324 ha of land are involved, including former meadows, playing fields, woodland, two lakes and a number of ponds, which provide a variety of landscape features and wildlife habitats. The southern 6 km of the Cole valley within the city is being similarly improved by the Millstream Project and the Cole Valley Walkway is to be officially opened in June 1996.

Rather closer to the city centre, environmental improvements are being made to the River Rea, which was severely affected by urbanization during the nineteenth century. The provision of access to the canalized sections of the Rea had begun in 1975 when a short section of public footpath was created along the river adjacent to Cannon Hill Park by the Severn Trent Water Authority. This approach has now been extended to the whole of the Rea valley, which is being opened up as part of the city's policy of developing a network of footpaths and cycle routes. The first 5 km section of the Rea Valley Cycle and Pedestrian Route was opened in 1991, with a further 1.6 km extension in 1992. This forms part of the Strategic Cycle Route Network which the city decided to develop in 1987. Eleven named routes are planned, using river walkways, canal towpaths, minor roads and cycle lanes along major routes, and all include off-road sections. It is intended that these should extend to all parts of the city and should have potential for both commuting and recreational use. Some 60 km had been completed by 1996, one third of which was off-road, and it is intended to increase this to 193 km by 2005 (Birmingham City Council 1995a). Links will also be provided with the National Cycle Network, which will eventually extend to 10,500 km and run through central Birmingham.

Leisure centres and sports facilities

National funding has similarly been available since the early 1970s for the provision of sports facilities. Like other British cities at this time, Birmingham was particularly lacking in facilities for indoor sports. The city's first gymnasium dates back to 1866 and the Birmingham Athletic Institute opened its facilities in the city centre in 1892 but, as late as 1970, the only purpose-built sports centre within the city was the private one on the campus of the University of Birmingham. The shortage of indoor facilities was so acute that the 1973 Structure Plan estimated a need for 19 such centres, as well as identifying a deficiency in other sports facilities (City of Birmingham 1973). The position has changed dramatically since then with the provision of a range of sport and recreation facilities, both indoor and outdoor. Important factors here have been the 'Sport for All' campaign and other national policies to encourage participation in sport and recreation, which have been supported by the provision of advice and grant-aid for facilities through the Sports Council.

The most striking change has been the development of leisure centres. The first public leisure centre in the present City of Birmingham was built by Sutton Coldfield on a greenfield site on the edge of Sutton Park and was incorporated into the city in 1974. The Wyndley Leisure Centre opened in 1971 and provides a range of indoor facilities, including a swimming pool, sports hall, squash courts, restaurant and sports shop. Although this provided a model for later developments, most such facilities in Birmingham were not created until the 1980s. These have been provided in two ways. Most numerous are the 21 community leisure centres on school sites established by the introduction of dual-use schemes, which are intended to make better use of existing publicly-owned facilities. All of these provide a multi-purpose sports hall, while some also offer swimming pools and other leisure and recreation facilities. Some of these facilities already existed or needed only modification, but others involved substantial new construction, for which national grant-aid was available. Dual-use schemes are based on the principle that school sports facilities should be available for community use out of school hours and they are jointly funded from the leisure services and education budgets; since 1994 they have been referred to as 'community leisure' facilities. The advent of grant-maintained schools caused initial problems as facilities in which the city had sometimes invested heavily were removed from its control. These problems have now been resolved, with all the community leisure centres being managed by the city as a single system, within which the use of facilities controlled by grant-maintained schools is provided on a contractual basis.

A number of freestanding leisure centres have also been constructed by the city. One of the earliest was the Aston Villa Sport and Leisure Centre opened in 1980 which forms part of a development including a superstore close to Villa Park. This was built with money provided by a partnership between the City Council, Aston Villa Football Club, the Sports Council, the Associated Dairies Group and the Department of the Environment's Inner City Programme. The main facility offered by the Aston Villa centre is a sports hall that provides nearly 2000 square metres of space, but some more recent leisure centres offer a wider range of leisure facilities. The Cocks Moors Woods Leisure Centre, for example, which was opened in 1987 on the edge of one of the municipal golf courses, offers not only a sports hall but also a free-form leisure pool equipped with a wave machine and flume, as well as a licensed bar and cafeteria (Fig. 21.3). Similar leisure pools have been built at two other centres and these, with their higher temperatures and informal poolside environment, are intended to provide a very different kind of recreational experience from the city's traditional swimming pools.

Fig. 21.3 Cocks Moors Woods Leisure Centre. The Cocks Moors Woods Leisure Centre was opened in 1987 on the edge on one of Birmingham's municipal golf courses. Its facilities include a sports hall and a free-form leisure pool with a wave machine and flume (photo: Geoff Dowling).

Three of these older pools have been closed because of obsolescence and three others have been replaced by those in leisure centres, but eleven have been retained and are still heavily used. Some of these have been refurbished, often with the addition of other facilities, like solariums and fitness centres, but others are in need of renovation. These traditional pools are the main way in which swimming opportunities are provided at the local level and are also particularly valuable to organised clubs which regard leisure pools as inappropriate to their needs. An important factor here is the lack of a 50-metre pool which is essential for competition at the higher levels. This question was addressed by the city when it drew up its strategy for swimming facilities in 1988, which recommended that the provision of a 50- metre pool in a central location should be given first priority. Such a pool would significantly increase the opportunities for 'serious swimming' in the city and would provide high-quality facilities for training and competition. Whereas swimming pools cater for long-established forms of recreation, the new multi-purpose sports halls and leisure centres provide opportunities for a much wider range of sports and fitness-related activities. Many of these can be enjoyed on a casual and informal basis, but they have also provided high quality facilities for a variety of organised sports. This has stimulated the growth of sports which, like badminton, squash and basketball, have always been practised indoors, but it has encouraged the development of indoor forms of outdoor games, especially five-a-side football, hockey and bowls. The flagship of Birmingham's indoor sports facilities is the National Indoor Arena, opened in 1991 on the edge of the central area, which is used for international, national and regional competition in a number of sports, including athletics. High-level competition also takes place at some leisure centres which, like that at Aston Villa, are equipped with moveable seating for spectators.

The attraction of leisure centres is that they provide a variety of social and recreational opportunities in a controlled environment that is independent of weather conditions and the hours of daylight. These advantages have also led to the development of specialized indoor facilities for some outdoor sports, usually by a combination of public and private funding and sometimes involving the use of converted buildings. Tennis has been a particular focus of such provision as a result of the Indoor Tennis Initiative launched in 1986 by the Lawn Tennis Association and the Sports Council and supported by the profits from the Wimbledon Championships. The Birmingham Tennis Centre at Billesley opened in 1994 and provides six indoor and eight outdoor floodlit courts. Indoor courts have also been built at two local clubs and at the privately-financed David Lloyd Club. Another sport which has become an increasingly popular indoor activity since the 1970s is bowling. Indoor facilities are available at some leisure centres, although there is currently only one specialized indoor bowling centre within the city, which occupies a converted DIY superstore. Indoor provision for a very different kind of sporting activity has been made at the Birmingham Climbing Centre, "The Rock Face". This privately-owned facility was opened in 1994 in a former builders' merchants near the city centre and offers a number of artificial climbing walls.

A similar capital-intensive approach has been adopted to the provision of outdoor sports facilities capable of supporting high levels of use. This has been achieved by the use of floodlighting and synthetic surfaces that are much more resistant to wear than traditional turf pitches. The capital costs of such facilities are high, but their maintenance costs are low, which increases their attractiveness because most grant-aid is available only for capital investment. They also have the advantage that their management costs can be reduced where they can be built adjacent to leisure centres. Birmingham's first floodlit artificial grass pitch was opened in 1981 in Highgate, an inner city area of great deprivation only 1.5 km from the city centre. Since then the city has built another seven all-weather pitches, mainly attached to leisure centres and partly financed through the government's urban aid programme. These are most heavily used for football, but the sport that has been most affected by their availability has been hockey, which is now played at the highest levels entirely on artificial surfaces. Birmingham also provides three synthetic athletics tracks, one at its Alexander Stadium, which is used for national and international events, and the others at two of its local leisure centres, Fox Hollies and Wyndley.

Urban regeneration and environmental improvement

The relationship between urban regeneration policies and the provision of recreational space is less immediately obvious, but it has made a significant contribution in some areas. The philosophy behind this is explained in the government's Environmental White Paper, which emphasises the value of 'greening urban areas' and argues that environmental improvement is a key element in the regeneration of local economies (Department of the Environment 1990). The significance of the urban programme is that it has given Birmingham and adjacent authorities access to external sources of funding for the provision of new recreational facilities and areas of open space. Various mechanisms have been used to channel central government funding into improvement schemes and in 1994 twenty separate urban aid programmes were brought together

Fig. 21.4 Climbing wall at the Ackers Trust. The Ackers Trust is an urban outdoor activities centre created from an area of derelict industrial land in Small Heath, only 4 km from Birmingham's city centre. It provides facilities for a range of outdoor activities, including two floodlit climbing walls, an artificial ski slope and a canoe training centre (photo: Geoff Dowling).

into a Single Regeneration Budget, to be administered by a new body, the Urban Regeneration Agency, usually known as English Partnerships. This name reflects the government's belief that partnerships between central government, local authorities, voluntary bodies, the private sector and the local community are the most effective way of improving the economy and environment of inner-city areas. Funding has been particularly directed at the reclamation of disused or derelict land, but the most important agencies in the West Midlands conurbation are the two urban development corporations (UDCs), which have planning powers and much broader interests. These are the Black Country UDC, established in 1987, and the Birmingham Heartlands UDC, which was set up in 1992 to take over the regeneration work in north-east Birmingham begun in 1989 by the Birmingham Inner City Partnership, a joint initiative between the city council and private developers.

Funding through the urban programme has been made available for both general environmental improvement, like landscaping, tree planting and the creation of public open space, and for more specialized recreational projects. Two such projects in two of the most deprived areas of Birmingham's inner city have used urban programme funding to convert areas of derelict industrial land into outdoor recreation facilities. Both have also received funding from Birmingham City Council and the Sports Council, as well as a number of other sources. The Birmingham Wheels Park originated in 1978 as a response to juvenile car-related crime and began as a collaborative venture between Birmingham City Council, the West Midlands County Council and the Probation service, with funding from the Manpower Services Commission. The site lies 2 km to the east of the city centre and was originally occupied by a brickworks and associated clay pits before it was taken over for tipping municipal waste. Initially only 2.7 ha of land was acquired, but this was later extended to 12 ha, which has been landscaped to provide opportunities for a range of motor-related sporting activities, including BMX racing, motorcycle scrambling, karting, stock-car racing and driver training. There is also an urban farm, a trim trail, an assault course and a nature trail.

An equally imaginative project was the foundation of the Ackers Trust in 1981 to re-develop a derelict industrial site in Small Heath, about 4 km to the south east of the city centre. The site, which extends to some 28 ha and is adjacent to the Grand Union Canal, has been used to create a major urban outdoor activities centre for use by both adults and school and youth groups. The on-site facilities include Birmingham's only artificial ski slope, an orienteering course and two large floodlit climbing walls (Fig 21.4), while a canoe training centre has been established using the canal basin, where both narrow boats and a residential centre are available. The Trust operates in the same way as outdoor activity centres in rural areas and offers a range of training courses using its specialist facilities, as well as providing opportunities for participation in more informal recreational activities. Since 1986, it has also managed a former industrial sports ground that forms part of the site and has been able to offer facilities for bowling, cricket and football.

A particular focus of the urban programme funding used for environmental improvement has been the canal system. There are 210 km of canal within Birmingham and the Black Country and the city itself lies at the heart of the national waterway system, which extends to some 3,200 km. Not only is there an extensive network within the built-up area, but the canals linking Birmingham with the Humber, Mersey, Severn and Thames estuaries meet close to the city centre. The potential of the canals as a recreational resource was recognized by Birmingham in its 1960 Development Plan and eventually acknowledged by the government in 1967 and the subsequent *Transport Act 1968* made provision for much of the system to be retained primarily

Fig. 21.5 Gas Street Basin, Birmingham (photo: Terry Slater)

for pleasure cruising and other leisure activities. A programme of improvement within the conurbation had begun by 1970, involving both preservation and restoration, but this tended to be piecemeal until the introduction of the Canals Improvement Programme in 1982. This was established by the Birmingham Inner City Partnership and jointly funded by the Department of the Environment, the British Waterways Board, Birmingham City Council and the former West Midlands County Council. The Programme has focused on both environmental improvement and the provision of increased recreational opportunities.

Because of their strategic location, the canals within the conurbation are much used by pleasure craft, especially during the summer months, but it is the 250 km of towpaths that support the highest levels of recreational use, especially for walking and cycling. Improvement work on the canal system and its immediate environment has been carried out throughout the conurbation, but is most striking in and around Birmingham's city centre (Fig 21.5). Here the City Centre Canal Walkway has been created by refurbishing 9.5 km of towpath through inner Birmingham, including both resurfacing work and the provision of new access points. Leaflets have been published for seven clearly identified towpath routes using this walkway and a number of similar routes have been designated elsewhere in the conurbation, including some circular walks, while Birmingham and Wolverhampton have been linked by the Birmingham and Black Country Canal Cycleway.

The potential of the canalside environment has also been recognized by making it the focus of development projects, some of which include leisure facilities. Construction work began in 1992 on Brindleyplace, which will provide 6 ha of shops, restaurants, offices and leisure facilities on the edge of Birmingham's city centre and adjacent to the International Arena and the International Conference Centre, both of which front onto the canal. The nearby Gas Street Basin has similarly been redeveloped to provide an attractive canalside area with restaurants and public houses (Fig. 21.5). Another major development project that uses the Birmingham and Fazeley Canal as its central feature, and includes the improvement of the canalside environment among its objectives, is the Waterlinks business village, which covers 134 ha of land 1.5 km to the north-east of the city centre. This is part of the much larger Heartlands urban regeneration area where a privately-led initiative supported by Birmingham City Council is working to create new employment opportunities, with a strong emphasis on environmental enhancement.

Developments in the public park system

The public parks and recreation grounds have provided a relatively stable element at a time of rapid evolution in Birmingham's recreational space system. In particular, their traditional function of providing an outlet for informal leisure activities in the open air remains a vital one, especially in the inner parts of the city. Similarly, they have continued to play an important role in the provision of facilities for organized sport, particularly football. The parks, in particular, have also retained their well-established functions relating to the entertainment, the arts and community activities. They therefore remain a popular venue for shows, sporting events, exhibitions, fairs, displays and public entertainments and community occasions of all kinds. This does not mean that they have remained unchanged. The public parks system has been affected by three kinds of change since 1965. The first relates to the perceived role of recreational space within the city. Parks and other areas of open space have increasingly been regarded as part of the broader environment, both in terms of their general amenity value and their function as a habitat for wildlife. This new approach is reflected in the fact that Birmingham's open spaces are now managed by a department of 'Parks and Nature Conservation'. It was also symbolized by the city's decision in the mid-1960s to remove the fences, hedges and railings along the road frontages of its parks and open spaces. The purpose of this change was to extend public access and open up new vistas, as well as reducing maintenance costs, but it had the effect of changing the character of the parks. No longer were they areas of controlled space within which behaviour could be carefully regulated by the use of byelaws enforced by park-keepers, although the last permanent staff were not removed from the parks until the mid-1980s. Their place has now been taken by a force of mobile rangers.

Changes have also resulted from changing recreational needs and growing public interest in the environment. Some public parks have therefore been modified to create a less formal and more natural environment that can provide a habitat for wildlife, as well as reducing maintenance costs and providing a greater variety of leisure experiences. Where funding has been available, this has led to programmes of tree-planting and landscaping, sometimes incorporating new path layouts and facilities like games areas, trim trails and nature conservation areas. In some respects, such modifications mean that many city parks and open spaces now offer a recreational environment similar to that of country parks, a similarity that is accentuated by the employment of conservation-trained rangers, the emphasis on footpaths and the provision of visitor centres and nature trails. At the same time, the older parks have largely retained their traditional layout and functions, although Cannon Hill Park has been enhanced by the Midland Arts Centre, which opened in 1967. This incorporates the arena theatre concept developed in the park in the years after the Second World War and provides art galleries, theatres, a cinema and other facilities.

These changes may be regarded as a response to changing attitudes and needs, but the third kind of change has been enforced by budgetary constraints. In spite of their recognised social importance, local authorities have not had the same access to central government funding for their urban parks as they have had for country parks, leisure centres, sports facilities and environmental improvements linked to urban regeneration. Similarly, there are not the same opportunities for partnership with the private sector because access is normally available without charge. The public parks have therefore been affected by reductions in local authority budgets and the withdrawal of staff, which have made it increasingly difficult to maintain the whole of what has become a very substantial estate to the same high standards. The result has been a loss of facilities and deterioration in levels of maintenance, while the parks have been starved of the investment needed for modernization and refurbishment. There is also widespread anxiety about the problems of vandalism and public safety in the parks, while the Garden History Society has expressed concern about the loss of their historic interest (Conway and Lambert 1993).

The problems affecting Britain's urban parks have been acknowledged by the government, which has given its support to a recent national study of their future, although without promising additional funding (Department of the Environment 1995). This study argues that the parks make an important contribution to the quality of urban life and that radical thinking is needed if the decline that has affected them since the 1960s is not to continue. It therefore recommends that local authorities should prepare strategies for the future development and management of their urban parks and that these should be a central element in urban regeneration policy and eligible for National Lottery funding (Comedia 1995). As far as funding is concerned, the Chairman of the National Heritage Memorial Fund has announced that it will welcome bids for the regeneration of city parks, which will become a major theme in the work of the Fund.

Birmingham is fortunate that, although it has similar problems to other cities, the basic infrastructure of its parks system remains intact and continues to provide a high quality recreational environment in many areas. Its parks also do not seem to have experienced the same decline in popularity as those of many other large cities. A recent survey suggested that 59 per cent of the city's population visited the parks on a regular basis and that there had been at least a six per cent increase in use between 1991 and 1995. It also revealed a high level of satisfaction with the parks, although there was concern about safety, particularly amongst inner-city residents, the elderly and ethnic minorities. This concern was reflected in a desire for the maintenance of staff on site, although this was perceived as being less important than the provision of better facilities. Children's playgrounds were identified as particularly valuable in encouraging family use (Forward Consultancy Initiative 1995). The purpose of the survey was to provide information about community needs as part of the city's preparation of a strategy for its public parks system that will be used in seeking funding for its future development. It is likely that this strategy will propose a concentration of resources on maintaining the quality of five 'centres of excellence', each of which is regarded as providing a unique service, and six 'premier parks', mainly around the outer edge of the inner city. These will be selected to ensure that there is at least one 'quality park' in each part of the city, while there will also be a number of 'community parks', where the aim will be to broadly maintain the present quality, although they may lose some of their amenities. The remaining areas, mainly recreational grounds, will be retained as open spaces, but will receive little investment.

A similar strategic approach is being adopted for the city's 65 playing field sites, which have also suffered because of lack of maintenance and the withdrawal of staff. Problems affecting changing accommodation, in particular, have led to a reduction of demand and complaints about the quality of the facilities available. Again the strategy is based on the concentration of resources on five 'premier sites' providing good quality facilities for a range of sports and supported by a staff presence on site. It is hoped to develop one of these as a regional centre of excellence for football. In addition, there will be a network of 'satellite sites' in each part of the city providing facilities of the standard required by the local football leagues. This rationalization process means that sites not selected for inclusion in these two categories may become disused, although most will be retained as open space.

Allotments and leisure gardens

Allotments have been providing an outlet for the use of leisure time in Birmingham since long before the first parks were established. Until the second half of the 19th century, the city was surrounded by 'guinea gardens' provided by private landowners. These were overwhelmed by development, but responsibility for providing such facilities was taken over by the corporation which, by 1914, controlled 4000 allotments. These were increased to over 12,000 plots covering nearly 500 ha in a war-time effort to increase food production, although many of these were temporary. During the inter-war period, the number of plots was stabilized at about this figure as the allotment movement became a powerful force and Birmingham, which regarded such provision as a social service, established a separate Allotments Committee in 1922. By 1938 there were 12,274 allotments on 147 sites, mainly on the outskirts of the city, with a total area 546 ha. In addition, there were some 4000 private allotments (Faulkner 1938). The largest municipal site at this time accommodated nearly 1000 tenants and it has been argued that the scale of provision reflected the city's interest in gardening (Briggs 1952).

During the Second World War the needs of food production again led to an increase in the number of allotments, which reached a peak of 20,414 in 1942, many on temporary sites. Even

Fig. 21.6 The Harry Thorpe Pavilion in the Meadow Road Leisure Gardens, Harborne. The Meadow Road Leisure Gardens occupy a site of 4.8 ha in Harborne and include the Harry Thorpe Pavilion. Professor Thorpe was Head of the Department of Geography in the University of Birmingham and Chairman of the Departmental Committee of Inquiry into Allotments. The publication of the Committee's report in 1969 paved the way for the redevelopment of many allotment sites into landscaped leisure gardens with improved facilities (photo: Geoff Dowling).

in 1950 there were still 16,377 plots covering 623 ha, although almost half of these were temporary, plus at least another 2500 private allotments occupying 91 ha (Black 1957). Subsequently there was a steady decline, mainly as result of the loss of temporary sites, but between 1967 and 1972 there was a decrease of 22 per cent in the number of permanent plots. Nevertheless, in 1972 there were still 8169 permanent allotments on 119 sites covering 307 ha, plus another 21 temporary sites. At about this time, there was a formal recognition that allotment sites, many of which were in a run-down condition, had the potential to be converted into attractive amenity areas following the recommendations of the Thorpe Committee (Thorpe 1969). The city therefore embarked on a planned programme of redeveloping these sites into 'leisure gardens' (Fig 21.6), the first of which opened in 1971 in Quinton (City of Birmingham 1973). Changing leisure patterns since then have led to some reduction in the demand for allotments, but in March 1996 the city still had 7310 plots, although 20 per cent of these were unoccupied and further rationalization is planned.

Recreational space in Birmingham in 1996

The period since 1965 has seen an increase of nearly 50 per cent in the amount of public recreational space in Birmingham (Fig 21.7), but most of this is accounted for by the inclusion within the city of the 970 ha of Sutton Park and a number of smaller parks and open spaces as a result of the 1974 local government reorganisation. Where there have been additions to the areas of recognized open space, these have mainly been small and are probably more than offset by the loss to development of private sports facilities, especially playing fields provided by industrial and commercial firms, some of which were of high quality. Not all such changes lead to an absolute loss of facilities. For example, Kings Norton Golf Club sold its course for development in 1973, but was able to use the proceeds to build a new course outside the city. Similarly, the provision of sports halls, synthetic pitches and other specialist sports facilities has given both individuals and clubs access to high-quality facilities, like many of the more than 50 clubs in the Birmingham Badminton League. Such provision has mainly been made by the public sector, although there has also been private-sector provision in some areas, including private health and fitness clubs. These new facilities have been very important for some sports, but others still rely mainly on private club facilities. For example, there are 46 clubs in Birmingham affiliated to Warwickshire Lawn Tennis Association, all but one of which have their own courts, while over 100 clubs in and around the city are affiliated to the Midlands Club Cricket Conference, most of which have their own grounds. Another addition to the recreation system in this period was Bartley Reservoir on the south-western edge of the city which, at 46 ha, is Birmingham's largest area of water. This was built in 1930 as part of the city's water supply system and opened up for sailing and windsurfing by the former Severn Trent Water Authority in 1985. It now supports a flourishing club and, like the other reservoirs within the conurbation, has proved a valuable recreational resource in a region notably lacking in extensive areas of open water (see Fig. 2.2).

The effect of these and other changes since 1965 is seen in the greater diversity of resources which now perform a recreational function and the extent to which these provide a wider range of recreational opportunities. It is no longer possible to think of recreational space in terms of a simple division between the municipally-provided parks, recreation grounds and swimming pools and the generally more limited range of facilities developed by private interests. Certainly the former elements have proved remarkably resilient in the face of continuing changes in leisure patterns, but they now need to be seen as only part of a wider system of recreational space. This is clearly recognized in Birmingham's *City Pride Prospectus* which describes its policy of developing 'an integrated and linked system of high quality open space throughout the city'.

This emphasis on informal recreation, especially walking, and the establishment of a footpath system linking together areas of both formal and informal open space is one of the most significant changes of the last quarter of a century. Together with the establishment of peripheral country parks, it has not only had the effect of providing access to the wider countryside beyond but also made it possible to enjoy a countryside recreation experience within the urban area. Similarly, the protection of green wedges and the creation of linear areas of open space enables rural wildlife to penetrate deep into the conurbation. Such an approach has the advantage that much can be achieved by combining limited public funding with voluntary effort, as well as attracting the support of the Countryside Commission whose current priority is the provision of footpaths and other facilities for informal recreation. It may also be interpreted as the continuation of a process begun a century ago when the acquisition of the Lickey Hills provided the people of Birmingham with their own little bit of readily-accessible countryside, which still retains a symbolic importance within the city.

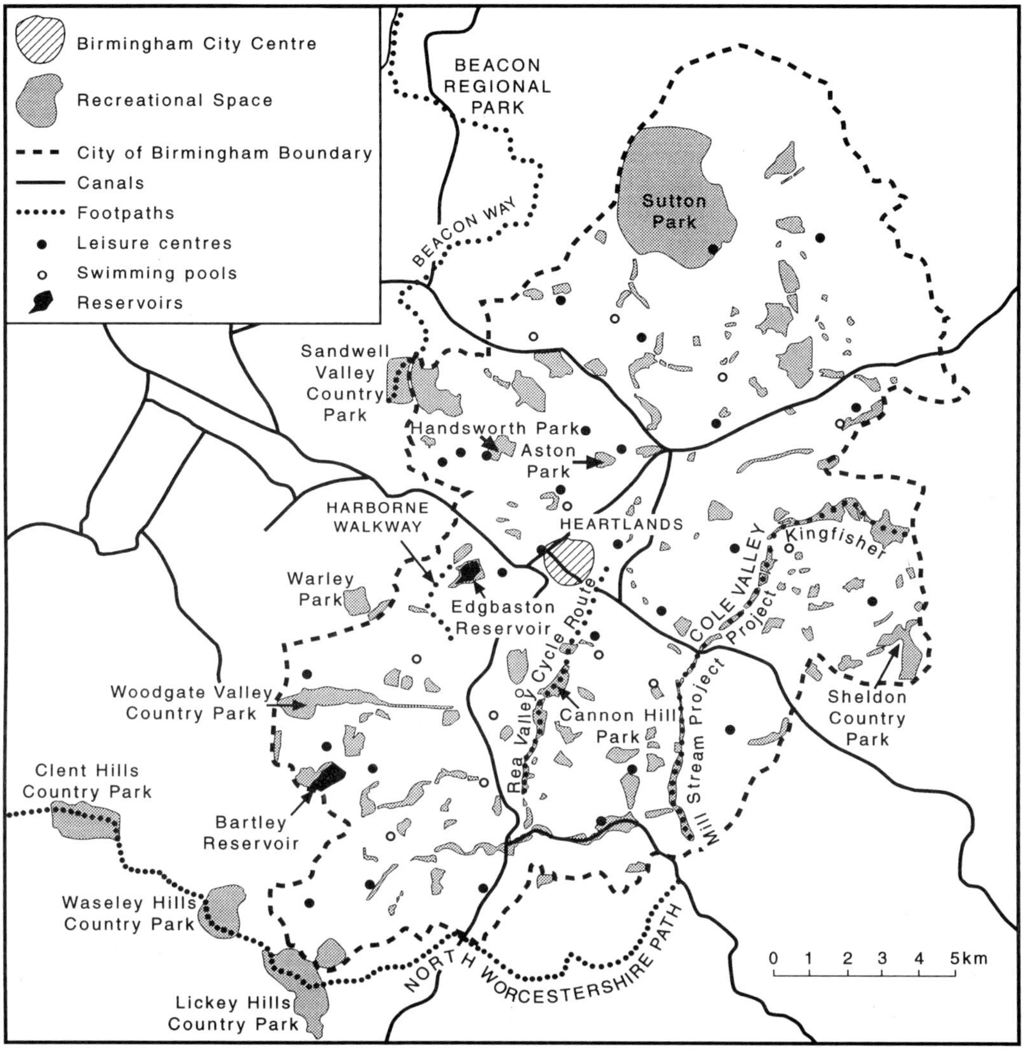

Fig. 21.7 Birmingham's recreational space system in 1996.

An important consequence of this approach is that recreational space is increasingly regarded as a multi-functional resource. This applies not only to the city's 3680 ha of publicly-owned open space, much of which is recognized as having nature conservation values, but also to built facilities. Fitness centres and other facilities have been grafted onto traditional swimming pools, while the sports halls, synthetic pitches and leisure centres are designed for multi-use. Even the Botanical Gardens now include a commercially-run business, banqueting and conference centre. Such provision has had the effect of raising people's expectations in terms of the quality of the leisure experience they seek and is clearly very popular. In 1974-5, there were some 8.2 million users of the city's leisure centres, of whom just over half were swimmers. The most popular, Wyndley Leisure Centre, alone attracted over one million users, only 200,000 more than Cocks

Moors Woods. These users included members of private clubs who rent sports halls, swimming pools, synthetic pitches and other facilities for practice and competition. At the same time, this availability of high-quality purpose-built facilities in a pleasant leisure environment has served to emphasize the problems caused by under-investment in the public parks, which have not been in receipt of targeted funding. In spite of this, Birmingham's parks have managed to attract increasing number of users, which is indicative of the extent to which they retain a central role in the provision of recreational opportunities.

This multi-functional approach is also reflected in administrative changes. Since 1994, Birmingham's allotments, parks and open spaces have been managed by the Department of Leisure and Community Services, which is also responsible for adult education, nature conservation and youth and community services of various kinds, as well as the city's libraries, museums, art galleries and community leisure centres. These responsibilities have also been affected by the greater emphasis on management and marketing made necessary by the local government changes of the 1980s, and particularly by Compulsory Competitive Tendering (CCT). CCT was made compulsory for a number of local government services in 1988, including recreation management and grounds maintenance. As a result, the city's swimming pools, golf courses and leisure centres outside the community leisure programme are managed by Birmingham Leisure Point, a 'Direct Service Organisation' wholly owned by the City Council. Similarly, its parks and recreation grounds are maintained by private contractors, although patrolled by its own ranger service, which is exempt from CCT.

Such changes have led to new attitudes and approaches to the provision of recreational opportunities, but these also reflect the increasingly entrepreneurial role city councils have been required to adopt in promoting the well-being of their communities. Like other post-industrial cities, Birmingham has become very conscious of the importance of environmental quality in attracting both visitors and investment. It also recognizes that its public parks, open spaces and leisure and entertainment facilities, as well as its architectural and cultural heritage, make a vital contribution to the image which it presents to the outside world.

These project-led developments have been accompanied by other initiatives intended to enhance the image of the city. In terms of general environmental improvement there has been greater emphasis on landscaping, tree-planting and floral displays in areas outside the park system, which have enabled the city to win first prizes in a number of different categories in the annual 'Britain in Bloom' competition. Similarly, the city has maintained its strong horticultural tradition and in 1995 won its fifteenth gold medal at the Chelsea Flower Show and the Wigan Cup for the best display by a local authority for the eighth time. Another traditional use of the city's parks and public spaces is the organisation of entertainments and events, which the city has recently developed into major spectacles. A crowd of 30,000 gathered in Centenary Square for the 1995 New Year's Eve Celebration, while Sir Simon Rattle will conduct the City of Birmingham Symphony Orchestra at the July 1996 Fireworks Fantasia in Cannon Hill Park, an event that attracted 40,000 people in 1995. The city has also sought to project its identity as a sporting venue, both in terms of its encouragement of participation in sport through its investment in leisure centres and other facilities and its ability to host major sports events at the National Indoor Arena, the National Exhibition Centre and the Alexander Stadium. These achievements were formally recognized in 1995 when the Sports Council designated Birmingham as an official 'City of Sport', which it is hoped will strengthen the city's ability to obtain funding for further major facilities, including the National Stadium and a 50-metre swimming pool.

As far as the future is concerned, much depends on the availability of public funding and the extent to which partnerships can be forged with other public, private and voluntary sector agency. The pressure on local authority capital budgets in recent years has meant that the provision of recreational space has become increasingly opportunistic and dependent upon jointly-funded initiatives. In particular, the emphasis on the provision of capital-intensive leisure facilities that characterized the 1980s came to an end some time ago, but this may return during the late 1990s as funds become available from the National Lottery. The Sports Council, which is one of the bodies responsible for distributing these funds, has been directed by the government to concentrate on the encouragement of sport in schools and the provision of specialist facilities for the active sports. Because of the competitive approach that is used to distribute such funding, Birmingham with its existing commitment to investment in sports is likely to benefit. Similarly, the Heritage Lottery Fund announced in early 1996 that £50 million was to be made available over the next three years to encourage local authorities to refurbish their public parks and other areas of urban open space. This may well provide an opportunity for Birmingham to introduce a new programme of investment in its inner-city parks, which still retain much of their Victorian splendour.

Acknowledgements

The author would like to thank all those who provided the information on which this chapter is based, especially Pat Gent, Information Officer, Sports Council (West Midlands), Jim Andrew of Birmingham Leisure Point and Peter Thomas, Head of Parks for the City of Birmingham.

References

Birmingham City Council 1993 *The Birmingham Plan: Birmingham Unitary Development Plan 1993* Birmingham City Council, Birmingham

Black H J 1957 *History of the Corporation of Birmingham, Volume VI (1936-1950): Part 2* Corporation of the City of Birmingham, Birmingham

Birmingham Post 1965 *Birmingham Post year book and who's who 1965-66* Birmingham Post and Mail Ltd, Birmingham

Bradnock F W ed 1965 *The City of Birmingham handbook to the departments of the Corporation* City of Birmingham, Birmingham

Briggs A 1952 *History of Birmingham, volume II: borough and city 1865-1938* Oxford University Press for the City of Birmingham, Oxford

City of Birmingham 1960 *Development plan: statement and maps, as approved by the Minister of Housing and Local Government 21st December 1960* City of Birmingham, Birmingham

City of Birmingham 1973 *Structure plan for Birmingham: written statement* City of Birmingham, Birmingham

Comedia in association with Demos 1995 *Park life: urban parks and social renewal* Comedia, Stroud, Glos

Conway H and Lambert D 1993 *Public prospects: historic parks under threat. A short report by the Garden History Society and the Victorian Society* Garden History Society and the Victorian Society, London

Department of the Environment 1990 *This common inheritance: Britain's environmental strategy* Cm 1200, HMSO, London

Department of the Environment 1995 *Park life: better parks, better cities* Department of the

Environment, London
Faulkner L W ed 1938 *City of Birmingham Official Handbook 1938* City of Birmingham Information Bureau, Birmingham
Forward Consultancy Initiative 1995 *A summary of parks use, non-use, service perceptions and satisfaction* unpublished report to Birmingham City Council
Thorpe H chairman 1969 *Departmental committee of enquiry into allotments* Cmnd 4166, HMSO, London
West Midlands County Council 1980 *County Structure Plan, Report of Survey: Recreation* West Midlands County Council, Birmingham

INDEX

C

D

G

H

R